Exam Ref 70-332: Advanced Solutions of Microsoft SharePoint Server 2013

Michael Doyle

Published with the authorization of Microsoft Corporation by:

O'Reilly Media, Inc.
1005 Gravenstein Highway North
Sebastopol, California 95472

ISBN: 978-0-7356-7810-1

1 2 3 4 5 6 7 8 9 QG 8 7 6 5 4 3

Printed and bound in the United States of America.

Microsoft Press books are available through booksellers and distributors worldwide. If you need support related to this book, email Microsoft Press Book Support at mspinput@microsoft.com. Please tell us what you think of this book at *http://www.microsoft.com/learning/booksurvey.*

Acquisitions and Developmental Editor: Kenyon Brown

Production Editor: Kara Ebrahim

Editorial Production: Box Twelve Communications

Technical Reviewer: Kyle Davis

Copyeditor: Box Twelve Communications

Indexer: Box Twelve Communications

Cover Design: Twist Creative • Seattle

Cover Composition: Karen Montgomery

Illustrator: Rebecca Demarest

This book is dedicated to David and Sandy Doyle.

—Michael Doyle

Contents at a glance

Contents

What do you think of this book? We want to hear from you!
Microsoft is interested in hearing your feedback so we can continually improve our books and learning resources for you. To participate in a brief online survey, please visit:

www.microsoft.com/learning/booksurvey/

Introduction

This book is primarily intended to help you prepare for Exam 70-332, "Advanced Solutions of Microsoft SharePoint Server 2013," but it's also intended to be a reference that you can consult during your experiences with SharePoint Server 2013. In many cases, the steps to perform a task are shown to help you feel comfortable with related questions on the exam as well provide a reference on how to perform the task in a real-life situation.

The level of detail in this book will often exceed what's required on the exam because of the very nature of it being an advanced solutions exam. This doesn't mean you won't come up with specific questions about the steps required to perform a task or requirements needed to install a service application. It does mean, however, that you don't need to focus on being able to spell out a command correctly or know exactly what parameter to pass it. You should focus on the concepts, the overall steps involved with a task, and the components needed for a solution. If you focus on these concepts and go through the tasks in this book, you will be well on your way to passing the exam.

This book is generally intended for exam candidates that have four or more years working with SharePoint Server and related technologies, such as SQL Server and Windows Server. Candidates should have hands-on experience with a multi-server SharePoint farm in the capacities of planning, implementing, and maintaining. This includes, but isn't limited to, the areas of high availability, disaster recovery, capacity planning, and exposure to SharePoint Online. Despite having multiple years of experience with a multi-server SharePoint farm, that you will have experience with all the technologies covered by the exam is doubtful; you should focus on the areas to which you have the least exposure. Also, any feature that has been added to SharePoint Server 2013 will likely receive additional coverage on the exam.

This book will help you prepare for the exam, but nothing can take the place of real-life experience. In an effort to make the exams closer to measuring knowledge of the product, they are going more and more to case studies and getting away from simple multiple-choice questions. You'll still see a number of traditional multiple-choice questions, but you'll also see questions where you have to place steps in order and questions where you have to choose the right set of items from a large list of possible items. In these cases, practicing the actual implementation of the functionality covered in this book will help you far more than just trying to memorize what is involved.

This book covers every exam objective, but it does not cover every exam question. Only the Microsoft exam team has access to the exam questions themselves and Microsoft regularly adds new questions to the exam, making it impossible to cover specific questions. You should consider this book a supplement to your relevant real-world experience and other study materials. If you encounter a topic in this book that you do not feel completely comfortable with, use the links you'll find in text to find more information and take the time to research and study the topic. Great information is available on MSDN, TechNet, and in blogs and forums.

Microsoft certifications

Microsoft certifications distinguish you by proving your command of a broad set of skills and experience with current Microsoft products and technologies. The exams and corresponding certifications are developed to validate your mastery of critical competencies as you design and develop, or implement and support, solutions with Microsoft products and technologies both on-premise and in the cloud. Certification brings a variety of benefits to the individual and to employers and organizations.

> ***MORE INFO*** **ALL MICROSOFT CERTIFICATIONS**
>
> **For information about Microsoft certifications, including a full list of available certifications, go to *http://www.microsoft.com/learning/en/us/certification/cert-default.aspx*.**

Acknowledgments

I'd like to thank the following people. I would like to especially thank Stepha, Maxson, and Carianna Doyle for being so patient with their father through this process. Also, I would like to thank Dr. L.J. Geiken for putting up with me being book-focused for so long and for being a great partner. I would finally like to thank the following people in the SharePoint community for encouraging my efforts (even if they didn't realize they were doing it): Dan Holme, Randy Williams, Debbie Ireland, Nick Hadlee, Brian Farnhill, and Christian Buckley.

Errata & book support

We've made every effort to ensure the accuracy of this book and its companion content. Any errors that have been reported since this book was published are listed on our Microsoft Press site at oreilly.com:

http://aka.ms/ER70-332/errata

If you find an error that is not already listed, you can report it to us through the same page.

If you need additional support, email Microsoft Press Book Support at mspinput@microsoft.com.

Please note that product support for Microsoft software is not offered through the addresses above.

We want to hear from you

At Microsoft Press, your satisfaction is our top priority, and your feedback our most valuable asset. Please tell us what you think of this book at *http://www.microsoft.com/learning/booksurvey*.

The survey is short, and we read every one of your comments and ideas. Thanks in advance for your input!

Stay in touch

Let's keep the conversation going! We're on Twitter: *http://twitter.com/MicrosoftPress*.

Preparing for the Exam

Microsoft certification exams are a great way to build your resume and let the world know about your level of expertise. Certification exams validate your on-the-job experience and product knowledge. While there is no substitution for on-the-job experience, preparation through study and hands-on practice can help you prepare for the exam. We recommend that you round out your exam preparation plan by using a combination of available study materials and courses. For example, you might use the Exam Ref and another study guide for your "at home" preparation, and take a Microsoft Official Curriculum course for the classroom experience. Choose the combination that you think works best for you.

Note that this Exam Ref is based on publically available information about the exam and the author's experience. To safeguard the integrity of the exam, authors do not have access to the live exam.

CHAPTER 1

Plan business continuity management

> **important**
> ***Have you read page xix?***
> It contains valuable information regarding the skills you need to pass the exam.

Downtime is something that nobody wants to think about, but it's a reality that any organization needs to plan for. This is the first chapter in this book because business continuity is something that you should plan for before you start building your SharePoint farm. Microsoft SQL Server and Microsoft SharePoint work together to provide various options for business continuity depending on your business needs. With the proper planning, your business can achieve a high degree of disaster recovery no matter what the situation requires. It all depends on the effort put into the planning and the resources that can be allocated to this endeavor.

Objectives in this chapter:

- Objective 1.1: Plan for SQL high availability and disaster recovery
- Objective 1.2: Plan SharePoint high availability
- Objective 1.3: Plan backup and restore

Objective 1.1: Plan for SQL high availability and disaster recovery

SQL Server is the foundation of any SharePoint 2013 farm. Getting your SQL installation ready is paramount to any disaster recovery or high-availability plan. Here, planning is of the utmost importance and is the area that's most likely at fault when something goes wrong. Poor planning at this stage can bring down the SharePoint farm for hours or even days. You can't plan for every potential disaster, but you can plan for items that you anticipate. Before starting with the objective topics, you need to understand gathering requirements and defining limitations.

This objective covers the following topics:

- Plan for SQL Server mirroring
- Plan for SQL Server clustering
- Plan for SQL Server AlwaysOn
- Plan for SQL Server log shipping
- Plan for storage redundancy
- Plan for login replication

Gathering requirements

Gathering requirements is definitely an art. It's a balance between spending too little time (which ends up in a poorly designed server farm) or spending too much time, causing project delays, and going over budget. The term poorly designed, in this sense, doesn't mean that it won't meet the needs of the organization, but instead that it might not match the business needs but addresses issues that don't really exist. Having a disaster recovery plan that works for everyone would be nice, but that simply isn't the case. To get started with gathering requirements, you must know the relevant terminology. The two most important terms associated with SQL Server high availability are Recovery Time Objective (RTO) and Recovery Point Objective (RPO).

EXAM TIP

You must be familiar with these terms and comfortable defining these requirements within the context of the SharePoint implementation.

RTO is usually a number that's heard when talking about uptime, such as 99.9 percent or something higher. Everyone wants a number that approaches 100 percent, but each 9 that's added causes the cost to go up exponentially. The number of 9's required depend heavily on the type of data being stored and who's accessing it from where. SharePoint 2013 isn't used to store transactional data, such as that stored by banks that process thousands of transactions every minute, so it doesn't have the same requirements. However, the content stored in SharePoint is often mission critical and requires a high RTO. When figuring your RTO requirements, you need to keep the business environment in context. Consider the following important questions:

- Does the data need to be available 24 hours a day, seven days a week, or are maintenance windows allowed?
- Is all content to be treated the same, or does different content have different sets of requirements?
- How is data to be archived when it's no longer timely?

RTO can't be determined just from a technological viewpoint. The opinions and requirements of business stakeholders also need to be taken into consideration. Also, the budget allocated to RTO must be considered. All these factors go into determining a realistic RTO.

Truly understanding RTO requires doing some math. Assuming that you're dealing with an organization that runs 24 hours a day, seven days a week, you can do the following math:

- An RTO of 99.9 percent means a downtime total of 8.76 hours in the whole year (365 days × 24 hours per day × .001).
- An RTO of 99.99 percent means a downtime total of less than 53 minutes in a year.
- An RTO of 99.999 percent means that less than 6 minutes of downtime is allowed for a whole year.

You can easily see that even the addition of one 9 can dramatically affect the high availability of your organization. For example, an RTO of 99.99 percent doesn't allow for the cumulative update of a server that might bring down the system. Therefore, you must have a plan that allows servers to be brought down without affecting the functionality of the system.

RPO isn't discussed as often but is just as important during the requirement gathering phase. You must have a true understanding of the data involved to determine the RPO. When determining the RPO, you should take into consideration the following details:

- Amount of data lost (for example, 30 minutes of loss)
- Cost to the company of lost data
- Cost to the company for the amount of time to recover

This means that if an outage causes a loss of 30 minutes of data, requires an hour to come back online, and then requires 30 minutes to replace the lost data, you are looking at an RPO of 2 hours. This reflects true outage time because it calculates the amount of lost productivity.

When you gather requirements, calculating and translating the number of lost hours into a dollar amount often helps. This is simply the RPO times the number of people affected times the average salary per hour of the people affected. You can use this kind of information to help gather support for high-availability initiatives.

Choosing a version of SQL Server

Because SQL Server comes in many versions, when planning high availability you need to determine which version to use. When installing SQL Server for a SharePoint 2013 farm, you currently have two version choices:

- The 64-bit version of Microsoft SQL Server 2012
- The 64-bit version of SQL Server 2008 R2 Service Pack 1

Both versions have options for high availability and represent viable installations for a comprehensive disaster recovery plan. The standalone version of SharePoint 2013 isn't part of this discussion because it shouldn't be used in an environment that requires high availability.

Future versions and revisions of SQL Server should work with SharePoint 2013, but that's not guaranteed. Any upgrade or update should be tested in a non-production environment before it's installed.

You need to choose a particular SQL Server version for many reasons. In many cases, moving to the most recent version isn't an option for various reasons including cost, ability to provide technical support, or lack of testing by the organization. However, one primary reason to choose SQL Server 2012 in regards to high availability is multi-subnet failover clustering, as defined in the next section.

> ***MORE INFO*** **HARDWARE AND SOFTWARE REQUIREMENTS FOR SHAREPOINT 2013**
>
> **See *http://technet.microsoft.com/en-us/library/cc262485.aspx#section4* for more information about hardware and software requirements for SharePoint 2013.**

Understanding multi-subnet failover clustering

Multi-subnet failover clustering allows each cluster node to reside in a completely different subnet. As a result, clusters can be farther away on the network as well as geographically dispersed. Geographically dispersed clusters are often referred to as *stretch clusters*. Because these clusters can't share data, a replication scenario must be enabled for the data in the cluster. Figure 1-1 shows a multi-subnet cluster.

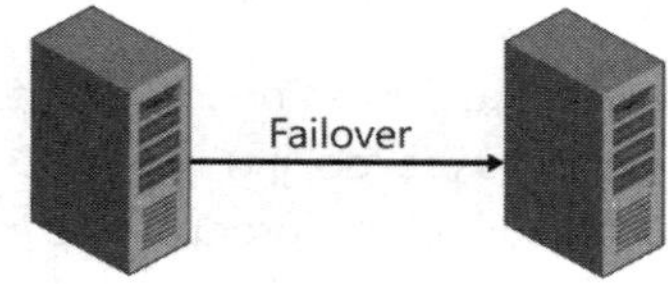

FIGURE 1-1 Example of multi-subnet failover cluster

Clustering—just one of several options that enable high availability—is discussed later in this chapter. Having multiple servers in each node is possible and, depending on the configuration, SQL Server can come online as long as one IP address is available.

Determining limitations

To avoid spending time and money designing a plan that can't be implemented, you need to know all the limitations that can affect your high-availability plan. Limitations can be grouped into two categories: non-technical and technical. Both must be considered in the creation of your high-availability plan.

Most limitations that you encounter have nothing to do with technology and can include but definitely aren't limited to the following:

- **Budget** Your budget can range from pessimistic to optimistic.

- **Power availability** Servers and backup devices require power that might or might not be available.
- **Heat** More servers might overheat the room, causing server failure.
- **Space availability** In the server room, racks require space that might not exist.
- **Training** This is critical to successful high-availability plans.
- **Network bandwidth** Different high-availability scenarios have varying bandwidth requirements.
- **Manpower** Servers require upkeep.
- **Politics** This is always involved.
- **Time** Implementing any high-availability scenario requires time.

Many of these limitations are out of the control of the individuals implementing the high-availability plan. Therefore, knowing these up front and which ones can be altered is important. For example, if the server room is in downtown Tokyo and is limited to a small space that's already full and challenging to cool, you need to take such limitations into consideration if the funds aren't available to rent more office space. The cloud helps alleviate many of these issues and should be considered, especially if one of the non-technical limitations becomes a critical issue.

After you identify the non-technical issues but before you plan for individual high-availability components, you need to look at the technical limitations. Some of these might include the following:

- **The recovery model** The simple recovery model doesn't allow for database mirroring, log shipping, and the ability to take backups of the transaction logs.
- **Network bandwidth and latency** Low bandwidth and latency can prohibit the successful implementation of most high-availability options.
- **FILESTREAM requirements** *FILESTREAM* can't be used with database snapshots or database mirroring. It can cause issues with other items such as transactional replication, log shipping, and backups.
- **Software limitations** Certain versions of SQL Server are required for some high-availability options. Make sure that the required version is available.

Now that you've looked at what's needed to gather requirements and identify limitations, you can concentrate on some of the high-availability options in SQL Server.

> ***NOTE*** **SINGLE-LABEL DOMAIN LIMITATIONS**
>
> **SharePoint 2013 doesn't support installations on single-label domains. Many features don't work correctly, including user profile import. For more information, refer to the Knowledge Base article at *http://support.microsoft.com/kb/2379373*.**

Planning for SQL Server mirroring

SQL Server mirroring provides an almost complete redundancy of the data used by SQL Server—*almost* because it depends on how SQL Server mirroring is configured. Another benefit is that SharePoint has fully supported database mirroring since version 2010, especially concerning content databases. Database mirroring is also fairly simple to set up and provides the following benefits:

- It increases data protection. Because a full copy of the database is available, mirroring greatly increases the likelihood of data survival.
- Database availability improves because SharePoint can use either database.
- Availability during upgrades means that you can upgrade one database at a time in a mirror.

As the benefits show, database mirroring provides a valid high-availability solution. It's also one of the most commonly used methods of providing high availability. The main drawbacks are cost (because it requires, at minimum, another SQL Server) and disk space (because it's a full duplicate, the storage requirements are now doubled). Assuming that you have the spare SQL Server (it doesn't have to be dedicated to this function) and the disk space, you still need to understand some terms so that you have a better understanding of how SQL Server mirroring works:

- **Principal database** This read/write database provides transaction log data to the mirrored database.
- **Principal server** The principal database resides on this server.
- **Mirror database** This database is a copy of the principal database.
- **Mirror server** The mirror database resides on this server.
- **High-performance mode** Because the database mirroring session operates asynchronously, data might be lost. This mode supports only forced switching.
- **High-safety mode** The database mirroring session operates synchronously and optionally uses a witness.
- **Forced switching** This manual process switches the database functionality to the mirrored database until the principal database can be recovered. SharePoint can be set up to do this automatically for content databases.
- **Witness** This SQL Server instance watches the principal and mirror to determine when a failover is required. It doesn't need to store data.
- **Transaction safety** This database setting determines whether a database mirroring session operates asynchronously or synchronously. The only options are FULL and OFF.
- **Manual failover** This occurs when a database owner forces the mirror to act at the principal, even though the principal is fully functional (as in a database upgrade situation).

- **Automatic failover** This occurs when a witness sees that the principal isn't functioning properly and causes the mirror server to become the primary server.

Looking at the terminology can help you determine what's happening in Figure 1-2. All three servers are communicating with each other, but only transaction log data is being sent from the principal server to the mirror server.

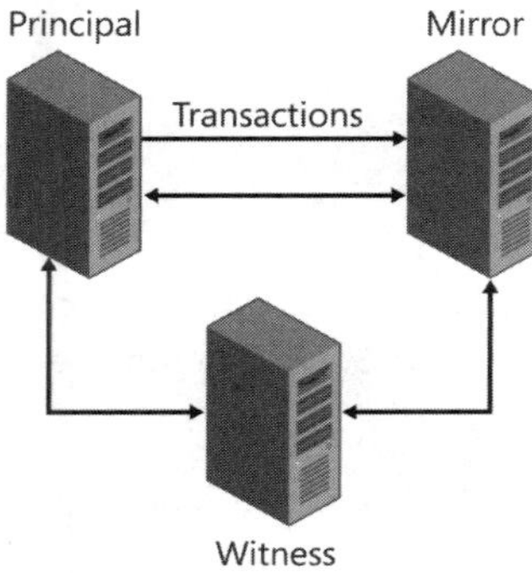

FIGURE 1-2 A high-safety database mirroring session with a witness

If you haven't dealt with database mirroring before, this can seem like a lot to take in at one time, but with a little practice it will soon make sense. Before you start actually setting up a mirror, you need to consider some significant requirements for database mirroring.

Determining mirroring requirements

Planning for high availability generally involves working with multiple groups. Normally, the person responsible for planning the SharePoint installation isn't the same person overseeing the SQL Server instance. The database administrator(s) involved must be aware of the following mirroring requirements:

- Full recovery model is required.
- Recommend latency of less than 1 millisecond is required.
- Recommend network bandwidth of at least 1 GB per second is required.
- Transaction logs can grow very large, so you need a plan for truncating them.
- The principal and mirror database must run the same version and same edition of SQL Server, although the witness can be any version, even SQL Server Express.
- Each mirroring session needs at least two threads, so make sure enough threads are available for SQL Server to run.

Latency and network bandwidth aren't strict requirements but can affect performance and lead to large losses of data if a catastrophic failure occurs on the principal database. You can adjust the number of threads in SQL Server, but each thread requires memory.

After you meet the preceding requirements, you can start creating some mirrors and testing them. You can set up mirrored pairs on existing SQL Server instances, but practicing in a production environment isn't recommended. Creating a mirror involves three main steps:

1. Back up the principal database and transaction log.
2. Restore the backed-up database on the mirror server.
3. Create the mirror connection.

The following section explains these steps in more detail.

Setting up a database mirror

You can create a database mirror using T-SQL commands or PowerShell commands, but for the purposes of illustration and for the exam, the following steps use SQL Server Management Studio:

1. Connect to the server that will serve as the principal server with SQL Server Management Studio, regardless of which version is being used.
2. Expand the database in the Object Explorer pane and right-click the database that is to be mirrored.
3. Choose Tasks and then choose Backup to launch the Backup Wizard.
4. Create a full backup of the principal database (to tape or disk, but disk is usually the easiest) as well as the transaction log.
5. Close the connection to the principal server.
6. Connect to the mirror server with SQL Server Management Studio.
7. Right-click the databases folder in the right navigation pane and choose Restore Database.
8. Restore the backed-up principal database to the mirror server. In the Options panel, select Restore With No Recovery and click OK.
9. Right-click the restored database after it's finished being restored. Choose Tasks and then navigate to the Restore submenu.
10. Select Transaction Log to open the Restore Transaction Log window.
11. Choose the principal database's backed-up transaction log.
12. Select Options in the Select a Page navigation panel and choose Restore With No Recovery.
13. Click OK to restore the transaction log.
14. Right-click the mirror database in the databases folder and choose Properties.
15. Click Mirroring in the Select a Page navigation pane.

16. Click Configuration Security to launch the Configure Database Mirroring Security Wizard.
17. Click Next to move to the Choose A Witness Server page. Choose the appropriate option depending on whether you want a witness server.
18. After you finish choosing options, click Next to open the Principal Server Options page.
19. Make sure the values for the principal server are correct and click Next.
20. On the Mirroring Server Instance page, select the mirror server if it isn't already there and click Next.
21. Click Connect to start the connection.
22. When the connection is established, click Next to open the Service Accounts page.
23. Enter the service account to use or leave blank to use the same service account.
24. Click Next to open the Complete the Wizard page.
25. Verify the settings and click Finish to save the settings.
26. On the Database Properties window, click Start Mirroring to begin the mirroring process.
27. After verifying that mirroring has started, click OK to close the dialog box. Both the mirrored and principal database should show that they are being mirrored in the database folder by having the word *Synchronized* next to them.

A database mirror should have been established if you followed these steps correctly and set up the SQL Server computers correctly.

Unless a witness is established, the mirror must be manually promoted to be the primary server. The primary database can be mirrored to an additional two SQL servers for a total of four copies. The additional demands on the memory and network need to be taken into consideration if this method is pursued. Each time a transaction occurs, it must be written to disk and then packaged up and sent across the network to be written again to another set of disks.

> ***REAL WORLD*** **GEOGRAPHICALLY DISPERSED MIRRORING**
>
> **I wanted to establish a database mirror for a production database located on the west coast of the United States with a SQL Server node located in London. It had a relatively low bandwidth and latency was relatively high, but I decided to try database mirroring because it would provide a geographically diverse location for the data and read-only queries. I did a test on a small test database and could mirror it, but the production database was bigger than 100 GB. The mirror was never successfully established due to the latency and bandwidth limitations of the connection. If something similar happens to you, log shipping might be an option, depending on the business requirements.**

Using permissions for database mirroring

SQL Server uses Transmission Control Protocol (TCP) to communicate between the servers involved in the mirroring process. TCP handles the moving of the transaction data as well as the monitoring of server health if a witness if being used. SQL Server database mirroring supports NT LAN Manager (NTLM), Kerberos, and certificates. Authentication occurs at the port level when the session is opened. Unless the network is secure, some sort of security should be used. SQL Server supports two types of encryption: Advanced Encryption Security (AES) and RC4.

> ***MORE INFO*** **DATABASE MIRRORING TRANSPORT SECURITY**
>
> **See *http://go.microsoft.com/fwlink/p/?LinkId=83569* for more information on Database Mirroring Transport Security.**

Regarding permissions, SharePoint requires additional steps for database mirroring to work. Setting up a database mirror doesn't add the permissions required on the master and msql databases. The Central Administration application pool account (as well as members of the farm administrators group) requires SQL Server logins and the following two fixed server roles be added to both databases:

- dbcreator
- securityadmin

Also, any application pool accounts, service application accounts, and default access accounts should have SQL Server logins on the mirrored database server. In essence, whatever SQL Server permissions are required by SharePoint on the principal server will also be required on the mirror in case of a failover. Creating a script to transfer these permissions is considered a best practice.

> ***IMPORTANT*** **PERMISSIONS FOR DATABASE MIRRORING**
>
> **A successfully created database mirror without the appropriate SharePoint permissions can result in an unsuccessful failover.**

Planning for SQL Server clustering

Planning for a SQL Server cluster involves considerable more planning than for SQL Server mirroring. With mirroring, you can use existing SQL Server computers and choose which database or database set you want to mirror. This allows selective high availability and reduced resource requirements. With a cluster, it is all or none.

A cluster is made of two or more SQL Server nodes that act as a single SQL Server instance. Therefore, the resource requirements are the same for each cluster node, except for the data storage, which is shared among all nodes. To get a better understanding of a cluster, look at what makes up a SQL Server cluster instance:

- A network name for the cluster instance
- One or more IP address for the cluster instance
- A combination of one or more disks in a Microsoft Cluster Service group
- At least one SQL Server instance with SQL Server Agent, Full-text Search service, Replication, and the SQL Server service
- Registry keys that provide checkpoints across the nodes
- Specific DLLs that handle the failover process

A SQL Server failover cluster is referred to by a single name. You don't connect to the individual servers but to the cluster instance name. On the network, the cluster appears as a single server. You must connect to the instance name rather than try to connect to a SQL Server's IP address or machine name. Internally, one node does all the interactions with applications and synchs up the other nodes. However, any of the nodes can become the primary node.

SQL Server clustering has specific hardware requirements, especially if the clusters are geographically dispersed. Latency and network bandwidth are limitations that can cause a cluster to fail. You can make a cluster work with unapproved hardware, but doing so isn't supported.

MORE INFO **WINDOWS CLUSTERING AND GEOGRAPHICALLY DISPERSED SITES**

See *http://go.microsoft.com/fwlink/?LinkId=116970* for more information on Windows clustering and geographically dispersed sites.

Storage Area Network (SAN) solutions work with SQL Server clusters, but some SAN solutions are incompatible with clustering. Check with the SAN manufacturer and with Microsoft to determine whether the available SAN solution is compatible.

Planning for SQL Server AlwaysOn

AlwaysOn is the new high-availability option available with SQL Server 2012. It's intended to provide a comprehensive disaster recovery and high-availability package to minimize downtime in organizations. AlwaysOn comes in two varieties:

- **AlwaysOn High Availability Groups** replace database mirroring.
- **AlwaysOn Failover Cluster Instances** replace database clustering.

Choosing which solution is best is similar to choosing between database mirroring and database clustering. The requirements are similar to their predecessors but provide additional enhancements. Because each solution is so different, this chapter looks at each one independently. AlwaysOn has had some improvements that might be significant enough to warrant an upgrade. Both AlwaysOn solutions rely on the Windows Server Failover Clustering (WSFC) infrastructure, which, combined with SQL Server, works to provide a robust high-availability platform.

AlwaysOn High Availability Groups

The AlwaysOn High Availability Groups technology is intended to replace database mirroring. It has all the benefits of database mirroring plus many more. Because many of the issues with hardware limitations have been addressed, it's a far more robust product than what was available in SQL Server 2008. Database mirroring is still available in SQL Server 2012, but it's being phased out over the next few releases. Some new features of AlwaysOn High Availability Groups are as follows:

- It can fail over a whole group of databases instead of just one at a time.
- It uses a virtual name to provide faster failover.
- Multiple secondary servers are supported, up to four.
- Asynchronous active log synchronization is available for solutions that require high latency.
- Built-in encryption and compression provide more secure and faster data transfer.
- Automatic page repair is available for corrupted pages.
- It provides a flexible failover policy with more control.
- It uses two synchronous secondary servers.

As you can see, quite a few features have been added to database mirroring. From this version forward, it's the recommended solution for high availability.

EXAM TIP

A database can use AlwaysOn High Availability Groups or database mirroring, but not both.

Using AlwaysOn High Availability Groups is a much more involved solution to implement and requires considerable configuration both on SQL Server as well as the Windows Server that it's installed on. You need to know the prerequisites involved when deciding whether AlwaysOn should be part of the SharePoint farm's high-availability solution. The prerequisites for configuring AlwaysOn High Availability Groups are as follows:

- A server with AlwaysOn installed can't be a domain controller.
- It can't be installed on a server with WOW64 (Windows 32-bit on a 64-bit server).
- Each server in the group has to be a node in a WSFC cluster.
- The WSFC cluster must contain sufficient nodes to support the availability group configurations.
- All applicable Windows hotfixes have been installed on every node in the WSFC cluster.

MORE INFO **ALWAYSON HIGH AVAILABILITY GROUPS**

See *http://msdn.microsoft.com/library/ff878487(v=sql.110).aspx* for more information on prerequisites, restrictions, and recommendations for AlwaysOn High Availability Groups.

WSFC is an advanced topic, but a general understanding of it is important to grasp the concepts of AlwaysOn High Availability Groups as well as AlwaysOn Failover Cluster Instances. The term *clustering* describes several different technologies used in planning and configuring SharePoint farms. Clearly stating which type of clustering is being used helps avoid confusion during the planning process.

WSFC is a Windows Server technology that supports high availability and disaster recovery for applications that sit on top of it, such as SQL Server and Exchange Server. Whenever a node in a cluster fails or is turned off for maintenance, it can automatically (or manually) transfer those services to another node in the cluster. In SQL Server, an AlwaysOn high-availability group becomes a WSFC cluster resource. WSFC then monitors the health of each node and initiates the failover processes. Although knowing every detail of how to configure a WSFC instance isn't necessary, understanding the terms helps with an overall comprehension of high-availability options. Some terms used with WSFC are as follows:

- **WSFC cluster** A group of independent servers that work together to provide high availability of services and applications such as SQL Server, Exchange, and/or SharePoint.
- **Failover cluster instance** A Windows Server service that manages an IP resource, a network name resource, and the application and/or services to be managed by the cluster. Rather than connect to an IP or computer name, an application connects to the IP resource or network name resource that crosses over all servers in the cluster.
- **Node** A server that's part of the cluster.
- **IP resource** An IP address (or IPv6 address) that refers to the cluster as a single entity.
- **Network name resource** Used in place of a server name or network name so that applications and servers can refer to the cluster as a whole.
- **Resource group** The set of resources typically required to manage an application or service as a single entity. Failover and fallback are done as a resource group.
- **Cluster resource** An object that can be "owned" by a node. It can be made online, offline, or transferred by a node but not shared by nodes.
- **Preferred owner** The node in a cluster that a resource group prefers to run on.
- **Possible owner** A node that a resource group can run on if the preferred owner is unavailable.

You can see, in these terms, many similarities between "typical" SQL Server clustering and WSFC. AlwaysOn High Availability Groups might seem to have more in common with traditional clustering than with database mirroring. In reality, the technology has some aspects of both, plus additional enhancements. One way to think about AlwaysOn high availability is that it works with WSFC to tie several resources together—database name, IP resource, network name resource, and SQL Server instance—so that they can act as a single entity regardless of what node is actively providing them.

MORE INFO WINDOWS SERVER FAILOVER CLUSTERING WITH SQL SERVER

See _http://msdn.microsoft.com/en-US/library/hh270278.aspx_ for more information on using WSFC with SQL Server.

AlwaysOn Failover Cluster Instances

The AlwaysOn Failover Cluster Instances (AlwaysOn FCI) technology replaces the SQL Server clustering technology available in earlier versions. As with any clustering technology, you need to consider many hardware and software issues before deploying. As with SQL Server clustering specifically, the entire instance fails over rather than just a single database or group of databases—something you need to consider when choosing a high-availability option. The following enhancements are available with SQL Server 2012 AlwaysOn failover clustering:

- Localized tempdb for improved performance
- Multi-site clustering across subnets to improve site protection (subnets are generally in the same physical location)
- Flexible failover policy
- Improved diagnostics

As with clustering, an AlwaysOn FCI relies on a single shared storage area, such as a WSFC group, a SAN, or a file share. This way, any one node can immediately take over for another node using the same set of data. Figure 1-3 shows how this can be represented.

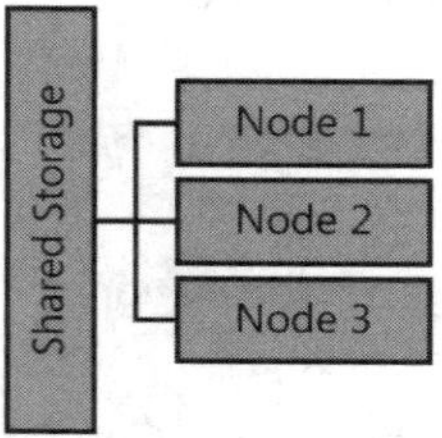

FIGURE 1-3 A visual representation of how each node in a cluster uses the same shared storage

Because AlwaysOn FCI uses shared storage, this represents a potential single source of failure. The underlying storage implementation is responsible for providing data redundancy, such as mirrored disks in physically different locations. An AlwaysOn failover cluster can work with an AlwaysOn high-availability group to provide both instance and database high availability.

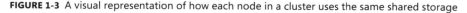

IMPORTANT AUTOMATIC FAILOVER

If an AlwaysOn FCI is in an AlwaysOn high-availability group with another cluster node, automatic failover isn't supported.

An AlwaysOn FCI runs in a WSFC resource group. Every node within the cluster maintains its own synchronized copy of the configuration data and checkpoint registry keys. Only one of the nodes "owns" the resource group at any time, but any node can be the owner. In case of a failure or an upgrade, another node takes over ownership. Failure can be the result of hardware failure, operating system failure, or an application. The SQL Server binaries are stored locally on each node for improved performance, but the services are managed by the WSFC and not started automatically.

A virtual network name (VNN) for the entire node provides a single connection point for applications to connect to the cluster. The VNN points to a single node in the cluster. In the case of a failover, the VNN points to a new node. The application is unaware of a node failure, and no modification is required on the client application for continued uptime.

AlwaysOn failover clustering can use multiple subnets for its nodes. Because a single IP address is required to provide unattended failover, a virtual IP address needs to be assigned to each subnet in the failover cluster. During a subnet failure, the VNN is updated in the DNS to point to the new subnet. Clients require no changes to point to the new subnet, but a slight amount of downtime will occur depending on the DNS configuration.

> ***MORE INFO*** **ALWAYSON FAILOVER CLUSTER INSTANCES**
>
> **See *http://technet.microsoft.com/en-us/library/ms189134(v=SQL.110)* for more information on AlwaysOn FCIs.**

Planning for SQL Server log shipping

SQL Server log shipping can be confused with database mirroring because both have similar functionality: The data from a primary server is sent to one or more secondary servers. Before looking at using SQL Server log shipping, you should look at the primary differences:

- Failover is always manual for log shipping.
- An infinite number of servers can receive log shipments.
- Failover duration is slow (many minutes) compared to database mirroring (seconds).
- In log shipping, transaction logs are backed up and then applied to secondary servers, rather than use TCP to transport changes.
- Role change is manual.
- Log shipping uses both committed and uncommitted transactions, whereas database mirroring only uses committed.

Here, you can see that the main points of concern in high availability are the necessity for a manual change of roles and the amount of time required for the secondary server to become the primary.

Because database mirroring and log shipping are so similar, knowing the terminology is important so that you can distinguish between the two. The following terms are used when discussing log shipping:

- **Primary server** This server contains the primary database.
- **Primary database** This database is backed up and shipped to the secondary databases. Also, all log shipping configuration is done on this database.
- **Secondary server** This server contains the secondary database.
- **Secondary database** This database receives the transaction logs and provides a copy of the database that can be used if the primary is unavailable. It has two states: RECOVERING and STANDBY. STANDBY provides a limited read-only version.
- **Monitor server** This optional SQL Server instance monitors the health of the log shipping process and provides backup information such as time of backups and alerts.
- **Backup job** This SQL Server Agent job, named Log Shipping Backup on the primary server, performs the backing up and notifying of the monitor.
- **Copy job** This SQL Server Agent job, named Log Shipping Copy on the primary server, transfers the backups to the secondary server(s) and notifies the monitor.
- **Restore job** This SQL Server Agent job, named Log Shipping Restore on the secondary server, restores the backup to the secondary, performs cleanup, and notifies the monitor.
- **Alert job** This SQL Server Agent job, named Log Shipping Alert, exists on the monitor. It sends alerts when a backup or restore job doesn't happen within a specified threshold.

NOTE **REMOVING A MONITOR SERVER**

If a monitor server is configured, you must remove log shipping from the primary before you can remove the monitor server.

You can always use log shipping to provide an additional copy of a database. If any databases need to be archived periodically, need a very high level of disaster recovery, or require remote read-only access, log shipping is an excellent option because it's relatively easy to set up compared to the AlwaysOn options. Before configuring log shipping, however, make sure that the following prerequisites are met:

- The full or bulk-logged recovery model is used for the primary database.
- An existing share for the backups must be available to the primary and secondary servers.

To get a better understanding of high-availability options, look at the steps on how to configure log shipping. You could use T-SQL to configure log shipping, but the following steps show only the method available via SQL Server Management Studio:

1. Open SQL Server Management Studio and connect to the database that will serve as the primary.
2. Right-click the database that you're configuring for log shipping and choose Properties.
3. Under the Select A Page section, click Transaction Log Shipping.
4. The right side of the dialog box shows the transaction log shipping options. Select the check box next to Enable This As A Primary Database In A Log Shipping Configuration, as shown in Figure 1-4.

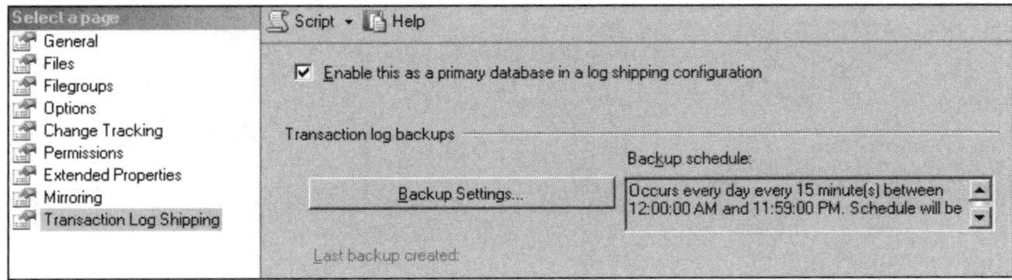

FIGURE 1-4 Selecting Enable This As A Primary Database In A Log Shipping Configuration so that the rest of the settings can be configured

5. Click Backup Settings to display the Transaction Log Backup Settings dialog box.
6. Enter a network path (such as *\\fileserver\backup*) of a location for the transaction logs and choose a local path if the folder is on the same server as the SQL Server. The SQL Server service account needs read and write permissions to the folder, and the SQL Server Agent service accounts of all secondary servers need read access.
7. Change the settings for Delete Files Older Than and Alert If No Backup Occurs Within to fit the requirements, or leave them as they are for now.
8. The backup job is given a default Job Name and schedule. Change the schedule, if you want, and click OK after reviewing all settings to create a SQL Server Agent job.

MORE INFO **BACKUP COMPRESSION**

Backup compression is available if SQL Server 2012 (or SQL Server 2008 Enterprise) is used. See *http://msdn.microsoft.com/en-us/library/bb964719.aspx* for more information on backup compression in SQL Server 2012.

9. Click Add in the Secondary Server Instances And Databases section.
10. Click Connect in the Secondary Database Settings dialog box to connect to the SQL Server instance that will serve as the secondary database.
11. In the Secondary Database field, choose an existing database or type the name of a database to create.

12. On the Initialize Secondary Database tab, choose one of the options. The default option generates a full backup of the primary database and restores it into the secondary database. It also creates the database if it doesn't exist. If Restore Options is chosen, folders other than the default can be chosen for the secondary database location of the data and log files.

13. On the Copy Files tab, enter the destination folder for the copied transaction logs (see Figure 1-5).

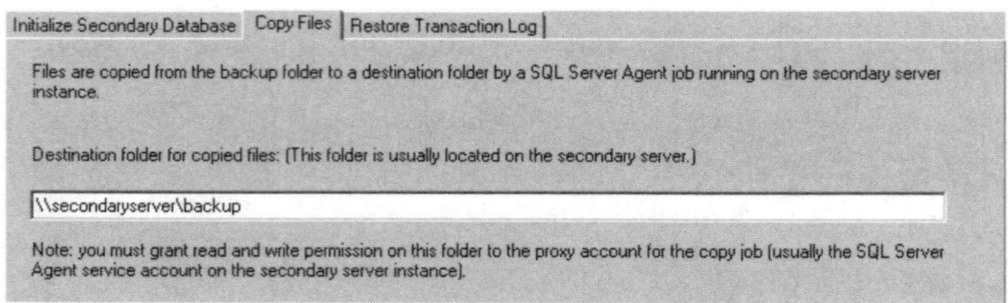

FIGURE 1-5 The Copy Files tab, on which you enter a location for the transaction log files

14. On the Restore Transaction Log tab, choose either No Recovery Mode or Standby Mode. Choosing Standby Mode disconnects anybody connected to the database when the restore of the transaction logs occurs. You also can choose to delay the backup (to counteract logical errors) and to have alerts sent if the restore doesn't occur within a given timeframe.

15. Click OK to close the Secondary Database Settings dialog box.

16. To add more secondary server instances, click the Add button.

17. If a monitor will be used to monitor the health of the primary server and the success of the transaction log shipments, select Use A Monitor Server Instance and configure the settings on the Settings tab. You can choose to impersonate the proxy account or use a specified account, as well as specify how long to keep the history of the jobs.

IMPORTANT **CHOOSING A MONITOR**

If you don't choose a monitor at this point, you must remove the transaction log configuration before you can add a monitor.

18. Click OK to start the configuration process.

IMPORTANT **ALTERNATE BACKUP METHODS**

If another job or maintenance plan is used to back up the transaction logs of the log shipping primary database, SQL Server Management Studio can't restore the transaction logs on secondary servers.

Failing over to a secondary database isn't as straightforward in log shipping as it is in database mirroring or one of the AlwaysOn technologies because of the time lag between the primary and secondary servers synching. Typically, the secondary database needs to be synchronized with the latest transaction logs before it assumes the duties of the primary server (unless a logical error occurs in which part of the database is corrupt and getting an earlier version of the data is necessary). Some transaction logs might not have even been copied to the secondary server and will need to be recopied (if possible). Failing over requires some additional manual steps, as follows:

1. Make sure that all backup files are available on the secondary server.
2. Apply transaction logs in order, starting with the oldest unapplied backup to the most recent backup.
3. Assuming that the primary server is still available, back up the transaction tail *WITH NORECOVERY* to leave it in a usable state.
4. Apply the transaction log tail to the secondary server to bring it up to date, if available.
5. Recover the secondary server and make it available to users.
6. Point applications to the secondary server, which can also be set up to be the primary server in log shipping.

> ***MORE INFO*** **FAIL OVER TO A LOG SHIPPING SECONDARY**
>
> **See *http://msdn.microsoft.com/en-us/library/ms191233.aspx* for more information on how to fail over to a log-shipping secondary.**

Figuring out when logical errors occurred in the database requires some effort. As long as a backup and the transaction logs are available, getting to a point before the logical error occurred should be possible. This is an important component in many disaster recovery plans because it minimizes the amount of lost data.

Database mirroring with log shipping

One major benefit to SQL Server log shipping is that it can be combined with database mirroring. This allows for redundancy not only in database storage but also in methods of maintaining that redundancy. For example, something happening to the database mirror (such as a corrupted DLL or latency issues) wouldn't stop log shipping from occurring. The net benefit is that you could still maintain up-to-date copies of your data. An additional benefit is that you can delay shipping logs in case an error occurs in the database itself that you don't want replicated. Just follow some basic guidelines:

- If you have only one copy, stick with database mirroring if the network bandwidth and latency allow.

- If you need more than one copy, do database mirroring for the first copy and transaction log shipping for the rest of them.
- If you need to guard against logical errors and database corruption, set up the log shipping to be delayed.

The general method of setting up database mirroring with log shipping is that the database mirror is established first, and then log shipping is established. It's not a requirement, however. The principal database in the mirror set should be the database that does the log shipping, but configuring the mirrored database for log shipping is also necessary. If the primary is offline for some reason, the mirror can continue the log shipping.

Setting up log shipping on the mirror with the exact same configuration as the principle is necessary. Because the mirror is in a restoring state, while the principle is active, the mirror won't interfere with the principle log shipping. Shipping logs to the primary or the mirror can cause failure and data inconsistency. All log shipping should go to servers not in the database mirror pair. Also, all servers should have access to where the transaction logs are backed up. Preferably this area is a network location but not physically on the same server as the principal server. Keeping the physical location separate provides for additional disaster recovery protection.

Planning for storage redundancy

Data redundancy is a cornerstone of any disaster recovery center. The amount of redundancy planning required depends on the data's importance, the budget allowed, and the speed at which the data must be recovered. A multitude of disasters can occur, such as the following real-world examples:

- Hardware fails (that is, hard-disk failure)
- Database corruption
- Natural disaster (fire, earthquake, flood)
- Unnatural disaster (vandalism, terrorism, theft)
- Upgrade of database fails, leaving it in an unrecoverable state
- Cyber attack

Data redundancy can help prevent a disaster from turning into a catastrophe, in which the data is permanently destroyed. Several methods are available for providing storage redundancy. This chapter goes over some of the most common methods, but any storage plan requires a large amount of resources to provide true data redundancy.

Database mirroring for data redundancy

Typically, you think of database mirroring as just providing a single copy of a database. This by itself can help prevent some disasters, such as hardware failure. A mirror in another physical location also can help recover from many of the other disasters (for example, that both locations would catch fire is highly unlikely). This provides a high level of redundancy as well as high availability. In some cases, a single copy of the database might not be sufficient. SQL Server 2008 and above allows for a database to be mirrored at least three times. This provides for four copies of the data in potentially four different physical locations—assuming that they have enough bandwidth to support the mirroring sessions.

As mentioned in the log shipping section, database mirroring along with log shipping can provide for a virtually unlimited number of copies of the database in various stages of recovery, depending on the network's capabilities and the servers involved. If the primary SQL Server node can't keep up with the processing of the database mirroring and the replication of the transaction log data, it will start to fail. The nature of the failure depends on the particular installation, but you're always constrained by the hardware limitations.

Database clustering for data redundancy

Using database clustering for data redundancy is also an option but doesn't provide the same level of redundancy as database mirroring (or the improved Microsoft SQL Server 2012 AlwaysOn version). Again, putting this solution into place requires much more restrictive hardware and software requirements. SQL Server supports up to 16 cluster nodes, depending on the SQL Server version and the hardware being used. The problem with clusters is that they all use common storage. This provides a single point of failure, depending on how the hardware is set up. Almost every cluster implementation will use a disk redundancy method such as RAID 0 (which is mirroring of the data disks) but you are still looking at physical location vulnerability unless the disks are being mirrored to a different location.

Backups for data redundancy

Backups don't provide high availability but can protect from database corruption. The more often you back up the data, the more current the latest uncorrupted version of the database. The issue with database mirroring and clustering is that any corruption is also copied. Database backups are essential to providing a comprehensive database redundancy plan.

Planning for login replication

Logins aren't replicated with the data unless the entire SQL Server instance is replicated. In the cases of database mirroring, log shipping and AlwaysOn high-availability group replication doesn't provide the SharePoint logins necessary for a successful failover. If a large number of servers are involved, maintaining the necessary logins can become a challenge. Even maintaining consistent logins between two servers can prove to be difficult. Nothing is more frustrating than performing an emergency failover and not having the logins in place to make the SharePoint instance function correctly. This isn't an issue with SQL Server clustering and AlwaysOn FCI because every node in the cluster is a copy of the whole server, not just the databases involved in replication.

You can create a script of SQL Server logins on the primary server and then run it on all secondary servers (mirror, secondary server, or member of an AlwaysOn high-availability group). Because scripting logins is a fairly involved process, you need to take great care when creating a script because different versions of SQL Server need slightly different scripts. Also, any errors in the script can result in a non-functional failover database. To test the logins properly on the secondary database, you need to initiate a manual failover.

> ***MORE INFO*** **TRANSFERRING LOGINS BETWEEN SQL SERVER INSTANCES**
>
> **Because a login script is fairly difficult to write, Microsoft has provided one in the Knowledge Base article at *http://support.microsoft.com/kb/918992*.**

Thought experiment

Choosing a high-availability database option

In this thought experiment, apply what you've learned about this objective. You can find answers to these questions in the "Answers" section at the end of this chapter.

You are told to design a high-availability solution for a group of content databases labeled as critical in the SharePoint farm. You are limited to using SQL Server 2008 R2 because of licensing and training concerns. The criterion is that if a content database fails, a failover must be available within 5 minutes. Two SQL Server instances are available for your use and are on the same network.

Develop a high-availability plan that meets these criteria.

Objective summary

- Gathering requirements and understanding the technical as well as the non-technical limitations are the first steps in developing a comprehensive high-availability solution.
- Database mirroring provides redundant data as well as high availability of database servers.
- Database clustering provides high availability of servers but not redundancy of databases—at least, not without additional efforts.
- You can combine log shipping with database mirroring to provide additional copies of the data in different stages.
- Using AlwaysOn High Availability Groups—the enhanced version of SQL Server database mirroring available in SQL Server 2102—is the preferred way to provide high availability.
- The AlwaysOn Failover Cluster Instances technology is the enhanced version of SQL Server clustering available in SQL Server 2012.
- When developing a high-availability SharePoint plan, you have to consider additional database permission requirements.

Objective review

Answer the following questions to test your knowledge of the information in this objective. You can find the answers to these questions and explanations of why each answer choice is correct or incorrect in the "Answers" section at the end of this chapter.

1. You've been requested to have downtime of an hour or less during the calendar year in an environment that runs 24 hours a day, seven days a week. What RTO should you strive for?
   - **A.** 99.9 percent
   - **B.** 99.99 percent
   - **C.** 99.999 percent
   - **D.** 1 percent
2. Which of the following Active Directory DNS names does SharePoint 2013 support?
   - **A.** contoso.com
   - **B.** contoso
   - **C.** Both A and B
   - **D.** None of the above
3. Which of the following is allowed with the simple recovery model?
   - **A.** Transaction log backups
   - **B.** Log shipping
   - **C.** Database mirroring
   - **D.** Clustering
4. You have a small but critical content database that needs high availability. Which option would provide the most resource-efficient, high-availability option?
   - **A.** Clustering
   - **B.** Log shipping
   - **C.** Database mirroring
   - **D.** They are all the same
5. AlwaysOn High Availability Groups has been chosen as the high-availability option for your SharePoint farm installation. Which of the following needs additional configuration to make this possible?
   - **A.** One Windows Server node that's part of the group
   - **B.** SQL Server
   - **C.** All the Windows Server instances that are part of the group
   - **D.** SharePoint 2013

Objective 1.2: Plan for SharePoint high availability

Having a high-availability plan for SQL Server is essential to disaster recovery and business continuity, but planning for SharePoint high availability is just as important. If SharePoint goes down, you still aren't functional no matter how many copies of the SQL Server database you have. The goal of this objective is to ensure that an adequate SharePoint high-availability plan is in place for your business needs.

This objective covers to the following topics:

- Plan for service distribution
- Plan for service instance configuration
- Plan for physical server distribution
- Plan for network redundancy
- Plan for server load balancing
- Plan for SQL Server aliases

Planning for service distribution

Unless you are dealing with a very small server farm, you need to distribute SharePoint services across several servers for performance as well as consider high availability. SharePoint has many different services roles that you can distribute across servers. Any SharePoint server can assume any of the roles with some configuration changes, giving SharePoint the ability to be an extremely robust and highly available system if it's configured correctly. A SharePoint server can provide these kinds of services:

- Web Front End (WFE)
- Search server
- Application server

Figure 1-6 shows how the services fit together and connect to SQL Server. Note that each service can have several servers—for example, a SharePoint 2013 farm could have five WFEs, three search servers, and two application servers. The number of different configurations depends totally on the resources available and the demands of your particular SharePoint environment.

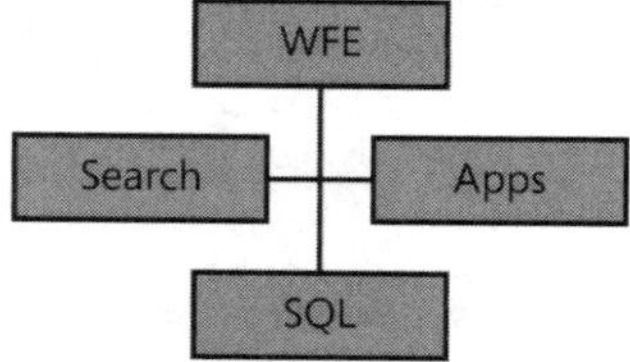

FIGURE 1-6 How each SharePoint Service connects with the database as well as the WFE

Web Front End

The WFE's job is to deliver content via Microsoft Internet Information Services (IIS). A SharePoint farm can have an endless number of WFEs. For the load to be balanced across all the WFEs, additional configuration is needed. All the WFEs need to respond to the same vanity URL or IP address if they will provide the same content with the same URL. You can also leave one or more WFEs on standby in case of failure or maintenance. In any case, if no functioning WFE is available, end users will find SharePoint down. Ensuring that a WFE is available is the first step in any SharePoint high-availability plan.

Search server

A SharePoint Search server crawls and indexes SharePoint content as well as returns query requests. These tasks don't all have to reside on the same server, and depending on how much content is being indexed, one search server might not be able to handle all the search functions. Separating the search server from the WFE provides the single biggest performance improvement (in a farm that has SQL Server on a separate server); otherwise, putting SQL Server on its own server would provide the biggest improvement. The search server is made up of a number of components that can be distributed across multiple servers to provide high availability:

- **Crawl component** crawls content (SharePoint or other content such as websites or file shares) and extracts crawled properties and metadata to send to the content processing component.
- **Content processing component** receives information from the crawl component, and then processes and sends it to the indexing component. It also interacts with the analytics processing component and is responsible for mapping crawled properties to managed properties.
- **Indexing component** receives information from the content processing component and writes it to the index. It also handles queries and sends back results to the Query processing component.
- **Query processing component** handles incoming query requests and sends them to indexing component for results. It also handles optimization of queries.
- **Analytics processing component** analyzes what users are querying on and how they interact with the results. This information is used to determine relevance, generate recommendations, and generate search reports.
- **Search administration component** manages administrative processes as well as changes to the search topology, such as adding or removing search components and servers.

You can distribute the search service components across multiple servers to provide high availability as well as improve performance. The Search Application Topology page in Central Administration shows which components are running on which servers (see Figure 1-7).

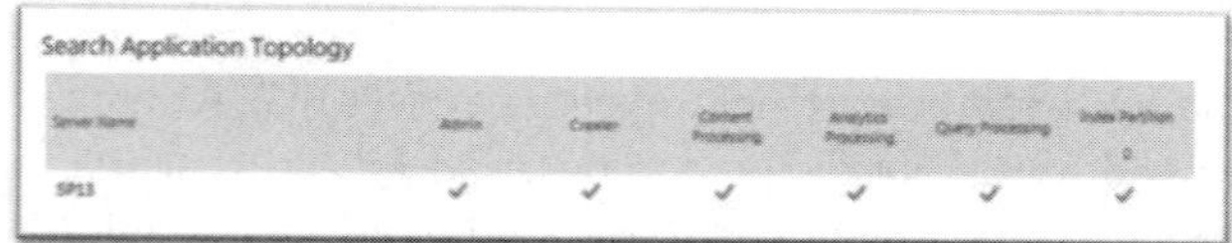

FIGURE 1-7 Each search component running on the server named SP13

The importance of each component varies in how it relates to high availability. Even if all search components were non-functional, SharePoint would still serve up content through the WFE. Of course, when a user tries to do a search, it comes back as the search service being unavailable, depending on which services are down. For example, the crawling component could be unavailable, but search would still return results; those results just become out of date until the crawling component is restored. To determine the high-availability plan for search services, you must first define what the high-availability goals are.

Application server

A SharePoint 2013 farm can have one or more servers that perform the application server service. Any server in the SharePoint farm can be an application server, and you can have a SharePoint server with the sole functionality of a single service application. For example, if your organization relies heavily on Excel, services can benefit from having a SharePoint server dedicated to Excel Services because it's a resource-intensive application. Determining which applications will need the most resources can be difficult because doing so depends on usage. Because any SharePoint server can provide application services, a high-availability plan can target multiple servers as failover options.

Planning for service instance configuration

A SharePoint Server can handle one or more service instances. Typically, the services moved from the WFE are the search service and application services such as Excel Services, but any service can be moved from the primary SharePoint instance. Generally speaking, search will be the most resource-intensive service to be considered for separation from the primary SharePoint server.

To configure the services available on a particular SharePoint 2013 server, follow these steps:

1. Open Central Administration.
2. Under System Settings, click Manage Services On Server.
3. The Services On Server page shows all the services running on the server. To configure a server, choose Change Server from the Server drop-down list in the upper-right corner.
4. On the Select Server page, select the desired server and click OK.
5. Back on the Services On Server page, choose Start or Stop for the appropriate services, as shown in Figure 1-8.

Service	Status	Action
App Management Service	Started	Stop
Business Data Connectivity Service	Started	Stop
Central Administration	Started	Stop
Claims to Windows Token Service	Started	Stop
Distributed Cache	Started	Stop
Document Conversions Launcher Service	Stopped	Start
Document Conversions Load Balancer Service	Stopped	Start
Lotus Notes Connector	Stopped	Start
Machine Translation Service	Started	Stop
Managed Metadata Web Service	Started	Stop
Microsoft SharePoint Foundation Incoming E-Mail	Started	Stop
Microsoft SharePoint Foundation Sandboxed Code Service	Started	Stop
Microsoft SharePoint Foundation Subscription Settings Service	Stopped	Start

FIGURE 1-8 Part of the Services On Server page, showing some of the services that can be started or stopped

The distribution of search services and application services depends on the organization's individual business requirements. A properly prepared high-availability plan allows for redistribution of services depending on the analysis of server demand. You can always add another SharePoint server in the future to offload demand, but many physical and financial requirements need to be taken into consideration during the planning stages. For example, if the server room has no space to add another SharePoint server, that should be noted in the high-availability plan.

Planning for physical server distribution

Physical distribution of servers occurs for two primary reasons:

- **For high availability during a disaster** If a disaster occurs in one building, physical distribution can keep services available.
- **For performance** If the SharePoint farm is servicing users in a wide, geographically dispersed region with varying bandwidth capabilities, physical server distribution can help improve performance. This is particularly true for WFEs. Putting a WFE locally in each region can greatly enhance performance from an end user's perspective.

During the planning phase, you can do the following to prepare for disaster recovery and plan for performance:

- Diagram the physical location of all servers, including those that host any virtual machines.
- During the pilot phase, record server usage (memory and CPU) so that distribution of services can be adjusted.
- Modify the architecture based on performance benchmarks and physical separation of critical services.
- After deployment, modify architecture (physical and virtual servers) as needed based on continuous measurements.

When you're planning for physical server distribution, taking a look at the underlying physical storage of data is important. Data is typically stored on a Redundant Array of Inexpensive Disks (RAID) or Storage Area Network (SAN). These two technologies represent the vast majority of disk configurations used in high-availability systems. The configuration of these technologies can greatly affect the high availability of the SharePoint farm (as well as the SQL Server implementation). To better understand how these technologies affect the SharePoint implementation, take a deeper look into how each one of them works.

SAN

A Storage Area Network is a set of disks and tapes that can be viewed as a single entity. Accessed at the file block level, a SAN appears as a locally attached drive rather than as a remote storage unit. The disks and tapes that are part of the SAN can be in physically distant locations, as opposed to traditional network attached storage (NAS), which usually must be located within a few meters of each other. Knowing the terminology associated with a SAN helps with potential exam questions as well as when discussions about physical storage planning occur. Several SAN-related terminology items are as follows:

- **SAN Fabric** refers to the hardware that connects the servers to the storage disks and tapes.
- **LUN** The logical unit number represents a logical group of disks and/or tapes. A LUN can be used as a single drive or as multiple drives.
- **Fiber Channel** This high-speed networking terminology is often used by SAN implementations.

Implementing a SAN is vendor-specific, so exact specifications are beyond the scope of this book. Generally, a SAN is usually much more expensive to implement but gives the best performance for physically separated storage. In fact, SAN solutions have been successfully implemented on storage devices that are many miles apart. Successful implementations over such distances requires cooperation with a network provider that can provide sufficient network bandwidth and the technologies for transport required (such as Fiber Channel) to make SAN a viable option.

RAID

Redundant Array of Inexpensive Disks (RAID) is a storage system that can be part of an individual server or a standalone set of disks that can be accessed by a number of different servers. You can set up RAID in a number of different varieties (referred to as *levels*), but typically only a few are relevant to storage planning. The RAID levels are as follows:

- **RAID 0** Referred to as *disk striping* because it writes blocks of data across multiple disks. This provides performance improvements by allowing data to be written to multiple disks at the same time but doesn't provide any data redundancy.
- **RAID 1** Often referred to as *disk mirroring* and requires at least two disks. Every bit of data written to one disk is written to the other. The disks don't have to reside in the physical location but usually must be close for latency reasons.

- **RAID 5** Known as *data striping with parity.* Data is written over a minimum of three disks with parity information that can help rebuild information if a disk is lost. A RAID 5 disk array can lose one disk and still keep performing with no data loss (at reduced functionality) until a disk can be replaced.
- **RAID 10** Sometimes called RAID 1+0. This level provides the benefits of both RAID 1 and RAID 0. It's composed of two sets of disks, each in the RAID 0 configuration. This RAID configuration is one of the most commonly implemented today.

To have any sort of physical separation of data, either RAID 1 or RAID 10 must be used. The ability to physically separate the disks in these two RAID options means that the drives can be placed in different racks, maybe even in different rooms. RAID 5 provides some protection in that a single disk can be lost and no data will be lost.

EXAM TIP

Familiarity with RAID 0, RAID 1, RAID 5, and RAID 10 is expected, as well as why you would choose one type of RAID storage over the others.

Planning for network redundancy

Network redundancy means that communication pathways exist, even if a particular link goes down. Because many real-world examples are known of when links go down, planning for them can help keep the SharePoint farm up and running. The following are examples of issues that arise where network redundancy is necessary to maintain service:

- Ethernet port has hardware failure.
- DNS server crashes (hard drive, operating system, software, and so on).
- Router has a hardware failure.
- Switch has a hardware failure.
- IP address is accidentally reused.
- Denial-of-service (DOS) attack is made against an IP address.

The exam doesn't expect you to be a certified network engineer, but you should be aware of these issues and how to plan for them. You should also be prepared to offer suggestions on how network redundancy can help to improve the overall uptime of the SharePoint farm. Many technologies are available to help improve network redundancy, but most of them are beyond the scope of this book. However, one that falls within the realm of this exam is Network Load Balancing (NLB).

NLB is most often discussed when WFEs are discussed. With this method, a single IP address or vanity URL can be used to connect to a set of WFEs (a user connects to only one server at a time, no matter which server). Noting that Central Administration can also be load balanced is important, although it's typically installed on only one server (best practices are that it's running on more than one SharePoint server even if it's not load balanced). NLB is configured outside of SharePoint on each server in the NLB group.

Because NLB operates at the network driver level, the TCP/IP stack isn't aware of it. Figure 1-9 shows how the communication layers are stacked to help get a better understanding of how the layers communicate with each other.

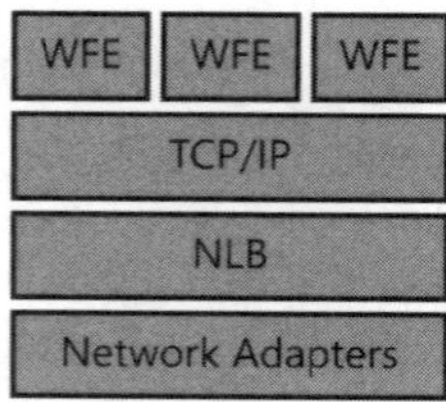

FIGURE 1-9 Communication stack showing how NLB sits below TCP/IP, indicating that the WFE isn't aware of it

Figure 1-9 clearly shows that the WFEs aren't aware of the network load balancing occurring because items in the stack are aware only of layers immediately below or immediately above.

Now that you have a graphical understanding of how NLB works in the communication stack, you can focus on how it's implemented from a practical standpoint. The following steps, for Windows Server 2008 R2, show how to configure NLB:

1. Install Network Load Balancing on each server (it's an optional component of Windows Server) by going to Start | Administrative Tools | Server Manager.
2. In the Features Summary section of the Server Manager main window, choose Add Features.
3. In the Add Features Wizard, select the Network Load Balancing check box and click Next.
4. On the Confirm Installation Selections page, click Install.
5. After NLB is installed, you can configure it by opening the Network Load Balancing Manager (Start | Administrative Tools | Network Load Balancing Manager).
6. Right-click Network Load Balancing Clusters and select New Cluster (see Figure 1-10) to launch the New Cluster Wizard.

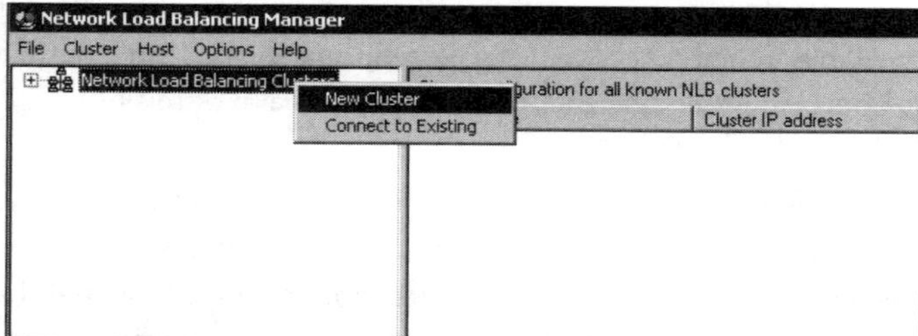

FIGURE 1-10 Selecting New Cluster in the Network Load Balancing Manager

7. On the Connect page, enter the host name of the first server to be part of the cluster (the name of the server being configured) and click Connect to list all available network addresses. (If you have only one network adapter and only one IP address is configured for that adapter, only one choice will be listed.)
8. Select the network IP address to add and click Next.
9. On the Hosts Parameters page, select a Priority (unique host identifier). The host with the lowest priority number takes precedence when no port rules are in effect (start with number 1 and work downward unless a specific server is set as the default).
10. If you need to add IP addresses, click the Add button. Otherwise, click Next.
11. On the Cluster IP Addresses page, enter the shared IP address (or addresses). This IP address is used by end users to connect to SharePoint. Then click Next.
12. On the Cluster Parameters page, select Unicast (if your servers have only one NIC card in them, choose Multicast). This way, the cluster's Media Access Control (MAC) address is used for each network adapter, rather than the individual MAC addresses. Click Next.
13. On the Port Rules page, click Edit and add the appropriate port rules, if necessary. Click Finish when done.
14. To add more servers to the cluster, go back to the Network Load Balancing Manager, right-click Network Load Balancing Cluster, and choose Connect To Existing. Fill in the details as was done for the first server and repeat for each server that is to be part of the cluster.

IMPORTANT **NLB AND DHCP**

Network Load Balancing can't use Dynamic Host Configuration Protocol (DHCP). IP addresses must be static.

NLB must be installed on every server that's part of the NLB cluster before it's added to via the Network Load Balancing Manager tool. After NLB is configured, if an individual server goes down, the load is automatically redistributed among the remaining servers. NLB determines whether a server is up via a "heartbeat" that each server sends out. If the Network Load Balance Manager doesn't receive a "heartbeat" for 5 seconds (by default), it assumes that the server is unresponsive and routes requests to the other servers in the NLB cluster. This is referred to as a *convergence*, and the server with the lowest priority number takes over as the default. If the server that was down (unresponsive heartbeat) comes back online during the convergence, it becomes part of the group. If it doesn't, it must be added back in via the NLB Manager tool. The convergence takes only a few seconds, so the total outage (assuming that a user was accessing the downed server) should be about 7–10 seconds. For other users, the cluster is down for only a few seconds.

You can add or remove a server from the NLB cluster at any time. This greatly improves uptime of the SharePoint server farm and allows for maintenance of servers with minimal downtime. NLB provides a number of additional features in Windows Server 2008 R2, including the following:

- An NLB cluster can have up to 32 servers.
- You can add hosts without bringing the cluster down.
- You can bring a host down for maintenance without downtime.
- A downed host can recover within 10 seconds.
- You can define port rules for individual websites, giving great flexibility on how the load is distributed.
- You can perform remote administration from anywhere on the network.
- No additional hardware is required.
- NLB allows for multiple IP addresses.

> ***MORE INFO*** **NLB OVERVIEW**
>
> **To learn about more NLB features, see** ***http://technet.microsoft.com/en-us/library/cc725691.***

Planning for SQL Server load balancing

Using SQL Server load balancing with Active/Active clustering isn't supported. *Active/Active* refers to two separate SQL Server instances using each other as failovers. This is different in that a single SQL Server instance uses one or more cluster nodes as failovers in case the primary node fails. Database mirroring or AlwaysOn high availability still relies on a single SQL Server instance to receive transactions and then push them out to secondary servers so that both methods rely on a single SQL Server instance to interact with for transactions. Log shipping also has a single server as a bottleneck for inputs because the secondary servers only receive content and can't be used for write transactions unless a failover is initiated. Even if clustering is set up, it still relies on a single server to receive the transactions and then replicate them to the other servers.

Planning for SQL Server load balancing is an advanced topic and requires considerable planning and resources. Generally, giving the primary SQL Server node more memory and network bandwidth resources gives more of a benefit than trying to load balance several SQL Server instances. One option for balancing some of the load is to use linked servers. This allows for a database that resides on one SQL Server instance to appear as it is on another SQL Server instance. The following section describes this option in more detail.

Linked servers

Linked servers are most useful in situations where the data can be separated into distinct databases. This is perfect for SharePoint, which can put sites into separate databases. A web application can have any number of databases, which, by using linked servers, can be distributed across multiple SQL Server nodes. Most resources involved in a database transaction are related to writing and reading data from the disk. Having multiple SQL Server instances allows for the distribution of this time-expensive operation. Connecting a linked server is fairly straightforward, but looking at the steps involved is worth the effort for a better understanding of how linked servers work:

1. Open Microsoft SQL Server Management Studio on the database server that SharePoint connects to.
2. In the Object Explorer window, expand the Server Objects folder.
3. Right-click Linked Servers and select New Linked Server as shown in Figure 1-11.

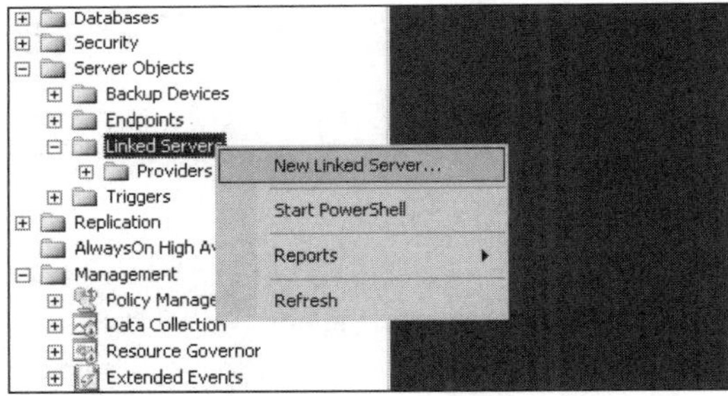

FIGURE 1-11 Creating a new linked server in SQL Server Management Studio

4. In the New Linked Server dialog box, select SQL Server under Server Type.
5. In the Linked Server text box, enter the name of the server to be linked.
6. Back in the Select A Page section on the right side of the screen, select Security.
7. In the Local Server Login To Remote Server Login Mappings section, add the login for the account under which the web application runs.
8. Click OK.

The linked server should now be connected and available for use. Limit linked servers to content databases that receive relatively little use, such as archived records. Queries against linked servers require distributed transactions, which are relatively expensive in memory and network bandwidth. The balance between disk operations and storage requirements need to be weighed against the distributed transaction costs.

MORE INFO **CREATE LINKED SERVERS**

See *http://msdn.microsoft.com/en-us/library/ff772782.aspx* for more information on creating linked servers.

Federated database servers

For SharePoint implementations that require high availability of SQL Server databases, federated database servers represent a viable solution for data that can benefit from horizontal partitioning. This highly advanced database subject requires significant planning and in-depth knowledge of SQL Server. Each SQL Server node in a federation group is managed independently, but all nodes cooperate to provide data as though from a single server.

MORE INFO **FEDERATED DATABASE SERVERS**

Although the federated databases present themselves as a single server instance, they have internal differences. See *http://technet.microsoft.com/en-us/library/ms190381(v=sql.105).aspx* for more information.

Planning for SQL Server aliases

A SQL Server alias allows for SharePoint to switch from one SQL Server instance to another should a disaster occur. SharePoint does this by connecting to the alias rather than directly to the SQL Server instance. If that SQL Server instance goes down, SharePoint can be pointed to a mirrored instance and be back up by just changing the details of the alias.

NOTE **LOCATION OF SQL SERVER CLIENT CONNECTIVITY COMPONENTS**

SQL Server aliasing is done on the client computer (SharePoint Server node), not on SQL Server itself. Each SharePoint server needs the SQL Server client connectivity components installed on it.

You can create a SQL Server alias in just a few steps. The following steps create an alias on a SharePoint 2013 server with Microsoft SQL Server 2012 client connectivity components installed on it:

1. From the Start menu of the SQL Server instance, navigate to Microsoft SQL Server 2012 | Configuration Tools | SQL Server Configuration Manager.
2. Expand SQL Native Client 11.0 Configuration.
3. Right-click Aliases and select New Alias.
4. Fill in the values for Alias Name and Server, as shown in Figure 1-12. Leave the Protocol as TCP/IP and the Port No as blank.

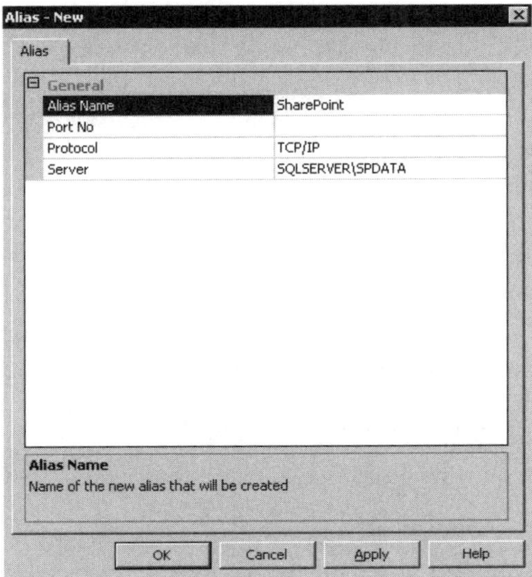

FIGURE 1-12 Alias dialog box from the SQL Server Configuration Manager

5. Click OK.
6. Repeat the preceding steps for SQL Native Client 11.0 Configuration (32bit). This is for *thunking* (converting 32-bit instructions to 64-bit instructions and vice versa) when communicating with SQL Server.
7. Repeat steps 1-6 for each SharePoint server.

After you configure each the SharePoint 2013 server with the appropriate alias, you can install the SharePoint 2013 farm. Where it asks for the database server, enter the alias rather than the actual server name. If you've already installed your SharePoint farm, you need to run the SharePoint Products Configuration Wizard and choose Disconnect From This Server Farm on the Modify Server Farm Settings page. After you disconnect, you can rerun the SharePoint Products Configuration Wizard and connect to an existing SharePoint farm by using the alias instead. Clicking Retrieve Database Names should bring back the existing configuration database. You also need to supply the farm passphrase and a port number (or use the one that's generated). Finally, all respective SharePoint services need to be restarted.

> ***IMPORTANT*** **REMOVING THE USER PROFILE SYNCHRONIZATION SERVICE**
>
> **The Forefront Identity Manager (FIM) Services on the SharePoint server responsible for the User Profile Synchronization becomes disabled if you detach it from the existing SharePoint farm. You need to set the start mode for the FIM services manually from Disabled to Automatic.**

If the SQL Server Configuration Management client tools aren't available on the SharePoint server, you can create an alias using the SQL Server Client Network Utility as follows:

1. Run the following application:

```
c:\windows\system32\cliconfig.exe
```

2. On the Alias tab, click Add.
3. Select TCP/IP from the Network Libraries section.
4. Type the alias in the Server Alias text box.
5. Enter the Server Name in the Connection Parameters section.
6. Leave the Dynamically Determine Port check box selected and click OK.
7. Run the 64-bit version (*c:\windows\syswow64\cliconfig.exe*) and repeat steps 1–6.
8. Repeat all these steps for each SharePoint server.

When these steps are complete, the aliases are complete and a farm can be installed or reconnected as described earlier.

If you're using database mirroring, AlwaysOn High Availability Groups, or log shipping, you should install SharePoint using a SQL Server alias to enable switching to a new SQL Server instance. The only high-availability options that don't benefit from an alias are database clustering and AlwaysOn Failover Cluster Instances. This is because if one node goes down in a cluster, another node takes over, but the SQL Server instance name stays the same. This doesn't prohibit an alias from being used in a clustering environment; in fact, it's encouraged in case the cluster itself fails and a backup needs to be restored to a new SQL Server while the cluster is restored.

Thought experiment

Balancing a network load across multiple WFEs with high-availability databases

In this thought experiment, apply what you've learned about this objective. You can find answers to these questions in the "Answers" section at the end of this chapter.

You have been told to create a SharePoint farm that should have multiple Web Front Ends and connect to a single mirrored SQL Server instance. You want to develop a solution that distributes the load across the WFEs and allows for switching over to the mirrored database if the primary SQL Server node fails or is down for maintenance. With the WFEs, the primary goal is to have high availability of front-end servers; the secondary goal is to have the processing load distributed across the servers, giving end users more responsive interactions with the SharePoint farm.

What two technologies would you implement to make this happen?

Objective summary

- SQL Server aliases provide a quick way to point SharePoint to a new database server.
- SharePoint services can be distributed across any number of SharePoint servers.
- You can use Network Load Balancing to distribute the network load over several Web Front Ends to provide performance improvements and high availability.
- Linked servers provide a way to distribute SQL Server data for databases with low usage.
- SharePoint services fall under three main categories: Web Front Ends, Search, and Application server.

Objective review

Answer the following questions to test your knowledge of the information in this objective. You can find the answers to these questions and explanations of why each answer choice is correct or incorrect in the "Answers" section at the end of this chapter.

1. You want to create SQL Server aliases as part of your high-availability plan. On which of the following will you need to configure this?
   - **A.** All the SQL Server instances that are part of the SharePoint farm
   - **B.** SharePoint servers that access SQL Server data
   - **C.** Both A and B
   - **D.** Neither A nor B
2. A SharePoint server can be which of the following roles?
   - **A.** Web Front End
   - **B.** Search server
   - **C.** Application
   - **D.** Any or all of the above
3. You want to distribute the network load on your SharePoint Web Front Ends (WFEs). On which of the following will you need to configure this?
   - **A.** Central Administration
   - **B.** NLB on each WFE
   - **C.** In the IIS Manager
   - **D.** All of the above
4. Where does Network Load Balancing (NLB) sit in the communication stack?
   - **A.** Right below the WFE layer
   - **B.** Below the network adapter layer
   - **C.** Right below the TCP/IP layer
   - **D.** Above the WFE layer

5. Which of the following would provide data redundancy at the hardware level?
   - **A.** RAID 0
   - **B.** RAID 1
   - **C.** RAID 5
   - **D.** RAID 10

Objective 1.3: Plan backup and restore

Backup and restore are essential to any disaster recovery plan. You need to consider many factors when developing a comprehensive backup and restore plan. RTO and RPO are the drivers that should determine the methods and frequency of backups, but in a SharePoint farm, making sure everything required for a full recovery is properly backed up is also essential. This objective goes over the essential components of the SharePoint installation, backup and recovery methods, and the frequency that each component should be backed up.

This objective covers the following topics:

- Establish a SharePoint backup schedule
- Establish a SQL Server backup schedule
- Plan a non-production farm content refresh
- Plan for a farm configuration recovery
- Plan for service application recovery
- Plan for content recovery

Establishing a SharePoint backup schedule

SharePoint needs to be backed up independently of SQL Server. You can back up SharePoint in a couple different ways, but to understand what a SharePoint backup versus a SQL Server backup means, you need to look at the SharePoint components that need to be backed up:

- Farm configuration
- IIS Settings
- Files in the web application
- Farm solutions
- The entire SharePoint hive
- Server topology (which servers are performing which functions)
- IP Settings
- Certificates
- Any Dynamic Link Libraries (DLLs) stored in the Global Assembly Cache (GAC)

The farm configuration is stored in the central administration database but should also be backed up independently of the normal SQL Server backups. This provides several benefits, including marking a farm configuration as a "golden" copy so that if corruption happens to the configuration, you're not trying to figure out when the last uncorrupted copy was backed up. Also, the backup can be kept local, which makes restoration easier for the SharePoint administrator. In many organizations, the person responsible for the SharePoint farm doesn't have the rights (and perhaps training required) to restore a SQL Server database. A SharePoint farm backup allows that person to restore a farm configuration independently.

When deciding on a schedule, the recovery model is important to consider. By default, SharePoint content databases have the full recovery model, which provides a greater level of recovery but takes up more hard drive space. To better understand the recovery model, look at the options in Table 1-1.

TABLE 1-1 Available recovery model options

Recovery model	Description	Recovery options
Simple	Automatically reclaims log space so that log space requirements are minimal.	Changes since the most recent backup aren't protected. Only the most recent backup can be recovered.
Full	Requires log backups. Log files can be used to recover to data up until failure.	You can recover to a point in time assuming that backups are complete.
Bulk Logged	Between Full and Simple. Requires log backups. Reduces log space by using minimal logging requirements.	You can use this to recover to the end of any backup. Point-in-time recovery isn't supported.

Most databases use either the Simple or Full recovery model. If you are using the Simple recovery model, backing up the data more frequently is important so that the amount of data lost is minimized. The main issue with the Simple recovery model is that it's not available if high-availability options such as database mirroring or AlwaysOn High Availability Groups are being used.

Using Central Administration backup

The primary tool used to back up a SharePoint 2103 farm is the Backup Tool available in Central Administration. You can use this easy-to-use graphical interface tool to back up the farm configuration as well as well as content databases. This tool has several types of backup types available:

- The complete farm with data and configuration
- Differential
- Configuration only
- Component level

NOTE USING DIFFERENTIAL BACKUPS

Differential backups are only for content databases. To restore, you need the full backup as well as the differential backup. Also, if you have large content databases (more than 100 GB each), the backup process could take a long time.

Central Administration backup provides a simple interface, but you need to consider some exceptions when using it. Although it's a great tool to use to back up farm configuration information, it should be used with caution as part of your content database backup strategy. Central Administration Backup can write to only a file location, not to tape, so enough file space must be available to handle the backup. Because it doesn't automatically get rid of old backups, they can add up quickly, depending on the type of backup. Finally, Central Administration has no built-in way to schedule backups. The only reason to use Central Administration Backup for content databases would be for archiving purposes. However, it's a valid backup strategy for having a locally available backup of the configuration data.

Configuration-only backups will be the primary function of the Central Administration Backup tool because no other built-in tool provides backups of configuration data with such completeness. This doesn't mean that it backs up all the configuration information necessary to restore a SharePoint server. Several important items aren't backed up by the Backup tool:

- **ISS settings not set by SharePoint** The IIS Microsoft Management Console (MMC) snap-in provides a backup mechanism that you can use to back up IIS settings. Although some overlap will occur, having this backup available is important in case settings need to be restored.
- **SSL Certificates** These need to be saved as individual files.
- **Anything in the SharePoint hive** The entire SharePoint hive needs to be saved (at least the templates folder) periodically, after you make major changes such as adding features or change any existing files, such as *docicons.xml*. The entire *Inetpubs* directory also can be saved. This takes off any files related to web application folders. You should document which services are running on each server and keep this information in a location not on your SharePoint server farm.
- **Files in the Global Assembly Cache** Files put into the GAC (DLLs in farm-level solutions) should be saved in a directory under a subfile that gives the version. All these files should be stored in a location that's not part of the SharePoint farm and in a different physical location from the database servers and the SharePoint farms. If a farm needs to be restored, redeploying the farm solutions should restore the DLLs.
- **Files in the web application folder** These should be manually copied to a safe location and documented.
- **Which servers are running which services** This information should be noted manually in a configuration document.

These settings should be backed up separately for each server in the SharePoint farm.

Backing up just the SharePoint configuration is straightforward with the Central Administration user interface. Follow these steps:

1. Navigate to Central Administration using a farm administrator account.
2. Click Backup And Restore.
3. Under Farm Backup And Restore, click Perform A Backup.
4. Select the very first check box that has the word Farm (see Figure 1-13).

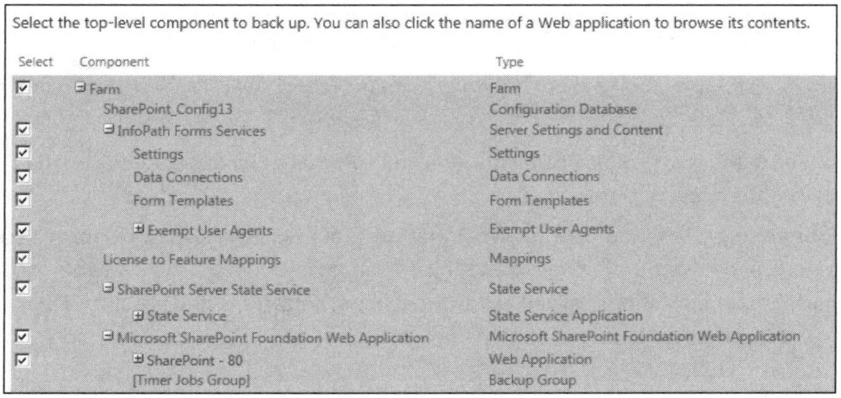

Select the top-level component to back up. You can also click the name of a Web application to browse its contents.

Select	Component	Type
☑	⊟ Farm	Farm
	SharePoint_Config13	Configuration Database
☑	⊟ InfoPath Forms Services	Server Settings and Content
☑	Settings	Settings
☑	Data Connections	Data Connections
☑	Form Templates	Form Templates
☑	⊞ Exempt User Agents	Exempt User Agents
☑	License to Feature Mappings	Mappings
☑	⊟ SharePoint Server State Service	State Service
	⊞ State Service	State Service Application
☑	⊟ Microsoft SharePoint Foundation Web Application	Microsoft SharePoint Foundation Web Application
☑	⊞ SharePoint - 80	Web Application
	[Timer Jobs Group]	Backup Group

FIGURE 1-13 Selecting all available components in a farm backup

5. Click Next.
6. For Backup Type, leave Full selected.
7. In the Back Up Only Configuration Settings section, select the Back Up Only Configuration Settings option.
8. For the Backup File Location section, enter a UNC path (for example, *server**backup*) in the Backup Location box.
9. Double-check your settings and click Start Backup to begin the backup process. The next page displays the status of the progress as soon as the timer job is started. When everything in the Progress column says that it's completed, the backup is done.

IMPORTANT **ALLOWING SPACE FOR BACKUPS**

When the Central Administration user interface is used, it calculates the space required to finish the backups and throws an error if not enough space is available. It tends to overcalculate because of the backup size of the truncated log files if you are using the simple recovery method.

SharePoint creates a folder in the backup location (such as *spbr0000*) each time a backup is performed. When you do a restore, you need to know which folder to choose to restore the proper backup. In the specified backup folder is a *spbrtoc.xml* file that specifies the backups available and when they occurred. Within each backup folder are two files that explain the contents of the folder—*spbackup.log* and *spbackup.xml*—in case you need to examine the contents of what was backed up.

You can also use PowerShell to perform SharePoint backups in a similar way as Central Administration because it provides the equivalent functionality. It's useful if you will be repeating the same type of backup or if you plan to automate any backup function. Being familiar with the syntax of the PowerShell backup commands is important:

```
Backup-SPFarm -BackupMethod <Full|Differential> -Directory <UNC Path> [-Configuration
Only] [-Force] [-Item <named component>]
```

If you save scripts that you use regularly, you can run them whenever needed rather than have to rewrite them every single time.

SharePoint also provides an object model that programmers can use to perform backups. This will be more involved than would benefit most organizations, but it's available for more complex farm implementations as well as third-party organizations that want to develop tools to provide comprehensive backup solutions.

Establishing a SharePoint backup schedule

A SharePoint backup schedule varies from a SQL server backup schedule. It should be driven by change, not by time. Whenever a significant environmental change occurs, you should perform a backup. Sometimes this might happen multiple times in a day, and sometimes weeks or months might pass without a need to back up SharePoint. This means that a manual process must be involved to start the backup process.

The following are some examples of when a full SharePoint backup should be performed:

- Right after installing and/or upgrading SharePoint and all the configurations are completed
- Before and after the addition or removal of a server to the farm
- Before and after significant services are added or removed (for example, adding or removing Project Server)
- Before and after installing any cumulative update (CU) or service pack
- Before attempting any upgrade

These backups can't be scheduled and should be performed by a SharePoint administrator. A snapshot of the server provides additional protection if you are using a virtual machine (VM); a backup of the entire server via disk or tape if you aren't using a VM provides additional protection and options for recovery. These backups do require significantly more resources than just backing up the pertinent information required for SharePoint.

A scheduled backup of the farm is also a good idea and should be part of high-availability planning. Central Administration doesn't allow for scheduled backups, so you need to use another method. For example, you can create a PowerShell script and then set up a Windows timer job to automate it.

Establishing a SQL Server backup schedule

SQL Server is where SharePoint stores the bulk of the content that needs to be backed up. If you can recover a content database, you can build a new SharePoint server and attach to it, thus recovering the data within. Determining a SQL Server backup depends on a number of factors, including some that will be out of your hands but must still be considered:

- Technologies available, such as Microsoft Data Protection Manager (DPM)
- Size of the content databases to be backed up
- Relative importance of the data
- How long to keep backups
- Resources available to do backups
- Timing of backups
- Time to restore backups

A typical scenario would be doing a full backup once a week and doing a differential every day during the week. This scenario would generally be used in an environment that backs up the databases to tape or to a shared storage area such as a SAN. (Tape has the benefit of being cheaper, but a SAN provides a quicker recovery time.) As part of the backup schedule, the service level agreement (SLA) should be determined. Using differentials saves money but requires more time to restore because the most recent full backup must be restored before you can restore a differential.

If a VM is being used for SQL Server, backups of the individual content databases should still be used because restoring a single content database from a VM is impossible. The backup VM could be used to bring up a temporary instance, and then a single content database could be saved from it and restored to the production database.

Planning a non-production environment content refresh

An up-to-date reproduction of your production environment is a great asset in development and testing. Every cumulative update and service pack should be tested in a non-production environment that matches as closely as possible the production environment. In many situations, however, this is prohibitively expensive. Not every single SharePoint server in the production farm needs to be reproduced in the non-production environment, but if at all possible, the reproduction should include all the production environment content. This is to allow for an environment that's as close to the real thing as possible without having a perfect replica.

If you are dealing with VMs, the process is much easier than if you are dealing with physical servers. You can simply take a snapshot of the servers involved and copy them over into the non-production environment replacing any out of date servers.

A non-production environment consists of at least the following items:

- Domain controller
- At least one SharePoint server
- SQL Server database(s)

With these three items, you can create a non-production environment with a high degree of certainty that your solutions, cumulative updates, or service packs behave similarly to the production environment.

> ***IMPORTANT*** **MAINTAINING A CONSISTENT ENVIRONMENT**
>
> **All servers should have the exact same operating systems that exist in the production environment. This means the same versions, updates, service packs, and so on.**

Keeping content refreshed is tricky if development is being done in the non-production environment (as is typical). Often, development is being stored in the content database. Items such as all client-side scripts, changes to master pages, workflows created out of the box (OTB) or with SharePoint Designer, changes to .aspx pages, and so on are all stored in the content database. A simple database restore would wipe all this work out unless everything had been re-created in the production environment before the content refresh. In these situations, determining how and when to refresh the content is up to the individual organization.

If you want a non-production environment with almost current (depending on the frequency of the updates but potentially less than an hour old) data all the time, you can use Content Deployment. SharePoint provides Content Deployment OTB. This can be used to keep a non-production environment current with scheduled data. Content Deployment can found in Central Administration or can be run via PowerShell or the SharePoint object model. For the purposes of the exam, this book focuses on the Central Administration method. Later, this book explores in detail the content deployment methods and configuration.

Planning for farm configuration recovery

Earlier, this chapter went over how to back up a farm configuration. Assuming that you backed up your configuration at that time, you can now recover it. Some settings have to be recovered manually, but you can start with recovering the farm configuration by using the built-in configuration restoration method in Central Administration. Because the Central Administration restore method uses a graphical UI that presents a visual representation of what's being restored, you will less likely restore something unintended.

A configuration backup must be done from a full backup and not a differential. (A differential backup is applicable only to content databases.) To better understand the process, you need to look at the steps involved:

1. In Central Administration, click Backup And Restore and then select Restore From A Backup.
2. The most recent backup path should be listed with the backup sets found. If the backup you need isn't in that location, enter the Backup Directory Location and click Refresh.
3. Select the backup that you want to restore, as shown in Figure 1-14, and then click Next.

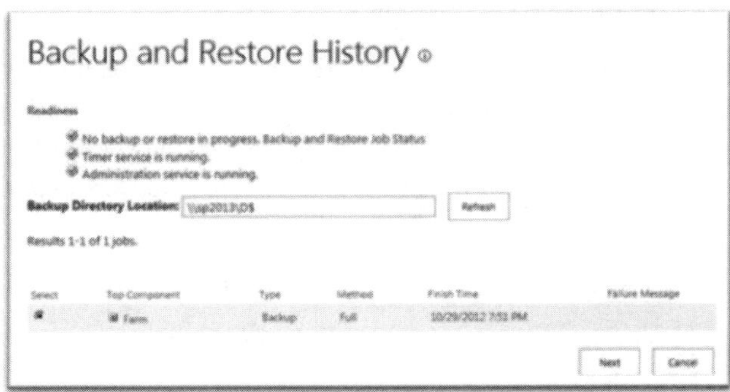

FIGURE 1-14 Selecting a specific backup to restore

4. SharePoint displays a list of all the components available for restore. Select the check boxes of the desired content to restore. If you are doing a full configuration restore from a configuration-only backup, choose Farm to select everything below it and then click Next.
5. The next page that appears depends on what you chose in step 4. To replace the current configuration, choose Same Configuration. A warning message appears, saying that all components will be overwritten. Click OK to continue.
6. Click the Start Restore button to begin the restore. A timer job is created, and you are redirected to the Backup And Restore Status page.
7. Click Refresh to view the progress. When everything in the progress column says *Completed*, the restore is done.

> ***IMPORTANT*** **RESTORATION CONSIDERATIONS**
>
> **Double-check all your settings before clicking Start Restore. The restore could take a while, and during this time the SharePoint farm is unavailable. Don't try to restart or stop the restoration process after it starts—it could leave your farm in an unstable condition.**

Planning for service application recovery

You can use Central Administration to back up components. If you need to be able to recover an application, you should have backed them up as described earlier in this objective. If you have done a full farm backup, you can simply choose an individual component to restore (such as Excel Services) from the entire backup. Ensuring that you have backed-up settings since any major changes to a service application were made is important. If you have a current backup, the restoration process is fairly straightforward via Central Administration. Even if you back up service applications, you should store in a location that's not in SharePoint a documented list of which services are on which servers.

Central Administration provides individual component backup. For example, if you want to back up only the Machine Translation services, you could use the OTB backup-and-restore services to back up just this one component so that it can be recovered quickly. For the purposes of illustration, the following steps restore a single service application, a previously backed-up instance of the InfoPath Services:

1. Navigate to Central Administration and click the Backup And Restore link.
2. Click Restore From A Backup under the Farm Backup And Restore section.
3. Select Farm\InfoPath Form Services from the list of backup jobs, as shown in Figure 1-15, and then click Next.

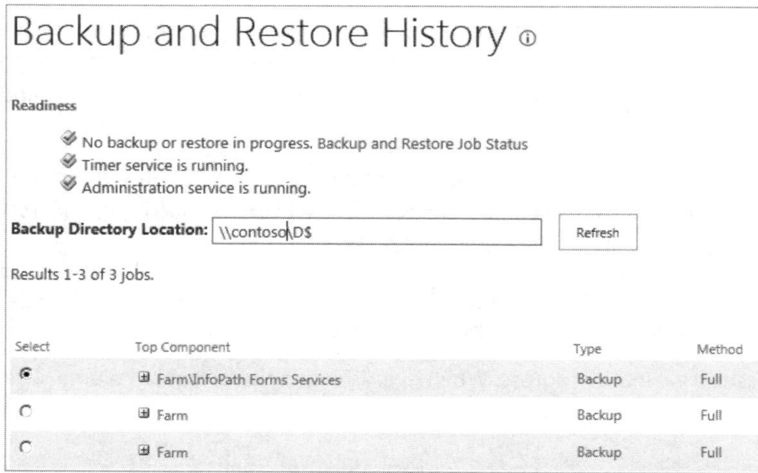

FIGURE 1-15 Choosing the InfoPath Form Services from the jobs in Backup and Restore History

4. Select InfoPath Forms Services on the Select Component to Restore page, and then click Next.
5. On the Select Restore Options page, select Restore Content And Configuration Settings under Data To Restore and choose Same Configuration under Type Of Restore.

6. Click Start Restore.
7. When the Backup And Restore Status page appears, click Refresh to check the status of the restore. When the restore is complete, everything under Status should show as completed.

Planning for content recovery

Several viable options are available for recovering content. Each one has its pros and cons, but they can all provide a full recovery of all the content from a content database. This section covers the following options:

- Recovery via *Restore-SPSite*
- Content database recovery via SQL Server
- Recovery via Central Administration

Backing up a content database with SQL Server or backup-and-restore products such as Data Protection Manager (DPM) by Microsoft is a standard disaster-recovery protocol. When a restore is required, you can restore over the existing content database, in which case everything that has been changed since the backup is lost, or you can restore to a new database, in which case you can look at the backed-up data and choose what you want to recover. This feature is extremely useful if you just want to recover certain parts of the content database, such as a corrupted site or list.

> ***NOTE*** **USING STSADM**
>
> ***STSADM*** **is still available and can work to export and/or import websites. It's no longer the preferred method, though, because PowerShell is available.**

Recovering a specific list or document library is best done using additional software because a list or document library template is limited to 25 MB by default. DPM enables you to back up and restore individual libraries and lists. If a library or list is below the limit, a list or library can be saved as a template (with content) to a temporary location by going through the galleries section of the site collection settings page. When it's saved to the temporary location, you can upload it to the production SharePoint farm and restore it in the proper location. If a library or list exceeds the SharePoint specified limit, another product needs to be used, such as Microsoft DPM.

> ***MORE INFO*** **USING MICROSOFT DPM**
>
> **See** ***http://technet.microsoft.com/en-us/library/cc424951.aspx*** **for more information on how to use Microsoft DPM to back up and recover lists and document libraries.**

Recovering a database using Restore-SPSite

If a content database has been restored to a temporary location, you can use the PowerShell commands *Backup-SPSite* and *Restore-SPSite* to recover an entire site collection. The *Restore-SPSite* syntax is as follows:

```
Restore-SPSite [-Identity] <String> -Path <String> [-AssignmentCollection
<SPAssignmentCollection>] [-Confirm [<SwitchParameter>]] [-ContentDatabase
<SPContentDatabasePipeBind>] [-Force <SwitchParameter>] [-GradualDelete
<SwitchParameter>] [-HostHeaderWebApplication <String>] [-WhatIf [<SwitchParameter>]]
```

> ***MORE INFO*** **RESTORE-SPSITE**
>
> **See *http://technet.microsoft.com/en-us/library/ff607788.aspx* for more information on the *Restore-SPSite* PowerShell command.**

If the backed-up site collection is being restored over an existing site collection, you must use the *-Force* option to overwrite the site collection and everything that has changed since the backup. Use caution when restoring large site collections; doing so could cause the SharePoint farm to be nonresponsive or to respond slowly. Also, the operation must have enough memory to finish. If not enough memory exists, the restore fails.

Depending on the size of the site collection, the restore operation could take hours through the PowerShell command. Thorough testing should be done to establish expectations and determine whether the SharePoint farm's capabilities meet the business requirements.

Recovering a database via SQL Server

Recovering a database with SQL Server involves two options: You can restore a whole content database, replacing an existing one, or you can restore a content database to a new name. Restoring an existing content database with a different name enables you to extract certain pieces of data as well as review the data against the current set of data. If you try to attach the content database to the same SharePoint farm that's using the current content database, SharePoint won't allow two databases with the same ID. Therefore, when you mount the database, you need to assign it a new ID. This can be done with the following PowerShell command:

```
Mount-SPContentDatabase [-Name] <String> [-WebApplication] <SPWebApplicationPipeBind>
[-AssignNewDatabaseId]
```

Example:

```
Mount-SPContentDatabase "Contoso Sales" -WebApplication http://contoso/sales
-AssignNewDatabaseId
```

MORE INFO **MOUNT-SPCONTENTDATABASE**

See *http://technet.microsoft.com/en-us/library/ff607581.aspx* for more information on the PowerShell command *Mount-SPContentDatabase*.

Recovering a database using Central Administration

Even with a different database ID, you shouldn't attach the database to the same web application as the one that contains the existing content database because the URLs will be the same for both databases. Create a new temporary web application to attach the database (the preferable solution) or attach it to a different existing web application that doesn't have the same tree structure.

You can use PowerShell to restore content from an unattached database backup. This way, you can avoid attaching with a new ID and still allow for data restoration. The PowerShell command for this is as follows (after the database is restored to SQL Server):

```
Get-SPContentDatabase -ConnectAsUnattachedDatabase -DatabaseName <DatabaseName>
-DatabaseServer <DatabaseServer>
```

After the PowerShell command finishes, you can recover the data using Central Administration as follows:

1. Log onto SharePoint 2013 Central Administration with a farm administrator account that also has db_owner rights on the SQL Server instance where the restored database resides.
2. Click the Backup And Restore link.
3. On the Backup And Restore page, click Recover Data From An Unattached Content Database in the Granular Backup section.
4. On the Unattached Content Database Data Recovery page, enter the name of the unattached database in the Database Name box and the name of the SQL Server instance it's on in the Database Server box.
5. Select the database authentication to use.
6. Select the Browse Content option and click Next.
7. On the Browse Content page, select the site collection, site, or list that needs to be restored and click Restore. The restoration should be complete at this point.

MORE INFO **RESTORING CONTENT FROM UNATTACHED CONTENT DATABASES**

See *http://technet.microsoft.com/en-us/library/hh269602.aspx* for more information about restoring content from unattached content databases in SharePoint 2013.

EXAM TIP

The exam expects familiarity with restoring content from an unattached database. The PowerShell syntax involved with restoring content from an unattached database is one of the few commands you should memorize.

Restoring a content database over an existing one using SQL Server totally replaces the existing database. Before doing this, make sure that that's what you want, because all data between the last backup and the restore is lost. You should be familiar with the process of restoring a database and the steps involved. Assuming that you have used SQL Server to back up a database, you can restore a database using the following steps:

1. Open Microsoft SQL Server Management Studio.
2. Expand the Databases folder in the Object Explorer.
3. Right-click the database you want to restore.
4. Choose Tasks | Restore | Database, as shown in Figure 1-16.

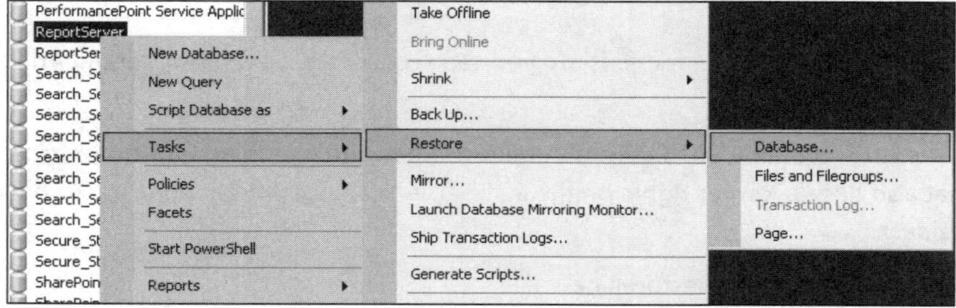

FIGURE 1-16 The Restore Database option in Microsoft SQL Server Management Studio

5. In the list of Backup Sets To Restore, select the backup set to restore and then click OK. The dialog box remains open and shows progress until the task completes or fails. Depending on the database size and the server speed, it could take minutes or hours.
6. After the restore finishes successfully, click OK in the dialog box that appears. The database is now ready to use.

IMPORTANT **EXCLUSIVE ACCESS FOR RESTORATION**

Exclusive access to a database is necessary to be able to restore it. If this is a SharePoint database, you have to stop any processes that use it (for example, stop the web application that's using the database).

This restore option uses the defaults and is sufficient for most database restoration needs.

MORE INFO RESTORING CONTENT DATABASES IN SHAREPOINT 2013

The other task options—Files and Filegroups, Transaction Log, and Page—available on the Restore Database dialog box are more advanced restoration options not covered in this book, but you can find out more about them at *http://technet.microsoft.com/en-us/library/ee748604.aspx#proc3*.

Thought experiment

Choosing the proper database recovery model

In this thought experiment, apply what you've learned about this objective. You can find answers to these questions in the "Answers" section at the end of this chapter.

Your assignment is to decide which recovery model would be best for the content databases in the SharePoint farm. The SQL Server nodes in the farm run on an AlwaysOn FCI group. The decision for high availability is often out of the hands of the designer of the SharePoint farm and in this case was made by the database administrators at your organization. The content databases range in size but go up to 200 GB each, and the expected size of the databases occupies from 60 percent to 70 percent of the space available on the storage allocated to the SharePoint farm. The only decision you have concerning the content databases is which recovery model to choose: Simple or Full.

Which model would make the most sense based on these restrictions?

Objective summary

- SQL Server and SharePoint backup schedules are completely separate entities that need individual planning.
- Testing the amount of time to recover and the acceptable RTO and RPO will drive backup schedules.
- Keeping a non-production environment as close to the production environment is crucial for testing any changes and for developing solutions with minimal impact.
- The configuration of a SharePoint farm occurs in several different areas that need to be backed up and maintained separately.
- You can restore SharePoint content using various methods, including SharePoint Central Administration, PowerShell, and SQL Server.
- You can use Central Administration to back up and restore individual service applications.

Objective review

Answer the following questions to test your knowledge of the information in this objective. You can find the answers to these questions and explanations of why each answer choice is correct or incorrect in the "Answers" section at the end of this chapter.

1. You need to back up the farm configuration. What are valid options?
   - **A.** Backup and Restore in Central Administration
   - **B.** PowerShell *Backup-SPFarm* method
   - **C.** *Stsadm* commands
   - **D.** All of the above
2. You are backing up SQL Server content databases, and a particular database needs point-in-time recovery. Which recovery model is required for the database?
   - **A.** Bulk logged
   - **B.** Simple
   - **C.** Full
   - **D.** Any of the above will work
3. A backup of a content database is restored to the production SQL Server. It needs to be attached to the SharePoint farm so that the backup data can be compared to production data. For that to happen, what needs to happen to the restored database?
   - **A.** It can simply be added as a content database in Central Administration.
   - **B.** It must be attached with a new database ID using a command-line function.
   - **C.** It can't be attached to the same SharePoint farm.
   - **D.** It can be attached with Central Administration but not to the same web application.
4. Which of the following isn't/aren't backed up by a configuration-only backup of the SharePoint farm via Central Administration?
   - **A.** SSL Certificates
   - **B.** DLLs in the Global Assembly Cache (GAC)
   - **C.** IIS-specific settings not manage through SharePoint
   - **D.** All of the above

5. Which of the following can be backed up as individual components using Central Administration?
   - **A.** Global search settings
   - **B.** SharePoint Server State service
   - **C.** InfoPath Forms services
   - **D.** All of the above

Chapter summary

- High availability for SQL Server data is the cornerstone for any SharePoint disaster recovery plan, and you can choose from a wide range of options.
- High availability for SharePoint data not stored in databases should be planned for separately as part of a comprehensive disaster recovery plan.
- Technologies such as Network Load Balancing (NLB) can help to ensure a high level of availability of SharePoint content.
- Resources and criticality of data dictate frequency of backups (both of databases and SharePoint-specific products).
- You can use Central Administration Backup to back up SharePoint-specific items such as service applications and settings.
- Some items, such as IIS settings, aren't backed up by SQL Server backups or Central Administration Backup and must be maintained separately.

Answers

This section contains the solutions to the thought experiments and answers to the lesson review questions in this chapter.

Objective 1.1: Thought experiment

In this scenario, database mirroring provides the best option. It provides high availability, and the 5 minute failover is well within the amount of time needed to fail over to the secondary database. Using AlwaysOn High Availability Groups isn't a good solution because SQL Server 2008 R2 is the available server and, based on the training and version, isn't a viable option. Clustering isn't an option because it doesn't provide high availability of the content databases, and log shipping isn't a good option due to the amount of time it takes to manually move over to a new database.

Objective 1.1: Review

1. **Correct answer:** B
    - **A. Incorrect:** An RTO of 99.9 percent means more than 8 hours of allowed downtime.
    - **B. Correct:** An RTO of 99.99 percent means a maximum of 53 minutes downtime in a 24-hour-a-day, seven-days-a-week environment.
    - **C. Incorrect:** An RTO of 99.999 percent (or *five nines* as it's referred to sometimes) means a downtime of less than 6 minutes—an admirable but expensive goal.
    - **D. Incorrect:** An RTO of 1 percent means the farm would be down 99 percent of the time—obviously not a desirable goal.
2. **Correct answer:** A
    - **A. Correct:** SharePoint 2013 supports multiple label domains.
    - **B. Incorrect:** SharePoint 2013 doesn't support single-label domains.
    - **C. Incorrect:** Only A is correct.
    - **D. Incorrect:** A is the correct answer.
3. **Correct answer:** D
    - **A. Incorrect:** Transaction log backups can't use the simple recovery model.
    - **B. Incorrect:** Log shipping can't use the simple recovery model.
    - **C. Incorrect:** Database mirroring can't use the simple recovery model.
    - **D. Correct:** Clustering is unaware what recovery models are used on what databases.

4. **Correct answer:** C

   A. **Incorrect:** Clustering can't be used to provide high availability for just a single content database. It's also the most expensive and complicated way to provide high availability in this situation.

   B. **Incorrect:** Transaction log shipping is a valid option here but isn't as effective as database mirroring.

   C. **Correct:** Database mirroring is an excellent choice for providing high availability for an individual database.

   D. **Incorrect:** Not all high-availability options are equal.

5. **Correct answers:** B and C

   A. **Incorrect:** WSFC must be configured on *all* the Windows Server instances running AlwaysOn High Availability Groups.

   B. **Correct:** SQL Server must be configured as well as the Windows Server instance it's running on.

   C. **Correct:** All Windows servers need to be configured that will be part of the AlwaysOn high-availability group.

   D. **Incorrect:** SharePoint 2013 doesn't need to be aware of an AlwaysOn high-availability group because it's aware of it only as though it were a single SQL Server.

Objective 1.2: Thought experiment

You need to deal with two issues in this thought experiment. The first is how to distribute the load across multiple WFEs. Network Load Balancing (NLB) is an excellent choice for this because it not only provides a way to distribute the processing load across several servers, but it also automatically detects when a Windows Internet Name Service (WINS) server becomes unavailable. This solves both the primary and secondary goals of the WFE requirement. The database failover goal can be solved by using SQL Server aliases. Because you know that SQL Server is being mirrored, you can modify the alias to point to the secondary or WINS server if the primary goes down or has been brought down for maintenance. Therefore, the combination of NLB and SQL Server aliases should provide a solution that meets the business goals outlined.

Objective 1.2: Review

1. **Correct answer:** B
   - **A. Incorrect:** Servers running SQL Server don't need aliases created on them.
   - **B. Correct:** All SharePoint servers that connect to the database need to be configured to use SQL Server aliases.
   - **C. Incorrect:** Only the SharePoint servers need to be configured to use SQL Server aliases.
   - **D. Incorrect:** To use SQL Server aliases in a SharePoint farm, they must be configured on the SharePoint servers.
2. **Correct answer:** D
   - **A. Incorrect:** WFE is one role a SharePoint server can assume but not the only one.
   - **B. Incorrect:** Search server is a processor-intensive role, but the SharePoint server that assumes this role can do others as well.
   - **C. Incorrect:** Application server is also an intensive role, but a SharePoint server can also handle more than just this role.
   - **D. Correct:** A SharePoint server can take on any or all of the roles listed above.
3. **Correct answer:** B
   - **A. Incorrect:** Central Administration is unaware that NLB is being used, yet NLB is the recommended way to distribute the load across multiple WFEs.
   - **B. Correct:** Configuring NLB on each SharePoint server WFE is the recommend way to distribute the load.
   - **C. Incorrect:** IIS isn't involved in configuring an NLB cluster.
   - **D. Incorrect:** Because B is the only correct answer, D can't be the answer.
4. **Correct answer:** C
   - **A. Incorrect:** The WFE layer communicates with the TCP/IP layer.
   - **B. Incorrect:** The network layer is the lowest layer in the communication stack.
   - **C. Correct:** Network Load Balancing (NLB) is between the TCP/IP layer and the network adapter layer.
   - **D. Incorrect:** The layer above the WFE is the interaction between the user and the WFE.

5. **Correct answers:** B and D
   - **A. Incorrect:** RAID 0 is writing data across several disks at the same time for increased performance in disk operations.
   - **B. Correct:** RAID 1 is disk mirroring, in which two exact copies of the data exist.
   - **C. Incorrect:** RAID 5 is like RAID 0 but with data parity so that a disk can be lost, but it provides no data redundancy.
   - **D. Correct:** RAID 10 has the benefits of RAID 0 and RAID 1.

Objective 1.3: Thought experiment

In this scenario, you are presented with a difficult decision. Because the SQL Server high-availability plan is out of your hands, you have only the choice of which recovery model to use for the SharePoint farm content databases. Clusters aren't aware of what recovery model individual databases use, so the only factor involved is how much disk space is being used and if point-in-time recovery is required. Because point-in-time recovery wasn't specified as a requirement, you can use the Simple recovery model to save space because the logs are truncated every time the database is fully backed up. Alerting the people involved that point-in-time recovery isn't possible in this scenario is always prudent. This is based on using SQL Server backups and not a third-party backup process.

Objective 1.3: Review

1. **Correct answer:** D
   - **A. Incorrect:** Backup and restore in Central Administration is a valid option, but it's not the only one.
   - **B. Incorrect:** PowerShell is only one of the valid options for backing up the farm configuration.
   - **C. Incorrect:** *STSADM* is still available in SharePoint 2013, although it's recommended that commands be executed via PowerShell.
   - **D. Correct:** All the preceding options are valid ways to back up the farm configuration.
2. **Correct answer:** C
   - **A. Incorrect:** Bulk logged backups can restore only to last backup.
   - **B. Incorrect:** Simple backups can restore only the entire backup.
   - **C. Correct:** The Full recovery mode is the only option that allows for point-in-time restore.
   - **D. Incorrect:** Because C is the only correct answer, this one can't be correct.

3. **Correct answer:** B

   A. **Incorrect:** An error occurs if you try to attach a content database with the same ID.

   B. **Correct:** To attach a backed-up content database to the same SharePoint farm, it must have a new ID (for example, using the PowerShell command *Mount-SPContentDatabase* with the *AssignNewDatabaseId* parameter).

   C. **Incorrect:** A content database can be attached as long as it has a new ID.

   D. **Incorrect:** Whether it's within the same web application or not doesn't matter. A content database with the same ID can't be attached within the same SharePoint farm.

4. **Correct answer:** D

   A. **Incorrect:** SSL certificates aren't backed up by the Central Administration tool, but it's not the only correct answer in the list.

   B. **Incorrect:** Again, DLLs aren't backed up as part of the Central Administration farm backup (either configuration only or full).

   C. **Incorrect:** IIS-only settings are backed up separately from the SharePoint farm.

   D. **Correct:** All the preceding answers are correct and not backed up via the SharePoint Central Administration tool (either the configuration only or the full backup).

5. **Correct answer:** D

   A. **Incorrect:** Global Search Settings can be backed up individually, but it's just one of the right answers.

   B. **Incorrect:** SharePoint Server State Service is just one of the right answers.

   C. **Incorrect:** InfoPath Forms Services is just one of the right answers.

   D. **Correct:** All of the preceding options are correct.

CHAPTER 2

Plan a SharePoint environment

Planning a SharePoint environment depends on which of the many roles the environment calls for. SharePoint is a broad platform that can be used for myriad applications or combinations of applications. This chapter covers some of the core functionality of the SharePoint platform and how to handle the workload involved with implementing these solutions. The core components of a SharePoint environment cover the areas of search, social, Web Content Management (WCM), and Enterprise Content Management (ECM). These core components of the SharePoint platform require careful planning and implementation. This chapter covers these aspects as well as how they relate to the exam.

Objectives in this chapter:

- Objective 2.1: Plan a social workload
- Objective 2.2: Plan and configure a search workload
- Objective 2.3: Plan and configure a Web Content Management (WCM) workload
- Objective 2.4: Plan an Enterprise Content Management (ECM) workload

Objective 2.1: Plan a social workload

The social workload demands on a SharePoint 2013 farm vary widely from one organization to the next. The biggest factor is how emphatically the organization embraces the social aspects of SharePoint. The social components can increase demands on database storage, search resources, and bandwidth resources.

SharePoint 2013 has changed the architecture of how the social components are implemented. The changes represent several technical challenges that you need to plan for, but social components bring on additional political challenges that you need to account for in the successful implementation of any SharePoint farm.

This objective goes over how to plan for the various social components of the SharePoint 2013 farm. The non-technical parts of implementing social computing aren't directly tested on the exam, but you will be tested on how to implement the changes brought on by these political decisions.

This objective covers the following topics:

- Planning communities
- Planning My Sites
- Planning social permissions
- Planning user profiles
- Planning activity feeds
- Planning connections

Planning communities

New in SharePoint 2013, Community Sites provide forums for people to ask and answer questions, post information, comment on posts, and be rewarded for their efforts in the form of points, earned badges, and gifted badges. Those familiar with the Microsoft forums should see many similarities. Much of the functionality in those forums has been built into the SharePoint Communities Sites. Additional components found in social networks, such as "liking" a post, are also included. This set of functionality can be extremely powerful in encouraging the sharing of knowledge and contributing of content. It's also most effective when the forum aligns with real business goals; building a community site just for the sake of trying to encourage social computing doesn't use communities effectively and will most likely fail.

You can add community features to an existing site, but a Community Site template is available. Discussion lists and the community features also have a bit of overlap. Therefore, SharePoint 2013 users have the following three options for community features:

- Add a discussion list to an existing site.
- Enable the community feature on an existing site.
- Create a community site based on the template.

The choice depends on the business needs, but if your organization needs a center of knowledge sharing, a community site is typically the way to go. If an existing site needs the Community Sites features, you can turn them on by following these steps:

1. Navigate to the site that needs the community features enabled.
2. Go to the site settings of the site.
3. Select Site Features under Site Actions.
4. Click Activate in the Community Site Feature section, as shown in Figure 2-1.

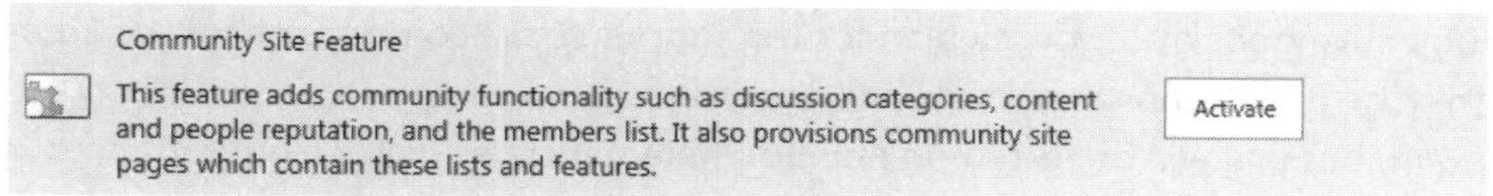

Community Site Feature
This feature adds community functionality such as discussion categories, content and people reputation, and the members list. It also provisions community site pages which contain these lists and features.
Activate

FIGURE 2-1 Activating the Community Site feature

IMPORTANT ENABLING THE COMMUNITY SITE FEATURE

The SharePoint Server Standard Collection feature must be enabled before the Community Site template appears among the available site templates, even if the template has been made available through the Page Layouts And Site Templates options under Look And Feel in Site Settings. By default, this feature isn't turned on.

Enabling the Community Sites feature creates lists, creates pages, and shows Web Parts that work with the community features:

- Discussions list
- Badges list, which contains the badges available for contributing members
- Community Members list
- Categories list
- Administration settings page
- Categories page
- Members page
- About page
- Community Home page
- What's Happening Web Part, which displays the number of members, discussions, and replies
- Top Contributors Web Part, which displays the members who contribute the most to the community site
- My Membership Web Part, which displays an individual's contributions to the community site
- Manage Web Part, which allows moderators and site owners the ability to change settings to the community site, such as how many points posts are worth

These items are available if the feature is turned on at the site level of an existing site or if a new site is created with the Community Site template. A community site has all the functionality of a normal SharePoint 2013 site, such as document management, versioning, permissions, auditing, and so on. The preceding items allow for an interactive forum experience, but some dependencies exist for an even more enhanced experience. The optional service applications of the SharePoint 2013 farm that provide additional functionality are as follows:

- **User Profile service application** This allows for a tie-in to users' newsfeeds and allows for mentions (an @ sign followed by a person's name). A user following another user can see whenever that followed user goes up in reputation, posts a discussion item, gets a like, or gets a reply marked as a best reply. When implemented in the same environment as My Sites, a community site can be accessed on the Sites page.
- **Metadata service application** This allows for hash tags to be used (an # sign followed by a keyword) in posts and replies.

- **Search service application** This isn't necessary but is required if searching of the community site is needed.

EXAM TIP

The exam isn't just a simple multiple-choice test that has been the hallmark of many past exams. It poses several questions that require placing steps in the correct order that they should occur. For example, enabling the Metadata service application is necessary before you can use hash tags.

The types of members for a site can be broken down into four different types: owner, moderator, contributor, and visitor. Typically, forums are open for contributions from all members, but in some situations only a certain group of users can contribute to a forum but a larger audience can view the contributions. A specialized help desk might be an example of this, where only members of the technology team can contribute.

Moderators are the key set of users in a community site. They serve as the site's shepherds. They can create and delete categories, edit and delete posts, mark replies as "best replies," and configure reputation settings. They are also responsible for monitoring content, if that is enabled. (Of course, they can manually monitor it, but allowing the community to report offensive content is much more effective.) To enable monitoring of offensive content, follow these steps:

1. On the home page of the community site, click Community Settings in the Community Tools section of the page (assuming that you are a moderator or owner).
2. Select Enable Reporting Of Offensive Content (see Figure 2-2).

Reporting of offensive content

Select this feature to allow community members to report abusive content. Administrators and Moderators can review reported material and then either remove it or reinstate it.

☑ Enable reporting of offensive content

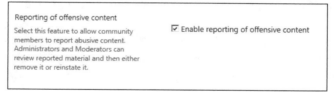

FIGURE 2-2 Enabling the reporting of offensive content

3. Click OK to continue and save settings.

Now, all moderators receive email when a user identifies a post or reply as offensive. Having users report offensive content is considered a best practice because it minimizes the amount of time moderators have to keep an eye on the content.

NOTE **OUTGOING EMAIL SETTINGS**

Outgoing email settings must be enabled in Central Administration for the moderator to receive emails about offensive content.

On the same page as Enable Reporting Of Offensive Content is a setting called Established Date. This date is shown on the About Page and can be used for sites created before the Community Site template existed. With this setting, users can see how long content has been contributed.

Anyone who has created a blog site should be familiar with the categories, and the idea is the same with Community Sites. Part of the planning process should involve creating categories appropriate for the site. Correct categories help visitors find the information quickly and efficiently.

Reputation settings

Reputation settings are one of the most important parts of setting up a community site. With proper planning, you can determine the correct setting values so that you won't have to change them in the future. Users prefer knowing what the settings are and that they don't change frequently. This helps users know what the goals are and what is required to achieve them. Keeping settings consistent is considered a best practice, and unless you have an overwhelming reason to change them, leave the settings alone. If reputation settings need to be configured or changed, they can be by following these steps:

1. On the community site home page, click Reputation Settings in the Community Tools section.
2. In the Rating Settings section, choose whether you want contributors to be able to rate a post or reply. If you choose Yes, you will need to select the rating system of either Likes or Stars.
3. Choose whether to have member achievement points system enabled by selecting Enable Member Achievements Point System. If it's selected, you must specify the points allocated for each activity (see Figure 2-3).

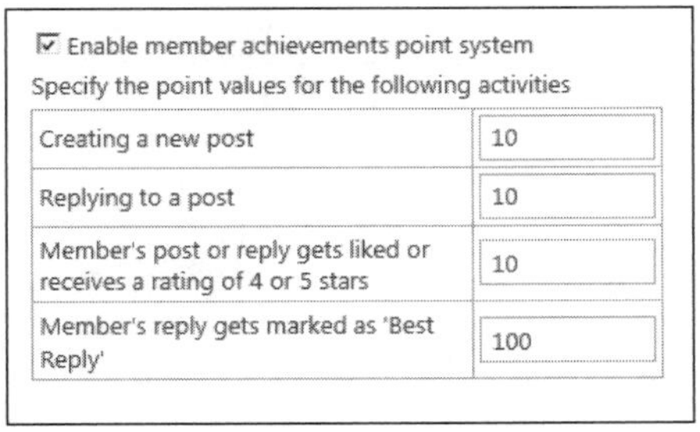

☑ Enable member achievements point system

Specify the point values for the following activities

Creating a new post	10
Replying to a post	10
Member's post or reply gets liked or receives a rating of 4 or 5 stars	10
Member's reply gets marked as 'Best Reply'	100

FIGURE 2-3 Default points for a community site that has the member achievement points system enabled

4. If the member achievement points system is enabled, you must configure the levels in the Achievement Level Points section. The five levels show defaults ranging from zero to ten thousand, but you can type any numeric value.

5. Again, if the member achievement points system is enabled, you can choose Achievement Level Representation, which displays either an image representing a contributor's level or corresponding text of the level. To change the level text, choose Display Achievement Level As Text.

6. Click OK when done to change the reputation settings.

By default, the reputation settings are enabled, and users start receiving points as soon as they start contributing—unless you change the settings. Removing points from a site causes end-user confusion.

Badges

Users receive badges for their contributions to the community site. Badges are a symbolic award for a user's efforts. They can be tied into actual recognition in the form of business goals being met and/or monetary rewards to make them even more effective.

Badges come in two different varieties:

- They can be *earned*. These are the "levels" in the member achievement points system.
- They can be *gifted* by community site moderators or site owners.

A badge is simple text displayed next to the user's name on the community site. As a moderator of the site (or site owner), you can create or gift a badge. To create badges, follow these steps:

1. On the community site home page, click Create Badges in the Community Tools section of the page.

2. Click New Item. Figure 2-4 shows the two predefined badges, Expert and Professional.

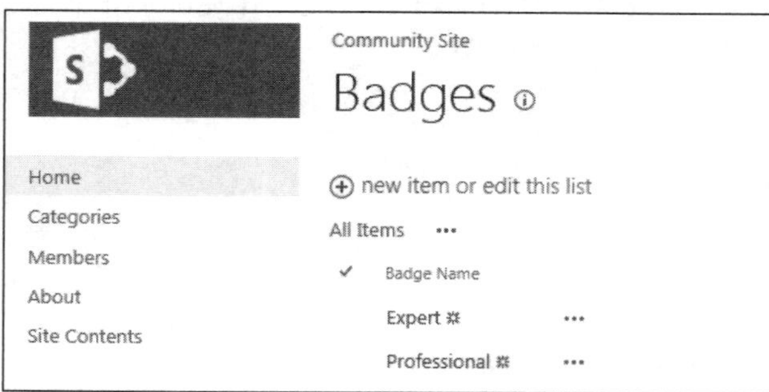

FIGURE 2-4 Badges administration page

3. Type the name of the badge in the Badge Name field.

4. Click Save.

Badges can be any sort of text but should reflect some sort of legitimate business goal. This depends on the organization, of course, but badges that truly reflect levels of effort mean more to the end user.

Now that you've created badges, you can gift them to individuals. Gifting is totally up to the site moderators and can be done at any time. To gift badges, follow these steps:

1. On the community site home page, click Assign Badges To Members in the Community Tools section of the page.
2. In the list, select who should be given badges by clicking to the left or right of the member name. (Clicking a member directly takes you to that member's information.)
3. On the Moderation tab, click the Give Badge icon.
4. Choose the badge to gift from the Gifted Badge drop-down list.
5. Click Save.

The badge now appears with the member's name so that when other people see the member in the top contributors' area or the member's page, they see the badge as well. The member's page also shows when the user joined, how many discussions she has started, how many replies have been made, and how many have been marked as best replies. The photo of the member also appears if the User Profile service application is enabled and the user has uploaded a picture.

> ***NOTE*** **GIFTED BADGE LIMIT**
>
> **A member can have only one gifted badge at a time.**

> ***MORE INFO*** **COMMUNITIES**
>
> **See *http://technet.microsoft.com/en-us/library/jj219805(v=office.15).aspx* for more information on communities in SharePoint Server 2013.**

Planning My Sites

The My Sites feature has changed a lot between SharePoint 2010 and SharePoint 2013. The two most notable places of change are the look and feel as well as the addition of the SkyDrive, which has replaced the individual content area. The two main areas of My Sites are still the My Site host and the individual site collections. The interaction between Microsoft Office 2013 and the site collections (accessed by clicking SkyDrive from anywhere within SharePoint) will most likely lead to a much higher usage of the site collections and therefore require a greater degree of planning. Planning for the My Site host and for the SkyDrive locations should be done separately and is addressed that way in this section.

My Site host

The My Site host is a site collection based on the My Site Host site collection template. Although the My Site host doesn't have to be created in its own web application, in all but the smallest of implementations it should have its own. This way, multiple content databases can be added as needed to accommodate for the growth of the individual site collections, as well as to allow for separate administration.

Creating the My Site host is done in the same way as in SharePoint 2010. Assuming that a web application has been created and that alternate access mapping has been configured, you can create the My Site host by following these steps:

1. On the home page of Central Administration, click Create Site Collections in the Application Management section.
2. Change the web application to the one created for the My Site host in the Web Application section.
3. Type a title in the Title section and a description in the Description field.
4. Leave the Web Site Address alone. It should be at the root of the web application.
5. In the Select Experience Version section, leave 2013 selected.
6. On the Enterprise tab, select My Site Host.
7. Enter a primary and secondary site collection administrator.
8. In the Quota Template section, choose an appropriate quota or create a new one.
9. Click OK.

The My Site host should be created shortly after you click OK.

User photos are stored in the content database of the My Site host like they were in SharePoint 2010. When a user uploads a profile picture, it's converted into three thumbnails—small, medium, and large—in three different subfolders in the Profile Pictures folder. (The original isn't saved.) These thumbnails don't take up much space—less than 40 or 50 KB per person—so storage concerns should be minimal for photos unless the number of users is extremely high (10,000 users would still be less than 1 GB). However, in SharePoint 2013, attachments can be added to posts. These attachments are stored in the My Site host content database and, depending on how frequently people add attachments and the limit of upload size, the database could grow rather large. The default upload size for a web application is 250 MB. Be careful when adjusting this size because it affects all the site collections (SkyDrive locations) under it.

After a My Site host is created, you need to configure it in Central Administration so that the farm knows about it. You can configure it only after the User Profile service application is started, as discussed later in this objective. After the User Profile service is started and the My Site host is created, you can configure the host as follows:

1. Navigate to Central Administration.

2. Click Manage Service Applications in the Application Management section.
3. Click the User Profile Service Application link (this might be called something else if it was created with a different name).
4. On the Manage Profile Service page, click the Setup My Sites link in the My Site Settings section.
5. Type the preferred search center location for the My Site host in the Preferred Search Center text box. (If a search center hasn't been created, this can be left blank until that task is completed.)
6. Choose a scope for finding people in the Search Scope For Finding People drop-down list. (The scope People is created by default when the Search service application is created.)
7. Choose a scope for finding documents in the Search Scope For Finding Documents drop-down list. The scope All Sites should be available.
8. In the My Site Host Location text box, enter the URL of the My Site host.

> ***NOTE*** **SETTING THE MY SITE HOST URL**
>
> **The value in the My Site Host URL in Active Directory section can't be set directly. It has to be set on the Exchange Server node with a PowerShell script that contains the location of the My Site host URL. This enables Exchange Auto Discovery.**

9. In the Personal Site Location section, enter where personal sites should be located. If the location hasn't been created yet, a wildcard inclusion managed path needs to be created in the My Site host web application.
10. Choose a Site Naming Format option. If the My Site host has users from only one domain, leaving the default User Name option is adequate.
11. Select whether users can choose their language in the Language Options section. Options depend on which language packs are installed.
12. The Read Permissions Level section lists who has read permissions to the personal site collections when they are created. Changing this value affects only sites created going forward.
13. Choose the appropriate Security Trimming Option, as shown in Figure 2-5, to determine which links to show in notes, activity feeds, ratings, and social tags based on whether the user has permissions to the linked item. The options include showing all the links, trimming all the links that users don't have permission to access, or trimming ones only in certain directories.

Security Trimming Options

Links in activity feeds, ratings, social tags and notes can be hidden from viewers without permissions to see them. Checking links can delay them from appearing on My Sites.

◉ Check all links for permission

○ Check only specified links for permission

Enter URL hierarchies to be checked for permission. Enter each URL on a new line:

Example: https://contoso/

Enter URL hierarchies to be displayed regardless of permission. Enter each URL on a new line:

Example: https://contoso/public_blogs/

○ Show all links regardless of permission

FIGURE 2-5 Security Trimming Options in My Site Settings

14. Choose whether to enable newsfeed activities in the Newsfeed section. You can also choose whether to include SharePoint 2010 activities.
15. In the Email Notifications section, choose whether users should get My Site-related emails (such as when a person posts on a site). If this setting is enabled, you need to provide a sent-from email address; it doesn't need to be a real email address but should be one that isn't blocked or sent to the junk folder.
16. In the My Site Cleanup section, choose whether to have delegation and who the secondary owner is. When a user profile is deleted, the corresponding site collection is deleted after 14 days. The person's manager and/or secondary owner can access the site to retrieve data before the 14 days are up.
17. In the Privacy Settings section, choose whether to make My Sites public. This determines whether users' social information—such as whom they follow and their newsfeed—is visible to other users.
18. Click OK to save settings.

EXAM TIP

Exchange Auto Discovery enables the SkyDrive option (making it easier for users to save in their site collections) in Office 2013 and mobile devices. The PowerShell script must be run on an Exchange Server node before autodiscovery is enabled.

Trusted My Site host locations

If more than one My Site host will be used, you need to configure Trusted My Site Host Locations. A trusted location can be on the same farm or a different farm. Audiences determine which user goes to which My Site host. The audiences used to configure the trusted locations need to be mutually exclusive; otherwise, confusion could result. To configure a trusted site location, follow these steps:

1. Navigate to Central Administration and click Manage Service Applications in the Application Management section.
2. Click the User Profile service application.
3. Click Configure Trusted Host Locations.
4. Click New Link.
5. Enter the URL of the trusted host in the URL text box.
6. Type a title in the Title text box.
7. Type the optional Description and Image URL.
8. In Target Audiences, choose the Audience (or audiences) that should use the trusted My Site host.
9. Click OK.

The reasons behind creating multiple My Site hosts are varied. One of the most common is because of distance. For example, an organization might have offices around the world and want users to access their SkyDrive sites from a local SharePoint farm for better performance (latency and bandwidth are still issues that must be planned for). That way, users could use a SharePoint site located in a geographically distant location but when they click SkyDrive or About Me, they are taken to their local SharePoint farm. Another reason could be that an organization wants different My Site variations based on what kind of employee uses it. You could have a My Site host for regular employees and a different one for contractors.

Personal site collections (SkyDrive)

After My Sites are configured on the My Site Settings page, you still need to enable self-site creation before users can create their own site collections. The content area of a user's personal site collection is the SkyDrive location for the individual. Follow these steps:

1. Navigate to Central Administration and click Manage Web Applications under the Application Management section.
2. Click the web application in which the My Site host site collection resides.
3. Click Self-Service Site Creation in the Web Applications section of the ribbon.
4. In the Site Collections section, choose a quota to apply. If a quota other than the Personal Site quota is to be used, you need to create it before performing these steps.
5. In the Start A Site section, leave the Be Hidden From Users option selected. Users shouldn't be able to create sites other than their SkyDrive sites.

6. The options Site Classification Settings and Require Secondary Contact should be dimmed. Click OK to finish.

Put thought into creating a quota for individuals. Changing which quota is used for self-service creation doesn't affect sites that have already been created. Those must be changed manually (if so desired). The quota itself can be changed, though.

EXAM TIP

Setting up self-service creation is an important step that could potentially be on the test. Even in the non-case study questions you might be asked a question similar to putting the steps of configuring a My Site Host in the correct order.

Personal site collection creation is handled differently in this version of SharePoint, which can affect the planning of My Site rollout. Personal sites are now created asynchronously in SharePoint 2013 as opposed to synchronously in SharePoint 2010. When a personal site (SkyDrive Pro location) is requested, it's put into one of two queues:

- **Interactive queue** Filled by requests from a user clicking a link in the browser that would require a personal site to be created such as clicking SkyDrive or Newsfeed
- **Non-interactive queue** Filled if a user tries to access SkyDrive through Office 2013 or if code is used to prepopulate sites

The reason behind using a queue is that creating a personal site collection is a relatively resource-expensive operation. Requests are handled via a timer job that fires every minute and handles up to three requests at a time. This way, SharePoint 2013 won't stop responding if it suddenly gets many personal site-creation requests at the same time. The interactive and non-interactive queues receive the same weight. So, if 100 are in the non-interactive queue and six are in the interactive queue, SharePoint processes three from the non-interactive queue, then three from the interactive queue, three more from the non-interactive queue, and so on until both queues are empty. This is so that if the sites are being created with code and someone clicks SkyDrive, they still get a fairly quick response rather than be stuck at the end of what could be hundreds or thousands of requests.

One important step is left in preparing to launch the My Site host. You need to determine the number of content databases needed. Moving site collections from one database to another is always possible, but by doing some proper planning, you can avoid this labor-intensive process involving downtime of the personal sites. Best practices still suggest a maximum of 200 GB per content database for backup, restore, and performance reasons. This might be extended through the use of certain hardware, but keeping content databases a manageable size is still a good idea. Because each personal site is a site collection, determining the number of content databases needed is fairly straightforward with the following math:

Number of databases = (Personal Site Quota × number of users) / 200 GB

Therefore, if you had a thousand users each with a 5 GB quota, you would need 25 content databases if users are expected to fully use their quotas. Personal site collection usage based on SharePoint 2010 will likely be erroneous based on how SkyDrive is integrated into Office

2013 and how pervasive it is in SharePoint 2013 sites (unless it is removed with branding). Usage will vary by organization and user, but the preceding formula should guarantee that content databases remain within suggested limits.

> ***IMPORTANT* PERSONAL SITE QUOTAS**
>
> **By default, the Personal Site Quota is 100 MB, with a warning that occurs at 80 MB. This size is fairly small in today's world of storage, so you probably want to adjust this to meet your organization's business needs before users starting running out of storage and needing assistance from technical staff.**

Planning social permissions

Social permissions are set in several places within the SharePoint environment. Proper planning helps enable those users who need the social components as well as keep those users who don't (such as temporary employees or contractors, depending on the organization's needs) from using the social components. Most social permissions are driven by political agendas instead of performance reasons, but you need to take some performance considerations into account.

Social data is stored and indexed for searching, which consumes resources. SkyDrive could also take up considerable resources and can be limited by allowing only the users that need it through permissions. Audiences also come under social permissions. Although they don't prohibit users from accessing files, they can be used to change what is shown to users and to route them to their home My Site host.

Audiences

Audiences are a way to group people by an attribute in their profile. This can be by office, title, or any of the profile properties. In My Sites, audiences are generally sorted by region or by employee type. Creating an audience is fairly easy:

1. Navigate to Central Administration and click Manage Service Applications under Application Management.
2. Click the User Profile service application.
3. Click Manage Audiences under the People section.
4. Click New Audience on the View Audiences page.
5. Type a name in the Name field. (The Description and Owner fields are optional.)
6. Choose Satisfy All Of The Rules or Satisfy Any Of The Rules and then click OK.
7. Choose User or Property (this example uses Property).
8. Choose the Property (such as Office Location).

9. Choose the Operator (such as Contains or Not Contains).
10. Enter a value in the Value text box.
11. Click OK to open the View Audience Properties sheet.
12. Click Compile Audience to compile the audience immediately; otherwise, it will be compiled during the next compile audience timer job.

After audiences are compiled, they can be used in the trusted My Site host locations to distribute users among various My Site hosts. Users can be in multiple audiences, but for My Site hosts the audiences should be mutually exclusive.

EXAM TIP

Creating audiences is a necessary step in setting up My Site host locations (and could potentially be on the exam). This step occurs after the My Site hosts are created but before they are publicly available.

Social permissions

Social components require that users have specific permissions. Three distinct permissions are controlled in the User Profile Service Application area. The following permissions are accessed under the Manage User Permissions link of the People section:

- Create Personal Site (required for personal storage, newsfeed, and followed content)
- Follow People and Edit Profile
- Use Tag and Notes

Users need all three permissions to be able to fully access all the social components of SharePoint 2013. Typically, the group of NT Authority\Authenticated Users is added by default. Permissions assigned in the Manage User Permissions dialog box are additive. For example, if a user doesn't have the Use Tag and Notes permissions but Authenticated Users has the Use Tag and Notes permissions, they still have those rights. If you want to prohibit users from using the social features, the default user groups have to be removed, and the groups that need social permissions have to be added. In some situations, a social permission needs to be removed entirely; for example, if an organization decides that it doesn't want users to be able to use tags and notes, it removes them in the Permissions For User Profile Service Application dialog box (see Figure 2-6).

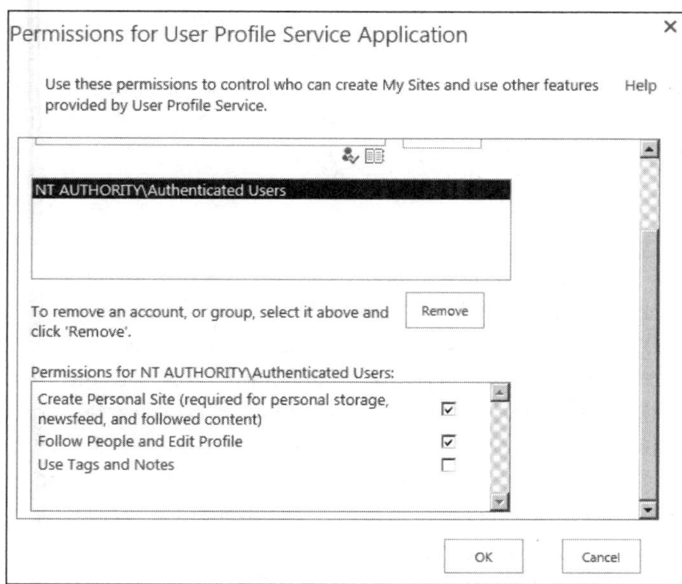

FIGURE 2-6 Permissions for User Profile Service Application dialog box

By using these permission levels, you can limit social components to just the users that need them. You also can phase in social features as training and political concerns allow.

Some changes have been made in the permissions of user profile properties in SharePoint 2013. SharePoint 2010 had four levels of permissions for profile properties, but SharePoint 2013 has only two: Everyone and Just Me. The reduction in the number of options available was an effort to streamline the choices available to the end user. If a profile property has its permissions set to editable, users are limited to just two choices. With any social network, the easier something is for users to use, the more likely they are to use it. To modify the permissions for a user profile property, follow these steps:

1. Navigate to Central Administration and click Manage Service Applications under Application Management.
2. Click User Profile Service Application.
3. Click Manage User Properties under the People section.
4. Choose the property that needs to be modified and click it. From the drop-down list, select Edit.
5. In the Policy Setting section, set the Default Privacy Setting.
6. Click OK to save the changes.

Some properties, such as First Name, can't be altered, but any added field can be changed. The choice of which properties are available to everyone is driven by the organization's political concerns. For example, an employee ID might be brought in through Active Directory that should be visible only to the employee. This employee ID can then be used to populate fields and even be used for single sign-on (SSO) solutions based on such an ID.

Planning user profiles

User profiles are the crucial component for social components. Getting user profiles populated is one of the key components in setting up a SharePoint farm. Importing these user profiles from Active Directory (AD) is similar to the way SharePoint 2010 populated profiles. It's still not a trivial task, however. For SharePoint to use profiles that it pulls from AD, the User Profile service needs to be started, a User Profile service application needs to be created, and then the User Profile Synchronization service needs to be started. When the User Profile service starts, you need to create a User Profile service application. Three databases associated with this service application are created when the User Profile service application is created:

- **Profile Database** Stores user profile and organization data
- **Synchronization Database** Used for configuration and staging of synchronization data from sources such as AD
- **Social Tagging Database** Stores social tags and notes

You can use the Configuration Wizard to create the User Profile service application, but creating it manually or via a script is the better way to go. This way, you can name the databases rather than let SharePoint name them with a GUID. It also allows for greater control over the options, such as specifying a My Site host location, selecting which application pool to use, and identifying a failover database server.

Before creating the User Profile service application, you should create the My Site host. Doing so isn't essential, but it does save some time by creating the managed path for you. Follow these steps:

1. Navigate to Central Administration and click Manage Service Applications under the Application Management section.
2. Click New and then click User Profile Service Application (see Figure 2-7).

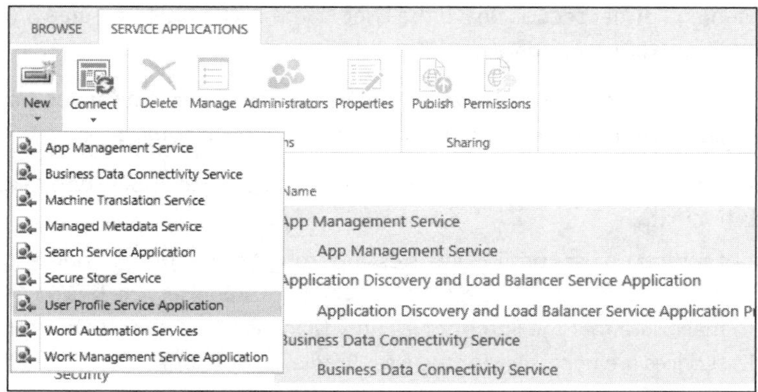

FIGURE 2-7 Creating a User Profile Service Application on the Manage Service Applications page

3. In the Name text box, type a name for the service application.
4. In the Application Pool section, choose an existing application pool or create a new one. Creating a new one is generally recommended but not required.
5. In the Profile Database section, type the name of the SQL Server node and the name you want to call the profile database (stay with Profile DB unless required by governance to use a different name). Also choose the Database Authentication Method (use Windows Authentication unless directed to do otherwise).
6. Still in the Profile Database section, enter a Failover Database Server if database mirroring is set up.
7. Repeat steps 5 and 6 for the synchronization database (preferably using Sync DB for the database name) and for the social tagging database (again, stay with the recommended database name if possible).
8. From the Profile Synchronization Instance drop-down list, choose the server that will run the profile synchronization. Only one server can run this process.
9. In the My Site Host URL text box, type the URL of the My Site host that you created earlier, click Create A New Site Collection if you want to create one at this time, or leave it blank if you want to create a My Site host later.
10. In the My Site Managed Path text box, type the location beneath the My Site host where personal sites for users (SkyDrive locations) will be created. This applies only if a My Site host has already been added.

11. In the Site Naming Format section, leave the User Name option selected unless you will have users from different domains.
12. For the Default Proxy Group, you probably want this to remain Yes unless you have a reason a web application shouldn't use this User Profile service application.
13. Click Create to start the creation process. The User Profile service application takes a minute or so to create.

The second part of setting up user profiles involves importing profiles from a source such as Active Directory. You first need to start the User Profile Synchronization service, but before you do that, you need to make sure that the Forefront Identity Manager (FIM) services are correctly configured. Two FIM services are necessary for the User Profile service spplication to run:

- Forefront Identity Manager Service
- Forefront Identity Manager Synchronization Service

Both services are disabled by default when SharePoint is installed. SharePoint enables them and configures the account associated with them when the User Profile Synchronization service is started.

EXAM TIP

Correctly configuring the FIM services is a key first step in setting up a User Profile imported from Active Directory. That they are changed from disabled to automatic is also a key component both in real life and potentially the exam.

Properly setting up the FIM service account is important. If the User Profile Synchronization service is started before the FIM services are configured, you might need to restart the computer before it can be provisioned correctly. The User Profile service also needs to be running. After the User Profile service and FIM services are configured, you can start the User Profile Synchronization service as follows:

1. Navigate to Central Administration and click Manage Services On Server under System Settings.
2. Click Start on the User Profile Synchronization Service line.
3. A service account name and password appears. This account will run the User Profile Synchronization service and will need local admin rights when it's provisioned. Click OK.
4. On the Manage Services On Server page, the User Profile Synchronization Service line should say *Starting*. Startup can take up to 15 minutes or so. Wait until it has finished and says *Started*.
5. Return to the Central Administration home page, click Manage Service Applications under Application Management, and then click User Profile Service Application.

After the User Profile Synchronization service starts, you need to configure a connection to pull in profiles from AD. Before you can do so, however, you need to choose or create an account that will be used to communicate with between SharePoint and AD. This account needs special privileges in AD—specifically, it needs the Replicating Directory Changes permission. If the account doesn't have this level of permissions, the synchronization still starts, but changes in AD aren't reflected in the user profiles. This permission must be granted on a domain controller using the Active Directory User and Computers tool under the Administrative Tools section of the Start menu.

MORE INFO **GRANTING AD DS PERMISSIONS**

See *http://technet.microsoft.com/en-us/library/hh296982.aspx* for more information on how to grant Active Directory Domain Services permissions for profile synchronization in SharePoint Server 2013.

EXAM TIP

The Replicating Directory Changes permission is required for the account that's synchronizing profiles from AD. This requirement will potentially be in a multiple-choice question or be a step in configuring user profile synchronization. The actual steps required to enable this permission most likely aren't covered.

If you need to export changes in a user's profile to AD, the synchronization account also needs Grant Create Child Objects and Write permissions to the organizational unit (OU) being synchronized with user profiles. One of the most common examples of when this would be needed is when My Site photos are used to populate Outlook and Lync via the *thumbnailPhoto* field in AD. That way, a single source of photos can be used for all three programs, plus any other program that can pull data from AD. Planning for the synchronization is discussed later in the "Planning connections" section.

MORE INFO **GRANTING CREATE CHILD OBJECTS AND WRITE PERMISSIONS**

See *http://technet.microsoft.com/en-us/library/hh296982.aspx#RDCchild* for more information on how to grant Create Child Objects and Write permissions.

Planning activity feeds

SharePoint 2013 has several items that can appear in the Activity Feed. Users can follow users, tags, sites, and conversations. Users can also post on a user's site or mention them in posts, which causes an item to appear in their activity feed. Two significant changes reflect the influence of social networks on SharePoint. The first is the *mention*. You can put an "at" sign (@) in front of a person's name to make the post appear in the person's newsfeed. The second one is the hash tag (#), which a user can put in front of a word in a post. Putting the hash sign in front creates a tag that users can follow. If a user is following that word, the post appears in that person's newsfeed. For example, if a user posts something about SharePoint and another user is following the keyword SharePoint, they see that on their newsfeed, as shown in Figure 2-8.

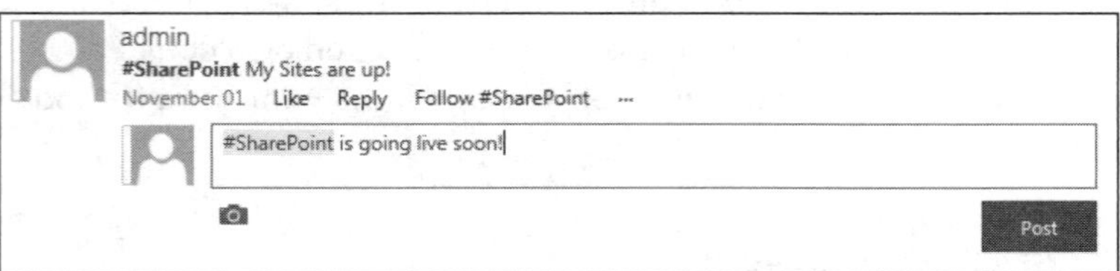

FIGURE 2-8 Using a hash tag to indicate a keyword and the option to follow the keyword

Following keywords is made even easier by a link that appears at the top of a conversation with the keyword associated with the word *Follow*. Because following keywords is so easy, you can expect a large increase in the number of tags followed. Tags are indexed and can be searched on. All this activity increases the load on the SharePoint server and needs to be taken into account when designing the farm.

The Outlook Social connector also shows the activity for individuals. These feeds are pulled from SharePoint periodically and stored in Outlook, requiring both memory and CPU resources. The number of people using the Outlook Social connector will vary depending on the organization, but this should factor into preparing for the load on the SharePoint server.

The number of profile properties that can be followed and therefore appear in the activity feed affect the resources required and need to be planned out. Also, some properties are excluded from the activity feed for political reasons. For example, in certain organizations, the title of a person can reflect their salary; as a result, an organization might decide that changes in a person's title only promotes gossip and distracts people from their jobs. Users might also benefit from some profile properties that aren't set up to be followed. To change whether a profile property appears in the SharePoint 2010-compatible newsfeed, follow these steps:

1. Navigate to Central Administration and click Manage Service Applications in the Application Management section.
2. Click the User Profile service application.
3. Click Manage User Properties in the People section on the Manage Profile Service page.
4. Click the property name of the user profile property to be changed (for example, Title) and select Edit from the drop-down menu.
5. Select or clear Show Updates To The Property In Newsfeed (Only Compatible With SharePoint 2010 Newsfeeds) and click OK to save.

The number of items that a user follows and the frequency of change in these items determine the load on the activity feed. Although the frequency of change is determined by usage and can't be easily controlled, you can limit the number of items followed. Users can follow three main items and have their changes appear in their activity feeds:

- **People** Default limit (and maximum) is 1,000 people who can be followed per user.
- **Documents** Default limit (and maximum) is 500 documents that can be followed per user.
- **Sites** Default limit (and maximum) is 500 sites that can be followed per user.

You can limit each of these items. Changing the number of items that can be followed is a farm-level change and affects all users. Organizations with a large number of users and/or a large farm with many documents and sites might want to limit the number of items that can be followed, as follows:

1. On the Manage Profile Service page, click Manage Following in the My Site Settings section.
2. Type values for the Maximum Number Of Followed People, Maximum Number Of Followed Documents, and Maximum Number Of Followed Sites (see Figure 2-9).
3. Click OK to save your changes.

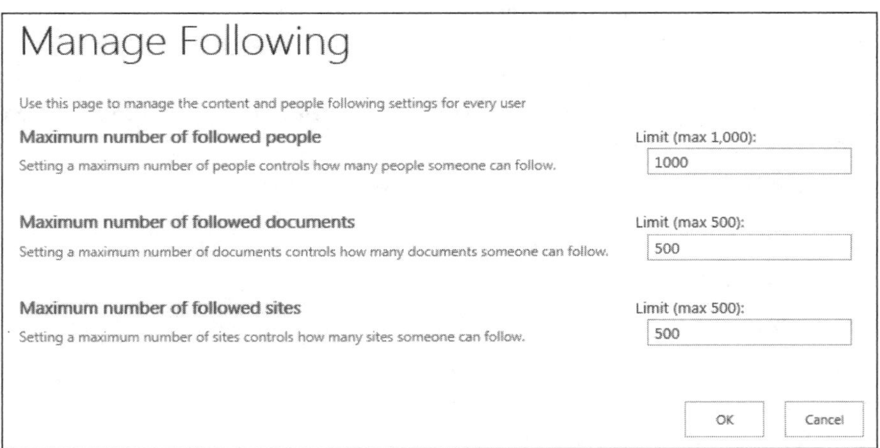

Manage Following
Use this page to manage the content and people following settings for every user
Maximum number of followed people
Setting a maximum number of people controls how many people someone can follow.
Limit (max 1,000):
1000
Maximum number of followed documents
Setting a maximum number of documents controls how many documents someone can follow.
Limit (max 500):
500
Maximum number of followed sites
Setting a maximum number of sites controls how many sites someone can follow.
Limit (max 500):
500
OK
Cancel

FIGURE 2-9 Manage Following page that shows the number of items followed that can be limited at the farm level

These limits are fairly high (and already at the maximum) for most people. You can't increase them, but you might want to lower them to increase the performance of the SharePoint server.

You can access feed information on a user's My Site. SharePoint 2013 offers several feeds, each with a different set of overall feed data that you can filter so that users can see the most appropriate data:

- **Newsfeed** The default view when visiting a user's My Site profile, it shows the last 20 recent activities for entities that the user follows.

- **Everyone** This feed shows the last 20 posts or replies across all users.
- **Activities** This feed shows all activities associated with a user, including system-generated activities, and not just recent activities.
- **Likes** This feed lists posts or replies that the user has liked.
- **Mentions** Whenever a user is mentioned in a post or reply, the item appears in this feed.

> ***MORE INFO*** **PLANNING FOR FEEDS AND DISTRIBUTED CACHE SERVICE**
>
> **See *http://technet.microsoft.com/en-us/library/jj219572.aspx#planfeeds* for more information on how to plan for feeds and for the Distributed Cache service.**

Distributed Cache allows for fast retrieval of activity-related items across all the components of SharePoint by caching recently accessed items. In fact, Distributed Cache has a dedicated cache referred to as the Feed Cache, whose sole purpose is to store activities and conversations for use by feeds on My Sites. Distributed Cache comes in two modes: Dedicated and Collocated.

Dedicated mode is recommended for the best performance, but it requires a server solely dedicated to being a Distributed Cache server. *Collocated* is when one or more SharePoint servers are running the Distributed Cache service as well as other services. A server running Distributed Cache in Collocated mode should stop all non-essential services to reduce the competition for memory resources.

Starting the Distributed Cache service on a SharePoint server is fairly straightforward:

1. Navigate to Central Administration.
2. Click Manage Services On Server under the System Settings section.
3. Find the Distributed Cache line and click Start.

Unlike SharePoint 2010, SharePoint Server 2013 can use Distributed Cache to cache the login token. This means that if Network Load Balancing (NLB) is being used, a user won't lose his login information if he goes from one Web Front End (WFE) to another. In SharePoint 2010, the NLB servers had to be set up to have *affinity* (where a user would go back to the same WFE). Although this would work, it wasn't true load balancing. With the login token cache, any WFE that receives a request for resources can access the security token, validate the user, and provide him with the resources requested (assuming that that user has permissions).

The Distributed Cache service is built on Windows Server AppFabric, which implements the AppFabric Caching service. This service must be installed on the Windows Server running SharePoint before it can be used. Luckily, Windows Server AppFabric is one of the prerequisites that must be installed before the SharePoint installation.

EXAM TIP

A new feature in SharePoint, Distributed Cache will most likely be on the exam in some way. Important concepts to remember are the mode, the login token cache, and the feed cache. Knowing how to enable Distributed Cache is also important.

MORE INFO MICROBLOG FEATURES, FEEDS, AND THE DISTRIBUTED CACHE SERVICE

See *http://technet.microsoft.com/en-us/library/jj219700.aspx* for more information on microblog features, feeds, and the Distributed Cache service in SharePoint Server 2013.

Planning connections

After the User Profile service application is created and the User Profile Synchronization service starts, you can use the selected account with sufficient permissions to create synchronization connection to a directory service. This connection needs to pull in just the users who are supposed to have profiles. This means that inactive users, test users, non-human users, and/or non-full-time employees might need to be filtered out.

MORE INFO PLANNING WORKSHEETS

Because creating a synchronization connection involves so many options, you should plan it out with worksheets. Luckily, worksheets have already been created to help you plan. See *http://www.microsoft.com/en-us/download/details.aspx?id=35404* to download and use these planning worksheets.

Every user who needs a profile must have an identity in a directory service. A unique identifier needs to exist that identifies the user (such as the account name in AD) so that the user can be synchronized as a unique person. A directory service doesn't have to be Active Directory, although this is the most common. Directory services come in three different types:

- Windows-based authentication (such as AD)
- Forms-based authentication
- Claims-based authentication

Claims-based or forms-based authentication requires that a trusted provider be used; with Windows-based authentication, no trusted provider is needed. Several different types of connections can be made to directory services, including these built into SharePoint Server 2013:

- Active Directory (AD)
- Active Directory Logon Data
- Active Directory Resource
- Business Data Connectivity

- IBM Tivoli Directory Server (ITDS)
- Novell eDirectory
- Sun Java System Directory Server

EXAM TIP

While knowing that a number of different types of connections can be used is important, you aren't expected to have in-depth knowledge of non-Windows directory services for the exam.

Such a varied set of directory services exists in case SharePoint runs in a non-Windows environment or users come from a third-party source. SharePoint Server 2013 is an enterprise solution that needs to work in a wide variety of environments. For purposes of illustration, you need to see how to create a Synchronization Connection with AD as the directory service:

1. Navigate to Central Administration and click Manage Service Applications under the Application Management section.
2. Click the User Profile service application to open the Manage Profile Service page.
3. Click Configure Synchronization Connections in the Synchronization section.
4. On the Synchronization Connections page, click Create New Connection.
5. In the Connection Name text box, type a connection name that's meaningful to SharePoint administrators (for example, **active users**).
6. Choose Active Directory in the Type section.
7. In the Connection Settings section, type a forest name in the Forest Name text box. This needs to be the complete forest name; remember that single-label domains aren't supported.
8. In the same section, choose whether to autodiscover a domain controller. If you choose not to, type the domain controller's name in the text box provided.
9. From the Authentication Provider Type drop-down list, choose Windows Authentication (Forms Authentication and Trusted Claims Provider Authentication are the other options). Because you're using Windows authentication, you don't need to provide an Authentication Provider Instance.
10. Type the account name with the additional AD permissions in the Account Name text box.
11. Type and confirm the password in the appropriate text boxes.
12. Choose the port and whether to use SSL. For most implementations, leave the port at 389.
13. Click Populate Containers and wait for the box below it to populate.

14. In the containers box, expand the tree and select the container(s) that contain the users to import. You might have to work with other groups in your organization to determine which containers have the users who need to be imported.
15. Click OK to save the changes.

> ***MORE INFO*** **PLANNING PROFILE SYNCHRONIZATION**
>
> **See *http://technet.microsoft.com/en-us/library/ff182925(office.15).aspx#connections* for more information on how to plan profile synchronization for SharePoint 2013.**

When a synchronization connection is created successfully, you can apply filters. You can use a filter to exclude certain users, such as contractors or temporary employees. Filters can also be used to narrowly define a set of users for a particular connection. For example, if only a subset of users from a specific office location needed profiles, a filter could limit the number of users imported. Most often filters are used to filter out inactive users. Not deleting users from AD in case they return is often a policy, so they can be given the same account that they previously had.

Filters are based on the attributes imported in the synchronization. The set of attributes will vary from organization to organization. To better understand how filters are used, follow these steps to create one:

1. Navigate to Synchronization Connections and choose the connection that needs to be modified. Clicking the name should show a drop-down menu; select the Edit Connection Filters option.
2. In the Exclusion Filter for Users section, choose the attribute to be filtered on. This determines the available Operators. Also choose whether the attribute is an AND or an OR operation.
3. Choose the desired operator, such as Equals or Contains.
4. Type in the value to filter on in the Filter text box.
5. Click Add to add the filter.
6. Continue adding filters until all applicable filters are applied.
7. Repeat steps 2-6 for groups in the Exclusion Filter for Groups section if you want to filter groups.
8. Click OK to finish and save the filters.

Now, the only thing left is to create a synchronization schedule. You first need to perform a full import and validate that the correct number of users are returned and that the mapped fields are populated correctly. Typically, a full synchronization isn't required, but it's necessary when the connection is first created. To synchronize a profile, follow these steps:

1. Navigate to the Manage Profile Service page and click Start Profile Synchronization.

2. Choose Start Full Synchronization.

3. Click OK to start the synchronization process.

The process might not start immediately, but should start within a minute. The process could take a long time to complete, depending on the number of users and the performance of the server doing the profile synchronization. Full synchronization is a resource-intensive operation and should be done only when absolutely necessary.

After the process completes (check the Profile Synchronization Status on the Manage Profiles Service page to see whether it says *Idle*), look at the number of user profiles to ensure that they match the expected number.

You can determine a profile synchronization schedule based on business requirements and the capabilities of the SharePoint server running the profile synchronization service. An incremental profile synch isn't overly taxing on the system and can be run quite often. You might want to consider an incremental synch if changes in Active Directory need to be reflected in SharePoint within a certain time frame.

> ***NOTE*** **PROFILE PROPERTIES CHANGE ITERATION**
>
> **When a profile property changes in Active Directory, you need to perform two steps for the information to be fully iterated through the SharePoint environment:**
>
> 1. **Perform an incremental synchronization.**
> 2. **Have the Search service crawl the user profiles for the changes to appear in search.**
>
> **To determine the maximum amount of delay, the time between incremental profile synchronizations needs to be added to the time between incremental crawls of user profiles by the Search service.**

You can set up an incremental profile synchronization after the connection is verified. Changes can't be made while the User Profile service is being synchronized; you must wait until the current synchronization process finishes. Incremental synchronization is handled with a timer job created in the SharePoint environment, which you can set up as follows:

1. Navigate to the Manage Profile Service page.

2. Click Configure Synchronization Timer Job in the Synchronization section.

3. In the Recurring Schedule section, choose how often the synchronization should run. Most organizations run it at least daily, but hourly or even every few minutes is a valid option because it's a fairly low-resource operation except in the largest of organizations.

4. Click OK or Run Now.

Now the profiles should be synchronized with AD regularly. Periodically, you should check individual users to ensure that changes are being replicated.

Thought experiment

Planning for a My Site deployment

In this thought experiment, apply what you've learned about this objective. You can find answers to these questions in the "Answers" section at the end of this chapter.

You are implementing a farm for which the User Profile service application has been provisioned and the User Profile Synchronization service has started. You are assigned to set up the My Site host with the appropriate number of content databases. The business requirements also call for a quick response time on activity feeds because the organization wants to promote the social features of SharePoint 2013. Finally, you need to accommodate 5,000 users who need SkyDrive space of 1 GB each.

How many content databases are needed for the My Sites? What should be done for optimal activity feed performance from an end user's perspective?

Objective summary

- Community sites are an effective way to encourage input in a forum-type environment but should be configured on creation.
- You should thoroughly plan out the My Site host before users start creating personal sites.
- The User Profile service application and User Profile Synchronization services require careful planning before they are implemented.
- The AD account needs additional permissions to be able to import users.
- Active Directory is just one of many directory services available for importing users.
- Establishing connections to directory services and providing the correct filters are necessary to keep extraneous user profiles out of SharePoint.
- Distributed Cache can greatly improve the performance of Activity Feeds and the end-user experience.

Objective review

Answer the following questions to test your knowledge of the information in this objective. You can find the answers to these questions and explanations of why each answer choice is correct or incorrect in the "Answers" section at the end of this chapter.

1. A community site has been created and a user has been given a badge. How many total badges is the person allowed to have?
   - **A.** As many as they receive
   - **B.** One
   - **C.** Three
   - **D.** Five
2. What is the default upload limit for an individual file in a My Site host?
   - **A.** 10 MB
   - **B.** 50 MB
   - **C.** 250 MB
   - **D.** 1 GB
3. On what server would an account be granted the Replicating Directory Changes permission (used in profile synchronization with AD)?
   - **A.** A domain controller
   - **B.** The SQL Server that SharePoint uses
   - **C.** Any SharePoint server
   - **D.** The SharePoint server that runs the profile synchronization
4. Which authentication method doesn't require a trusted provider?
   - **A.** Forms-based authentication
   - **B.** Claims-based authentication
   - **C.** Windows-based authentication
   - **D.** All of the above
5. A user can follow many items in SharePoint 2013, and changes to these followed items appear in their activity feed. SharePoint allows the limiting of how many items users can follow for performance reasons. Which of the following items can be limited on a farm?
   - **A.** The number of people followed per user
   - **B.** The number of documents followed per user
   - **C.** The number of sites followed per user
   - **D.** All of the above

Objective 2.2: Plan and configure a search workload

Searches typically consume the most resources of any component in the SharePoint farm and often require one or more servers dedicated just to handle the demands. Because of the resources that searches consume and the end-user expectations, you need to know how to plan for them both for real-world implementations and for this exam.

This objective covers the following topics:

- Planning and configuring search result relevancy
- Planning and configuring index freshness
- Planning and configuring result sources
- Planning and configuring the end-user experience
- Planning and configuring a search schema
- Analyzing search analytics reports

Planning and configuring search result relevancy

Search is at the very core of SharePoint. Users type terms in the search box and expect relevant results to be returned. Although SharePoint does a great job at indexing and querying those results, it still needs some human interaction to help it determine the most relevant results.

Many factors can be used to help determine what results are the most relevant. SharePoint takes into consideration the item that's searched on and what users click to refine the results that seem the most relevant, but many other factors can be configured so that certain results can be pushed to the top. The following items can be configured to help improve search relevancy:

- Building a thesaurus
- Defining a custom entity extraction
- Adding query rules and suggestions
- Designating authoritative pages

You can use each of these items to help end users find the results they need as quickly as possible so that they can spend more time doing their job and less time searching for the data. This section covers how to configure and plan for increasing search result relevance using the items in the preceding list.

Building a thesaurus

A thesaurus uses synonyms to help expand the results that SharePoint returns. For example, SharePoint 2013 could be a synonym for SharePoint Server 2103 and SP2013. After the synonyms are loaded into the SharePoint server, a search on any one of the three items would bring back results for all three items. The synonyms can be all in one language or expanded to other languages.

The thesaurus is created and maintained outside SharePoint, using a program such as Microsoft Excel to help generate comma-separated (CSV) files that are imported into the SharePoint system. When you create a thesaurus, remember that each SharePoint farm is limited to one thesaurus file.

Creating a thesaurus requires some manual effort, but the steps are pretty straightforward. When the SharePoint Search service application is up and running, you can create a file to be used to import the synonyms. A synonym consists of three key components:

- **Key** Single-word or multiple-word key that triggers the expansion of search components
- **Synonym** Word or phrase that's included when the key word or phrase is searched on
- **Language** Optional component with an abbreviation for the language of the synonym

The simple CSV file that needs to be created has *Key,Synonym,Language* as the first line and the key, synonym, language combinations listed as individual lines below the first line. The following is an example:

```
Key,Synonym,Language
SharePoint 2013, SharePoint Server 2013, en
SharePoint 2013, SP2013, en
```

After you create and save the file as a CSV file with Windows Notepad, Microsoft Excel, or a third-party product, you can then import it into the SharePoint Search configuration as follows:

1. Verify that the account being used is an administrator for the Search service application.
2. Start the SharePoint Server 2013 Management shell (PowerShell for SharePoint) and type the following command, where <*Path*> is the location of the CSV file:

   ```
   $searchApp = Get-SPEnterpriseSearchServiceApplication
   Import-SPEnterpriseSearchThesaurus -SearchApplication $searchApp -Filename <Path>
   ```

When the thesaurus is imported and validated, whenever someone types the keyword, the synonyms are appended to the search so that all items in the group are returned. To help build a thesaurus, the words that people search on should be tracked so that a SharePoint administrator (or preferably a librarian) can look at the results and help to build a more accurate thesaurus.

MORE INFO **CREATING AND DEPLOYING A THESAURUS**

See *http://technet.microsoft.com/en-us/library/jj219579* for more information on how to create and deploy a thesaurus in SharePoint Server 2013.

Defining custom entity extractions

Custom entities are used to refine search results. For example, if the Contoso company had three levels of certification available to its users, it might want refiners to be displayed whenever the certification or part of the certification was typed into the search box. If the word *expert* was entered into the search engine, *Contoso expert* might appear as a refiner. This would help users find information on how to become a Contoso expert.

Defining custom entity extractions is similar to creating a thesaurus—you need to create a CSV file and then import it. The imported file is referred to as a *custom entity extraction dictionary*. As with the thesaurus, the file must follow a certain format, but with custom entity extractions, only two fields of data exist:

- **Key** A word or phrase that defines the custom entity
- **Display form** The refiner name (optional)

This is a little simpler than the thesaurus in that it doesn't have a language component. An example of the CSV file is as follows:

```
Key, Display form
Expert, Contoso Expert
Contoso, Contoso Expert
```

After you create the CSV file with a program such as Notepad or Excel, you can import it into the SharePoint environment. The steps for importing the CSV file are similar to the method used in importing a thesaurus:

1. Create the CSV file based on the preceding example.
2. Open the SharePoint 2013 Management Shell.
3. In the Management Shell interface, type the following command, where <*Path*> is the path to the CSV file and <*Dictionary name*> is the name of the type of the custom extraction dictionary:

```
$searchApp = Get-SPEnterpriseSearchServiceApplication
Import-SPEnterpriseSearchCustomExtractionDictionary -SearchApplication $searchApp
-Filename <Path> -DictionaryName <Dictionary name>
```

The dictionary name depends on the type of custom extraction dictionary. You can use one of the following values:

- *Microsoft.UserDictionaries.EntityExtraction.Custom.Word.n*, where n=1, 2, 3, 4, or 5
- *Microsoft.UserDictionaries.EntityExtraction.Custom.ExactWord.1*
- *Microsoft.UserDictionaries.EntityExtraction.Custom.WordPart.n*, where n=1, 2, 3, 4, or 5
- *Microsoft.UserDictionaries.EntityExtraction.Custom.ExactWordPart.1*

MORE INFO **CUSTOM ENTITY EXTRACTOR TYPES**

See *http://technet.microsoft.com/en-us/library/jj219480(v=office.15)#CustomDictionaryTypes* for an overview on custom entity extractor types.

You can extract custom entities from managed metadata. Here, a managed property such as the Title or Body field can be used to create refiners of the custom entity. To make this happen, follow these steps:

1. Validate that the account being used is an administrator of the Search service application.
2. Navigate to Central Administration and click Manage Service Applications in the Application Management section.
3. Click the Search service application.
4. Click Search Schema in the Queries And Results section.
5. On the Managed Properties page, find the property to associate with the custom entity extraction.
6. Point to the managed property, click it, and then click Edit/Map Property.
7. On the Edit Managed Property page, edit the settings in the Custom Entity Extraction section. Select the dictionary for the custom entity extraction dictionary that you've imported, and then click OK.

The entity extraction requires a full crawl to implement. After the refiners are created, you can use Refinement Web Parts to include them on the search results page. Follow these steps:

1. On the page that the Refinement Web Part is to be configured, validate that the user making the changes is a member of the Designer group of higher.
2. Edit the page on which the refinement page resides.
3. Edit the Refinement Web Part.
4. Click Choose Refiners in the Properties For Search Refinement section.
5. Select one or more managed properties containing extracted entities that you want to use as a refiner from the list and click Add.
6. In the Configure section, configure how you want the refiner to appear and click OK.

When the refinement panel is configured, the custom entities should appear if the values match the entities in the custom extraction dictionary.

Adding query suggestions

Query suggestions (or *search suggestions*, as they are often referred to) help give users suggestions as they type text into the search box. This functionality is seen in almost all popular search engines used today.

SharePoint automatically generates query suggestions over time. The default is that when an item is searched on and then clicked six times, it then becomes a query suggestion. For example, if someone types **Microsoft** in the search engine, *Microsoft SharePoint* might appear as a query suggestion below the search box. A query suggestion appears only if at least one word that has been typed appears in the query suggestion.

As part of planning for search relevancy, you can add or prohibit query suggestions manually as part of the search configuration. Manually added query suggestions exist at the Search application level and appear in all search boxes across all site collections.

To add query suggestions, you must first create a text file that has one query suggestion per line. You can create this simple text file with Notepad or a similar product. After you create the file, you can add the query suggestions as follows, using an administrator account for the Search service application:

1. Navigate to the Search service application in Central Administration.
2. Click Query Suggestions in the Queries And Results section.
3. For the Language For Suggestion Phrases, select the language of the query suggestions to be imported. The list shows only the languages for which language packs have been added.
4. In the Always Suggest Phrases section, select the Import From Text File option.
5. Browse to the query suggestions file that you created and click OK.
6. Click Save Settings.

After the file is uploaded, the query suggestions in the provided list appear when a user types in the search box (if the query suggestions are turned on). If you want to remove all manually added query suggestions, you can upload an empty text file to erase all query suggestions for the language chosen.

IMPORTANT **OVERWRITING A QUERY SUGGESTION FILE**

Importing a query suggestion file overwrites any existing suggestions that exist in the search system (per language). Therefore, keeping a master query suggestion file is recommended.

Excluding query suggestions is also possible. The reasons behind excluding items are driven by business reasons, but SharePoint allows for these exclusions. When a phrase is added to the exclusion list, it never appears as a query suggestion. The text file to be used is similar to the file used for query suggestions in that one query phrase exists per line. The steps involved are as follows:

1. Navigate to Central Administration and click Manage Service Applications in the Application Management section.
2. Click the Search service application.
3. In the Queries and Results section, click Query Suggestions.
4. For the Languages For Suggestion Phrases, select the language of the query exclusions (one file per language).
5. In the Never Suggest Phrases section, click Import From Text File.
6. Browse to the file to be imported and click OK.
7. Click Save Settings.

Query suggestions (and the ability to exclude individual query suggestions) are turned on by default, but you can turn them on or off within SharePoint Server 2013. The process is fairly straightforward and can be accomplished with a few steps:

1. Navigate to the Search service application with an account that has administrative rights.
2. Open the Query Suggestions page in the Queries and Results section.
3. To enable query suggestions, select the Show Search Suggestions check box or leave it cleared to disable query suggestions
4. Click Save Settings to enable the changes.

The changes made are at the Search service application level and affect all search boxes in all site collections across the farm. Users expect query suggestions because they are familiar with popular search engines. Therefore, leave these on unless you have a specific business reason for them to be turned off.

After query suggestions are uploaded, you can export them to a text file. This is useful for maintaining query suggestions and for sharing them with other farms. This is done on the same page as importing the query suggestion text files.

MORE INFO **MANAGING QUERY SUGGESTIONS**

See *http://technet.microsoft.com/en-us/library/jj721441* for more information on managing query suggestions in SharePoint Server 2013.

Designating authoritative pages

SharePoint uses authoritative pages to rank certain pages or sites above others. For example, an organization might decide that *http://contonso/documents* is a more important site than *http://contoso/archive* (because an archive site is probably less relevant than a working site). Defining authoritative pages is probably one of the most important steps that can be taken in making more relevant pages rise to the top of the search results. Rank is determined by how many times an item has been chosen from a search results query as well as how far it is away from an authoritative site or page. Closeness is determined by how many clicks it would take to get to the document from the authoritative page.

You can also enter non-authoritative sites into the SharePoint system. These pages or sites would then be pushed to the bottom of the search results list. This is useful for sites (such as archives) that need to be indexed, but the results shouldn't be at the forefront of the search results. These sites are pushed to the bottom of the search results not matter how often they are chosen.

Determining which sites or pages are authoritative (or non-authoritative) is the role of someone who's familiar with the SharePoint environment as well as the organization using SharePoint. Because finding a single individual for this task is difficult, it will probably require working with individuals who have in-depth knowledge of different areas of the SharePoint farm. One way to define authoritative pages is to create a page with links to sites deemed important and/or relevant. Sometimes this is simply the home page, but for more precise search results, creating a page for both authoritative results and non-authoritative results is beneficial.

Authoritative pages can be entered into the SharePoint system but require farm-level rights, whereas a page can be used so that a subject-matter expert or experts can update a SharePoint page without having access to Central Administration. Pages or sites can be deemed authoritative (or not) by following these steps:

1. In Central Administration, navigate to the Manage Service Applications page in the Applications Management section, using an account with administrative rights on the Search service application.
2. Click the Search service application.
3. Click Authoritative Pages to open the Authoritative Pages page.
4. Add the pages with the most authority in the Most Authoritative Pages text box under the Authoritative Web Pages section. Separate the sites and/or pages so that each line has only one URL.

5. In the Second-Level Authoritative Pages text box, type the URL of any pages seen as second-level. Repeat for the third-level authoritative pages.
6. In the Non-Authoritative Sites section, add the URLs of the sites to be demoted (all sites that start with this URL will also be demoted).
7. To adjust rankings immediately, click Refresh Now in the Relevance Rankings Analytics section. Otherwise, rankings will be refreshed later.
8. Click OK to save the changes.

After the changes are made and the rankings are calculated, users should start getting results ordered by the rankings in relation to the authoritative pages. These settings should be reviewed periodically so that the rankings can be adjusted based on how the SharePoint farm is used. This review is necessary to provide users the most relevant and up-to-date results possible and therefore saving them time and money.

Planning and configuring index freshness

Whenever a document is added, it doesn't appear in the search results until it's crawled and indexed. The same is true with document changes: They don't appear until the content source is crawled. The more often a content source is crawled, the more up to date the results will be. SharePoint 2013 now includes an option to continuously crawl a content source. Of course, crawling continuously is a resource-intensive task, and the server or servers doing the crawling need to be up to the task.

> ***IMPORTANT*** **SHAREPOINT 2013 QUERY SERVER CHANGES**
>
> **Changes made to SharePoint 2013 mean that the server responsible for handling search queries needs more resources. This was an effort to move some of the work away from the SQL Server. Therefore, moving the query functionality to its own server provides significant performance improvements.**

Continuous crawling is started at 15 minute intervals by default. This interval can be changed using PowerShell. Before continuous crawling can be used, it must be enabled according to content-source level (applicable only to the SharePoint sites' content-source type). To enable continuous crawling, follow these steps:

1. Navigate to Central Administration with an account that has administrative rights to the Search service application and click Manage Service Application in the Application Management section.
2. Click the Search service application.
3. Click Content Sources in the Crawling section.
4. Choose a content source to modify, or create a new one and click the content source.
5. In the Crawl Schedule section, select Enable Continuous Crawling.

6. Click OK.
7. On the Content Sources page, verify that the Status column shows *Crawling Continuous*.

Enabling continuous crawling means that search results can appear before a crawl is completed because adding a document starts a new crawl that might finish before the first crawl. A user can add a document and have it appear in the search results within seconds of it being added, which can greatly improve the end-user experience and help users find the most current information as soon as possible. The only thing to consider is the amount of resources consumed by the search server. For large content source and limited search server resources, enabling continuous crawling might not be an option. After continuous crawling is enabled, the server should be monitored to see how memory and CPU resources are affected.

MORE INFO **MANAGING CONTINUOUS CRAWLS**

See *http://technet.microsoft.com/en-us/library/jj219802.aspx* for more information on managing continuous crawls in SharePoint Server 2013.

EXAM TIP

New in SharePoint 2013, continuous crawling is the best way to keep search content as fresh as possible. You can expect to see this concept on the exam in some way, both among the multiple-choice questions as well as in the case studies.

Planning and configuring result sources

Result sources help limit crawls to subsets of the SharePoint farm. They have replaced the scopes used in previous SharePoint versions. Correctly configuring the result sources can help maximize the efficiency of the search servers.

SharePoint's default result source is Local SharePoint Results, which is set up for you when you create the Search service application. Whenever a Search Driven Content Web Part is added to a page, it uses the default result source. If business rules specify that a specific result source is used, you can change the default at the Search service application level, the site collection level, and the site level. To change the default result source at the Search service application level, follow these steps, using an administrator account for the Search service application:

1. Navigate to Central Administration and click Manage Service Applications in the Application Management section.
2. Click the Search service application.
3. In the Queries and Results section, click Result Sources.
4. In the Manage Result Sources section, select the result source that will be the default. Click the arrow that appears and select Set as Default.

You can create result sources at the farm, site collection, and site levels, but this book focuses only on the farm level. To create or modify result sources at the site collection level, navigate to the site collection settings and click Result Sources in the Site Collection Settings section. To modify or create result sources at the site level, navigate to the site setting and click Result Sources under the Site Settings section.

To create a new result source at the farm level, follow these steps, using an administrator account for the Search service application:

1. Navigate to Central Administration and click Manage Service Applications in the Application Management section.
2. Click the Search service application.
3. In the Queries and Results section, click Result Sources.
4. On the Manage Result Source page, click New Result Source.
5. On the Add Result Source page, type the Name and Description in the General Information section.
6. In the Protocol section, select one of the following protocols for retrieving results:
   - **Local SharePoint** The default; provides results from the Search service application
   - **Remote SharePoint** Provides results from another farm
   - **OpenSearch** Provides results from other sites that use the OpenSearch 1.0/1.1 protocol
   - **Exchange** Provides results from Microsoft Exchange Server
7. In the Type section, choose SharePoint Search Results or People Search Results.
8. In the Query Transform field, you can choose to leave the default (searchTerms) as it is, or you can use a different transform method. You can also use QueryBuilder to help build queries using specific filters.
9. In the Credentials Information section, select the authentication type that you want to use to connect to the result source.

IMPORTANT **EXCHANGE WEB SERVICES**

The Exchange Web Services Managed API must be installed on the computer that's running the Search service if Exchange results are desired.

Result sources enable you to bring a variety of different search results into the SharePoint search experience, so that users can use SharePoint as a single source for all their search needs. However, you still need to plan out the result sources.

EXAM TIP

SharePoint 2013 can no longer create scopes; result sources have replaced them. The scopes of All Results and People exist as part of the SharePoint installation. As part of the exam, knowing that creating a scope wouldn't be a step for anything is important. You should also be aware that result sources can integrate different sources so that results appear in the same set of search results.

Gone is the ability to create scopes and have them appear in the drop-down list next to the search box (although migrated scopes will still be usable). Users now click the result scope they want to use. The result scopes shown on a search page are configured on the page from the result scopes that have been made available. For example, on the Enterprise Search results page, the default result sources of Everything, People, Conversations, and Videos are listed below the search box (see Figure 2-10).

FIGURE 2-10 Result types shown right below the search box on the Enterprise Search Center results page

The result sources are listed in a Search Navigation Web Part (the result types shown under the search box are actually just links to pages configured to display a particular result source by changing the query values of the Search Results Web Part). Clicking one of the result types changes what appears in the search results box connected to the Search Navigation Web Part. The displayed result sources are determined by the search settings, not by the Search Navigation Web Part. To modify the result sources, follow these steps:

1. Navigate to the search results page to be modified and click Site Settings under the Settings icon.
2. Click Search Settings in the Search section.
3. In the Configure Search Navigation section, you can add or remove links. The sort order also can be configured, as shown in Figure 2-11. Click OK to save any changes.

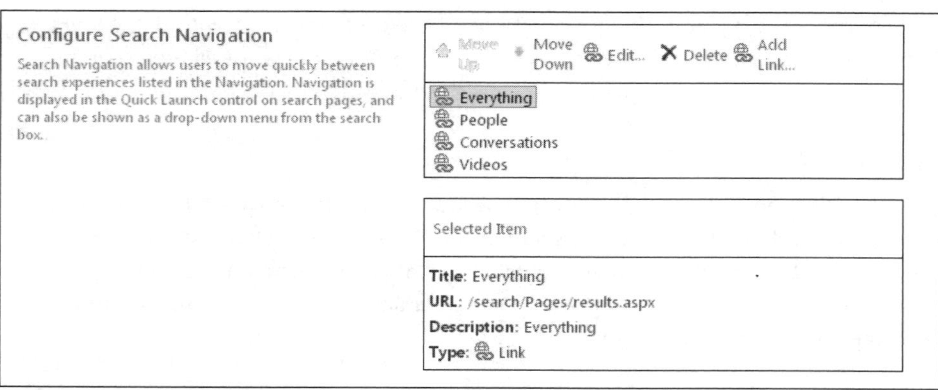

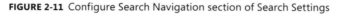

FIGURE 2-11 Configure Search Navigation section of Search Settings

Before adding new links, you have to create the pages. The Search Results Web Part is where you choose the result source, but you can configure many other query options. You don't need to know how to configure each of these options for the test, but you should have a general understanding of the options available. Some options that you can configure (by clicking Change Query in the Search Results Web Part settings) are as follows:

- Select a result source
- Add a keyword filter
- Add a property filter
- Query text to use and/or append
- Choose refiners
- Choose which property to search on
- Choose a ranking model
- Configure dynamic sorting
- Whether to use query rules
- Whether to use asynchronous or synchronous loading
- Whether to rewrite URLs for product catalog items

As you can tell by the number of options, the ability to configure the search results has been greatly expanded. A high degree of customization can mean the results will take a while to be fully returned. In such cases, asynchronous loading would provide a more user-friendly experience.

EXAM TIP

While most of the exam is concerned with configuring solutions in Central Administration, some items—such as result types—cross over because they can be configured at site, site collection, or farm level. To make these changes, you need to understand what kinds of permissions are required. For example, site collection administrators still can't create a farm-level result source unless they also have farm-level permissions.

Planning and configuring the end-user experience

SharePoint 2013 has completely revamped the way search results appear. In SharePoint 2010, designers had to work with a huge XSLT file to modify the results. Now designers can target individual types of items and have them display differently, with specific metadata displayed and HTML that can be modified to show links and/or graphics in addition to the content. You can modify each item type in distinct files rather than modify the whole XSLT file. This way, multiple developers can work independently, potentially speeding up development as a result. SharePoint 2013 also uses query rules to alter the results being returned. This can be used to promote certain content or to change the result set based on the query entered.

You can use all these items together to provide a richer and better targeted search experience. They can even be used to provide a different result set for different individuals. For example, engineers could have different search result experiences than contractors.

This section covers how to use query rules, display templates, and result types to configure the search experience (result sources were covered in the previous section). Going through each of these, even if you aren't the person having the search experience, will help you both on the exam and in understanding the architecture behind them.

Query rules

Query rules are used to change what's returned in a search result set. You can use query rules to promote certain results, show additional results, and fine-tune rankings. A query rule is made up of conditions, actions, and publishing. These three components combine to make a rule that determines the content of the search results for a specified amount of time.

To get a better understanding of query results, you should start by creating one. You can set query results at the Search service application level, the site collection level, and the site level. At the Search service application level, you can add or modify query rules as follows:

1. In Central Administration, click Manage Service Applications in the Application Management section.
2. Click the Search service application to open the Search Administration page (or click the list of Search service applications).
3. In the Queries And Results section, click Query Rules to open the Manage Query Rules page (see Figure 2-12).

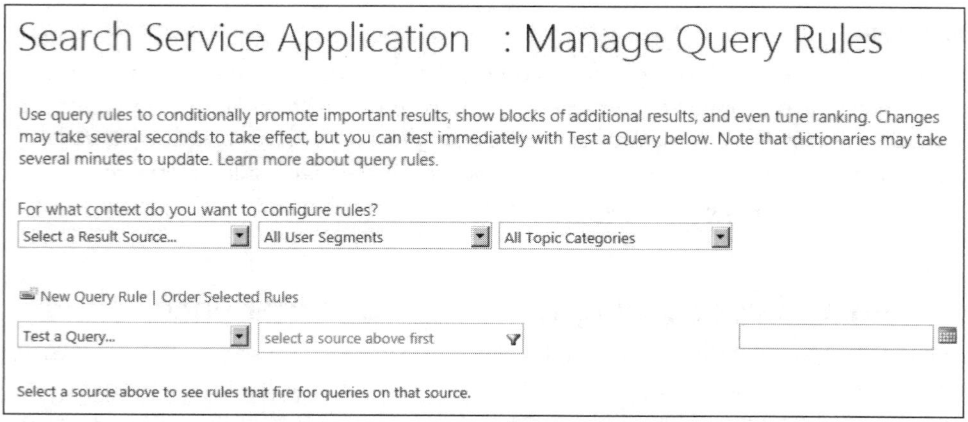

Search Service Application : Manage Query Rules

Use query rules to conditionally promote important results, show blocks of additional results, and even tune ranking. Changes may take several seconds to take effect, but you can test immediately with Test a Query below. Note that dictionaries may take several minutes to update. Learn more about query rules.

For what context do you want to configure rules?

Select a Result Source... | All User Segments | All Topic Categories

New Query Rule | Order Selected Rules

Test a Query... | select a source above first

Select a source above to see rules that fire for queries on that source.

FIGURE 2-12 The Manage Query Rules page in Search Administration

The first step in building a query rule is to determine what the conditions are. Not enough room is available to go over all of them, but here are some examples of possible conditions. First, look at some of the possible results sources:

- All Sources
- Wiki
- Documents
- Pages
- Local People Results

After you choose a result source, you need to select a user segment and a topic category. Then you can create a query rule for the context by clicking New Query Rule. You can then configure the rule by following these steps:

1. Type a name for the rule in the Rule Name text box (the context will show under the box).
2. In the Context section, choose one of the following possible query conditions from the drop-down list:
   - Query Matches Keyword Exactly
   - Query Contains Action Term
   - Query Matches Dictionary Exactly
   - Query More Common in Source
   - Result Type Commonly Clicked
   - Advanced Query Text Match
3. Depending on which query condition is chosen, you can fill in options, such as providing the text for Query Matches Keyword Exactly.
4. Continue adding conditions by clicking Add Alternate Condition, if you want.

5. Choose which action to take:
   - Add Promoted Result
   - Add Result Block
   - Change ranked results by changing the query
6. In the Publishing section, choose when to make the query rule active or inactive by selecting a Start Date and End Date. You also can choose to review the rule on a certain date by setting the Review Date and entering a Contact.
7. Click Save to save the changes.

Back on the Manage Query Rules page, you can test a query by typing some text in the Find Rules That Fire For A Query text box. You can also sort the queries by different types, such as inactive rules, thus simplifying the task of finding and modifying the query rules. Adding a query rule doesn't make it take effect right away, but you can still test it immediately. You can use the same steps at the site collection and at the site level for targeted query results.

Display templates

Display templates enable particular search result items to be displayed differently. For example, if the item in question had the content type of Press Release, it could be displayed differently than a normal document (perhaps by having an icon associated with it and showing some additional metadata, such as Company). You can create display templates with straight HTML. This sort of control is a vast improvement over SharePoint 2010, where this sort of modification required modifying a huge XSLT file (more than 600 lines). Display templates are made up of the follow file types:

- An HTML file
- A JavaScript file that's generated when the HTML file is uploaded

Everything needed for the display template is defined within the HTML file.

The easiest way to create a display template is to modify an existing one. A variety of templates are available in SharePoint 2013 in the Master Page Gallery of a site collection. To find the Display Template folder and save an example, follow these steps:

1. Navigate to the top level of a site collection and click Site Settings.
2. In the Web Designer Galleries section, click Master Pages And Page Layouts.
3. Click Display Templates on the Master Page Gallery page.
4. Because this discussion concerns search, click the Search folder.
5. Navigate to an item that closely matches the one you want to design a template for (for example, use *Item_Person.html* for a person-based template) and hover over it for the drop-down arrow.
6. Click the arrow and choose Download A Copy.

After you download the file, you can make changes to it and then upload it back to the display template in the Master Page Gallery. The file is fairly long but is much less complicated than the XSLT file that you had to modify for the people results page in SharePoint 2010.

After you create a display template, you need to create a result type so that SharePoint knows when to use it.

Result types

Result types work with display templates. A result type determines which display template is used based on a set of rules configured for the result type. Using content types, result sources, and managed properties to define rules for the result type provides some interesting options for displaying results. Each rule can have multiple values, and the result type can have multiple rules; you have an unlimited number of combinations. For example, you can combine a content type with a managed property. A possible option would be to show a map (or link to a map) if the item contained a Street, City, and State field.

To create a result type, follow these steps:

1. Navigate to the Site Settings page of the site collection where you need to create the result types.
2. Click Result Types in the Search section.
3. On the Manage Result Types page, click New Result.
4. Choose the appropriate Result Condition and Result Action—for example, if the content type is Sales Report, display the Sales Report display template.
5. Click OK to save the results.

Now that the result type is connected to a display template, whenever that item comes up in search, the display template for that item appears with all the extra content and/or graphics associated with it.

EXAM TIP

Display templates and result types are a totally new way to modify the look and feel of search results. You probably won't need to know how to add HTML elements, but knowledge of the concepts and some details—such how a result type is made up of a condition and an action—is expected.

Planning and configuring a search schema

A search schema is composed of managed property mappings and managed property settings. Managed properties determine what's indexed and therefore available in the search results and for refiners. The content and metadata of a document or a list item is referred to as *crawled properties*. For crawled properties to be included in the search index, you must map the crawled property to a managed property. Only managed properties are written to the index and therefore available to be searched on.

You can map multiple crawled properties to a managed property. For example, you can map both Office and Location to the managed property Office. Therefore, when a user types *Office:Seattle*, it returns results for documents or lists with either the Office or Location property populated with the word *Seattle*. If a document or list item contains the Office and Location properties, the first property that the Search service encounters is used to populate the Office managed property. A crawled property can also be mapped to more than one managed property.

> ***MORE INFO*** **CRAWLED AND MANAGED PROPERTIES**
>
> **See *http://technet.microsoft.com/en-us/library/jj219630.aspx* for an overview of crawled and managed properties in SharePoint Server 2013.**

Some crawled property types generate a new managed property and mapping between the crawled and managed property. Whenever a site column is generated on a list or document library, a crawled property, a managed property, and the mapping between the two is automatically generated. Search application administrators can change the default mappings or create new ones. However, any changes to the default mappings require a full crawl of the content to take effect.

Multiple search schemas can exist. The main search schema is maintained in Central Administration in the Search service application. However, you can modify search schemas at the site collection and tenant levels. This means that site collection owners can manage the search experience at the site collection level by modifying the search schema. Site owners can view the search schema but can't modify it.

The search index is composed of a set of files in a set of folders on the search servers that have the index component on them. The content processing component processes crawled properties and stores the mapping information in the index. A variety of indexes can be queried. Whenever an item is changed, it must be reindexed after it's crawled. To reduce the reindexing load, SharePoint 2013 has introduced new index update groups:

- **Default** This group contains most of the managed properties. Everything that doesn't fit into one of the other groups falls into this group.
- **Security** This group contains the document Access Control List managed property.
- **Link** This group contains managed properties related to link data.
- **Usage** This group contains managed properties related to usage data.
- **People** This group contains managed property information related to people searches.

The default full-text index contains the contents of the managed properties. All searchable text is saved into the index. The full-text index is divided into weight groups that determine the importance of a managed property. The relevance ranking model determines what content is the most important and therefore appears higher in the search results. Two main full-text indexes exist (other than the default full-text index): one for SharePoint content and one for people-related content.

Because all the data that exists in the indexes is based on managed properties and how a crawled property is mapped to a managed property, you should go over how these are added to the Search service application. To add a managed property, follow these steps, using an account with administrative rights to the Search service application:

1. Navigate to Central Administration and click Manage Service Applications in the Application Management section.
2. Click the Search service application to open the Farm Search Administration page.
3. In the Queries and Results section, click Search Schema.
4. Click New Managed Property.
5. Type a Property Name and an optional Description in the Name And Description section.
6. In the Type section, choose the type of data for the property (such as Text, Integer, Decimal, or Date and Time).
7. In the Main Characteristics section, select all applicable items (Searchable, Queryable, Retrievable, Refinable, and so on).
8. In the Mappings To Crawled Properties section, click Add A Mapping.
9. Select a crawled property in order to map a property to the managed property and then click OK. Repeat this step to map additional crawled properties.
10. On the New Managed Property page, specify whether you want to include all content from all crawled properties mapped to this managed property and/or content from the first crawled property in the Mappings to crawled properties section.
11. In the Company Name Extraction section, optionally select the check box to enable custom entity extraction.
12. Click OK to save changes.

> ***IMPORTANT*** **CREATING REFINERS**
>
> **When creating a managed property to be used as a refiner, it must be both Refinable and Queryable.**

If you want to change the mappings, you can edit managed properties in the same area they are created. If you want to change the name, you can create a new one and, if necessary, delete the old one (if it's not in use, it can be changed safely).

Use caution when deleting a managed property. Users can no longer run queries using the property, any query rules based on that property will no longer work, and it will break any custom search applications or Web Parts that use the property. If you're not sure whether it's used, don't delete it until you can find out.

Now that you've created a managed property, you can attach crawled properties to it. Again, just because a property is crawled doesn't mean it's searchable. It must be mapped to a managed property and/or included in the full-text index. To map this property, follow these steps, using an account with administrative rights:

1. Navigate to and click the Search service application to open the Search Administration page, and then choose the particular Search service application to administer.
2. Click Search Schema in the Queries And Results section.
3. Click Crawled Properties to open the Crawled Properties page and find the property you are looking for by scrolling or using the filter (see Figure 2-13).

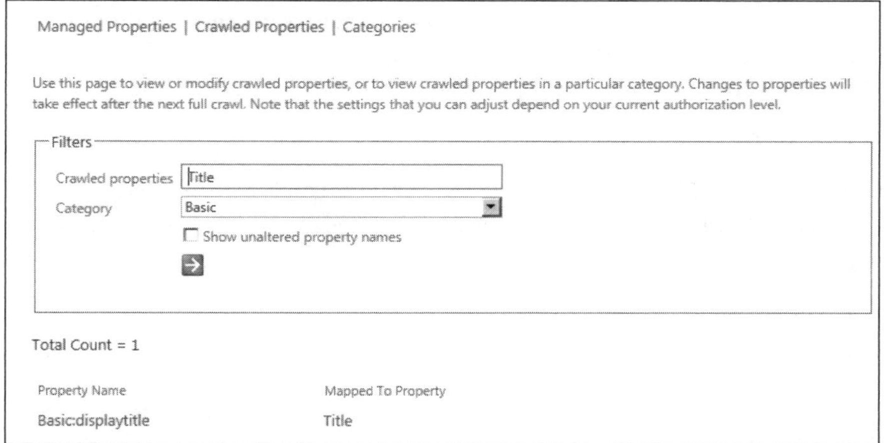

FIGURE 2-13 Crawled Properties page, with Title and Basic as the filters used to find the Title property

4. Hover over the Property Name to be edited and select Edit/Map Property from the drop-down menu.
5. In the Mappings To Managed Properties section, click Add A Mapping.
6. Choose a managed property from the Select A Managed Property list (you can narrow down the list by using the Find box) and click OK.
7. Repeat these steps for every managed property to be mapped to the crawled property.

8. Check to see whether the crawled property should be in the full-text index. If it's in the full-text index, it's available for querying without using a managed property (overuse of this can result in poor performance of the search engine).
9. Click OK to save changes.

Each crawled property has a category. Categories help organize the crawled properties so that they're easier to find and group, but they also provide a way to modify all the crawled properties in a category at the same time. For example, all the crawled properties in the Basic category could be set to Searchable. To view or edit property categories, follow these steps, using an account with administrative rights:

1. Navigate to and click the Search service application to open the Search Administration page, and then choose the particular Search service application to administer.
2. Click Search Schema in the Queries And Results section.
3. Click Categories to open the Categories page.
4. Hover over the category name to be viewed or edited and click the drop-down arrow so that you can select Edit Category (clicking a category takes you to the crawled properties page, with that category filled in for the filter).
5. View or change the Category Name in the Name And Information section.
6. Modify the four options available in the Bulk Crawled Property Settings as necessary:
   - Map all string properties in this category to the Content managed property
   - Searchable
   - Queryable
   - Retrievable

   Optionally, you also can Delete All Unmapped Crawled Properties.
7. Click OK to save changes.

Changes made to a category affect all the crawled properties in that category. Therefore, choose these settings carefully because they can have unintended consequences on items in the search index.

> ***MORE INFO*** **MANAGING SEARCH SCHEMAS**
>
> **See *http://technet.microsoft.com/en-us/library/jj219667.aspx* for more information on managing search schemas in SharePoint Server 2013.**

EXAM TIP

Several changes have been made to the categories for crawled properties. These changes are significant enough that they might appear in test questions. Be aware of which items, such as Searchable and Queryable, can be set across all crawled properties within a category.

Analyzing search analytics reports

Search analytics are important because they let users know how Search is being used and therefore how it can be modified to help users find what they want more efficiently. The analytics processing component analyzes crawled items and how users interact with Search. This is referred to as search analytics, which you can use to determine which items are searched on most often, how many times no results appear, and what users end up clicking. The analytics architecture consists of three main parts:

- **Analytics Processing Component** runs the analytics jobs.
- **Analytics reporting database** stores statistical information. Data from this database can be used to create Excel reports or to provide data to third-party products.
- **Link database** stores information about searches and crawled documents.

The Analytic Processing Component runs two different types of analyses: search analytics, which analyzes how content is crawled and added to the search index, and usage analytics, which analyzes user actions such as clicked or viewed items.

Search analytics

Search analyses extracts information such as links and anchor text from the crawled content. This data is processed and stored in the search index. Extracted data is stored in the Link database with information on how users click search results. This information is then used to improve relevance and rank. It's also used for reporting. Several types of analyses are done in search analytics:

- **Search Clicks** This type analyzes what a user clicks in the search results and is used to increase or decrease the relevancy of items in the search index. The click data is stored in the Link database.
- **Click Distance** This type analyzes the distance between an authoritative page and the item by the number of clicks between the two.
- **Social Tags** This type analyzes searches by social tags (words or phrases). By default, these aren't used for refinement or rankings.
- **Anchor Text Processing** This type analyzes how items are interlinked. The text associated with the link is also included in the analyses. The results help determine rank and relevancy.

- **Social Distance** This type focuses only on users who follow people. The analysis calculates following to two levels: the people the user follows and then which users those people follow. Analyses are used to sort people by social distance.
- **Search Reports** Various search reports are created based on items such as top queries, no results queries, and number of queries.
- **Deep Links** These are based on what people actually click in the search results.

Usage analytics

Usage analytics are based on user actions such as clicking an item in search results or typing into a search box. Statistics are calculated on these actions and stored in the Analytics reporting database. Out of the box, SharePoint monitors and stores information about these events and provides some default reports. To get a better understanding of the analyses done in usage analytics, consider the different types of analysis performed:

- **Usage Counts** This type analyzes user events such as when a user clicks an item or views an item. The counts aren't just for search results but can also include clicks from Microsoft Office programs (such as Word) or from a SharePoint library.
- **Recommendations** This type analyzes how users interact with an item. For example, it tracks users who clicked the same item and can recommend items that they also clicked.
- **Activity Ranking** This type uses the rate at which items are clicked to determine relevancy. For example, if an item is ranked on total number of clicks, older items rise to the top, but if more recent clicks are weighed more, recent items can rise to the top. This helps new documents get a higher rank.

The data collected with usage analytics is also used to generate reports so that search administrators can analyze usage trends and fine-tune how items are searched. Two types of reports are created based on usage:

- **Popularity Trends** This Excel report shows daily and monthly counts for a site collection, site, or even a specific item.
- **Most Popular Items** This report shows usage for all items within a list or library. The rankings are sorted by either Recent or Ever. This report can help you determine, for example, the most viewed item in a library.

Thought experiment

Customizing search results

In this thought experiment, apply what you've learned about this objective. You can find answers to these questions in the "Answers" section at the end of this chapter.

You have been tasked with creating a custom result set that appears when anyone types the name of the CEO in the people search box. A specialized result item should contain the CEO's picture, short biography, and links to the organization's respective social networks, including its My Site. Additional results would appear below this customized item.

What steps would be necessary to create a viable solution?

Objective summary

- Search relevancy can honed with several tools available in SharePoint, including synonyms, query suggestions, and authoritative pages.
- Result sources have replaced scopes for defining search boundaries. They can be used to bring in search results from various different sources such as other farms, Exchange, and any source that uses OpenSearch 1.0/1.
- You can pair display templates with result types to provide customized search results for individual items to provide additional details, graphics, and links related to the search item.
- Managing crawled properties and managed properties is important in providing users queryable items as well as refiners.
- Frequent review of search analytics is essential to fine-tune the search results and address issues such as no-results queries.

Objective review

Answer the following questions to test your knowledge of the information in this objective. You can find the answers to these questions and explanations of why each answer choice is correct or incorrect in the "Answers" section at the end of this chapter.

1. A decision has been made to push search results from an archive site in the SharePoint farm to the bottom of the search results page. What is the best way to achieve this result?
   - **A.** Make the site a third-level authoritative site.
   - **B.** Make the site a non-authoritative site.
   - **C.** Remove the site from the search results.
   - **D.** Remove the site from the list of authoritative results.

2. By using search results sources, users can search on results pulled from which of the following sources?
   - **A.** SharePoint sites
   - **B.** Exchange
   - **C.** OpenSearch 1.0/1.1
   - **D.** All of the above
3. You can use categories to do all but which of the following?
   - **A.** Make all crawled properties within the category searchable.
   - **B.** Delete all unmapped crawled properties.
   - **C.** Make all crawled properties refinable.
   - **D.** Map all string properties within the category to Content managed properties.
4. If you wanted the refiner *Contoso Professional* to appear whenever a user types the word *Contoso* or the word *Professional* in the search box, which of the following would you use?
   - **A.** Thesaurus
   - **B.** Entity extractor
   - **C.** Query suggestion
   - **D.** Search analytics
5. You've created a display template for items that have the content type of Expense Report, and you want items of that content type to use the display template in the search results. What else must you create to make that happen?
   - **A.** Query rule
   - **B.** Result source
   - **C.** A new content type
   - **D.** Result type

Objective 2.3: Plan and configure Web Content Management (WCM)

Web Content Management (WCM) is just one of the many roles that SharePoint 2013 can be configured to perform. This objective covers how to plan and configure the elements that make up the WCM environment.

WCM typically refers to a site that's consumed by many people but for which only a few content authors are available. Users typically don't collaborate on content (although that is possible) because they would do so on a team site or similar situation. Having a WCM site doesn't preclude other types of content, but keeping internal and external content separated for security reasons is considered a best practice if the WCM content is to be consumed by external users.

When thinking about WCM, you need to consider a growing number of subjects, such as what types of devices are being used to view the content as well as what browsers to use. Also consider the publishing piece about how content is deployed and to where. Decisions about the preferred languages of the content consumers also need to be considered. All these items can't be covered in great detail in this book, but understanding the different components in SharePoint 2013 related to WCM for the exam is still important.

This objective covers the following topics:

- Planning and configuring channels
- Planning and configuring product catalog and topic pages
- Planning and configuring content deployment
- Planning and configuring variations

Planning and configuring channels

Channels are part of the publishing infrastructure of SharePoint 2013 and are configured for particular device types. For example, you might have a channel for laptops, one for tablets, and one for mobile devices. SharePoint 2013 uses user agent strings that the browser provides to determine which channel to use. Depending on the channel, SharePoint can provide different master pages and CSS files designed specifically for the device being used. This allows web content providers to provide content that crosses a variety of different devices. (However, this doesn't mean that content doesn't have to be tested on the target devices.)

To create a channel within a site collection, click the Device Channels link in the Look And Feel section of the Site Settings page. Optionally, you can use the Design Manager. A default channel is already part of the site collection; if a browser doesn't meet any specific channels, it will use the default one. A channel is defined by five properties:

- **Name** A required user-friendly name used to identify the channel
- **Alias** A required name used by code; must be 20 alphanumeric characters or fewer
- **Description** An optional description of the channel
- **Device Inclusion Rules** The required user agent string that determines which devices the channel is targeted for
- **Active** A check box to indicate whether the channel is active

NOTE MAKING A CHANNEL ACTIVE

When designing a channel, you are recommended to leave the channel inactive until it's ready to use so that users don't have a partially finished or non-functional user experience. To test a page using a specific channel, append *?DeviceChannel=alias* (where *alias* is the alias property defined in the channel definition) to the page being tested.

Each site is limited to 10 channels (for on-premises installations). The order in which these channels occur can affect what channel is applied to what device. The more specific rules need to be above the general ones because the rules are processed in the order that they occur. For example, if a channel for a Windows 7.0 Phone operating system was below a channel for all Windows Phones, the Windows 7.0 Phone operating system channel would never be used. You can order device channels by following these steps:

1. Click the Site Settings icon to open Design Manager.
2. Click Manage Device Channels.
3. Click Edit Or Reorder Existing Channels.
4. On the Items tab, click Reorder Channels.
5. Use the Move Up and Move Down buttons to order selected channels (the default channel can't be moved).
6. Click OK to exit.

After you create a channel, you need to associate a master page with it via the Site Master Page Settings. You can use the same master page for multiple channels. Channels can use a master page only if an approved version of the master page is available.

You can use device panels to display specific content on a particular device channel or set of channels. Doing so is particularly useful for trimming content for smaller devices such as mobile phones. Rather than use Cascading Style Sheets (CSS) to hide or alter content, you can use the device panels to prevent any rending of content, thus saving on resources, which can be of particular interest for users with limited bandwidth or bandwidth quotas. Typically, content that requires many resources—memory, CPU, bandwidth—is constrained to desktops and/or tablets.

MORE INFO PLANNING FOR DEVICE CHANNELS

See *http://msdn.microsoft.com/en-us/library/jj862343.aspx* for more information on how to plan for device channels in SharePoint Server 2013.

EXAM TIP

It is highly unlikely that channels will be covered on the test. The proliferation of different device types has made addressing the needs of the people using these devices a priority in the industry, and the test will reflect this.

Planning and configuring product catalogs and topic pages

SharePoint 2013 allows for any library or list to be designated as a catalog. This way, the list or library can be reused among publishing sites. Creating a catalog is easier by first creating a product catalog site collection via the Product Catalog template, which is part of the Publishing group. The Product Catalog templates aids in the creation of catalog items and topic pages (pages automatically created for catalog items). This site collection is created just like any other site collection in Central Administration. After it's created, you need to customize it for it to be a useful catalog. The Product Catalog template is part of SharePoint 2013 Enterprise Edition and isn't available in the Standard edition.

Product catalogs

After you create the site collection, you can find several options that can help guide you through creating a product catalog. The welcome page shown in Figure 2-14 lists the steps basically in order.

Welcome to your product catalog site!
The following tasks are typically required to set up your product catalog and make the data available to other site collections:

Create site columns
Create site columns for the item properties that describe your products, for example Color or Size.
When your product catalog site is crawled, the site columns will automatically become managed properties for search.

Manage site content types
Add site columns to the site content type *Product*.
If you have item groups that have very different item properties, consider creating additional site content types for each item group, inheriting from Product.

Manage item hierarchy in Term Store
Add terms to the term set *Product Hierarchy*. This term set represents how items in the product catalog are categorized. The Item Category site column is mapped to this term set.

Add catalog items
Add catalog items to the *Products list*.
Consider creating additional lists based on the amount and complexity of your catalog data.

Modify search properties
Modify the managed properties settings so that users of cross-site publishing can query for and refine on properties in the catalog.
Before you can modify the properties, the catalog items must be approved and crawled.

Products
Title | Item Number | Group Number | Language Tag | Rollup Image | Approval Status
There are no items to show in this view of the "Products" list.

FIGURE 2-14 Home page of a product catalog site collection

CREATING SITE COLUMNS

You first create site columns. You can use existing site columns, but you probably want to create some additional that are specific to the products in the catalog (such as make and model columns, if the products are cars). After all the site columns that describe the product are created, you can add them to the Product content type. (You can always add or remove site columns, but getting the catalog as close to final as possible is best because additional site columns can affect how the product is displayed.)

MANAGING SITE CONTENT TYPES

The second step is to modify the Product content type. Click Manage Site Content Types on the welcome page and scroll down to Product on the Site Content Types page. You can also make the changes directly by clicking the Product link in the Manage Site Content Types section. From here, you will add the product-specific site columns as follows:

1. Click the word Product under the Product Catalog Content Types heading.
2. Click Add From Existing Site Columns.
3. Choose the product-specific site columns from the Available Columns drop-down list and then click Add.
4. In the Update List And Site Content Types section, leave Yes selected so that the site columns are added to the product list and the Product with Image content type.
5. Click OK to save.

> ***IMPORTANT*** **MODIFYING THE PRODUCT CONTENT TYPE**
>
> **The Products list on the product catalog site actually uses the Product with Image content type by default. The Product with Image content type inherits from the Product content type, so you always want to update all content types inheriting from the Product content type to see the changes in the Products list.**

MANAGING ITEM HIERARCHY IN TERM STORE

The third step is to create the product hierarchy. Click the Manage Item Hierarchy In Term Store link (or by going through the site settings). The one you want to modify is under the Site Collection heading, followed by the site name and site catalog). This should have one term set called Product Hierarchy. Under the Product Hierarchy, you can enter an item that's all inclusive of the products (for example, if the products are cars and trucks, the highest level would be vehicles). Then you enter term sets and subterm sets as applicable. Figure 2-15 shows an example.

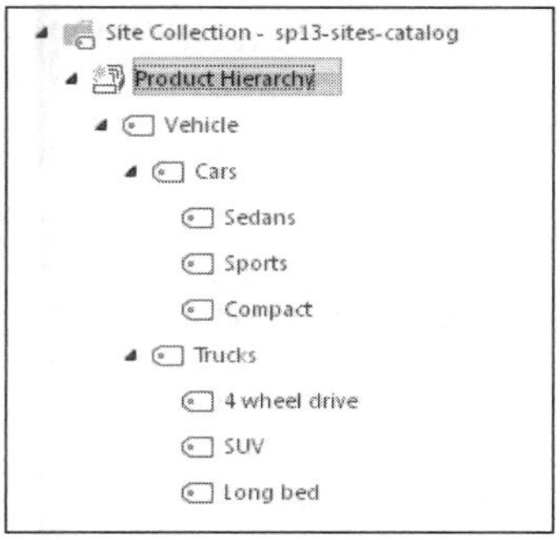

Site Collection - sp13-sites-catalog
Product Hierarchy
Vehicle
Cars
Sedans
Sports
Compact
Trucks
4 wheel drive
SUV
Long bed

FIGURE 2-15 Example of a Product Hierarchy for a product catalog

> ***NOTE*** **TERM STORE LOCATIONS**
>
> **Rather than use a term store located within the site collection, you should use a term store located at the farm level (one created by going to the Metadata service application in Central Administration rather than the Term Store link under Site Settings). This way, consumers of the product catalog (like with other site collections) don't need rights to the term store within the product catalog site collection.**

ADDING CATALOG ITEMS

After the categories are entered, they can be chosen when a user adds an item. Items are added by clicking the Products link on the welcome page and then clicking the new item or the plus arrow. The list can also be reached by clicking Add Catalog Items or the Products List link. The Products list has Product with Image as its default content type, but you don't have to insert an image if one isn't available. To add an item category, you can click the metadata icon next to the Item Category, or just start typing into the Item Category text box and have SharePoint provide suggestions. By default, the categories term set is closed and it doesn't allow unknown terms to be entered.

> ***IMPORTANT*** **APPROVAL OF PRODUCT LIST ITEMS**
>
> **By default, items entered into the Products list require approval. Until they are approved, they aren't visible to end users, aren't indexed, and don't appear in the search results.**

MODIFYING SEARCH PROPERTIES

The final step listed on the welcome page is the Modify Search Properties section. This reminds the creator(s) of the product catalog that the newly created site columns need to be added to the managed properties within the search schema so that they can be searched on. After this step and a full crawl of the content are performed, the product catalog is ready to be used or consumed. It can be used in the site collection that it exists or it can be consumed by other sites or site collections.

The settings for how the product catalog is to be consumed don't appear on the welcome page, but they can be found in the Library settings of the list itself. Several settings can be applied to a product catalog and should be planned out ahead of time, depending on how the product catalog will be used, how it will be searched on, and who can edit the items. To modify these settings, follow these steps:

1. Click Products on the welcome page.
2. Click List Settings on the List tab.
3. Click the Catalog Settings link.
4. Choose to enable or disable search indexing by clicking Advanced Settings Page in the Reindex list section (or trigger a full reindexing).
5. Choose whether to share the catalog among other sites and site collections by selecting the Enable This Library As A Catalog check box.
6. Select Enable Anonymous Access if you want users to have anonymous access to the product catalog.
7. Choose which fields will identify the catalog items (unique field or fields that identify unique items) and add them in the Catalog Item URL Fields section.
8. In the Navigation Hierarchy section, choose the column to use for navigation (typically, the Item Categories field).
9. Click OK to save changes.

> ***NOTE*** **CATALOG PROPERTIES**
>
> **If the library isn't enabled as a catalog, the options for anonymous access, catalog item URL fields, and navigation hierarchy won't be available.**

USING THE CATALOG

Assuming that you chose to share the product catalog with other sites and site collections, the product catalog can be consumed and displayed. The site collection that contains the product catalog needs to be crawled fully before it can be consumed. This might take a bit of time depending on how the crawl was set up. When the crawl is finished, the product catalog can be consumed. This is done within the site that's using the product catalog:

1. Navigate to the Site Settings page and click Manage Catalog Connections in the Site Administration section.

2. Click Connect To A Catalog on the Manage Catalog Connections page.
3. Choose or search for the product catalog. When you find it, click Connect.
4. Several options are on the next page, but the only ones that need to be filled in are in the Navigation Hierarchy section. Select the navigation field (for example, Item Category) and then choose the root term. You also want to choose the navigation level (Vehicles in this example), because you can't choose the Product Hierarchy level.
5. Click OK to save changes.

After a connection is established, SharePoint creates pages on which the catalog can be displayed and the navigation hierarchy used to navigate the product catalog. Several options could have been configured during the connection. Of note is the Catalog Item URL Behavior option, which you can use to make the catalog seem as though it's part of the consuming site. This is done by making the URLs relative to the consuming site. You also have the option of continuing to point to the source catalog. You even have the option to choose different master pages for the product catalog, but generally you want to use the master page of the consuming site so that it appears that it's actually one site. Catalog items can be used with variants as well. The language tag is part of the Product content type and can be used to filter product catalog items so that only items that match the browsers language are shown.

EXAM TIP

As a new component in the WCM abilities of SharePoint, product catalogs will likely be a source of at least one question on the exam. Key concepts are the use of term store data for navigation and that a product catalog can be consumed by another site or site collection.

Topic pages

You can use topic pages—category pages and catalog item pages—to display content from a metadata-driven term store (like the term store from the product catalog) without having to create a new page for each category or category item. This also allows for automatically created user-friendly URLs (unless that option is turned off). For example, if you used the example product catalog and had it consumed by a site called *http://contoso*, *http://contoso/trucks* and *http://contoso/trucks/Long-bed* would be category pages and *http://contoso/trucks/long-bed/2* (a Dodge Ram truck is the second item in the catalog) would be a catalog item page. (Notice the absence of *.aspx* or *.html* extensions on the page names.) These pages are created automatically and are based on page layouts that are also created for you. To get to these newly created pages, use the navigation provided by the metadata, which replaces the structural navigation (see Figure 2-16).

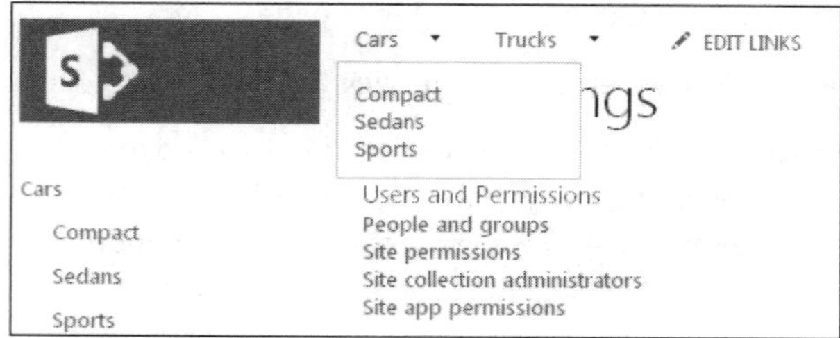

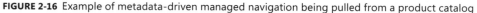

FIGURE 2-16 Example of metadata-driven managed navigation being pulled from a product catalog

You can set up managed navigation without using a product catalog and use it with any term store.

> ***MORE INFO*** **MANAGED NAVIGATION**
>
> **See *http://msdn.microsoft.com/en-us/library/jj163978(v=office.15).aspx* for more information about managed navigation in SharePoint 2013.**

Before any data actually appears on the topic pages, the pages must be published. Open the Site Settings page and click Master Pages And Page Layouts in the Web Designer Galleries section. On the Master Page Gallery page, look for the following two pages and publish a major version of them:

- *CategoryItem-<Top level Term Store Name>.html*
- *Category-<Top level Term Store Name>.html*

For the example, the files would be *CategoryItem-Vehicle.html* and *Category-Vehicle.html*, respectively. If you plan to change these layouts, edit the HTML pages. They are meant to be customized for your product catalog branding needs. If for some reason you want to edit the *.aspx* page directly, delete the HTML page layouts.

The category page is meant to help users find the products they are looking for. It has a Content Search web part that limits the results to the category and displays links to the catalog items. The catalog item page is meant to display one item as well as display the picture at the top with properties below it. With the navigation and the topic pages created, you are well on your way to designing a complete product catalog suitable for public consumption.

> ***MORE INFO*** **CROSS-SITE PUBLISHING**
>
> **See *http://technet.microsoft.com/en-us/library/jj635883.aspx* for an overview on cross-site publishing in SharePoint Server 2013.**

Planning and configuring content deployment

Content deployment is broadly defined, but in the context of WCM, this section focuses on cross-site publication, a new feature in SharePoint 2013, and Web Parts such as the Content Search Web Part that you can use to show content from the search index. Cross-site content deployment allows for publishing of site content across sites, site collections, and even farms. This varies from content deployment in SharePoint 2010 in which the entire site had to be deployed using the built-in SharePoint 2010 functionality.

The Content Search Web Part (CSWP) can show content from the search index, allowing content to be shown from other locations within the context of the site on which it's located. This is much different than using the Content Query Web Part in SharePoint 2010 in that it was confined to the site collection in which it was contained. The CSWP is configured to use a result source, either built-in or created. It can also be used to show results from a published catalog. Some of the default result sources are as follows:

- Documents
- Pages
- Pictures
- Recently changed
- Popular
- Items related to current user
- Wiki

After you choose the result source, you can restrict the returned items to the current site, the current site collection, or a URL, or you can leave it unrestricted, in which case it brings back everything from that result source. If no result source matches your needs, you can build a query from scratch. This is very similar to creating a result source. Considering this, you have a great amount of flexibility in the results that can be pulled back from the search results. An additional property of the CSWP allows for the search results to be further refined by tags. The following options are related to tags:

- Don't restrict by tag
- Restrict by navigation term of current page
- Restrict by current and sub-page navigation terms
- Restrict on this tag

Restricting by tags can provide many options, such as putting on a page that shows a particular wiki item. The CSWP could show videos related to the tag across a number of site collections and even different farms.

The CSWP also uses display templates, allowing for customization of how the results are displayed. The display templates are configured similarly across the SharePoint environment. This is essentially modifying HTML and JavaScript.

MORE INFO CONTENT SEARCH WEB PART

See *http://msdn.microsoft.com/en-us/library/jj163789(v=office.15)* for more information about the CSWP.

Traditional content deployment is still supported and is similar in function to the way it was in SharePoint 2010. The improvements in SharePoint 2013 involve a feature that determines whether a site collection can be deployed. Certain features must be removed before a site collection can be deployed via the built-in content deployment. If you try to deploy a site collection, you probably can't see any site collections to deploy by default because a feature at the site collection level needs to be activated. To prepare a site collection for deployment, follow these steps:

1. Navigate to Site Settings as a site collection administrator.
2. Click Site Collection Features in the Site Collection Administration section.
3. Click the Activate button next to the Content Deployment Source Feature feature.

EXAM TIP

The Content Deployment Source Feature is new in SharePoint 2013 and, like anything new, will receive special attention on the exam. Be aware of the feature and what it accomplishes as well how to disable features that prohibit content deployment.

When the Content Deployment Source Feature is activated, you can check whether the site collection is ready for content deployment. SharePoint 2013 lists items that prevent a site collection from being deployed. To find this list, follow these steps:

1. Navigate to Site Settings as a site collection administrator.
2. Click Content Deployment Source Status in the Site Collection Administration section. The Content Deployment Source Status page displays all features that you need to deactivate before content deployment is supported.

By default, a normal publishing site requires that quite a few features be deactivated before it can be deployed. Some of these can be deactivated by clicking the Deactivate link on the Content Deployment Source Status page. Some features are hidden and need to be deactivated by using PowerShell. The list might be very long and require that a lot of features be turned off. Some site templates, such as the Community Site, aren't even supported. The PowerShell command for deactivating features is as follows:

```
Disable-SPFeature -Identity <name of feature> -url <URL of site collection or site>
```

When the unsupported features are disabled, the site is ready for deployment. However, the farm receiving the content must be configured to receive content. By default, a

SharePoint 2013 farm is set up to reject any incoming content deployment jobs. To receive content deployment jobs, the SharePoint farm can be configured as follows:

1. On the destination server, navigate to Central Administration with an account that has administrator rights and click General Application Settings.
2. Click Configure Content Deployment in the Content Deployment section.
3. On the Content Deployment Settings page, select Accept Incoming Content Deployment Jobs.
4. Choose the import server to receive the incoming deployment jobs in the Import Server section. Make sure that the incoming server has enough disk space to handle the incoming jobs.
5. Optionally, specify the export server by selecting it in the Export Server section if it will be deploying content deployment jobs.
6. Choose whether https is required in the Connection Security section.
7. Choose whether to check for source status errors in the Source Status Check section.
8. Select a location for the temporary files involved in receiving content in the Temporary Files section. This drive location needs to have enough space to store the entire site collection being deployed.
9. In the Reporting section, choose how many reports to retain, and then click OK to save changes.

After the receiving SharePoint farm is configured to accept content deployment jobs from the deploying SharePoint farm, you can configure content deployment paths in Central Administration. The process involves creating a path for the content to be deployed and a job that determines how often the content will be deployed. To create a content deployment path, follow these steps:

1. Navigate to Central Administration and click Configure Content Deployment Paths And Jobs in the General Application Settings section.
2. On the Manage Content Deployment Paths And Jobs page, click New Path.
3. On the Create Content Deployment Path page, enter a name and description in the Name and Description settings.
4. Select the source web application and then the source site collection in the Source Web Application And Site Collection section.
5. Type the URL of the destination Central Administration server in the Destination Central Administration Web Application section.

6. Choose the authentication method, and then enter a user name and password that has Central Administration rights on the destination server in the Authentication Information section.
7. Choose the destination web application and the destination site collection in the Destination Web Application And Site Collection section.
8. Choose whether to deploy user names in the User Names section.
9. Choose what security information to deploy (All, Role Definitions Only, or None) in the Security Information section, and then click OK to save changes.

> ***IMPORTANT*** **DEPLOYING CONTENT DEPLOYMENT USING HTTP**
>
> **Communications over the http protocol (instead of https) can be intercepted by malicious users. Use https if the content being deployed is sensitive in nature.**

After the path is established, you can set up a job that runs on a specified schedule or on demand. The Manage Content Deployment Path And Jobs page shows the newly created path. Hovering over the name of the path and clicking it reveals options to Test Job, Run Now, and edit the Quick Deploy Settings. Follow these steps to configure the Quick Deploy Job settings after you choose the Quick Deploy Settings for the content deployment path:

1. In the Allow Quick Deploy Jobs section, choose whether to allow Quick Deploy Jobs.
2. Choose whether to use SQL Snapshots.
3. Select the content deployment schedule in the Quick Deploy Schedule section. The range is from 10 minutes up to 60 minutes.
4. Choose the users who can designate pages for Quick Deploy Jobs in the Users section.
5. In the Notification section, choose whether to send email when content deployment succeeds and/or fails and provide the email address to send the notifications to.
6. Click OK to save changes.

The content deployment job is now configured. To test the job to ensure that it works, choose Test Job in the content deployment path. The first time you deploy the job, choose Run Now. The first deployment can potentially take a while, depending on the size of the site collection. After the initial deployment, only changes are deployed, greatly increasing the speed of deployment.

Planning and configuring variations

Variations are used to target a person's preferred language based on their browser settings. For example, with variations, SharePoint can target a page for English speakers, another one for French speakers, and a third one for Japanese speakers. SharePoint would automatically route a person to the preferred page based on the preferred language of the browser being used. SharePoint 2013 also can do machine translation, using an external service to automatically translate content. This is a powerful new feature but, as with any translation service, reviewing the finished product is necessary to ensure accuracy.

Setting up variations is done at the site collection level. After variations are configured and labels are created, content is copied selectively from the source site to the language-specific sites. For variations to be used, you should start by configuring the variation settings:

1. Navigate to the Site Settings page with a site collection administrator account.
2. Click Variations Settings in the Site Collection Administration section on the Site Settings page. (This link is also accessible from the Variations Labels page.)
3. In the Site, List, And Page Creation Behavior section, choose Create Everywhere or Create Selectively, depending on the desired result whenever a site, list, or page is created.
4. In the Recreate Deleted Target Page section, choose whether to re-create a new target page whenever a source page is republished.
5. Choose whether to update any Web Part changes when the variation source page is propagated (Web Part changes are treated independently of page content).
6. Choose whether to send email notifications when a new site or page is created or updated by the variation system.
7. Click OK to save changes.

After setting the variation settings, you can configure the labels. Labels represent individual variations (languages) that will be created. Labels typically represent individual languages, such as French, German, Chinese, Japanese, and so on. Language packs can be used with variations but aren't required. Language packs provide translations for the SharePoint menu and ribbon items but don't translate the user-provided content.

> ***MORE INFO*** **DOWNLOADING LANGUAGE PACKS**
>
> **You can download language packs for SharePoint 2013 at *http://www.microsoft.com/en-us/download/details.aspx?id=35492*.**

You can add language packs at any time, but because they require some downtime of the SharePoint server, installing them at the beginning is best. Adding language packs also gives users an interface in the language they prefer, encouraging use and contribution.

The next step in using variations is to create labels. Labels—also created at the site collection level—determine the sites created by SharePoint. Sites created based on label are created beneath the source site automatically. The first label to be created is the source variation label from which other variations receive published content based on the individual label settings selected. To create labels after the initial label, follow these steps, using an account that has site collection administrator permissions:

1. Click Variation Labels in the Site Collection Administration section of the Site Settings page.
2. Click New Label on the Variations Labels page.
3. Select the site template language from the drop-down list in the Language section. This doesn't have to match the language of the variation.
4. Choose the locale from the drop-down list in the Locale section. This is the value used to redirect the browser based on the browser's language settings.
5. Click Continue.
6. On the Target Label page, type the URL appended to the source site in the Label Name box and an optional description in the Description text box.
7. Type a user-friendly and locale-appropriate display name in the Display Name text box.
8. In the Hierarchy Creation section, choose what types of content should be copied from the source site and click Continue.
9. On the Translation Options page, choose whether to allow human translation in the Create Translation Package section. This allows users to export content to an XLIFF file for human translation.
10. In the Machine Translation section, choose whether to allow machine translation (which needs to be configured in Central Administration before it's available on the page) and click Continue.
11. On the Target Label Behavior page, choose whether users manually sync updates from source variation pages or whether the operation is automatic. Also, in the Label Contact section, enter an email address to which notification is sent whenever variation content is created.
12. Click Continue to review the label settings on the Review Label Settings page, and then click Finish to save the changes.

> ***NOTE* CREATING A SOURCE VARIATION**
>
> **The first label created is the source variation. The process for creating this label is similar to creating other labels, except that a template (Publishing Site or Publishing Site with Workflows) needs to be chosen that won't have the translation options or the target label behavior options. This varies from which content is copied from to other variations (and possibly translated).**

You can continue to create labels for all the variations that you want. After you finish creating them, return to the Variation Labels page and click Create Hierarchies. The variations won't be available right away; they are created with timer jobs and will be ready to use soon, depending on the resources available. You can check the status on the Variations Labels page.

This page shows other information—such as locale, language, and whether it's the source—about all the labels created and allows them to be edited.

One great new function of SharePoint 2013 is the ability to support the automatic translation of content. Referred to as Machine Translation, it's configured in Central Administration similarly to other service applications. The Machine Translation service application requires a connection to the service providing the translation. After the Machine Translation service application is created, it needs to be configured, as follows:

1. Using an account that's a member of the Farm Administrators group, navigate to Central Administration and click Manage Service Applications in the Application Management section.
2. On the Manage Service Applications page, click the Machine Translation Service link (or whatever the machine translation service was named).
3. Specify which file extensions are to be excluded by clearing the box next to the extension in the Enabled File Extensions section.
4. Set the file limit size in kilobytes for binary files (such as Microsoft Word documents) and text files (such as HTML, *.txt*, and *.xlf* files) in the Item Size Limits section. Then set the maximum number of characters in Word documents allowed for the Maximum Character Count For Microsoft Word Documents setting.
5. In the Translation Process section, set the number of simultaneous processes that can run at the same time. These processes consume resources, so be careful not to set the value too high; also, be sure to monitor resource usage.
6. In the Translation Throughput section, set the frequency (in minutes) at which translations start in the Frequency In Which To Start Translations text box. Also, set the number of translation to start per translation process in the Number Of Translations To Start text box.
7. Set the maximum number of translation attempts in the Maximum Translation Attempts section.
8. In the Maximum Synchronous Translation Requests section, set the number of maximum translation requests per server (that's running the Machine Translation service) that can be run at one time.
9. In the Translation Quota section, indicate the maximum number of translation requests that can occur in a 24-hour period (or set it to unlimited). This can be done overall and per site subscription.
10. In the Recycle Threshold section, determine the number of documents to translate before the Machine Translation service restarts.
11. In the Office 97-2003 Document Scanning section, choose whether to disable Microsoft Office 97-2003 documents, and then click OK to save changes.

NOTE RESTARTING THE MACHINE TRANSLATION SERVICE

Many of the options in the Machine Translation service application require that the service be restarted manually to take effect. Doing this is recommended after you make any configuration changes and/or if site collections are having problems connecting to the Machine Translation service.

You need to consider many options when configuring machine translation. Depending on the amount of translation required, specifying a server (or two) as the designated translation server might be beneficial. Only those servers with the Machine Translation service started on them can process translation requests.

Translation services have come a long way in a short time, but that doesn't preclude checking the translated data for accuracy. Another way to address this is to set up a link for end users to report errors in translation.

EXAM TIP

Because machine translation is an important and powerful new feature in SharePoint 2013, you can expect it to be covered on the exam. Possible questions include using it as a step in setting up a WCM site as well as a possible short-answer question. Knowledge of how it fits in with variations is also to be expected.

Thought experiment

Choosing cross-site content

In this thought experiment, apply what you've learned about this objective. You can find answers to these questions in the "Answers" section at the end of this chapter.

You've decided that several sites in the SharePoint environment need access to a particular list that shows various items that can be purchased internally and externally. Each item to be purchased has several description fields and a picture. Your environment has a site that faces internally as well as externally and will be used to display these items.

What is the best way to create this content so that it can be shared across both internal and external site?

Objective summary

- You can configure channels to deliver specific branding to multiple devices.
- You can use product catalogs to provide list information across sites and site collections as well as to filter products specific to individual languages.
- The Content Search Web Part can be used to deliver targeted search results from across multiple sites, site collections, and even other farms.
- Content deployment has been made easier using the feature Content Deployment Source Feature and the Content Deployment Source Status page.
- Variations enable automatic publishing of content—and potentially automatic translation—for language-specific sites.
- Using Machine Translation services to enable the automatic translation of content in variations greatly reduces the amount of manual effort.

Objective review

Answer the following questions to test your knowledge of the information in this objective. You can find the answers to these questions and explanations of why each answer choice is correct or incorrect in the "Answers" section at the end of this chapter.

1. As an administrator of a WCM site collection, you want to use different master pages for different devices. Channels can be used to target custom master pages to which of the following devices?
   - **A.** A particular operating system that runs on smartphones
   - **B.** Tablets
   - **C.** Desktop running a specific operating system
   - **D.** All of the above
2. A product catalog is consumed by another site collection. What does the product catalog use for navigation of the catalog items?
   - **A.** Term set
   - **B.** Views
   - **C.** List Filter
   - **D.** Quick Launch

3. You've created a community site by using the Community Site template. What must you do for the community site to be deployed to another SharePoint farm?
    A. Activate the feature Content Deployment Source Feature on the community site.
    B. Disable the features on the Content Deployment Source Status page.
    C. Nothing. The Community Site template doesn't support content deployment and therefore can't be deployed using out-of-the-box OTB SharePoint.
    D. Both A and B.
4. You've decided to create variations to support the publishing content in a worldwide deployment across many languages. What built-in SharePoint functionality would you implement to translate content with minimal human effort?
    A. Machine Translation service application
    B. Nothing, because variations are automatically translated in SharePoint 2013
    C. Enable variation labels
    D. Export XLIFF files for translation

Objective 2.4: Plan an Enterprise Content Management (ECM) workload

Enterprise Content Management covers a wide variety of topics, but basically this objective is concerned with functions at the farm level that affect sites and site collections across several site collections. These functions involve dealing with records, configuring routing, using eDiscovery, and archiving items into repositories.

This objective covers the following topics:

- Planning and configuring eDiscovery
- Planning and configuring record disposition and retention
- Planning large document repositories

Planning and configuring eDiscovery

eDiscovery is generally referred to how litigators and records managers discover content in an electronic format. This involves searching through documents, emails, and websites across a wide variety of sources so that the content can meet the criteria for a legal case. SharePoint 2010 introduced the concept of putting a hold on an item such as a document, list item, or page so that no further modifications could be placed on it (nor could the item be deleted). Exchange 2010 also introduced a way to put legal holds on mailboxes so that a thorough search could be made on them without any content being modified or deleted. SharePoint

2013 works with Microsoft Exchange to establish an eDiscovery solution. The tasks involved with setting up eDiscovery in SharePoint 2013 involve the following:

- Configure communication between SharePoint and Exchange
- Configure the Search service to crawl all the relevant material
- Grant the appropriate permissions to crawl content
- Create an eDiscovery center

If content is to be discovered in Exchange using a SharePoint eDiscovery center, Exchange Server 2013 must be running. To discover content in the Exchange Server instance, make sure the following steps have been performed:

1. Ensure that the Exchange Web Service managed API is running on all the Web Front Ends (WFEs) that are running SharePoint 2013.
2. Configure a trust relationship between the SharePoint 2013 servers and the Exchange Server instance.
3. If content from Lync Server 2013 is to be discoverable, make sure that it's set up to archive to Exchange Server.
4. Perform the eDiscovery configuration steps for Exchange Server.

> ***MORE INFO*** **CONFIGURING EXCHANGE SERVER FOR EDISCOVERY**
>
> **See *http://technet.microsoft.com/en-us/library/jj218665(v=exchg.150)* for more information on how to configure Exchange Server for SharePoint eDiscovery Center.**

Content can be discoverable only if it's crawled and indexed by the Search service application associated with the eDiscovery center. If Exchange content is to be searched, it must be crawled as part of result source. Also, all sites and libraries within the sites must be made searchable for the eDiscovery center to be able to discover them.

Everything that needs to be searched must be accessible by the users involved in the eDiscovery. The recommended way to provide permissions is to create a security group of all concerned individuals and then grant permissions at the web application level. This is done by creating a user policy with full read (because you don't want the records modified) for each web application involved in the discovery process. Changing or adding a policy at the web application level starts a recrawl of the content contained with the web application, precluding the need to manually start a new crawl. Finally, the security group needs permissions to view the search crawl log. This is done using PowerShell.

> ***MORE INFO*** **SETTING PERMISSIONS ON THE SEARCH CRAWL LOG**
>
> **See *http://technet.microsoft.com/en-us/library/jj219817.aspx* for more information on how to use the PowerShell command *Set-SPEnterpriseSearchCrawlLogReadPermission* to set permissions on the search crawl log.**

After permissions are established and any Exchange Server permissions and crawls are set up, an eDiscovery center needs to be created. This center is a site collection that allows user to create and manage eDiscovery cases. The eDiscovery template requires that claims be used in the web application in which the center resides. It's created similarly to other site collections in Central Administration, using the eDiscovery template that resides in the Enterprise section.

> ***IMPORTANT*** **PERMISSIONS REQUIRED FOR EDISCOVERY**
>
> **If you're not going to use policies, make sure the eDiscovery security group is made a site collection administrator on each site collection in which discovery is to be done. Also, if you are discovering content on Exchange, the security group needs access to the Exchange Server mailboxes.**

After an eDiscovery site is created, you need to create a new case before you can start eDiscovery. Follow these steps:

1. On the home page of the eDiscovery site collection and with site collection administrator privileges, click Create A New Case.
2. Type a title and description in the Title And Description section.
3. In the Web Site Address section, enter a URL-friendly name for the site.
4. In the Template Selection section, choose the only template available—the eDiscovery Case template.
5. In the Permissions section, leave Use Same Permissions As Parent Site selected unless you have an overriding need to change it.
6. In the Navigation And Navigation Inheritance section, leave the defaults and click Create to start the creation process.

The site that's created has two major sections: one for Identify and Hold and one for Search and Export. The exam doesn't cover the end-user experience, so this book won't cover how to use these functions in detail, but seeing how these functions work is a worthwhile exercise to get a better understanding of how to plan for an eDiscovery site.

The ability to do in-place holds is a new feature in SharePoint Server 2013 that deserves some attention. It allows for items in SharePoint and Exchange Server to stay in place so that users can continue to work with them, but a copy of the content at the time the hold is placed is kept. This is in contrast to SharePoint 2010, which wouldn't allow content that had a hold on it to be modified or deleted. Now, an end user doesn't even have to know that the content is being held. An in-place hold occurs at the site level, and a preservation hold library is created that stores copies of any content modified or deleted after the hold is placed. If multiple in-place holds are established, the content could appear more than once in the preservation library.

MORE INFO EDISCOVERY AND IN-PLACE HOLDS

See *http://technet.microsoft.com/en-us/library/fp161516(office.15).aspx#in_place_holds* for an overview of eDiscovery and in-place holds in SharePoint Server 2013.

EXAM TIP

eDiscovery is a high-visibility feature that represents a very task-specific technology set. The ability to do in-place holds is an important concept. Expect at least one question about it on the exam. It's not a highly used feature because it addresses a niche market, but understanding the general workings of it is still important.

Planning and configuring record management

SharePoint Server 2013 includes a powerful set of features for managing records. Because of the very nature of records, setting up a record-management solution requires a considerable amount of planning. A record is generally considered a piece of evidence that an organization performed an activity or transaction. In SharePoint, a record is considered active until it's declared a record and can then be modified only if it meets certain policy requirements. You can make an item go from active to record in several ways:

- Manually declare an item as a record.
- Use a workflow to send a document to the record center.
- Define a policy that either declares an item a record or routes it to the record center.
- Use custom code based on the SharePoint object model to declare an item a record or route it to the record center.

Records generally have some sort of legal and/or archival nature to them, which means that as soon as an item becomes a record, it shouldn't be altered (or if it is, the alteration is recorded) and should have a retention period as part of it. The retention period determines how long the record should remain with the record management system. When planning for a record-management system, you need to consider the following:

- What should be considered a record
- The process of declaring an item a record and how it should be treated at that point
- How legal, regulatory, and business requirements affect records
- Retention policies for different record types
- What to do with expired records
- What types of records are managed
- Whether record declaration should be voluntary or mandatory

Record management typically isn't a single solution for most organizations. Various types of records could exist, such as print, audio, video, and even physical items such as art.

Although the exam focuses on SharePoint-specific solutions, including these other types in your overall plan is a beneficial exercise. You would first categorize the types of records that you need to manage and the details associated with them, such as kind of record, category, description, media, retention period, disposition, and a contact of the person(s) who oversees the records.

MORE INFO **PLANNING FOR RECORD MANAGEMENT**

See *http://go.microsoft.com/fwlink/p/?LinkID=179987&clcid=0x409* for an Excel worksheet to help plan for record management.

SharePoint 2013 has all the record-management features that existed in SharePoint 2010, plus the following additional capabilities:

- Site retention
- Site mailbox
- Record management in the cloud

Site retention is where the entire site is essentially treated as a record. In SharePoint 2013, a site can be "closed," which means that it's ignored by navigation and search crawls but can still be accessed via its URL. Closure of a site doesn't prevent its use; closure just makes the site harder to get to. Closure of a site collection, however, can make the site collection and all subsites read-only depending on the policy chosen.

Site closure is enabled via Site Policy, a site collection feature that must be enabled before site collection policies can be implemented. After you activate this feature, you can implement a site collection closure policy by following these steps:

1. Navigate to Site Settings at the site collection level (even policies applied to just a site are created at the site collection level), with a site collection administrator account.
2. Click Site Policies in the Site Collection Administrator section.
3. On the Site Policies page, click Create.
4. Enter a name and description for the policy in the Name And Description section.
5. Choose how to handle site deletion and closure (automatic or manual) in the Site Closure And Deletion section. Choosing one of the automatic options requires entering times—in days, months, or years—in which the deletion and/or closure should happen.
6. In the Site Collection Closure section, choose whether to make the site collection and all subsites read-only.
7. Click OK to create the policy.

After the policy is created, you can apply it at the site or site collection level for deletion policies and at the site collection level for closure policies. To apply site policies, click Site Closure And Deletion in the Site Administration section on the Site Settings page. You also can choose to close the site immediately if manual closure is desired.

Site mailboxes are integrated between Exchange Server 2013 and SharePoint Server 2013. In the past, documents and emails were usually kept into two distinct repositories. Site mailboxes use shared storage in both the Exchange and SharePoint spaces to provide end users a single place to access emails and related documents. Now emails can be dragged directly from Microsoft Outlook into SharePoint and can be treated as records, just like regular documents residing in SharePoint. Configuration of site mailboxes is required on both the Exchange Server side as well as the SharePoint side. Knowing how to set up site mailboxes in detail isn't required for the exam, but general knowledge of what is required might be. The following items are required in addition to SharePoint Server 2013:

- Exchange Server 2013
- Exchange Web Services API 2.0—and only version 2.0—installed on each WFE
- A mutual trust between Exchange Server 2013 and SharePoint Server 2013
- That the User Profile Synchronization service is configured on the SharePoint farm
- That the App Management service application is configured on the SharePoint farm
- That Secure Sockets Layer (SSL) is configured for the default zone on the SharePoint farm

MORE INFO **CONFIGURING SITE MAILBOXES**

See *http://technet.microsoft.com/en-us/library/jj552524(office.15).aspx* for more information on configuring site mailboxes in SharePoint Server 2013.

Site mailboxes should be configured and maintained on the SharePoint side. The lifecycle application can be used to automatically close and delete site mailboxes, giving users the chance to keep them open if needed. When a site mailbox is closed by the lifecycle application, it's retained for a period of time specified by the lifecycle policy. You should delete mailboxes only via the SharePoint interface, because deleting them on the Exchange Server instance causes orphans on the SharePoint server. On the Exchange Server side, only the mailbox size and the maximum size of an individual email can be set. These are set with PowerShell commands on the Exchange Server node.

IMPORTANT **DISASTER RECOVERY CONSIDERATIONS FOR SITE MAILBOXES**

Emails that are part of a site mailbox aren't backed up as part of the usual SharePoint backup. The emails need to be backed up on the Exchange Server side.

EXAM TIP

Although SharePoint 2013 now supports record management in the cloud, it's unlikely to be on the exam. Advanced solutions are geared toward on-premises solutions and often involve many connected servers. The 70-331 exam, "Core Solutions of SharePoint Server 2013," covers the cloud in more detail.

A *record center* is a site that you can create anywhere inside a SharePoint environment by using the Records Center template. The key components of the record center are the Drop Off Library and the Record Library. Documents sent to the Drop Off Library (via routing or uploading or code) are processed and then sent to the proper record folder (such as the Record Library or similar library) depending on the document's properties. This is known as *document routing*. Drop Off Libraries don't just exist in record centers, but in other site templates as well, and they can be used to route documents. The Drop Off Library requires the site level feature Content Organizer to be activated (the default in a record center). This enables the two site settings pages located under the following Site Collection Administration settings, which need to be configured before document routing can occur:

- Content Organizer Settings
- Content Organizer Rules

You need to consider a number of settings when planning for a record center or for sites using the Content Organizer:

- **Redirect Users To The Drop Off Library** Indicates whether users who are trying to upload a document to a library in the site are redirected to the Drop Off Library. Enabling this setting allows for the Drop Off Library to be the sole source for determining which library receives the record and therefore centralizing the location for rules.
- **Sending to Another Site** Allows documents to be sent to another site or site collection if that location has the Content Organizer feature turned on. Using this setting is useful if you want to create a central record management hub.
- **Folder Partitioning** Enables records to be split into folders after a certain limit is reached. Lowering the number of items per folder increases the display speed of the items in the browser.
- **Duplicate Submissions** Allows records with the same name to either be appended or added with an additional unique character at the end.
- **Preserving Context** Allows the original audit log and properties of the submitted content to be saved in an audit entry.

Another available option enables you to email role managers if a submission doesn't match a rule and/or when content has been left in the Drop Off Library. This allows for unattended monitoring of record activity. Also, a submission point enables other sites or email-messaging software to send content to this site (it's always the site URL followed by */_vti_bin/OfficialFile.asmx*).

Modifying the content organizer settings gets you ready to create rules. Content organizer rules route documents to the appropriate locations based on content types and property rules. To create a rule, follow these steps, using an account that has Full control:

1. Click Content Organizer Rules on the Site Settings page in the Site Administration section.
2. Click New Item on the Content Organizer Rules page.
3. Type a name that describes the rule in the Name text box.
4. In the Rule Status and Priority section, choose whether the rule is active and what priority it has. If an item matches several rules, the one with the highest priority is applied.
5. In the Submission's Content Type section, choose the content type that the rule is to run on. You can also enter alternate names for the content type if it's coming from other sites.

> ***NOTE*** **USING WILDCARD CHARACTERS**
>
> **Adding a rule with the * makes the rule run for all items that don't match another rule. Generally, you want to create as many record libraries as you think you will need before you start to create rules so that documents don't get stuck in the Drop Off Library or in a document library specified by the * wildcard character.**

6. In the Conditions section, add one or more property rules (for example, Department=Financial) to be used for rule matching.
7. In the Target Location section, choose the library or list to which the item will be routed. This section also includes an option to create folders based on unique properties—for example, for a Word document library that had a department property, folders would be created for each department that submitted records.
8. Click OK to create the rule.

Planning and configuring record disposition and retention

After an item is declared a record, you need to consider how long to retain it and how to dispose of it after it's no longer required for business or legal reasons. (The term "dispose of" is used here because it might not actually be deleted.) Retention plans are typically centered on the business and legal requirements for keeping documents around. The two main factors involved are disk space requirements and disaster recovery concerns.

Disposition involves several options. The most efficient is automatic deletion. For example, if a record has been around for seven years, it's deleted automatically. In this case, it would happen without user interaction and if, for some reason, a record was declared accidentally, it would be deleted without notice. Another method of disposition is to have automatic deletion with holds. In this case, a record would be deleted automatically unless a hold had been placed on it. The hold would be extended past the time for automatic deletion for a predefined period of time. Also, records might require human interaction and review before they are deleted. This disposition method is the safest (that is, least risky) but requires the most time and effort.

Site retention policies were discussed in the preceding section. A site itself can now have a deletion as well as a closure schedule. The policies associated with items within a site collection are defined at the site content level by default. To define a policy for site content, follow these steps:

1. Navigate to the Site Settings page of the site collection and click Site Content Types in the Web Designer Galleries section.
2. On the Site Content Types page, choose the site content type on which to apply a retention policy.
3. On the Site Content Type settings page, click Information Management Policy Settings in the Settings section.
4. Type a name and description in the Name And Administrative Description section.
5. Type a policy statement describing what policies to apply and why in the Policy Statement section.
6. In the Retention section, select the Enable Retention check box to display the retention options.
7. In the Non-Records section, click Add A Retention Stage.
8. In the Stage Properties sheet, specify what causes the stage to activate (amount of time or custom retention formula) and what action to take as soon as the stage is activated (move to recycle bin, permanently delete, declare a record, move to a new location, and so forth).
9. Choose whether to force the stage to recur after a certain period of time and then click OK to save the stage.
10. You can add more retention stages and choose whether you want to apply the same retention policy after it's declared a record. If a different stage is required for records of this content type, the stage(s) must be defined at this time.
11. Optionally, define Auditing, Barcodes, and Labels on this page. Then click OK to save changes.

You can override content type retention policies at the document library and list level. Overriding requires that the site collection level's Library and Folder–based retention is activated. After this is done, go to the library or list settings and then click Information Management Policy Settings. On the Information Management Policy Settings page, click the content type if more than one is associated with the list/library. On the Edit Policy page, enable retention as you would for a content type and then enter the appropriate retention schedule.

Planning large document repositories

With record management and eDiscovery, you need to plan for large document repositories. The definition of "large" is subject to debate, but you can take some steps to ensure that your SharePoint environment is responsive. The best way to determine the system's capabilities is to do some load testing, which helps determine the number and type of servers necessary to achieve the capabilities demanded by your business needs. Some of the tests that you can perform are as follows:

- Time required to upload a document
- Time required to update a document's properties
- Time required to route a document based on a workflow or policy
- Time required to download a document
- Time required to display a view of a document library
- Time required to return data with the Content Query Web Part such as highest rated, newest, or most recently modified
- Time required to query the repository based on document properties
- Time required to crawl the content

After you come up with a test that represents what the end user will experience and the load that will be placed on the servers, you can load the servers with test data to see whether the performance is what you expect. As with any test scenario, representing the load presented by real-life situations is difficult, but it can at least help you determine the hardware requirements.

One item that can decrease performance is the number of items in an individual document library or list. Although SharePoint can support lists/libraries containing tens of millions of items, performance degradation occurs, especially for the SQL Server node that contains the items. You need to test performance on the individual hardware and software that you expect to use, but CPU usage and memory are two items that need to be monitored.

The number of documents contained within a content database can also affect document uploading performance. A large part of this degradation can be mitigated with proper database maintenance. Most databases are set up to grow by a percentage so that when a 100 GB database, for example, needs to grow 10 percent, it must grow by 10 GB, but when it's a terabyte in size, it must grow by 100 GB. Obviously, growing a database by 10 GB would require a lot less time than growing it by 100 GB. Other maintenance tasks, such as keeping the index up to date as well as keeping a fresh set of statistics, helps improve performance.

Because most of the work involved with large document repositories is placed on the SQL Server nodes, you can achieve only a certain amount of performance increase by adding more WFEs. Each situation is different, but generally after two WFEs, the performance gain is minimal. Even during bulk uploads, the SQL Server node becomes the bottleneck. Data being sent to the SQL Server instance needs to be written to disk, and the speed at which this occurs depends on the input/output speed of the disks more than any other factor.

SharePoint sites tend to continue to grow, and planning for space to contain all this growth comes under capacity planning. Although document libraries and lists can contain millions of items, you might not want all that data in a single content database. Extremely large databases require a long time to back up and even longer to restore if something happens to them. Most organizations strive to find an effective setup that minimizes the number of databases and maximizes performance. Such a setup depends on a multitude of variables, including hardware, software, number of servers, network performance, and the business needs. You need to take care of capacity planning early on to handle the growth of large repositories so that the budget, space, and technical expertise can be available to meet the demand.

> ***MORE INFO*** **CAPACITY PLANNING**
>
> **See *http://technet.microsoft.com/en-us/library/ff758645.aspx* for more information on capacity planning for SharePoint Server 2013.**

Thought Experiment

Choosing cross-site content

In this thought experiment, apply what you've learned about this objective. You can find answers to these questions in the "Answers" section at the end of this chapter.

Your company is involved in a legal inquiry and needs to complete an eDiscovery on a set of SharePoint Server 2013 sites. You are asked what's needed to accomplish this with the minimal amount of disruption to end users. Ideally, end users wouldn't even be aware that an eDiscovery was taking place and could continue their work as usual.

What steps would you suggest, assuming that the company has a SharePoint Server 2013 farm?

Objective summary

- eDiscovery centers can be used to manage eDiscovery as long as the proper permissions are configured.
- Site closure enables site collections to be made read-only, and SharePoint treats the site as though it doesn't exist.
- Site mailboxes enable emails and documents to be stored together.
- Record management can occur on documents, list items, emails, and even sites.
- The full life cycle of records (creation, retention, and disposition) need to be taken into account when planning a record management system.
- Planning for large document repositories requires load balancing to determine the correct number and types of servers as well as storage requirements.

Objective review

Answer the following questions to test your knowledge of the information in this objective. You can find the answers to these questions and explanations of why each answer choice is correct or incorrect in the "Answers" section at the end of this chapter.

1. Permissions are a very important part of setting up an eDiscovery center. What rights do the people doing discovery on a set of site collections and Exchange mailboxes need?
   - **A.** Site collection administrator rights on all site collection involved in the discovery
   - **B.** Rights on the Exchange Server mailboxes being discovered
   - **C.** Just being a site collection administrator on the eDiscovery site collection gives a user all the rights necessary
   - **D.** Both A and B
2. You need to implement site mailboxes in your SharePoint ECM solution. On which of the following servers does this requires configuration?
   - **A.** All SharePoint WFEs
   - **B.** All SharePoint servers
   - **C.** All SharePoint WFEs and Exchange Server 2013 nodes
   - **D.** No server configuration is required

3. Which of the following items wouldn't be considered a record?
   A. Item in a list
   B. Document library
   C. Word document
   D. Email
4. When creating a retention schedule in SharePoint, you can choose to retain an item for a period of time. The amount of time specified can be in increments of all the following except which?
   A. Hours
   B. Days
   C. Months
   D. Years

Chapter summary

- Community sites use points and badges to reward users for contributing content.
- The User Profile service relies on the Forefront Identity Manager to synchronize user profile data.
- On-premises SkyDrive storage (SkyDrive Pro) for individuals is kept in their personal site collections.
- Users can now follow people, documents, and sites so they can keep track of related activity and be notified of suggested sites on their newsfeed.
- Search can be configured to display search result differently, based on the type of content returned and the properties associated with the item.
- Continuous crawling allows for recently added items to appear in search result within seconds of being added.
- Channels allow SharePoint content to be displayed differently, depending on the target device.
- eDiscovery allows in-place holds on content, allowing users to continue modifying content during the eDiscovery process.

Answers

This section contains the solutions to the thought experiments and answers to the lesson review questions in this chapter.

Objective 2.1: Thought experiment

In this thought experiment, you were presented with two main questions: How many content databases are required for My Sites? What is the best way to increase performance for the activity feeds?

You can answer the first question with some simple math, based on an assumption that no content database should be larger than 200 GB. Because each user is allowed 1 GB of space, you can assume 200 users per content database. This means 25 content databases for the My Sites, thus allowing for users to fully use their allotted space without moving site collections from one database to another.

The second question is concerned with activity feed performance. The best way to increase activity feed performance is to have a dedicated Distributed Cache server, a SharePoint 2013 server that runs only the Distributed Cache service. The other option is to have collated servers running the Distributed Cache service with every non-essential SharePoint service turned off. This gives the Distributed Cache service as much memory as possible, allowing for the fastest retrieval of activity feed data.

Objective 2.1: Review

1. **Correct answer:** B
    - **A. Incorrect:** The number of gifted badges is limited to one
    - **B. Correct:** Only one badge is allowed at a time.
    - **C. Incorrect:** Three is an erroneous number.
    - **D. Incorrect:** Five is the number of levels on earned badges but has no relation to gifted badges.
2. **Correct answer:** C
    - **A. Incorrect:** 10 MB isn't the default in SharePoint 2013 for a web application.
    - **B. Incorrect:** 50 MB was the default in SharePoint 2010.
    - **C. Correct:** 250 MB is the default in SharePoint Server 2013.
    - **D. Incorrect:** 1 GB isn't the default limit.

3. **Correct answer:** A

   A. **Correct:** AD permission-level changes are made on domain controllers, using the Active Directory and Users tool.

   B. **Incorrect:** Because SQL Server doesn't communicate directly to Active Directory during the synchronization process, it doesn't need enhanced permissions.

   C. **Incorrect:** SharePoint servers shouldn't be domain controllers and therefore don't have the necessary tools.

   D. **Incorrect:** The SharePoint server doesn't matter. Because none of them should be domain controllers, the permissions can't be given on those servers.

4. **Correct answer:** C

   A. **Incorrect:** Forms-based authentication isn't native to the Windows environment, so it needs a trusted provider.

   B. **Incorrect:** Claims can come from a wide variety of different sources, so a trusted provider is needed.

   C. **Correct:** Windows-based authentication is the only authentication method that doesn't require a trusted provider.

   D. **Incorrect:** Because C is the only correct answer, D isn't a valid answer.

5. **Correct answer:** D

   A. **Incorrect:** The number of users that can be followed can be limited. The default is 1,000, but it's not the only correct answer.

   B. **Incorrect:** The number of documents that can be followed can be limited. The default is 500, but it's not the only correct answer.

   C. **Incorrect:** The number of sites that can be followed can be limited. The default is 500, but it's not the only correct answer.

   D. **Correct:** The number of people followed, number of documents followed, and number of sites followed can all be limited at the farm level for users.

Objective 2.2: Thought experiment

In this scenario, you were asked how you would customize the search results for when a user entered the name of the CEO in the people results search box. This requires three steps:

1. You need to create a query rule with a context of local people results. This distinguishes when a user is looking for people results as opposed to a general search.
2. You need to create a display template, which enables you to customize how the results look for a particular item (in this case, the name of the CEO).
3. You need to create a result type so that the customized display template is displayed.

These three steps enable you to display the required results in the desired format.

Objective 2.2: Review

1. **Correct answer:** B
    - **A. Incorrect:** This is better than making it a first or second level authoritative site, but it's not the best answer.
    - **B. Correct:** Making a site a non-authoritative site would push it down to the bottom of the search results.
    - **C. Incorrect:** This would completely remove the site from the search results, which isn't the stated objective.
    - **D. Incorrect:** Although removing the site from the authoritative sites would lower them compared to other authoritative sites, the results wouldn't be pushed to the bottom.
2. **Correct answer:** D
    - **A. Incorrect:** SharePoint sites are the default for a results source but serve as only one of many result sources available.
    - **B. Incorrect:** Exchange Server is an available results source when the Exchange Web Services Managed API is installed on the SharePoint Search server. However, it's just one of several sources available.
    - **C. Incorrect:** Although OpenSearch 1.0/1.1 is an available source of search results, it's just one of several options available.
    - **D. Correct:** All the previous options are valid result sources.
3. **Correct answer:** C
    - **A. Incorrect:** Making all the crawled properties within a category searchable is one of the options available on the Edit Category page.
    - **B. Incorrect:** Delete all unmapped crawled properties is a button on the Edit Category page.
    - **C. Correct:** Making all crawled properties refinable isn't an option available on the Edit Category page.
    - **D. Incorrect:** Mapping all string properties in this category to Content managed properties is an option on the Edit Category page.

4. **Correct answer:** B

   A. **Incorrect:** The thesaurus is used to expand the results returned but doesn't have anything to do with refiners other than increasing the result set they can be pulled from.

   B. **Correct:** Entity extractors are used to create refiners based on word or phrases that are typed in the search box.

   C. **Incorrect:** Query suggestions appear as a user types in the search box, whereas refiners are shown after the results are returned and used to narrow the results.

   D. **Incorrect:** Search analytics can be used to determine whether refiners would be useful, but they don't create refiners.

5. **Correct answer:** D

   A. **Incorrect:** A query rule could be used to promote an item and/or expand a result set, but in this case it's not necessary.

   B. **Incorrect:** A result source is used to define subsets of the crawled content.

   C. **Incorrect:** The new content type isn't required because the one being used in the question has already been created, and another one couldn't be used to display the new template.

   D. **Correct:** The result type helps determine when a certain display template should be used.

Objective 2.3: Thought experiment

In this scenario, you were presented with a single main question: What is the best solution for providing consistent list content across multiple sites and site collection, both internally and externally? The answer is a product catalog site collection that enables a product catalog to be published across sites, site collections, and even SharePoint farms.

Because the content is to be shared internally and externally (meaning the Internet), a product catalog makes the most sense. A product catalog enables the consuming of content from a wide variety of sites and site collections, enabling editing of content in one location and publishing that content to every source that consumes it. Product catalogs are new in SharePoint 2013 and represent a new way to distribute content across multiple sites, site collections, and even SharePoint farms.

Objective 2.3: Review

1. **Correct answer:** D

   A. Incorrect: You can use channels to target specific operating systems on smartphones, but this is just one of the correct answers.

   B. Incorrect: You can use channels to target tablet devices, but other answers are correct.

   C. Incorrect: You can use channels to target operating systems that run on desktop computers, but this too is just one of the correct answers.

   D. Correct: Channels can target specific master pages to devices and/or operating systems listed in A, B, and C.

2. **Correct answer:** A

   A. Correct: A metadata term store set is used for navigation of the product catalog and is a required item when connecting.

   B. Incorrect: Views can be used to limit items shown from a list but not for navigation of a product catalog.

   C. Incorrect: List filters are used in addition to navigation and can be used to further filter a set of results.

   D. Incorrect: Quick Launch is a manually maintained way to navigate a site. It can link to other SharePoint pages or even pages outside SharePoint, but not for the navigation of a product catalog.

3. **Correct answer:** C

   A. Incorrect: Activating the Content Deployment Source Feature feature is the first step in preparing a site collection for deployment, but a community site isn't supported for deployment.

   B. Incorrect: The Content Deployment Source Status page shows the features that need to be disabled before a site collection can be deployed successfully, but the community site needs features unsupported by content deployment.

C. **Correct:** The Community Site template includes features unsupported for content deployment and therefore can't be deployed using OTB SharePoint.

D. **Incorrect:** Although A and B are required for preparing a site collection for content deployment, they work only for site collections that support deployment.

4. **Correct answer:** A

   A. **Correct:** Machine translation allows for the automatic translation of content into other languages with minimal human interaction based on the source site.

   B. **Incorrect:** Variations aren't translated automatically.

   C. **Incorrect:** Labels are used to create new sites and content, but no automatic translation is done.

   D. **Incorrect:** XLIFF files are exported for the purpose of human translation and therefore require a much higher degree of human interaction than machine translation.

Objective 2.4: Thought experiment

In this scenario, you were told to come up with a solution for an eDiscovery project that would cause minimal disruption to the end users allowing them to work undisturbed. You would start by creating a security group, an eDiscovery site collection, and a new case site:

1. Create a security group with everyone doing eDiscovery in it, and then create a user policy for the security group that had read rights to all sites involved in the eDiscovery.
2. Create an eDiscovery site collection, making the security group site collection administrators.
3. Create a case (which creates a site) by clicking Create New Case.

After the new case site is created, content can be identified and held. An in-place hold would cause the least amount of disruption to the end users enabling them to continue to work on their documents and lists without disruption. After items are identified and held, a search and export can make a copy of all identified items (including mailbox items, if that was configured during the identify process).

Objective 2.4: Review

1. **Correct answer:** D
   - **A. Incorrect:** Site collection administrator rights (or a web application–level user policy) are necessary to ensure that discovery can happen on all necessary site collections and subsites, but it doesn't cover the Exchange Server requirement.
   - **B. Incorrect:** Read rights on Exchange Server mailboxes are also needed but don't address the SharePoint permissions.
   - **C. Incorrect:** Rights given on the eDiscovery site collection have nothing to do with the permissions required on SharePoint site collections or Exchange Server mailboxes.
   - **D. Correct:** Both site collection administrator rights (or a user policy equivalent) and rights on Exchange mailboxes are needed for users to be able to use eDiscovery in this situation.
2. **Correct answer:** C
   - **A. Incorrect:** SharePoint WFEs require the Exchange Web Services API and a trust needs to be established, but the solution also requires Exchange Server to be configured.
   - **B. Incorrect:** Only the WFEs need to be configured, but this answer doesn't include the Exchange Server side.
   - **C. Correct:** Site mailboxes need configuration on both the SharePoint WFEs and the Exchange Server 2013 node before they can be enabled.
   - **D. Incorrect:** Site mailboxes aren't available without configuration on SharePoint and Exchange Server.
3. **Correct answer:** B
   - **A. Incorrect:** An item in a list can be considered a record, and SharePoint treats it as such.
   - **B. Correct:** Document libraries can contain records but are themselves not generally considered a record because their contents change similarly to a traditional file cabinet.
   - **C. Incorrect:** Word documents are one of the most common types of records.
   - **D. Incorrect:** Emails are considered records and can be treated as such in SharePoint by using site mailboxes.

4. **Correct answer:** A

   A. **Correct:** Hours isn't a valid option for a retention schedule in SharePoint. One day is the shortest amount of time that can be specified.

   B. **Incorrect:** Days is a valid option, and the shortest amount of time that can be specified is one day.

   C. **Incorrect:** Months is a valid option.

   D. **Incorrect:** Years is the longest valid option.

CHAPTER 3

Upgrade and migrate a SharePoint environment

Upgrading a SharePoint environment can be a complicated task, especially if you're running in an environment that allows only minimal downtime. People have come to rely on their SharePoint solutions to get their work done, and your job is to minimize the impact that the SharePoint migration has on their day-to-day functionality. SharePoint Server 2013 supports both the SharePoint 2010 and SharePoint 2013 user interfaces, allowing for a gradual transition to the SharePoint 2013 user experience depending on your organization's technical and business requirements. Depending on the level of customization of the earlier SharePoint environment, you might need to upgrade in stages to allow for changes in branding and custom solutions. This chapter goes over many of the issues and concerns of upgrading the SharePoint environment so that you can be prepared both for the related exam questions and for upgrading your environment in real life.

Objectives in this chapter:

- Objective 3.1: Evaluate content and customizations
- Objective 3.2: Plan an upgrade process
- Objective 3.3: Upgrade site collection

Objective 3.1: Evaluate content and customizations

This objective focuses on the tasks necessary to ensure a smooth transition between SharePoint 2010 and SharePoint 2013. SharePoint is a platform that uses a relational database to store most of its data. Users create custom solutions, branding is applied, code is written, and sometimes data is deleted, leaving orphans that need to be cleaned up. These customizations and possible database issues need to be addressed before a successful migration can be attempted.

You also need to consider how users authenticate and how the authentication method migrates. Claims authentication has opened up a whole new world of authentication, spawning custom authentication solutions that also need to be migrated.

Fortunately for those of you doing migrations, SharePoint Server 2013 provides several tools to help you get ready for your migration. These tools go a long way toward ensuring a successful migration, but don't make the mistake of upgrading without a fallback plan. Covering every single possible configuration that exists is impossible, and the potential always exists for a disaster to occur during the middle of the migration process. Always make sure that the SharePoint environment—the SharePoint server environment as well as all data files and any remote storage files—is totally backed up before initiating the migration process. With those tasks accomplished, you can safely proceed with the migration process.

This objective covers the following topics:

- Performing migration pre-check tasks
- Analyzing content database test results
- Configuring web application authentication for upgrades
- Resolving orphan objects
- Resolving missing files
- Resolving configuration issues

Performing migration pre-check tasks

You should perform a number of tasks before you start a migration. Following best practices, you should—ideally—make a full survey of the current environment before doing any other task. Making a thorough list of all your SharePoint components can help you determine what needs to be cleaned up before migration as well as the steps involved in the migration process. The following items need to be surveyed:

- All servers involved
- Service application databases
- Content databases
- Web apps
- Site collections
- Customizations
- Large lists
- Views
- Blocked file types

This list is intended to help you determine what needs to be upgraded as well as what items need to be redone on the SharePoint 2013 system (such as blocked file types).

MORE INFO **SHAREPOINT 2013 PRODUCTS PREVIEW UPGRADE WORKSHEET**

A spreadsheet is available to help guide you in this process. You can download the SharePoint 2013 Products Preview Upgrade worksheet from *http://go.microsoft.com/fwlink/?LinkId=252097*.

With SharePoint 2010, you could do an in-place upgrade from SharePoint 2007—meaning that you could install SharePoint 2010 on the same server as SharePoint 2007. SharePoint 2013 doesn't support in-place upgrades, which means that you have to install SharePoint 2013 on a different server from the one on which SharePoint 2010 is installed. For some organizations, this presents additional costs, but some benefits have been gained as well. This was done to separate the process of upgrading the software and databases with the process of upgrading the site collections.

EXAM TIP

For the exam, you will be expected to know that in-place upgrades aren't supported (a major shift from SharePoint 2010). The only valid upgrade path is the database-attach method.

The database-attach method requires that a separate farm be installed and configured before the migration process can begin. After this is accomplished, the databases need to be moved over and upgraded. All content databases can be upgraded, as can some of the service application databases. The following service applications can be upgraded to SharePoint 2013:

- Business Data Connectivity
- Managed Metadata
- Performance Point
- Secure Store
- User Profile
- Search Administration

MORE INFO **SERVICES UPGRADE OVERVIEW**

See *http://technet.microsoft.com/en-us/library/ee731990.aspx* for more information on the services upgrade overview for SharePoint Server 2013.

After you conduct a thorough survey, you need to clean up your environment (and make any necessary adjustments to the survey). First, you need to remove any underused or unused site collections. As part of the survey, you can determine the sites that are truly needed. Also, if any sites can be archived during this process, you can move them to content databases that can be migrated later (or possibly left on SharePoint 2010 until they have been disposed of). Make sure that you communicate with the site users during this process to ensure that the sites required for reporting, compliance, and other business needs aren't deleted.

The next stage of cleanup is to manage lists and document libraries. Lists or libraries with a large number of items should be trimmed, if possible. By default, list throttling is turned on in SharePoint 2013 just as it is in SharePoint 2010 and could cause problems if the lists are too large. Plus, now is a good time to look at your lists to see if some of the data can be deleted or archived, thereby speeding up the migration process when it occurs. Additional benefits include speeding up crawl times and decreasing the size of the search index, thus improving the overall quality of searches.

Also consider that lists with a large number of columns can actually cause an upgrade to fail. You can test a content database for this problem by running the following PowerShell command:

```
Test-SPContentDatabase
```

You should test all your content databases to ensure that no lists have too many columns. If you do have a list with too many columns, you can remove extraneous columns and run the command again, or you can leave the lists as they are rather than migrate them to SharePoint 2013.

Another potential source of trouble in migration is content databases with too many site collections. SharePoint 2010 had a hard limit of 15,000 site collections per content database and a default warning level of 9,000 site collections; SharePoint 2013 has a *suggested* limit of 5,000 site collections per content database and a default warning level of 2,000 site collections. If the number of site collections exceeds 5,000 in a content database that will be migrated, it could result in broken site collections and leave you in an unsupported situation. Deleting unneeded site collections is the best way to clean up a content database, but if all the site collections need to be migrated, you should create additional content databases and migrate some of the site collections over to the new databases. The maximum number of site collections per database can be changed, but more than 10,000 site collections isn't supported. A list of content database supported limits follows:

- 500 content databases per farm
- 200 GB of content per content database in general usage scenarios
- 4 TB of content per content database in specialized usage scenarios
- 60 million items per content database (documents and lists)
- 10,000 site collections

> ***MORE INFO*** **CONTENT DATABASE LIMITATIONS**
>
> **See *http://technet.microsoft.com/en-us/library/cc262787.aspx#ContentDB* for more information on the limits for content databases.**

Large numbers of document versions also can greatly increase the amount of time needed to migrate. Verify that you really need to keep all these versions before you waste precious migration time. Determining which versions to delete can be a large task that's best handled by governance and some programming. Individually removing versions from hundreds or thousands of lists and libraries can take considerable more resources than are available.

Removing unused items such as features, site templates, and web parts also increases the likelihood of a successful migration. The survey used in the earlier part of this objective can help you determine which of these items are being used. You can use the stsadm command EnumAllWebs to double-check that you aren't removing a web part or feature that's actually in use:

```
stsadm - enumallwebs -databasename <database name> -includefeatures -includewebparts
```

This command also lists setup files and event receivers associated with the web.

A couple types of sites aren't supported and must be removed before the upgrade:

- **PowerPoint Broadcast** Office web apps are now installed separately from the SharePoint environment.
- **FAST Search Center** FAST is no longer a separate product and therefore doesn't have a search center of its own. The FAST Search Center can continue to function after the upgrade in the SharePoint 2010 mode, but the user experience can't be upgraded to 2013. The Enterprise Search Center in SharePoint Server 2013 replaces the FAST Search Center.

Web Analytics also needs to be stopped. The architecture of Web Analytics is different in SharePoint 2013 and doesn't upgrade. The presence of Web Analytics information in content databases could cause errors during the upgrade.

EXAM TIP

The Web Analytics application needs to be stopped before databases are backed up for upgrade. The importance of this step makes it a prime subject for exam questions.

The preceding pre-check tasks can definitely help prepare you to begin the migration process; it's your job to make the SharePoint 2010 environment as clean as possible before the upgrade. For example, if the environment had originally been a SharePoint 2007 environment, make sure that all the visual upgrades are finished. This goes for any tasks that might have been left over from the previous upgrade. Deleting or archiving as much data as possible has additional benefits, such as a cleaner search experience and reduced crawl times, and you can save money on storage as well (both for storing the data and the backups).

MORE INFO **CLEANING UP AN ENVIRONMENT BEFORE AN UPGRADE**

See *http://technet.microsoft.com/en-us/library/ff382641.aspx* for more information on how to clean up an environment before an upgrade to SharePoint 2013.

Analyzing content database test results

The preceding section introduced the PowerShell command Test-SPContentDatabase, a tool that helps you determine whether the SharePoint content databases are ready to be migrated. Every content database needs to have Test-SPContentDatabase run against it and any migration-blocking issues resolved. You can run the command against attached and unattached content databases in two ways.

The first way is just against the content database. The full syntax here is followed by a description of the parameters:

```
Test-SPContentDatabase [-Identity] <SPContentDatabasePipeBind> [-AssignmentCollection
<SPAssignmentCollection>] [-DatabaseCredentials <PSCredential>] [-ExtendedCheck
<SwitchParameter>] [-ServerInstance <SPDatabaseServiceInstancePipeBind>] [-ShowLocation
<SwitchParameter>] [-ShowRowCounts <SwitchParameter>]
```

- **Identity** A required parameter that can be the name of the database or the database GUID
- **AssignmentCollection** A PowerShell parameter used to dispose of memory objects
- **DatabaseCredentials** A PSCredential object that contains the user credentials for SQL Server authentication
- **ExtendedCheck** A parameter that checks to make sure that the authentication methods match (claims or classic) in the different web application versions
- **ServerInstance** A parameter that specifies which SQL Server instance to use
- **ShowLocation** A parameter that shows locations where missing templates and features are being used
- **ShowRowCounts** A parameter that returns row counts for the various tables within the content database

> ***IMPORTANT*** **Although Test-SPContentDatabase doesn't alter any data in the content databases, it does require significant resources to run, especially if a rather large content database is used. This can make the content database unresponsive for a period of time, so running it only on unused databases or during low-usage periods (such as on the weekend or during off hours, depending on the organization) is recommended.**

The second method of using Test-SPContentDatabase involves testing a web application with a content database. This verifies customizations that are associated with the web application. The only difference in parameters is that Test-SPContentDatabase uses Name instead of Identity, and strings must specify the database name and the WebApplication (which can be the web app's URL or GUID). The full syntax is as follows:

```
Test-SPContentDatabase -Name <String> -WebApplication <SPWebApplicationPipeBind>
[-AssignmentCollection <SPAssignmentCollection>] [-DatabaseCredentials <PSCredential>]
[-ExtendedCheck <SwitchParameter>] [-ServerInstance <SPDatabaseServiceInstancePipeBind>]
[-ShowLocation <SwitchParameter>] [-ShowRowCounts <SwitchParameter>]
```

Example:

```
Test-SPContentDatabase -Name WSS_Content -WebApplication http://contoso
```

Test-SPContentDatabase lists all the issues that it found, whether an issue will block an upgrade, the issue's remedy, and the message of what the issue is. It returns the following items for each issue it finds:

- **Category** tells you what category the issue falls under, such as missing feature, configuration, or missing web part.
- **Error** is a true/false value indicating whether it's an error.
- **UpgradeBlocking** is a true/false value indicating whether it will prevent the upgrade from occurring.
- **Message** describes the issue that was found, such as Database [WSS_Content] Has Reference(s) To A Missing Feature: Id =[<GUID>].
- **Remedy** suggests a solution for the issue.
- **Locations** shows where the issue occurs, unless it's a global issue such as configuration.

EXAM TIP

On the exam, you will be expected to be familiar with Test-SPContentDatabase—one of the most important PowerShell commands—and how to use it. Make sure that you know the syntax of the major parameters and what results are brought back.

Configuring web application authentication for upgrades

The authentication methods of the web application must match when doing an upgrade. If you are migrating from a claims-based web application, the path is pretty straightforward because the default authentication method in SharePoint 2013 is claims. Running Test-SPContentDatabase on the content database that you want to upgrade can help you determine whether you need to configure the web application before the upgrade. If you need to do additional configuration, one of the issues found by running Test-SPContentDatabase should match the following criteria:

- **Category** should be Configuration.
- **Error** should be False.
- **UpgradeBlocking** should be False.
- **Message** should show that the web application is configured with Claims authentication mode and that the content database you are trying to attach will be used against a Windows Classic authentication mode.
- **Remedy** should show that an inconsistency exists between the authentication mode of target web application and the source web application. You need to ensure that the authentication mode setting in the upgraded web application is the same as what you had in the SharePoint 2010 web application.

If you are facing this issue, you should upgrade your SharePoint 2010 web application from classic-mode authentication to claims-based authentication before you upgrade. Converting the web application to claims-based authentication while still in the SharePoint 2010 environment allows for testing of claims before the migration and allows for any potential fixes before migration (such as making sure the search application still functions in claims-based mode). Converting it after the database-attach upgrade process is also possible. If for some reason you absolutely need to stick with the classic authentication method, you can create a SharePoint 2013 web application that uses classic authentication.

EXAM TIP

As part of the exam, you will be asked to put steps in order. Configuring your SharePoint 2010 web application for claims before you upgrade to a SharePoint 2013 web application that uses claims authentication is a perfect example of an upgrade step that must be done in a certain sequence.

Converting a SharePoint 2010 web application from classic-mode authentication to a SharePoint 2010 claims-based authentication involves the following steps:

IMPORTANT **You should approach this process with caution. If it fails, you might need to restore the whole web application from a backup and start over.**

1. Open the SharePoint 2013 Management Shell with an account that has the following permissions:
   - Member of the Administrators group on the server on which you are running the PowerShell commands
   - Securityadmin fixed server role on the SQL Server instance that contains the web application
   - Db_owner fixed server role on all databases to be updated
2. Enable claims authentication on the target web application by typing the following PowerShell commands, replacing *<WebAppUrl>* with the URL of the target web application:

```
$WebAppName = http://<WebAppUrl>
$wa = get-SPWebApplication $WebAppName
$wa.UseClaimsAuthentication = $true
$wa.Update()
```

3. Enable a site collection administrator on the claims-based enabled application, replacing *yourDomain\SiteCollectionAdminUser* with the account name for the site collection administrator:

```
$account = "yourDomain\SiteCollectionAdminUser"
$account = (New-SPClaimsPrincipal -identity $account -identitytype
1).ToEncodedString()
$wa = get-SPWebApplication $WebAppName
$zp = $wa.ZonePolicies("Default")
$p = $zp.Add($account,"PSPolicy")
$fc=$wa.PolicyRoles.GetSpecialRole("FullControl")
$p.PolicyRoleBindings.Add($fc)
$wa.Update()
```

4. Use the following PowerShell command to migrate users:

```
$wa.MigrateUsers($true)
```

5. After migration is completed, finish with the provisioning process by using the following PowerShell command (still in the same PowerShell window):

```
$wa.ProvisionGlobally()
```

After the web application is converted, it should be fully tested to ensure that the change to a claims-based authentication process was successful. This includes running a full crawl on the search service to ensure that the search account has the proper permissions. Validation of search results should also be done. If everything appears to be in order, migrating the web application to SharePoint 2013 is an easy process—as far as authentication goes.

IMPORTANT **The process of converting a web application to claims-based authentication is a one-way process. Going back to classic-mode authentication isn't supported and might require a full system restore (databases and SharePoint farms) to return to classic-mode authentication, if that's required.**

If you want a SharePoint 2013 web application that uses classic-mode authentication (such as a custom solution that requires classic-mode authentication that can't be rewritten due to budget and/or time constraints or comes from a third party), use PowerShell. Using classic-mode authentication requires an overwhelming need because claims-based authentication is the preferred method of authentication for SharePoint 2013 going forward. This process, via PowerShell, involves the following steps (when you create a web application via Central Administration, classic-mode isn't an option):

1. Open up the SharePoint 2013 Management Shell on a SharePoint 2013 server with an account that has farm-level administration rights.

2. Use the following PowerShell command to create the web application, where *<WindowsAuthType>* is either NTLM or Kerberos and the other options are similar to creating any other web application:

```
New-SPWebApplication -Name <Name> -ApplicationPool <ApplicationPool>
                                  -AuthenticationMethod <WindowsAuthType>
                                  -ApplicationPoolAccount <ApplicationPoolAccount>
                                  -Port <Port> -URL <URL>
```

After creating the classic-mode web application in SharePoint Server 2013, you will see a warning whenever you go to the web application page. This warning indicates that the web application is using the classic-mode authentication. This is to emphasize that claims mode is the preferred authentication mode.

Converting a SharePoint 2013 classic-mode web application to a claims-based web application is a fairly straightforward process. You need to open the SharePoint 2013 Management Shell with the proper permissions and run the following command:

```
Convert-SPWebApplication -Identity "http:// <servername>:port" -To Claims
-RetainPermissions [-Force]
```

Again, whenever you switch authentication modes, you should thoroughly test the web application to make sure that nothing permissions-related is broken. This is especially true for any search-related items.

MORE INFO **MIGRATING FROM CLASSIC-MODE TO CLAIMS-BASED AUTHENTICATION**

See *http://technet.microsoft.com/en-us/library/gg251985.aspx* for more information on how to migrate from classic-mode to claims-based authentication in SharePoint 2013.

Resolving orphan objects

Orphan objects are items that exist in a database but have no reference to an existing item—for example, a site that has no parent site, or a site collection or a document library that has no parent site. Orphaned objects can cause an upgrade to fail because when SharePoint reaches an orphaned item, it doesn't know where to put it. Orphaned objects can be caused by various reasons, such as the following:

- A database is corrupt. Corruption can occur at the disk level or logical level.
- Moving site collections from one content database to another can occasionally leave orphans.
- A site collection fails to be provisioned.
- The power fails during a write operation.
- Unsafe code causes a problem.

Regardless of how the orphans occurred, they need to be cleaned up before you upgrade. Before you dive into cleaning up the database, you should check your survey information against the list of sites found in each content database to locate missing sites and duplicate sites. You can get a list of all the sites in a content database by using the stsadm command enumallwebs:

```
stsadm -o enumallwebs -databasename <database name> [-databaseserver <database server
name>]
```

You also can use the enumallwebs command can to list all the features and web parts, as shown earlier.

After you determine orphaned or duplicate sites (and after you choose which one to keep), you should remove them by using the PowerShell command Remove-SPSite:

```
Remove-SPSite [-Identity] <SPSitePipeBind> [-AssignmentCollection
<SPAssignmentCollection>] [-Confirm [<SwitchParameter>]] [-DeleteADAccounts
<SwitchParameter>] [-GradualDelete <SwitchParameter>] [-WhatIf [<SwitchParameter>]]
```

IMPORTANT **All subsites below the site collection will be deleted.**

The Identity parameter can be either the URL of the site or the GUID that the enumallwebs command can obtain. The other important parameter to consider when dealing with a production environment is the GradualDelete parameter, which allows for a gradual rather than immediate deletion. A large site or site collection deletion can potentially make a SharePoint farm unresponsive for several minutes (or longer).

MORE INFO **USING REMOVE-SPSITE**

See *http://technet.microsoft.com/en-us/library/ff607948.aspx* for more information on the PowerShell command Remove-SPSite.

SharePoint 2010 provides some additional tools to help you detect and repair orphans. These tools can also help to repair other issues, such as the following:

- Removal of a site or subsite that has no parent site
- Removal of a list that has no parent list
- Removal of a list (including a document library) that has no parent site
- Removal of list items that have no parent list
- Removal of documents that have no parent document library
- Removal of web pages that have no parent site
- Missing security scopes on subsites, lists, and items

The available tools are the stsadm command databaserepair and the PowerShell Repair function that exists on database objects. Both tools show the corruption that exists and provide the option of repairing it. Before attempting any database repairs, however, you should always make a backup, as with any operation that changes the database significantly. The first tool to look at is the stsadm command databaserepair:

```
stsadm -o databaserepair -url <url name> -databasename <database name>
[-deletecorruption]
```

The deletecorruption parameter is required if you truly want to delete the corruption. Don't run this command while the database is being used during your company's usual production hours. You can also delete corruption with the SharePoint 2010 Management Shell (PowerShell). Both options are included here because stsadm and PowerShell coexist; although stsadm eventually will be deprecated, it's still widely used. The PowerShell method of deleting corruption is done by opening the SharePoint 2010 Management Shell and running the following commands:

```
$db = Get-SPContentDatabase "<content database name>"
$db.Repair($true)
```

If you want to use these PowerShell commands just to list the corruption, you would use $db.Repair($false) instead of $db.Repair($true). Use of these tools is highly recommended to remove orphans of various types before beginning the migration process.

EXAM TIP

Removal of orphans is listed as an exam objective for a reason. It is essential that all orphans are dealt with before migration begins. Both the stsadm method and the PowerShell method were included for completeness. Either method could show up on the exam. Stsadm is being deprecated, but it's still used extensively by SharePoint administrators.

Resolving missing files

Missing files can cause upgrades to fail or, if an upgrade succeeds, can cause sites not to work correctly and pages not to display correctly. SharePoint Server 2013 supports both the SharePoint 2010 experience as well as the SharePoint 2013 experience. It does this by maintaining both a 14 directory and a 15 directory (sometimes referred to as the *SharePoint hive* or *SharePoint folder*) under %COMMONPROGRAMFILES%\Microsoft Shared\Web server extensions. The SharePoint 2010 files are located under the 14 directory, and the SharePoint 2013 files are located under the 15 directory. This allows for both experiences to exist on the same farm but prevents an in-place upgrade.

All the customizations that you want to keep have to be brought over and installed on the SharePoint 2013 farm. This can cause some confusion over where some files should exist. SharePoint files reside in four main areas:

- **GAC** The Global Assembly Cache stores DLLs that are used by SharePoint as well as globally deployed solutions. These are located in the Windows directory.

- **SharePoint 14 folder** The files necessary for the SharePoint 2010 experience reside in this folder, which is found in the %COMMONPROGRAMFILES%\Microsoft Shared\Web server extensions\14 directory.
- **SharePoint 15 folder** This is the main folder for SharePoint 2013 files, which reside in the %COMMONPROGRAMFILES%\Microsoft Shared\Web server extensions\15 directory.
- **Inetpub** This folder is necessary on every WFE that serves up SharePoint content. The location for SharePoint files are under the inetpub\wwwroot\wss\VirtualDirectories directory.

> ***IMPORTANT*** **When a SharePoint 2010 solution is installed on a SharePoint 2013 farm, the files generally go in the 14 folder but are still be accessible to SharePoint 2013 websites until the site is upgraded to the SharePoint 2013 experience.**

These four directories will be where missing files need to be placed. Finding out what files are missing is often a difficult task. After installing all the customizations from your SharePoint 2010 farm to your SharePoint 2013 farm, you might want to make some comparisons to ensure that all necessary files were copied over. Luckily, you have tools available, such as Windiff and comp, to help you do this.

Using Windiff and comp

Windiff and comp are two tools from Microsoft Windows Server 2008 that can help you figure out what files are missing. For example, you could compare files between multiple WFEs to make sure that they are in sync. They can also help you figure out missing files between the SharePoint 2010 and SharePoint 2013 systems.

You use Windiff to compare two ACSII files (such as XML files) or two folders that contain ASCII files. The Windiff graphical tool is available on installation media under support\tools and needs to be installed before it can be used. You can view whether a file is different as well as use a view that allows for line-by-line inspection of files.

> ***MORE INFO*** **USING THE WINDIFF.EXE UTILITY**
>
> **See *http://support.microsoft.com/kb/159214* for information on how to use Windiff.exe.**

Comp is a command-line utility that you can use to compare both ASCII and binary files. Comp.exe should already exist on the server that SharePoint is installed on. Several options can be found by typing **comp /?** on the command line. The syntax is fairly straightforward. For example, if you want to compare the GAC of two different computers, you can run the following command on one of the two servers:

```
comp.exe C:\Winnt\System32\*.dll \\<other computer name>\C$\Winnt\System32\*.dll
```

Then you can use the results of the output to look for missing assemblies. This can also help determine whether you have the right version of the assembly.

Using the SharePoint Products Configuration Wizard for missing files

During the course of a SharePoint farm's life, some system files might go missing, become corrupted, or be modified. This can affect the migration and upgrade process, so keeping the originals in a backed-up location is important. On a SharePoint 2010 farm or a SharePoint 2013 farm, you can run the SharePoint Products Configuration Wizard to replace missing system files necessary to run SharePoint. Before you do this, of course, you should back up everything in the SharePoint folder as well as anything under the inetpub directory. This process checks for necessary files and replaces them if they are missing. It also checks and/or changes a host of other things, such as the web.config files, registry keys, and xml files.

> ***IMPORTANT*** **Running the SharePoint Products Configuration Wizard should be done with caution. It could cause a heavily customized farm to fail (for example, you altered files in the _layouts directory that you shouldn't have). Always make a full backup before running it.**

Resolving configuration issues

When migrating to SharePoint 2013 from a customized SharePoint 2010, you need to be concerned about a number of configuration issues. You can't simply copy over configurations, and the lack of an in-place upgrade means that all configuration customizations required have to be created on the SharePoint 2013 farm. The survey listed earlier in this objective can help you determine the configuration issues you need to copy over. The following configuration items might present issues:

- Trust between servers
- User Profile Service
- Forms-Based Authentication
- SPNs for Kerberos
- SSL certificates
- Special IIS settings
- Trusted locations for Excel
- Secure Store settings
- Network Load Balancing

This list is by no means exhaustive, but it gives you an idea about the kinds and amount of configuration required on a SharePoint farm. Diagnosing the cause of configuration issues can be one of the most difficult tasks in configuring a SharePoint farm. Fortunately, you have diagnostic tools available to help. This section focuses on the SharePoint Diagnostic Studio.

The SharePoint Diagnostic Studio is part of the SharePoint Administrator's Toolkit. At the time of this writing, the latest version is the SharePoint 2010 Administrator's Toolkit, which also works well with SharePoint 2013. The toolkit includes the following tools:

- SharePoint Diagnostic Studio 3.0 (SPDiag 3.0)
- User Profile Replication Engine 2010
- Load Testing Toolkit
- Security Configuration Wizard (SCW) manifests
- Content Management Interoperability Services (CMIS) connector for SharePoint Server 2010

> ***MORE INFO*** **DOWNLOADING SHAREPOINT ADMINISTRATOR'S TOOLKIT V2.0**
>
> **You should install the SharePoint Administrator's Toolkit to help diagnose a wide variety of configuration issues as well as other issues that can affect performance. See *http://www.microsoft.com/en-us/download/details.aspx?id=20022* to download the SharePoint Administrator's Toolkit v2.0.**

After you install the SharePoint 2010 Administrator's Toolkit, you can run reports and get diagnostic information by following these steps:

1. Navigate to the server that you want to diagnose. (Remote diagnosis is also available but requires a separate set of steps.)
2. Click Start | SharePoint 2010 Administration Toolkit | SharePoint Diagnostic Studio.
3. In the SharePoint Diagnostic Studio user interface, click New Project.
4. In the Create Project dialog box, enter the name of the current server and then click Create Project. This creates a project with the same name as the configuration database, with a .ttfarm extension.
5. Wait until the process finishes and returns you to the diagnostic studio. You might have to close the SharePoint Diagnostic Studio, return, and then click Open Project and choose the project you just created to view results.

> ***IMPORTANT*** **If you're creating a new project in the SharePoint Diagnostic Studio on a production system, be advised that it can cause a brief service outage. After the project is created, it can be run at any time.**

After you connect to the server, you can run a number of reports to help determine configuration issues. For instance, you can click Failed User Requests in the Availability section under Reports to determine which users have tried to access the SharePoint server and failed. This could show you that the authentication method in use isn't configured correctly. Another useful report in figuring out configuration issues (as well as other issues) is the ULS Trace

Issues report. This displays the ULS (Universal Logging Service) items in a grid-like format and can help diagnose a wide range of issues, including configuration issues.

Some issues, such as IIS configuration, are best tackled through the use of proper documentation. This is also true for SSL configurations, but SharePoint Diagnostic Studio can help you with this by identifying failed https requests. Tools can definitely help with identifying issues, but they can't always help with solving the issues, especially customizations such as forms-based authentication or third-party claims authentication methods.

Thought experiment

Migrating to a claims web application

In the following thought experiment, apply what you've learned about this objective. You can find answers to these questions in the "Answers" section at the end of this chapter.

You want to migrate a SharePoint 2010 web application to SharePoint 2013. The SharePoint 2010 web application uses classic-mode authentication, but you want it to use claims-based authentication after the migration because you know that claims-based authentication is the default authentication method for SharePoint 2013.

What are your options and what would be the benefits and/or drawbacks in each case?

Objective summary

- Test-SPContentDatabase is one of the most useful tools to identify issues that need to be resolved before migration.
- Authentication methods need to match for web applications that are being migrated.
- Claims-based authentication is the default authentication method in SharePoint Server 2013.
- Orphan removal (sites, subsites, lists, documents, and list items) is an important step in preparing for migration.
- Use of tools such as Windiff and comp can help identify missing files.
- You can use the SharePoint Diagnostic Studio to diagnose a wide range of issues, including configuration issues.

Objective review

Answer the following questions to test your knowledge of the information in this objective. You can find the answers to these questions and explanations of why each answer choice is correct or incorrect in the "Answers" section at the end of this chapter.

1. What is the recommend limit on the number of site collections that are contained within a single content database?
   - **A.** 200
   - **B.** 5,000
   - **C.** 10,000
   - **D.** 1 million
2. You want to migrate a classic-mode web application from SharePoint 2010 to SharePoint 2013. What are your options with regards to configuring authentication before the web application is migrated?
   - **A.** Convert the SharePoint 2010 to claims-based authentication and then upgrade.
   - **B.** Convert the SharePoint 2010 web application to claims-based authentication after the database upgrade.
   - **C.** Create a classic-mode SharePoint 2013 web application and then upgrade.
   - **D.** All of the above
3. What method name is used to remove orphan objects from a content database using the SharePoint 2010 Management tool?
   - **A.** deletecorruption
   - **B.** Test-SPContentDatabase
   - **C.** Repair
   - **D.** Upgrade-SPContentDatabase
4. Windiff.exe is a graphical Windows Server tool that you can use to compare files in different directories. What file types can it compare?
   - **A.** ASCII files
   - **B.** All binaries
   - **C.** DLLs
   - **D.** EXEs
5. The SharePoint Administrator's 2010 toolkit comes with which of the following items?
   - **A.** SharePoint Diagnostic Studio
   - **B.** User Profile Replication Engine
   - **C.** Load Testing Toolkit
   - **D.** All of the above

6. You want to install a feature so that it will be available for both the SharePoint 2010 experience and the SharePoint 2013 experience. How can you install it?
   - **A.** Use the PowerShell command Install-SPFeature a single time.
   - **B.** Use the PowerShell command Install-SPFeature twice, using the CompatibilityLevel parameter to install the feature for both experiences.
   - **C.** Features are automatically upgraded during the database-attach method.
   - **D.** Features are either compatible with the SharePoint 2010 experience or the SharePoint 2013 experience, but not both.

Objective 3.2: Plan an upgrade process

Migration to SharePoint Server 2013 can be quite an undertaking depending on the size and level of customization of your SharePoint 2010 installation. Because in-place upgrades aren't supported, you can't install SharePoint 2013 on top of SharePoint 2010. Removing a SharePoint 2010 installation and then installing SharePoint 2013 isn't recommended, either. SharePoint Server 2013 should be installed on a clean install of Microsoft Windows Server 2008 R2 or greater. These requirements to the upgrade process can provide additional difficulties for companies wanting to use the same hardware. Before beginning the upgrade, you should outline each step necessary to complete the upgrade with minimal impact and effort.

EXAM TIP

The exam will focus some of its questions on planning for this upgrade process. Questions will center on the topics discussed in this objective, but this information will also help you in your own upgrade process.

This objective covers the following topics:

- Planning removal of servers in rotation
- Configuring a parallel upgrade
- Configuring read-only access for content
- Configuring upgrade farms
- Measuring upgrade performance
- Planning an installation sequence

Planning removal of servers in rotation

Part of your migration process might include the removal of servers on the SharePoint 2010 farm so that they can be used in the SharePoint 2013 farm. This strategy would enable the gradual transition of content to the new server farm.

SharePoint servers shouldn't just be turned off. You need to remove the SharePoint 2010 servers in a way that allows the farm or farms to function as long as necessary for your organization's requirements. Several tasks might be involved in the removal process, such as the following:

- Moving Central Administration
- Moving Search
- Removing WFE from NLB
- Moving WFE functionality
- Moving Application Services
- Moving the User Profile Service

The most important issue to consider is keeping all the services necessary for SharePoint to function correctly to be running on at least one server at all times. This generally means turning on a service on a server before turning it off on another server. Central Administration is one service that must be functioning at all times for SharePoint to be functional. Luckily, Central Administration can be running on any server in the SharePoint farm and can even be on multiple servers at the same time.

Using Psconfig

One command-line tool that you can use to provision Central Administration is Psconfig, which provides an alternative to the graphical user interface and allows for scripting. For example, if you want to use Psconfig to provision the Central Administration web application on a server, you would open a command-line interface with farm-level permission and run the following command:

```
psconfig.exe -cmd adminvs -provision -port <port number>
             -windowsauthprovider onlyusentlm
```

EXAM TIP

psconfig is a powerful command-line utility that could very well be on the exam as a possible answer or choice. You should be familiar with it and the main functionality it provides.

The Psconfig command creates the Central Administration web application on the server it was run on, with the port number specified by *<port number>* and with NTLM used as the authentication mechanism. Using the enablekerberos parameter instead enable Kerberos on all Central Administration web applications in the farm.

Provisioning any web application is a resource-intensive operation and should be performed only during non-critical hours on production farms. Psconfig can also be used to unprovision a Central Administration web application:

```
psconfig.exe -cmd adminvs -unprovision
```

Of course, one Central Administration web application should be running at all times. Psconfig is a very useful command utility and can be used to do a whole host of configuration items that are useful for the configuration of the SharePoint farm.

> ***MORE INFO*** **PSCONFIG COMMAND-LINE REFERENCE**
>
> **You can find the Psconfig command-line reference at *http://technet.microsoft.com/en-us/library/cc263093.aspx*.**

Servers that run parts of the Search service application need their components removed or moved, depending on the search topology. The Search service requires three components that can exist on different servers: the Search Administration service, the Crawl component, and the Index Partition and Query component.

The Crawl component and the Index Partition and Query component can exist on one or more servers. If you want to move one of these components, you can do so through Central Administration by following these steps (this isn't necessary if components already exist on more than one server):

1. Navigate to the Search service application.
2. Click Farm Search Administration | Modify Topology.
3. Under New, choose the component to be moved.
4. Choose the server to which the component is being moved, the associated database, and location (on the server where the component is being created) of files the component creates.
5. Click OK and wait for the component to be created.

After the new search component is created, you can delete the one from the server that's being removed from rotation. This can also be done in Central Administration. To accomplish this, go back to the Modify Topology page and click the component to be removed. An option to delete the component will become available.

> ***IMPORTANT*** **Creating and removing search components can take a very long time—up to an hour or more in some cases. The process will degrade SharePoint performance, especially on the server being affected, so you need to take this into consideration if your SharePoint farm is in production.**

You can remove the Search Administration component in Central Administration also. The Search Administration component for a Search service application can exist on only one server. To move the Search Administration component, follow these steps:

1. Make sure that the SharePoint Server Search service is running on the destination server.

2. Navigate to the Search service application.
3. Click Farm Search Administration | Modify Topology.
4. Click Administration Component in the Admin section.
5. Click Edit Properties.
6. Change the server hosting the Search Administration component by choosing one of the servers from the Administration Component Server drop-down list.
7. Click OK to save changes.

Removing services

After you remove a server's components, you should stop all the services on it before you remove it. Central Administration provides a visual display of all the SharePoint services that you can use to stop them. You can also stop them by using the PowerShell command Stop-SPServiceInstance (or start with Start-SPServiceInstance), but these commands require the GUID of the service instance, which you can obtain with the command Get-SPServiceInstance. To stop all the services with Central Administration, follow these steps:

1. Navigate to Central Administration with a farm administrator account.
2. Click Manage Services On Server in the System Settings section.
3. Select the server on which you want to stop services from the Server drop-down list.
4. Under the Action column, click Stop for each service running on the server, waiting until each service stops before proceeding to the next one.
5. Leave the page after all services on the server are stopped.

After you stop all the SharePoint services on the server to be removed, you can go to the actual server and ensure that all the SharePoint services (in the Services MMC) are stopped. At this point, you can safely remove the server (in this case, only search services were running on the server).

> ***IMPORTANT*** **After removing any server from a SharePoint farm, you should perform a thorough test to ensure that any functionality the server was providing is still there.**

Moving User Profile Synchronization

The User Profile Synchronization (UPS) service is a special case in that it must be stopped before it's started on another server. The UPS service can't run on more than one server at a time. Before moving the UPS service, you should make a full backup of the farm (using the built-in Central Administration backup tool) and the related UPS databases (defaults are Profile DB, Synch DB, and Social DB). To move the UPS by using Central Administration, follow these steps:

1. On the server to which the UPS is being moved, make sure that the Forefront Identity Manager Service and the Forefront Identity Manager Synchronization Service are set up identically to the server that currently hosts the UPS.
2. Verify that the account being used to perform this process is a member of the Farm Administrator's group and is a member of the local Administrator's group on the server on which you want to install the UPS. (The account can be removed from the local Administrator's group after the UPS is started.)
3. Navigate to Central Administration on the server that's currently running the UPS and click Manage Service Applications in the System Settings section.
4. On the User Profile Synchronization Service line, click Stop to stop the current UPS service.
5. Navigate to the server on which you want to start the UPS service and open Central Administration.
6. Click Manage Service Applications in the System Settings section.
7. On the User Profile Synchronization Service line, click Start.
8. Wait several minutes until the UPS service starts.
9. Navigate to Manage Service Applications in the Application Management section on the home page of Central Administration.
10. Click User Profile Service Application (or whatever you named it) on the Service Applications page.
11. In the Synchronization section on the User Profile Service Application page, click Start Profile Synchronization.
12. Start a full profile synchronization on the Start Profile Synchronization page.

> ***MORE INFO*** **MAINTAINING UPS SETTINGS**
>
> **See *http://technet.microsoft.com/en-us/library/ff681014.aspx* for more information on how to maintain User Profile Synchronization settings in SharePoint Server 2013.**

Removing other servers

You can take out of rotation servers that provide service applications (other than Search and User Profile Synchronization) by simply starting the services they provide on other SharePoint servers in the farm and then stopping them on the server to be removed. This is assuming that the services they provide aren't being consumed by other SharePoint farms. This scenario would involve reestablishing the connection after the service is moved. You first would want to unpublish the service and then stop it. After that, you would start the service on the server providing the service and then publishing it from that server. This would require establishing trusts as well, if they don't already exist. You should plan for an outage associated with publishing and consuming the service to avoid loss of services during production hours.

EXAM TIP

Unpublishing a service application that's being consumed by other SharePoint Server farm(s) is a good example of a step that should be performed in a certain order and might be on the exam. You will often be asked to place items in the order in which they should be performed.

Configuring parallel upgrades

The upgrade path to SharePoint 2013 requires the use of the database-attach upgrade method. This process can take a long time, especially if you are upgrading one database at a time. Luckily, content databases can be upgraded in parallel. Before looking at the process of configuring a parallel upgrade, you should look at the different phases of the upgrade process. The process typically follows this order:

1. Create the SharePoint Server 2013 farm.
2. Copy databases to the new farm.
3. Upgrade the service applications.
4. Upgrade the content databases.
5. Upgrade site collections.

Notice that the content databases should be upgraded after the service applications. Database upgrades are a resource-intensive process, but enabling them to proceed in parallel can decrease the amount of time it takes. The number of databases that can be upgraded in parallel depends on the type of hardware being used.

IMPORTANT **Before you begin the upgrade process, you must make sure that the account being used to attach the database is a member of the db_owner fixed database role on the database being upgraded.**

Content databases are attached to a web application. If you have more than one content database that needs to be attached to the web application, the one that contains the root site collection needs to be the first one attached. A content database needs to be connected to a web application with the following PowerShell command:

```
Mount-SPContentDatabase -Name <Database Name> -DatabaseServer <Server Name>
-WebApplication <URL>
```

MORE INFO USING MOUNT-SPCONTENTDATABASE

See *http://technet.microsoft.com/en-us/library/ff607581.aspx* for more information on how to use the PowerShell command Mount-SPContentDatabase.

The act of mounting the database to the web application begins the upgrade of the database to SharePoint 2013. You can monitor the progress of the upgrade by navigating to the Upgrade Status page in Central Administration. After you upgrade the first content database and verify its success, you can begin the parallel upgrade of the remaining content databases. To perform parallel upgrades of the content databases, follow these steps:

1. Open a command prompt on the SharePoint server on which you want to initiate the upgrade process.
2. Run the Mount-SPContentDatabase PowerShell command to begin the database upgrade of the next content database to be upgraded.
3. Wait several minutes to allow the upgrade process to begin and to avoid database locks.
4. Open a new command prompt (one for each database being upgraded) and repeat steps 2 and 3 for the next database.
5. Repeat steps 2 through 4 for each additional content database that needs to be upgraded.

EXAM TIP

Mount-SPContentDatabase is one of the few PowerShell commands that you are expected to know in detail. You can expect to see the command as an option in an exam question or used in a case study.

The speed of the parallel upgrades depends on the hardware capabilities of the servers involved and the databases being upgraded. Upgrading very large content databases individually is advisable because the parallel upgrade process can result in a slower upgrade experience. If you plan to upgrade many content databases at the same time, you should monitor the performance on both the SQL Server instance where the databases are being upgraded and the SharePoint server where the database upgrade is initiated. The following factors can affect the speed of the upgrade process:

- SQL Server disk performance
- SQL Server CPU and memory
- Web Server CPU and memory
- Network performance
- Content database complexity (number of site collections, documents, versions, and so forth)

- Number of subsites
- How data is organized (for example, lots of lists take longer than a few lists with lots of items)

> ***MORE INFO*** **PLANNING FOR PERFORMANCE DURING AN UPGRADE**
>
> **See *http://technet.microsoft.com/en-us/library/cc262891.aspx* for more information on how to plan for performance during an upgrade to SharePoint 2013.**

Configuring read-only access for content

Migrating content in a production environment is a tricky process that takes careful planning and scheduling to minimize the impact on production as well as keep people from losing any work. The loss of work can be minimized by making the content databases read-only before they are migrated. A communication plan should be in place to let users know before the content databases are made read-only so they can prepare by saving their work ahead of time. Any open documents can't be saved after the database is made ready-only, which results in lost work unless users save the items to another location.

The method used to make content read-only varies depending on your needs (such as making site collection read-only before making the content database read-only). For example, if you have a huge number of site collections (such as personal sites), you probably want to make just the content database(s) read-only, but if you have a set of heavily used site collections within a content database, you might want to make the site collections read-only first so that the content can be made read-only gradually. Site collections can be made read-only by following these steps:

1. Navigate to Central Administration with a Farm Administrator account.
2. Click Application Management and then click Configure Quotas And Locks in the Site Collections section.
3. Choose the site collection that is to be made read-only in the Site Collection section and then choose Read-Only (Blocks Additions, Updates, And Deletions), as shown in Figure 3-1.

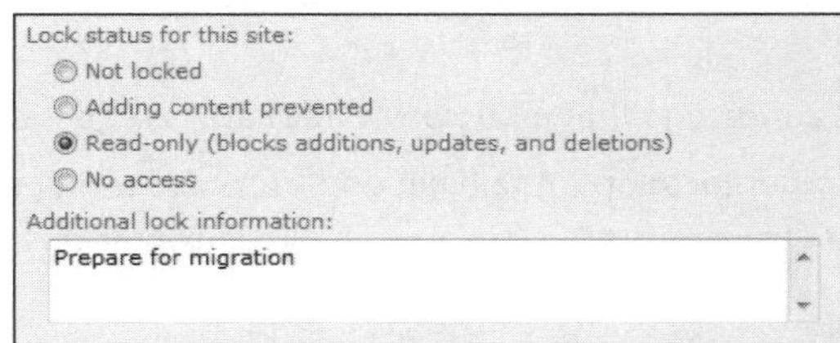

FIGURE 3-1 Setting a site collection to read-only

4. Add information in the Additional Lock Information text box and click OK to save changes.

You can also use PowerShell to set a site collection to read-only:

```
Set-SPSite -Identity "<URL of site collection>" -LockState "ReadOnly"
```

> ***MORE INFO*** **LOCKING OR UNLOCKING SITE COLLECTIONS**
>
> **For more information on how to lock or unlock site collections, see *http://technet.microsoft.com/en-us/library/cc263238(v=office.14).aspx.***

Setting a site collection (or a content database) to read-only affects the end-user experience for that content. Many items that allow for addition and/or modification of data are removed from the user interface, to help prevent users from trying to add or modify content. Some items that are removed or disabled are as follows:

- Edit and New Page are disabled on the Site Actions menu.
- Check In, Check Out, New Document, Upload Document, Delete Document, and other options are disabled on the Library Tools tab for Documents.
- The ribbon isn't displayed on the Search page (and FAST Search page).
- Create View, Modify View, New Row, Form Web Parts, and other options are disabled on the Library Tools tab for Library.
- For Permissions New, Remove Users from Group, and Settings are disabled.

If users aren't warned ahead of time, making a site read-only will most likely result in a lot of confusion because users will see the items as broken and will report them as such. Other items will appear to be available, but the OK button will be disabled. This can cause some concern as well, but at least the functionality is removed so that users won't get an error. However, some items will display an error message if they are clicked:

- Clicking Restore Selection, Delete Selection, or Empty Recycle Bin in the Recycle Bin causes an Access Denied error.
- Clicking Create for sites or workspaces causes an Access Denied error.
- Trying to apply a theme causes an Access Denied error.
- Clicking Create New Content in Site Libraries and Lists displays a message that an unexpected error has occurred.
- Clicking Customize Form displays a message that a Microsoft InfoPath is required.

Additional error messages appear in other locations. Again, let end users know that such errors might show up and that they aren't truly errors but are a result of the content being read-only.

MORE INFO USER EXPERIENCE ON READ-ONLY SITES

See *http://technet.microsoft.com/en-us/library/ee517786(v=office.14).aspx* for more information on the User experience on read-only sites (SharePoint Server 2010).

To set the entire content database to read-only, you can go through SQL Server. Setting a content database as read-only makes the entire set of site collections contained within as read-only. Follow these steps:

1. Log onto the SQL Server instance with an account that has the db_owner fixed database role on the content database to be made read-only.
2. Open SQL Server Management Studio and connect to the SQL Server for the SharePoint farm.
3. Right-click the content database to be made read-only in the Object Explorer and choose Properties.
4. Click the Options link in the Select A Page section.
5. Find the Database Read-Only property under the State section and change the property to True.
6. Click OK to save changes.
7. Repeat steps 1 through 6 for all content databases that need to be set to read-only.

The end-user experience will be similar to that when a site collection is made read-only through Central Administration, so you still need to alert users. After you make a content database read-only, it can be copied safely to the SQL Server instance that's being used for SharePoint 2013. Attaching a database with the Mount-SPContentDatabase PowerShell command makes the database read-write.

EXAM TIP

The very act of connecting a content database to the SharePoint 2013 farm changes it from read-only to read-write. No additional steps need to be taken.

As mentioned earlier, when you attach a content database using the Mount-SPContentDatabase it begins the upgrade process (and hence can't remain read-only). The content database and all the site collections within are ready to use after the database is attached and upgraded, but it's still in the SharePoint 2010 user experience. Each site collection needs to be upgraded to the SharePoint 2013 user experience individually. This can be done by the site collection administrators or by the farm administrators.

MORE INFO ATTACHING AND RESTORING A READ-ONLY CONTENT DATABASE

See *http://technet.microsoft.com/en-us/library/ee748633(v=office.15).aspx* for more information on attaching and restoring a read-only content database in SharePoint 2013.

Configuring upgrade farms

The SharePoint 2013 farm should be configured before content is upgraded. This helps ensure that the content is ready to use after the upgrade process. The first step after you install SharePoint 2013 on the servers in the farm is to start applying the configuration needed based on the survey information that you gathered earlier during the pre-upgrade data-gathering step. Some of the configuration items that need to be reviewed and documented before migrating content databases are as follows:

- Authentication methods on all applicable web applications
- Alternate Access Mappings
- Managed paths
- Email settings
- Self-service site management settings
- Quotas
- Farm-level customizations

After the farm is configured with these items, the service applications needs to be configured if they will be upgraded. Service applications require special consideration when being upgraded and need to be addressed individually.

You need to perform a few important steps after the SharePoint 2013 farm is installed. Before you start configuring the service applications, you should install the language packs for SharePoint 2013. Even if you aren't upgrading the service application, you should install the language packs before you start upgrading any of the content databases. After you install the language packs, you should run the SharePoint Products Configuration Wizard.

MORE INFO INSTALLING OR UNINSTALLING LANGUAGE PACKS

See *http://technet.microsoft.com/en-us/library/cc262108* for more information on how to install or uninstall language packs for SharePoint 2013.

After the language packs (if any) are installed, the service applications should be upgraded and/or configured. One of the first steps is to configure the Secure Store Service, which requires that you have the passphrase. If you don't know the passphrase, you can refresh the key and then back up the Secure Store database. The passphrase is required so that you can use it in the SharePoint 2013 farm.

MORE INFO **CONFIGURING THE SECURE STORE SERVICE**

See *http://technet.microsoft.com/en-us/library/ee806866.aspx* for more information on how to configure the Secure Store service in SharePoint 2013.

The next important step has to do with the User Profile service. If you want to upgrade the User Profile Sync database, you need to export the encryption key for the User Profile Synchronization service application. This key is stored separately from the database. This key must be imported into the SharePoint 2013 environment after you upgrade the User Profile service application. This fairly complicated process typically isn't performed on servers, so the following steps are for the export process:

1. Open a command prompt on the server that runs the User Profile Synchronization service with an account that's a member of the Administrators group.
2. Change the directory to %Program Files%\Microsoft Office Servers\14.0\Synchronization Service\Bin at the command prompt.
3. Run miiskmu.exe from the command prompt.
4. In the Microsoft Identity Integration Server Key Management Utility wizard, make sure that Export Key is selected.
5. Click Next, and then enter the farm administrator account into the Account Name text box and the password for the account in the Password text box.
6. In the Domain text box, enter in the domain name of the farm administrator account.
7. Enter the filename and location of the export file in the Specify Export File Name And Location text box and click Next.
8. Click Finish and then close the dialog box.

You should now have an encryption key that can be imported into the SharePoint 2013 farm. After the User Profile databases are upgraded using the database-attach method, you need to import the key into the SharePoint 2013 environment on the server that runs the User Profile Synchronization service (the server that runs the FIM services).

MORE INFO **CREATING A SHAREPOINT 2013 FARM FOR A DATABASE-ATTACH UPGRADE**

See *http://technet.microsoft.com/en-us/library/cc263026* for more information on how to create the SharePoint 2013 farm for a database-attach upgrade, including exporting the User Profile Synchronization service encryption key.

Before you upgrade any content databases, you must upgrade all the service applications that need to be migrated. Any service applications that aren't being migrated also should be created before the content database upgrades. The following service applications can be upgraded:

- Managed Metadata service
- Search service
- User Profile service
- Secure Store service
- PerformancePoint Services service
- Business Data Connectivity (BDC) service

NOTE **UPGRADING THE BUSINESS DATA CONNECTIVITY SERVICE APPLICATION**

The Business Data Connectivity service is available for upgrade from SharePoint 2010 to SharePoint Foundation 2013 and SharePoint Server 2013. The other service applications can be upgraded only from SharePoint Server 2010 to SharePoint Server 2013.

The process of upgrading service applications follows a general set of rules for each application. After the service application databases are copied over to the new server, you can perform the following steps to upgrade them:

1. Start the service instances. (You can start all but the SharePoint Search service instance via Central Administration; you must use PowerShell to start the Search service.)
2. Create the service applications and upgrade the databases. This must be accomplished via PowerShell commands.
3. Create proxies for all service applications except Business Data Connectivity (which automatically creates its own proxy).
4. Verify that the proxies exist in the default group.

After the User Profile service application is created, you need to import the encryption key that you exported earlier. The same command, miiskmu.exe, can be used to import it on the SharePoint 2013 server. After you import the encryption key, you can start the User Profile Synchronization service.

MORE INFO **UPGRADING SERVICE APPLICATIONS**

See *http://technet.microsoft.com/en-us/library/jj839719.aspx* for more information on how to upgrade service applications to SharePoint 2013.

Measuring upgrade performance

A test farm is the best way for you to test the performance of upgrading your content databases. Getting your test farm to be an exact replica of your production farm might not be possible, but you can still get a fairly decent measurement of performance if your SQL Server instance in the test environment is close to the one that will be in production and you're using actual backups of your content databases. Performance varies greatly for content databases of the same size, depending on how the data is organized. You can't say that a database that's twice the size will take twice as long; it could take the same amount of time or go many times longer. The only way to properly determine how long a content database or set of content databases takes to upgrade is to measure how long it takes to upgrade them on a test environment. After you create your test environment, you can start measuring the performance of the upgrades and determine whether actions need to be taken to improve performance before the actual migration.

> ***MORE INFO*** **CONFIGURING SHAREPOINT SERVER IN A THREE-TIER FARM**
>
> **See *http://www.microsoft.com/en-us/download/details.aspx?id=30386* to download the test lab guide titled "Configure SharePoint Server 2013 in a Three-Tier Farm."**

After you create a test farm and configure it to be as close to production as possible, you can copy over the content databases you want to test by first backing them up and then copying them over to the SQL Server instance to which you want to attach them. Some of the items that you should keep track of are as follows:

- Amount of time to upgrade a single content database
- Amount of time to upgrade using parallel upgrading
- Memory usage on the SQL Server instance
- CPU usage on the SQL Server instance
- Disk space on the SQL Server instance

The amount of time required to upgrade content databases (whether singly or in parallel) is fairly straightforward because you simply monitor how long it takes.

You should also measure how much disk space is used during the upgrade process; a lot of temp space is potentially used by the paging file, the temp database, and the transaction log on the database that's being upgraded. You might have to shrink the log file by backing up the database after it's upgraded and then checking for empty space on both the log file and the data file. Depending on your SQL Server hardware, you could gain significant improvements simply by adding more memory. To monitor CPU and memory usage, follow these simple steps:

1. Navigate to the SQL Server instance being monitored.
2. Right-click the taskbar and choose Start Task Manager.

3. Click the Performance tab to see the usage percentages for the CPU and memory.

4. Click the Resource Monitor for more detailed information.

To start the Resource Monitor by itself, type **resmon.exe** in the Start text box. The Resource Monitor allows for some very detailed information about several performance-related items, such as the following:

- CPU
- Memory
- Disk
- Network

The Overview tab gives you an overview of all four performance items, as shown in Figure 3-2.

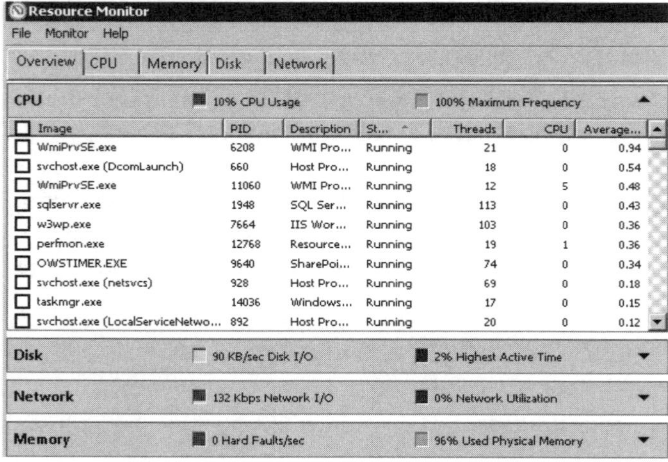

FIGURE 3-2 Overview tab in Resource Monitor

From the Resource Monitor you can determine what's causing your bottleneck. In Figure 3-2, physical Memory is topping out at 96 percent. Depending on which operation is using that much memory, you could determine that if you added more memory, performance would increase.

You should test all your scenarios of content database upgrades—and site collection upgrades, if those are to be done as part of the upgrade—to determine how long you can expect the upgrades to take. This helps with user expectations, the amount of downtime, and possible ways to improve performance.

MORE INFO **TROUBLESHOOTING RESOURCE AVAILABILITY**

See *http://technet.microsoft.com/en-us/library/dd883276(v=WS.10).aspx* for a getting-started guide on resource availability troubleshooting.

EXAM TIP

The Resource Monitor is one of the main tools used to measure performance on Microsoft Windows Server and is probably the first tool you would use to diagnose performance issues.

Planning an installation sequence

You need to consider many factors when determining an installation sequence for your SharePoint farm. The main factor is whether you plan to use all new hardware or reuse some (or all) of the existing hardware. Three main components must exist before you can start creating or migrating content:

- SQL Server (database component)
- Web front end (WFE)
- Application Server component

All these components can exist on the same server (a standalone installation), but because this exam is about advanced solutions, assume that at least the SQL Server installation is on a separate server:

- SQL Server should be the first server configured because you can't install SharePoint 2013 without a SQL Server database. You can use the same database for SharePoint 2013 as you do for SharePoint 2010, although doing so will put quite a strain on the server if both SharePoint installations are trying to use it at the same time.
- The second server that needs to be installed is the one hosting Central Administration that's also a WFE. This doesn't have to be a WFE in the long term, but SharePoint needs a web site to host Central Administration.
- The third component to be installed is the Application Server. It can exist on the same server as the WFE, although typically it would be on its own server in a three-tier system.

You might want to combine these roles if you plan to reuse the SharePoint 2010 servers in your new farm. A whole set of brand-new servers (and the cost of the software that goes on them) can be cost-prohibitive.

EXAM TIP

Determining the order of installation might be on the exam. It's definitely a listed exam topic and fits well with one of the ordering types of questions. The questions aren't designed to trick you, but pay special attention to the wording on any sort of question that asks you to put steps in order.

As you move content databases and web applications off SharePoint 2010, you can reuse the servers on the SharePoint 2013 farm. The sequence depends on the organization's needs and the load on each web application. For example, after you move over a heavily used web application, you might decide to allocate a WFE or two to the SharePoint 2013 farm. Whenever you move a server from the SharePoint 2010 farm, you should do a fresh install of the Windows Server software to help keep any setting or DLL conflicts from occurring.

> ***MORE INFO*** **INSTALLING SHAREPOINT 2013**
>
> **See *http://technet.microsoft.com/en-us/library/cc303424.aspx* for more information on how to install SharePoint 2013.**

Thought experiment
Upgrading content databases

In the following thought experiment, apply what you've learned about this objective. You can find answers to these questions in the "Answers" section at the end of this chapter.

You have been assigned the task of upgrading the SharePoint 2010 content databases to SharePoint 2013. You have a root site collection database that's about 20 GB, one very large content database, and a dozen or so small content databases.

What process would you use to upgrade all the content databases in the shortest amount of time possible?

Objective summary

- The removal of a server from a SharePoint farm should be planned to avoid loss of services.
- Parallel upgrades can greatly speed up the process of upgrading to SharePoint 2013, depending on the type of hardware being used.
- You can make both site collections and content databases read-only so that a gradual stoppage of production use can occur.
- You need to upgrade service applications before you can upgrade content databases.
- Use the Resource Monitor to test the resource required to migrate content and diagnose any bottlenecks.
- Installation of servers needs to be planned out to provide optimal performance during the migration of content.

Objective review

Answer the following questions to test your knowledge of the information in this objective. You can find the answers to these questions and explanations of why each answer choice is correct or incorrect in the "Answers" section at the end of this chapter.

1. You can use the command-line utility Psconfig to perform which of the following functions on a SharePoint farm?
   - **A.** Unprovision a SharePoint Central Administration web application
   - **B.** Install features
   - **C.** Provision SharePoint product services
   - **D.** All of the above
2. When you are connecting databases to a web application for the purposes of upgrading to SharePoint 2013, in which order should you connect them using the PowerShell command Mount-SPContentDatabase?
   - **A.** Largest first, because it takes the most time to upgrade
   - **B.** The one with the root site collection first
   - **C.** Smallest first, so that the web application can be available as soon as possible
   - **D.** It doesn't matter because they can be upgraded in parallel
3. You can make an individual site collection read-only with all except which of the following?
   - **A.** Central Administration
   - **B.** The PowerShell command Set-SPSite
   - **C.** SQL Server
   - **D.** The stsadm command setsitelock
4. Which of the following can be upgraded to SharePoint 2013?
   - **A.** PowerPoint Broadcast sites
   - **B.** Web Analytics
   - **C.** User Profile service application
   - **D.** A FAST search center
5. The Resource Monitor can be used to monitor all except which of the following?
   - **A.** CPU usage
   - **B.** Time to complete a content database
   - **C.** Network latency
   - **D.** Memory usage

6. Which services can run on only one server in a SharePoint 2013 farm?
   A. User Profile Synchronization service
   B. Excel Calculation Services
   C. Central Administration
   D. Machine Translation service

Objective 3.3: Upgrade site collection

The upgrade process in SharePoint 2013 is separated into two parts: Upgrade the content database and then upgrade the site collections in the content databases. When the content database upgrade process is complete, the site collections are left in the SharePoint 2010 user experience. The separation of these two steps makes the content database upgrade process significantly faster than it was in SharePoint 2010.

This objective covers upgrading site collections to the SharePoint 2013 experience. The upgrade of site collections can be done by the farm administrator or by the site collection administrator, if the farm administrator has allowed for self-service upgrades.

This objective covers the following topics:

- Performing a health check
- Analyzing and resolving health check results
- Planning and configuring available site collection modes
- Planning and configuring site collection upgrade availability
- Planning and configuring evaluation mode
- Planning and configuring site collection upgrade queues and throttling

Performing a health check

You should run a health check to determine any issues before upgrading a site collection to the SharePoint 2013 user experience. Health checks can be done by the site collection owner. They are also automatically run in repair mode (as covered later in this objective). The pre-upgrade health check examines a site collection by using several health check rules, reports back on the issues that need to be resolved, and (in many cases) suggests how to fix them. Health checks use the following rules:

- Check for files that were customized (or unghosted) within the site collection or one of the subsites.
- Ensure that all default galleries are available.
- Validate that the template on which the site collection is based is available.

- Check for any unsupported multi-user interface (MUI) elements to ensure that they exist and are referenced correctly.
- Make sure that any language packs used by the site collection are available and referenced correctly.

Before you start using the health check process, make sure that all configurations and customizations have been performed on the SharePoint 2013 farm. Of course, the content database on which the site collection resides must be upgraded to SharePoint 2013 before any health check on the site collections can be performed. To run the pre-upgrade health check on an individual site collection, follow these steps:

1. Navigate to the Site Settings page of the site collection to be analyzed with an account that's a site collection administrator.
2. In the Site Collection Administration section, click Site Collection Health Checks.
3. Click Start Checks on the Run Site Collection Health Checks page.

When you run the health check, you should see a list of the items that were checked and any issues that need to be fixed. The health check can be run repeatedly so that you can be sure the site collection is ready to be upgraded to the SharePoint 2013 experience.

EXAM TIP

Running the pre-upgrade health check on the site collections to be upgraded to the SharePoint 2013 experience is an important step in the upgrade process. You can expect to see this step on the exam.

You can also perform the pre-upgrade health check by using PowerShell. The health check can be run in two modes: test mode and repair mode. If you want to run in test mode, the account running the PowerShell command must have the securityadmin server role on the SQL Server database and the db_owner role on the content databases that are being analyzed. The account must also be a site collection administrator or be given the full read permission. The following PowerShell command performs the health check in test mode:

```
Test-SPSite -Identity <SiteURL> [-Rule <RuleID>]
```

The RuleID is available if you want to run the command for just an individual rule. If the Rule parameter isn't specified, all the rules are applied.

You can also run the pre-upgrade health check in repair mode. The account running the health check in repair mode must also have the same rights as running the health check in test mode except that it needs to be a site collection administrator or have full control over the site collection being analyzed. The syntax for the PowerShell command to run the health check in repair mode is as follows:

```
Repair-SPSite -Identity <SiteURL> [-Rule <RuleID>]
```

If it can, repair mode tries to repair the issues that it finds (such as unghosting a file and setting it to the default). When a site has all its issues resolved, it can be upgraded to an evaluation site or directly to the SharePoint 2013 user experience.

> ***MORE INFO*** **RUNNING SITE COLLECTION HEALTH CHECKS**
>
> **See *http://technet.microsoft.com/en-us/library/jj219720(v=office.15)* for more information on how to run site collection health checks in SharePoint 2013.**

Analyzing and resolving health check results

The pre-upgrade provides information on the issues that it found that will affect the upgrade as well as a way to correct them in some cases. Running the health checks in the site settings of the site collection by clicking Start Checks displays the lists of issues it found, grouped by the rule that found it. For some of the items, you are given an option to fix it. For instance, in the Customized Files section of the report, you could see a line such as the following:

```
http://contoso/search/Pages/default.aspx - Reset page to default
```

Reset Page To Default is a link that can be used to ghost the file (set it to default). Simply clicking that link takes you to the Reset To Site Definition page (see Figure 3-3), where you are given the option of resetting that one page or resetting all the pages in the site to the site definition version.

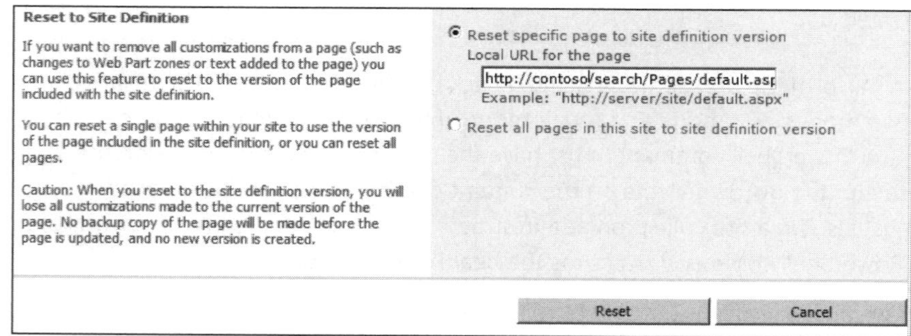
Reset to Site Definition
If you want to remove all customizations from a page (such as changes to Web Part zones or text added to the page) you can use this feature to reset to the version of the page included with the site definition.
You can reset a single page within your site to use the version of the page included in the site definition, or you can reset all pages.
Caution: When you reset to the site definition version, you will lose all customizations made to the current version of the page. No backup copy of the page will be made before the page is updated, and no new version is created.
Reset specific page to site definition version
Local URL for the page
http://contoso/search/Pages/default.asp
Example: "http://server/site/default.aspx"
Reset all pages in this site to site definition version
Reset
Cancel

FIGURE 3-3 Reset To Site Definition section

Choosing the Reset All Pages In This Site To Site Definition Version option causes you to lose all the customizations, and you can't get them back unless you retrieve them from the original SharePoint 2010 site.

EXAM TIP

Be aware of the issues concerning upgrading to the SharePoint 2013 user experience and resolving them. Resetting all pages to site definition is automatic if the Repair-SPSite PowerShell command is used.

A customized page isn't a serious issue because it affects only that one page. The look and feel of the page might be affected depending on the level of branding and customization, but it won't stop the upgrade. However, you might discover some other issues that can cause your site collection not to function. One issue that the health checker looks for is conflicting content types. SharePoint 2013 has many new content types that might conflict with ones that were created in your SharePoint 2010 sites. A typical example of this would be the Video content type, which is used in SharePoint 2013 for better multimedia support but is also one that many organizations might have created. Having two content types with the same name would cause issues. This type of issue could even affect the site's functionality. To rename the existing site content type, follow these steps:

1. Navigate to Site Settings of the site that contains the content type to be renamed.
2. Click Site Content Types in the Web Designer Galleries group.
3. Click the name of the content type to be renamed on the Site Content Types page.
4. Change the name of the content type in the Name text box.
5. Click OK to save changes.

In the health check report, you can click Tell Me More to get additional information that can help to resolve these issues. Whenever you make changes that affect the health check issues, you should rerun the health check to verify that you've solved all your issues.

If you have a missing gallery (such as site columns that could have been corrupted or accidentally deleted), SharePoint 2013 attempts to rebuild it for you when you do the health check. If an error occurs, you might have to delete it and try to rerun the health check to get it repaired. Any custom data in the gallery could potentially be lost. This data can be recovered from the SharePoint 2010 site collection, assuming that it's still available (and not corrupted or deleted).

One rule run by the health checker makes sure that all the content types have parents. If content type is found to be orphaned, you need to do one of the following:

- Delete the orphaned content type
- Associate the content type with another parent
- Re-create the missing parent and then reattach the orphan

Modifying content types can be done on the Site Settings page by clicking Site Content Types in the Galleries section. Orphans could be the result of accidentally deleting a parent site content type, or perhaps of adding and removing a solution that relied on content types, but the solution not removing cleanly.

The absence of a site template can cause the upgrade to the SharePoint 2013 experience to fail. This might occur for a couple of reasons:

- The site template has been accidentally deleted (you can delete the site template after the site is created without affecting the site itself).

- The site template might not be available for the language in which the site was created.

In any case, the absence of a site template needs to be resolved before upgrading to the SharePoint 2013 experience. If for some reason the site template isn't available, the site needs to be re-created using an available site template. This issue might require the importation and export of data (lists and document libraries) to succeed.

Missing language packs are another issue that must be resolved before a site collection can be upgraded to the SharePoint 2013 user experience. The pre-upgrade site collection health check shows which language packs aren't available and which must be installed. If the language pack you need isn't available for some reason, you can't upgrade until it is available. (Most, if not all, language packs should be available on the Microsoft download site.)

The last health check rule that's run by the health check tests for unsupported MUI references. The MUI allows for user interface items such as the ribbon, navigation bars, and column headings to appear in the default language of the user's browser. These issues will probably be similar to those found in the missing language pack rule, but the MUI check might cause additional issues to surface. You won't be prevented from upgrading to the SharePoint 2013 if issues are found, but the functionality of being able to use multiple languages will be affected until the language pack is found and installed.

Planning and configuring available site collection modes

By default, site collection administrators are allowed to upgrade their site collections to the SharePoint 2013 experience whenever they want. This might or might not be what your organization wants. Some site collections will need extensive testing before they are upgraded, and the decision of when to upgrade the site collection shouldn't fall within the site collection administrator's realm. Sites that might fall under this group might include the following:

- **Heavily customized sites** These sites are prime candidates for not allowing site collection administrators permission to upgrade. A site should go through thorough testing before it's upgraded.
- **Critical sites** These sites are critical for day-to-day business needs and can't endure any sort of downtime during production hours without disrupting the organization's function.
- **Very large sites** For these sites, the upgrade process could put undue strain on the SharePoint farm, causing it to be sluggish (or even non-responsive) during production hours.

Identification of sites that need to be upgraded by the farm administrator should be identified early (before the content database upgrade) to ensure that a site collection isn't accidentally upgraded to the SharePoint 2013 experience.

When a site collection is available for upgrade, a banner appears at the top of the site collection, indicating that it's available for upgrade but hasn't been upgraded (see Figure 3-4).

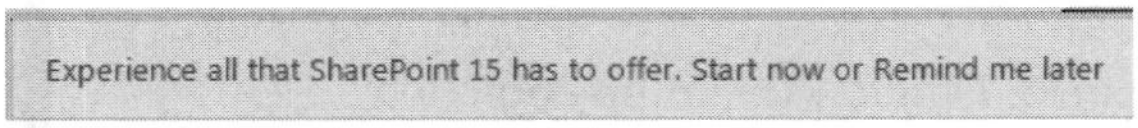

Experience all that SharePoint 15 has to offer. Start now or Remind me later

FIGURE 3-4 Upgrade option banner on pre-upgraded site collections

The reminder delay and the maintenance link can both be modified using PowerShell commands. Your organization's needs determine the amount of time and the link to be used and can vary as much as you want. The modifications are at the web application level and are modified by using the following PowerShell commands:

```
$webApp=Get-SPWebApplication <Web App URL>
$webApp.UpgradeReminderDelay <Value in Days>
$webApp.UpgradeMaintenanceLink='<Link to Maintenance Page>'
```

The reminder delay is in number of days as indicated in the code. That is the only option available; no option exists for a particular site collection. Remember that only site collection administrators can see the reminder.

Farm administrators can determine the site creation mode for an application as well. The options are to be able to create site collection in 2010 mode, 2013 mode, or allow the site collection administrator to be able to choose either one. The choice depends on your business needs and the schedule of migration to the SharePoint 2013 user experience. You can determine which versions of the SharePoint experience are supported for a web application by using the following PowerShell command:

```
$webApp=Get-SPWebApplication <Web App URL>
$webApp.CompatibilityRange
```

You are returned a minimum and a maximum compatibility range as well as the default compatibility level. The SharePoint 2010 experience is compatibility level 14, and the SharePoint 2013 experience is compatibility level 15. Those are your only two choices in SharePoint 2013. If you want to modify the range for a web application, you can do this with PowerShell by specifying a range (RangeName) for a web application. The available RangeName options are as follows:

- OldVersions
- NewVersion
- AllVersions

You can use the following PowerShell commands to limit a web application to either the SharePoint 2010 experience or the SharePoint 2013 experience:

```
$webApp=Get-SPWebApplication <Web App URL>
$webApp.CompatibilityRange=[Microsoft.SharePoint.SPCompatibilityRange]::<Range Name>
$webApp.Update()
```

This way, you can limit web applications to just having one of the SharePoint experiences available or switch back to allowing for both SharePoint options available. Going forward, limiting it to just the SharePoint 2013 user experience is probably wise so that the next upgrade will be smoother. Of course, knowing the future is impossible, but keeping your sites as current as possible is always a good idea when looking toward future upgrades.

> ***MORE INFO*** **MANAGING SITE COLLECTION UPGRADES**
>
> **See *http://technet.microsoft.com/en-us/library/jj219599.aspx* for more information on how to manage site collection upgrades to SharePoint 2103.**

Planning and configuring site collection upgrade availability

Part of the planning process for upgrading to the SharePoint 2013 experience involves determining which sites will allow site collection administrators to do self-service upgrades and which sites won't. By default, self-service version-to-version upgrades are available to site collection administrators, as long as the throttle limits for content haven't been exceeded. You should use PowerShell to control the self-service ability on site collections if you want to keep site collection administrators from upgrading their site collections themselves. The following PowerShell commands can be used to disable self-service upgrade on an individual site collection:

```
$site=Get-SPSite <URL>
$site.AllowSelfServiceUpgrade=$FALSE
```

If this command is run, the site collection in the <URL> parameter will require that the upgrade to the SharePoint 2013 experience be done by the farm administrator. If you want to turn self-service upgrades back on, just replace $FALSE with $TRUE in the preceding command.

If you have many site collections to disable (or enable) for an entire web application, doing so manually would take a long time. You can use piping to enable or disable self-service site collection upgrades via a single PowerShell command. The syntax for disabling an entire collection is as follows:

```
Get-SPWebApplication "<Web App URL>" | Get-SPSite -Limit ALL | ForEach-Object{ $_.AllowS
elfServiceUpgrade=$FALSE}
```

The command might take a while, depending on the number of site collections contained within the web application. This command also covers all content databases used by the web application. Depending on your business needs, you might want to turn off all site collections and then turn back on just the ones that you want users to be able to self-service. In any case, this command allows bulk control of version-to-version self-service upgrades.

Generally, you should plan an upgrade to the SharePoint 2013 experience in stages. The default is for everything to be turned on so that site collection administrators can use self-service upgrade. This causes a lot of confusion if end users haven't had any training, because they will encounter both the SharePoint 2010 and the SharePoint 2013 experiences. This means they will have two different user interfaces to deal with because it's highly unlikely that all the site collection administrators will decide to upgrade at the same time.

> ***IMPORTANT*** **TURNING OFF SELF-SERVICE UPGRADE**
>
> **The act of upgrading a content database to SharePoint 2013 makes it writeable. Therefore, you should turn off the self-service upgrade ability before allowing site collection administrators access if you want to control when the upgrade occurs.**

Planning and configuring evaluation mode

If you have any questions about how your site collection will look in the SharePoint 2013 experience, you should use an evaluation site first. An evaluation site provides a preview of how a site collection will look after it's upgraded to the SharePoint 2013 experience. Site collection administrators and farm administrators can request an evaluation site.

Requesting an evaluation site for each site collection will end up being quite tedious for most farms, but representative site collections can be evaluated to determine how other sites will look and perform when they are upgraded. An evaluation site leaves the site to be upgraded alone so that you're in no danger of losing functionality.

An evaluation site is set to expire (and be deleted) after a certain amount of time; the default is 30 days. You can change this value depending on your organization's needs. An evaluation site is also be deleted when the site collection it's based on is upgraded to the SharePoint 2013 experience.

> ***IMPORTANT*** **Data that's modified and/or created in the evaluation site isn't replicated back to the production site collection. This is also true for the other direction: Data modified in the production site collection isn't replicated to the evaluation site collection.**

Evaluation sites are created by using a snapshot or by using backup and restore, depending on the SQL Server version used by the SharePoint farm. The SQL Server snapshot option is available for SharePoint installations that use either the Microsoft SQL Server Enterprise edition or Microsoft SQL Server Datacenter edition. If another version is used, the backup and restore APIs are used. The main difference is that SQL Server snapshots don't require an outage, but the backup and restore APIs require that the site collection be made read-only during the backup process, keeping users from writing to the database during the backup process. Users are notified of the read-only status through System Status Notifications.

The creation of evaluation sites can be a resource-intensive process, using up valuable SQL Server disk space as well as CPU and memory resources. By using PowerShell, farm administrators can determine whether site collection administrators can request an evaluation site collection. This is done at the site collection level via the SPSite object. You can use the following PowerShell syntax to disable the ability to request an evaluation site collection:

```
$site=Get-SPSite <URL of site collection>
$site.AllowSelfServiceUpgradeEvaluation=$FALSE
```

> ***MORE INFO*** **USING THE ALLOWSELFSERVICEUPGRADEEVALUATION PROPERTY**
>
> See *http://msdn.microsoft.com/en-us/library/microsoft.sharepoint.client.site.allowselfserviceupgradeevaluation.aspx* for more information on the AllowSelfServiceUpgradeEvaluation property.

If a site collection can have an evaluation site, its site collection administrator can request an evaluation site by following these steps:

1. Navigate to the Site Settings page as a site collection administrator.
2. Click Site Collection Upgrade in the Site Collection Administration section.
3. On the Step Up To SharePoint 2013 page, click the Try A Demo Upgrade link.
4. Click Create Upgrade Evaluation Site Collection in the Create Upgrade Evaluation Site Collection section.
5. Click Close.

The evaluation site collection is put into a queue, and the site collection administrator is emailed when the evaluation site is available. The request is added to the timer job Create Upgrade Evaluation Site Collection, which is run once daily (between 1 AM and 1:30 AM locally, by default). This means that up to 24 hours can pass before the evaluation site collection is available. One Create Upgrade Evaluation Site Collection timer job is created per web application, so if you want to change the timer job to create a more responsive experience, you need to modify all the timer jobs for each application. The changes required depend on your business needs and can vary per web application.

Farm administrators can request evaluation site collections by using the PowerShell Request-SPUpgradeEvaluationSiteCollection command. The account requesting the evaluation site collection needs the following permissions:

- The db_owner role on the content database in which the evaluation site collection is being created
- The securityadmin fixed server role on the SQL Server instance that contains the content database where the evaluation site collection is being created
- Membership in the Administrators group on the server on which the PowerShell command is being run
- Site collection administrator permissions or full control of the site collection

The syntax for the PowerShell command to request an evaluation site collection is as follows, where the URL of the site collection refers to SharePoint 2010 site collection that you want to evaluate:

```
Request-SPUpgradeEvaluationSiteCollection -Identity <URL of site collection>
```

EXAM TIP

Creating an evaluation site is much different from the Visual Upgrade process that was part of the SharePoint 2010 upgrade. The changes made in the evaluation site aren't reflected in the production site. You can expect to be quizzed on some aspect of the creation of an evaluation site on the exam.

Planning and configuring site collection upgrade queues and throttling

Giving site collection administrators the ability to upgrade site collections to the SharePoint 2013 user experience can take a large load off farm administrators by allowing site collection administrators to determine when a site collection is ready to be upgraded. When the site upgrade process is initiated, a job is created and placed in a queue, even if the process starts immediately. The job is removed from the queue when it is finished or has failed. If the job is stopped midstream for some reason, such as hardware failure or service unavailability, the job is restarted as soon as the timer service can start it.

Farm administrators can manage the queue. Sites can be added, removed, or manually upgraded. Each web application has its own queue, and farm administrators can view the sites in each queue for each content database associated with the web application. To manage the site collection upgrade queue, the account being used should have the following permissions:

- Membership in the Administrator group on the server where the PowerShell commands will be run
- The securityadmin fixed server role on the SQL Server instance where the content databases to be queried are located
- The db_owner role on any database to be updated

After the necessary permissions are validated, farm administrators can use PowerShell commands to control the queue. To view all the site collections (those in progress, those completed, and those failed) in the queue for a content database, use the Get-SPSiteUpgradeSessionInfo PowerShell command:

```
Get-SPSiteUpgradeSessionInfo -ContentDatabase <Content Database Name>
                             -ShowInProgress -ShowCompleted -ShowFailed
```

MORE INFO **USING GET-SPSITEUPGRADESESSIONINFO**

See *http://technet.microsoft.com/en-us/library/fp161278.aspx* for more information on the PowerShell command Get-SPSiteUpgradeSessionInfo.

If you want to see the sites now being processed, use just the ShowInProgress parameter and leave off the others. To see whether a site collection is now in the queue, use the

Get-SPSiteUpgradeSessionInfo command by passing it the URL of the site to be queried, as follows:

```
Get-SPSiteUpgradeSessionInfo -Site <URL of site>
```

You can add site collections to the queue manually by using the PowerShell command Upgrade-SPSite. You might want to do this for several reasons. For example, if you've turned off self-service upgrades, you need to add the site collections to the queue manually. If you have a site that you want to upgrade but the throttle limit has been exceeded, you can override the throttle with the command and allow for the site collection to be upgraded sooner that it would be otherwise.

Be aware of a couple of considerations when using Upgrade-SPSite:

- By default, Upgrade-SPSite performs build-to-build upgrades, so the VersionUpgrade parameter must be specified to get it to do a version-to-version upgrade.
- When a version-to-version upgrade is done with Upgrade-SPSite, the site collection health checks are run automatically in repair mode.

The syntax for adding a site collection to the upgrade queue using the PowerShell command Upgrade-SPSite is as follows:

```
Upgrade-SPSite <URL of site> -VersionUpgrade -QueueOnly
```

The absence of the QueueOnly parameter causes the upgrade process to start immediately. If you want to put all the site collections for a web application into the upgrade queue, you can use the piping feature of PowerShell.

> ***MORE INFO*** **USING UPGRADE-SPSITE**
>
> **See *http://technet.microsoft.com/en-us/library/fp161257* for more information on the PowerShell command Upgrade-SPSite.**

After a site collection is moved to the queue, it can be removed with the following PowerShell command:

```
Remove-SPSiteUpgradeSessionInfo -Identity <URL of site>
```

You might want to use this command if you've added a lot of site collection upgrades by using piping but want to remove a few site collections from the list, such as ones that might have lots of customization and need more testing or will take a very long time to upgrade. Doing so might save a lot of typing time. If you use this method, put it all in a script so that it can be run all at the same time.

> ***MORE INFO*** **USING REMOVE-SPSITEUPGRADESESSIONINFO**
>
> **See *http://technet.microsoft.com/en-us/library/fp161276.aspx* for more information on the PowerShell command Remove-SPSiteUpgradeSessionInfo.**

The process of upgrading site collections to the SharePoint 2013 experience can consume significant server resources, such as disk space, CPU, and memory. To minimize the impact that upgrading can have, farm administrators can throttle the number of site collections that can be in the upgrade queue at any specific time by upgrading the site collection manually; farm administrators can also override this manually by starting an upgrade with the Unthrottled parameter.

Farm administrators can use PowerShell to view the throttle settings of a web application. The SiteUpgradeThrottleSettings property of the SPSite object returns the throttle values of the site:

```
$webApp=Get-SPWebApplication <web app URL>
$webApp.SiteUpgradeThrottleSettings
```

The results from running these PowerShell commands should look similar to the following results:

```
AppPoolConcurrentUpgradeSessionLimit : 5
UsageStorageLimit                    : 10
SubwebCountLimit                     : 10
Name                                 :
TypeName                             : Microsoft.SharePoint.Administration.
                                       SPSiteUpgradeThrottleSettings
DisplayName                          :
Id                                   : a3097994-1acb-4947-9979-7889d6305e1d
Status                               : Online
Parent                               : SPWebApplication Name=SharePoint - 80
Version                              : 722459
Properties                           : {}
Farm                                 : SPFarm Name=SharePoint_Config
UpgradedPersistedProperties          : {}
```

A lot of data is listed here, and what's being throttled isn't readily apparent because throttles are built in at the web application, content database, and content levels. The following list shows the items and their default values:

- **Web Application level** The default is five concurrent site collection upgrades per web application instance (per web server).
- **Content Database level** The default is ten concurrent site collection upgrades per content database.
- **Content level** If a site collection has more than 10 MB of content or more than ten subsites, the default is that the site collection can't be upgraded via self-service.

That three different throttle options are available can provide for tricky scenarios because the most restrictive throttle will win out. For example, if you have one web application, one WFE, and one content database, you could process only five concurrent version-to-version upgrades at one time, assuming that they were all under the content-level throttle threshold. Most site collections will exceed the content throttle threshold because 10 MB is a very low limit for a site collection, and ten subsites is also a low limit for most production site collections (except for personal sites).

EXAM TIP

That you can throttle version-to-version upgrades in three different areas lends itself to some interesting test questions. You need to have a good grasp on what can be throttled and how changing the throttle of one area affects the other areas.

Throttle settings can be set in two areas: in the web application and in the content database.

The first area is the web application, where you can set the limits for concurrent session, storage, and subsites by modifying the property values of the SPSite object. The properties related to throttling are as follows:

- **AppPoolConcurrentUpgradeSessionLimit** The maximum number of concurrent upgrade sessions allowed in the app pool
- **SubwebCountLimit** The maximum number of subsites allowed in a site collection allowed for self-service upgrades
- **UsageStorageLimit** The maximum amount (in megabytes) allowed for a site collection to be upgraded with self-service

You can use PowerShell to change these limits, but keep in mind that version-to-version upgrades can consume considerable resources. SharePoint might even become non-responsive if the load becomes too heavy. The syntax for changing the properties is shown in the following PowerShell script, where <*value*> is an integer:

```
$webApp=Get-SPWebApplication -URL <URL of web application>
$webApp.SiteUpgradeThrottleSettings.AppPoolConcurrentUpgradeSessionLimit=<value>
$webApp.SiteUpgradeThrottleSettings.SubwebCountLimit=<value>
$webApp.SiteUpgradeThrottleSettings.SubwebCountLimit=<value>
$webApp.Update()
```

If site collection administrators exceed the throttle settings for the AppPoolConcurrentUpgradeSessionLimit, the version-to-version upgrades are placed in the queue and processed when a spot becomes available. If the SubwebCountLimit or UsageStorageLimit is exceeded, a farm administrator must perform the upgrade via PowerShell; otherwise, the throttle limits must be changed. Content-level throttles prohibit self-service upgrades, and only a farm administrator can upgrade the site collections that exceed the throttle limits.

MORE INFO **UNDERSTANDING SPSSITEUPGRADETHROTTLESETTINGS PROPERTIES**

See *http://msdn.microsoft.com/en-us/library/microsoft.sharepoint.administration.spsiteupgradethrottlesettings_properties.aspx* for more information on SPSiteUpgradeThrottleSettings properties.

The second area where throttling can occur is with the content database. Each content database can have its own throttle rule that works with the web application throttle limits. If a content database has a lot of site collections or if you want to minimize the effects of upgrades, you should consider modifying the throttle from the default of 10. The appropriate throttle limit is best determined by performing thorough throttle testing in a test environment that's close to the production environment.

You can view the throttle settings for a content database by using PowerShell commands. The permissions required for the account used for viewing or modifying the throttle limits are as follows:

- Needs to have the securityadmin fixed database role on the SQL Server instance where the content database resides
- Needs to have the db_owner fixed database role on the content database if it is to be modified
- Needs to be part of the Administrators group on the server where the PowerShell commands are to be run

The number of concurrent sites that can be upgraded is shown by the ConcurrentSiteUpgradeSessionLimit of the SPContentDatabase object. The syntax for the script is as follows:

```
$db=Get-SPContentDatabase <Database Name>
$db.ConcurrentSiteUpgradeSessionLimit
```

PowerShell commands can also be used to modify the throttle settings. The syntax is similar to the following:

```
$db=Get-SPContentDatabase <Database Name>
$db.ConcurrentSiteUpgradeSessionLimit=<value>
```

Content databases, such as the ones that store personal sites, can have thousands of site collections. These content databases should be considered for throttling. Typically, site collections are upgraded in bulk because most users find out at about the same time. The special case of personal sites (SkyDrive Pro locations in SharePoint 2013) is that each individual in the organization is a site collection administrator. Either these users need some training, or the site collections need the version-to-version upgrade performed for them. If you plan to allow self-service upgrades on personal site collections, you want to look at the throttle values on both the content databases and the web applications to make sure that the upgrades don't affect the overall performance of the SharePoint farm.

MORE INFO **USING SPCONTENTDATABASE.CONNCURRENTSITEUPGRADESESSIONLIMIT**

See *http://msdn.microsoft.com/en-us/library/microsoft.sharepoint.administration.spcontentdatabase.concurrentsiteupgradesessionlimit(v=office.15).aspx* for more information on the ConcurrentSiteUpgradeSessionLimit property of SPContentDatabase.

Thought experiment

Upgrading personal site collections

In the following thought experiment, apply what you've learned about this objective. You can find answers to these questions in the "Answers" section at the end of this chapter.

You work for an organization that has several thousand employees, and each employee has a personal site collection. All these site collections are located in one large content database. Each personal content site can have up to 250 MB of content. Also, the farm has four WFEs that can be used to access the personal sites. Through your testing, you've determined that the farm can handle 20 version-to-version upgrades to the SharePoint 2013 experience concurrently.

What changes do you need to make on the farm to enable users to perform self-service upgrades to the SharePoint 2013 experience and for up to 20 concurrent upgrades be processed at the same time?

Objective summary

- The pre-upgrade check helps you identify (and in some cases resolve) issues before upgrading to the SharePoint 2013 experience.
- Determine early which site collections you will allow site collection administrators the ability to have self-service upgrades to the SharePoint 2013 experience.
- Self-service upgrades can be turned on or off in bulk at the web application level by using PowerShell commands.
- Evaluation sites can help determine the look and feel of a site collection before it's upgraded to the SharePoint 2013 experience.
- Evaluation sites are copies of the production data, and changes in either site aren't reflected in the other.
- Farm administrators can determine whether self-service upgrades should be made available to site collection administrators.
- Site collection version-to-version upgrades are throttled by default, but throttle settings can be modified as needed.

Objective review

Answer the following questions to test your knowledge of the information in this objective. You can find the answers to these questions and explanations of why each answer choice is correct or incorrect in the "Answers" section at the end of this chapter.

1. The PowerShell command Test-SPSite can be used to do which of the following functions?
   - **A.** Test a site collection for possible upgrade issues.
   - **B.** Test a site collection for possible upgrade issues and fix the issues if found.
   - **C.** Test an individual subsite for possible upgrade issues.
   - **D.** All of the above
2. By using the pre-upgrade health check on a site collection, you have discovered that you have a content type with the same name. What should you do to resolve this issue?
   - **A.** Delete the pre-existing content type.
   - **B.** Rename the pre-existing content type.
   - **C.** Upgrade to the SharePoint 2013 user experience and then delete the newer content type.
   - **D.** Nothing additional is required. SharePoint 2013 will fix it for you.
3. By default, SharePoint 2013 allows you to create what kind of site collections within an upgraded content database?
   - **A.** Only SharePoint 2013 experience site collections.
   - **B.** Only SharePoint 2010 experience site collections, until all site collections are upgraded to the SharePoint 2013 experience.
   - **C.** Both SharePoint 2013 and SharePoint 2010 experience site collections can be created.
   - **D.** No site collections can be created in an upgraded site collection.
4. You've just finished attaching the backup of a SharePoint 2010 content database to a SharePoint 2013 web application and verified that it functions on the new farm and that the health checks are clean. You now want to upgrade to the SharePoint 2013 experience using PowerShell. Which command-line syntax can you use for your site collection *http://contoso*?
   - **A.** Upgrade-SPSite http://contoso.
   - **B.** Upgrade-SPSite http://contoso -VersionUpgrade.
   - **C.** Upgrade-SPSite http://contoso -VersionUpgrade -QueueOnly.
   - **D.** Nothing is needed. When the health check runs clean, it will automatically upgrade to the SharePoint 2013 experience.

5. You have a web application with 20 site collections that are all contained in one content database that needs to be upgraded to the SharePoint 2013 experience. Three WFEs are available, and the default throttle limits are in place. How many site collections can be upgraded at the same time without overriding the throttle limits (and so that the site collections don't exceed the content throttle limits)?
   - **A.** 20
   - **B.** 15
   - **C.** 5
   - **D.** 10
6. As a site collection administrator, you've requested an evaluation site collection. When can you expect the evaluation site to be available (as long as the default settings are in place)?
   - **A.** Within 24 hours
   - **B.** Within an hour
   - **C.** Within 5 minutes, plus the time it takes to process
   - **D.** Immediately

Chapter summary

- The default authentication method for SharePoint 2013 web applications is claims.
- Upgrading from SharePoint 2010 to SharePoint 2013 is a two-step process. No in-place upgrade is supported.
- The first step in the upgrade process should be cleaning up and cataloging your existing SharePoint farm.
- Service applications should be upgraded before moving over to content databases.
- A health check is used to determine whether site collections are ready to be upgraded to SharePoint 2013 mode.
- SharePoint 2013 supports both SharePoint 2010 mode and SharePoint 2013 mode site collections.
- Evaluation sites are temporary and content isn't kept in sync with production sites.

Answers

This section contains the solutions to the thought experiments and answers to the lesson review questions in this chapter.

Objective 3.1: Thought experiment

In this thought experiment, you were told to decide how to proceed with upgrading to a SharePoint 2013 claims-based authentication web application from a SharePoint 2010 classic-mode authentication web application. You have a couple of options here:

- You could convert the SharePoint 2010 web application to a claims-based authentication web application. This would allow you to solve any issues that came up with that process (such as Search not working) while still in an environment that you are familiar with and while avoiding the compounding of the issues with those involved with the upgrade process. The downside of this process is that the conversion is a one-way process; if it fails and you are working on a production environment, the environment could be down for quite a while until the issues are resolved.
- You could migrate the web application to a claims-based SharePoint 2013 web application and then do the conversion on the migrated content databases (converting to claims and upgrading simultaneously). The benefit of this process is that the conversion can take place on a SharePoint server that's probably not in production, and it might provide enough time to deal with any conversion issues as well as any upgrade issues. The drawback is that it might prove more difficult with the combined issues (assuming that some exist) and, as with the first solution, the conversion to claims is a one-way process. Best practices indicate that you should migrate to claims while still in the SharePoint 2010 environment.

If for some reason you still want to stick with classic-mode authentication, you can create a classic-mode authentication web application using the SharePoint 2013 Management Shell.

Objective 3.1: Review

1. **Correct answer:** B
   - **A. Incorrect:** 200 is the limit for number of content databases in a single SharePoint 2013 farm.
   - **B. Correct:** 5,000 is the recommend limit for the number of site collections in a single content database.
   - **C. Incorrect:** Although up to 10,000 site collections per content database is supported, it's beyond the recommend limit of 5,000.
   - **D. Incorrect:** A million is way off. However, up to 60 million items (documents and list items) are supported per content database.

2. **Correct answer:** D

   A. **Incorrect:** This valid path for upgrading allows for troubleshooting any issues with claims-based authentication before the upgrade, but it's just one of the valid methods.

   B. **Incorrect:** This supported method is just one of the valid methods.

   C. **Incorrect:** This is just one of the valid methods and should be used only if you have a strong reason to keep the web application in classic mode.

   D. **Correct:** All three of these methods are valid.

3. **Correct answer:** C

   A. **Incorrect:** Deletecorruption is a parameter used with the stsadm command data-baserepair.

   B. **Incorrect:** Test-SPContentDatabase can help you determine issues with content databases, but it's not used to remove orphaned objects.

   C. **Correct:** Repair is the method of a content database object used to remove or-phaned objects using the SharePoint 2010 Management Shell.

   D. **Incorrect:** Upgrade-SPContentDatabase doesn't remove orphaned objects. It can detect them, however, but is used only to resume a failed upgrade or begin a build-to-build upgrade.

4. **Correct answer:** A

   A. **Correct:** Windiff compares only ASCII files such as XML, text, ASPX, INI, CSS, HTML. and other similar type files.

   B. **Incorrect:** Binaries aren't compared by Windiff, but other programs such as comp and third-party products can do so.

   C. **Incorrect:** DLLs are binaries and therefore not handled by Windiff.

   D. **Incorrect:** EXEs are binaries and therefore not handled by Windiff.

5. **Correct answer:** D

   A. **Incorrect:** The SharePoint Diagnostic Studio is part of the administrator's toolkit, but so are the rest of the options.

   B. **Incorrect:** The User Profile Replication Engine, which allows the copying of User Profile Information from one SharePoint farm to another, is part of the toolkit, but so are all the other options.

   C. **Incorrect:** The Load Testing Toolkit, which can be used for SharePoint 2010 as well as SharePoint 2013, is part of the toolkit, but so are the other options.

   D. **Correct:** All the preceding options are part of the SharePoint Administrator's 2010 Toolkit.

6. **Correct answer:** B

   A. **Incorrect:** When you install a feature on a SharePoint 2013 farm, it defaults to the max version level. This can be SharePoint 2013 or SharePoint 2010. If you install it only once, it will be available only for the max version level.

   B. **Correct:** The feature needs to be installed once for the max version level and once for the other version. The CompatibilityLevel parameter is used (14 for SharePoint 2010 and 15 for SharePoint 2013) to force the install into the version necessary.

   C. **Incorrect:** Features aren't upgraded by SharePoint 2013. They have to be upgraded using Visual Studio or another tool.

   D. **Incorrect:** Features can generally be used in SharePoint 2010 or SharePoint 2013; however, some will have to be rewritten to be compatible with SharePoint 2013. Features are not incompatible by default.

Objective 3.2: Thought experiment

In this thought experiment, you were assigned the task of doing an upgrade on several content databases in the shortest amount of time possible. The first step would be to upgrade the content database that contains the root site collection. Second, upgrade the large content database and wait for that process to complete. Third, upgrade the rest of the content databases in parallel. Because they are smaller content databases, they should upgrade in parallel without issue.

Objective 3.2: Review

1. **Correct answer:** D

   A. **Incorrect:** You can unprovision a SharePoint Central Administration web application with the command psconfig.exe -cmd adminvs –unprovision, but it is just one of the right answers.

   B. **Incorrect:** Features can be installed by using the command psconfig.exe -cmd install features, which registers any SharePoint Products and Technologies features located on the file system, but this is just one of the right answers.

   C. **Incorrect:** Psconfig can be used to provision services on standalone installations (but not farm installations). This is just one of the right answers.

   D. **Correct:** All the preceding answers are correct, although C is a bit tricky in that it applies only to standalone installations, which aren't covered on this exam.

2. **Correct answer:** B

   A. **Incorrect:** Connecting the largest database first can minimize the total amount of time, but not necessarily, and if it doesn't contain the root site collection, it could fail.

   B. **Correct:** The content database that contains the root site collection should first be connected with the command Mount-SPContentDatabase so that other site collections can be connected to the root.

   C. **Incorrect:** The root site collection must be available before any of the other site collections can be accessed.

   D. **Incorrect:** Because B is the correct answer, D can't be correct.

3. **Correct answer:** C

   A. **Incorrect:** You can use Central Administration to set an individual site collection to read-only in the Quotas and Locks section.

   B. **Incorrect:** You can use the PowerShell command Set-SPSite to set a site collection to read-only, using the -LockState "ReadOnly" parameter.

   C. **Correct:** SQL Server can't be used to set an individual site collection as read-only. It can be used only to set an entire content database as read-only.

   D. **Incorrect:** The stsadm command setsitelock can still be used, even though it is deprecated.

4. **Correct answer:** C

   A. **Incorrect:** PowerPoint Broadcast sites aren't upgradable to SharePoint 2013 because Office Web Applications is no longer an integrated application.

   B. **Incorrect:** Web Analytics uses a different architecture in SharePoint 2013 and therefore can't be upgraded. In fact, it should be turned off before any content databases are backed up for migration.

   C. **Correct:** The User Profile Service application is one of the service applications that can be upgraded.

   D. **Incorrect:** The FAST Search center can't be upgraded. FAST is no longer a separate product in SharePoint 2013.

5. **Correct answer:** B

   A. **Incorrect:** You can use the Resource Monitor to monitor CPU usage.

   B. **Correct:** The amount of time that it takes to complete a content database upgrade needs to be measured manually or with some other program.

   C. **Incorrect:** You can use the Resource monitor to monitor network latency.

   D. **Incorrect:** You can use the Resource Monitor to monitor memory usage.

6. **Correct answer:** A

   A. **Correct:** Only one server can be running the User Profile Synchronization service per farm.

   B. **Incorrect:** The Excel Calculation service can be run on any and/or every server in the SharePoint farm.

   C. **Incorrect:** The Central Administration service can be run on any server in the SharePoint farm. Although Central Administration is usually run on only one server, having it on multiple servers provides redundancy.

   D. **Incorrect:** Machine Translation service can be run on multiple servers.

Objective 3.3: Thought experiment

In this thought experiment, you were asked to determine what changes were required so that 20 concurrent version-to-version upgrades can occur on the content database where the personal sites are located. Because the farm has four WFEs, the throttle limit is 20 by default for the web application that's hosting the personal sites. Theoretically, it can support 20, assuming that the requests are spread across the four servers. You might want to increase the number of concurrent session per app pool to account for uneven distribution of self-service upgrade requests though. Two hard limits need to be changed:

- The first is the limit on the content database. The default is 10 concurrent upgrades per content database, so this value needs to be changed to 20 because all the personal sites reside on the same site collection. End users could still request that their personal site be upgraded to the SharePoint 2013 experience, but requests that couldn't be handled immediately would be put on the queue.
- The second is the content limit, which is a real concern because the default is 10 MB per site collection and the personal site collections have a limit of 250 MB. This will cause many issues because end users will get different self-service options. Those with less than 10 MB of data can upgrade their site collection to the SharePoint 2013 experience, but those with more than 10 MB can't. The throttle for content needs to be changed at the web application level to 250 MB so that each user has the same experience and can use the self-service upgrade. This is because content-level throttles prohibit self-service upgrades, whereas the other throttles just put the upgrade on the queue and don't prohibit the self-service upgrade process.

Objective 3.3: Review

1. **Correct answer:** A
   - **A. Correct:** You can use the PowerShell command Test-SPSite to test site collections for possible issues to the upgrade process.
   - **B. Incorrect:** You can't use the PowerShell command Test-SPSite to repair issues, but you can use the PowerShell command Repair-SPSite to repair some of the issues (such as setting customized sites back to their defaults).
   - **C. Incorrect:** You can't use the PowerShell command Test-SPSite to target an individual subsite. It can target only a site collection.
   - **D. Incorrect:** Because the only correct answer was A, D has to be incorrect.
2. **Correct answer:** B
   - **A. Incorrect:** Deleting the content type will cause issues if it's used by a list, library, or the parent of another content type.
   - **B. Correct:** Renaming the site content type allows you to keep the functionality of the pre-existing content type.
   - **C. Incorrect:** Trying to upgrade the site collection to the SharePoint 2013 user experience will cause an error.
   - **D. Incorrect:** This type of error needs to be resolved manually.
3. **Correct answer:** C
   - **A. Incorrect:** Unless the farm administrator has turned off the ability to create SharePoint 2010 site collections, they can still be created within an upgraded (or new) content database.
   - **B. Incorrect:** SharePoint 2013 site collections can be created in an upgraded content database unless explicitly turned off by the farm administrator.
   - **C. Correct:** Both the SharePoint 2010 user experience and the SharePoint 2013 user experience are supported in SharePoint 2013 by default.
   - **D. Incorrect:** Site collection can be created in upgraded content databases in the same way as they are in new content databases.

4. **Correct answers:** B and C

   A. **Incorrect:** By default, the Upgrade-SPSite command does a content-to-content upgrade and not a version upgrade.

   B. **Correct:** This command upgrades the site collection to the SharePoint 2013 experience because it has the VersionUpgrade parameter specified.

   C. **Correct:** This command upgrades the site collection to the SharePoint 2013 experience because it has the VersionUpgrade parameter specified. The additional parameter QueueOnly means it will go in the queue rather than be run immediately.

   D. **Incorrect:** The process of upgrading to the full SharePoint 2013 experience is a two-stage process. The upgrade is a manually started process that must be initiated either by the farm administrator or a site collection administrator.

5. **Correct answer:** D

   A. **Incorrect:** Twenty would be the answer if you had no throttling.

   B. **Incorrect:** Fifteen seems like it would work because of the three WFEs, but the amount is limited by the content database throttle of ten.

   C. **Incorrect:** Five would be the answer if you had only one WFE.

   D. **Correct:** Ten is the correct answer because the content database throttle is the limiting factor.

6. **Correct answer:** A

   A. **Correct:** Evaluation sites are generated by a timer job that runs once daily. Therefore, it can take up to 24 hours before an evaluation site gets created.

   B. **Incorrect:** An hour would only be correct if the Create Upgrade Evaluation Site Collection timer job were changed to one hour instead 24 hours.

   C. **Incorrect:** If the timer job was changed to run every five minutes, this would be correct as long as the system resources were available.

   D. **Incorrect:** Evaluation sites aren't created right away. They are created via a timer job process that runs every 24 hours by default.

CHAPTER 4

Create and configure service applications

Service applications enable SharePoint to go beyond simply providing content in a browser-based format. They extend SharePoint and provide a framework where other applications can provide services while getting the benefits of SharePoint. With service applications, SharePoint can use the power of Microsoft Office applications such as Excel, Access, and Word right in the browser.

Service applications go even farther by allowing other SharePoint farms to consume certain services from other farms, so those farms can provide dedicated services such as Search or Word document conversions. This frees up the other farms to provide other services and allows for less duplication of services as well as a potentially more secure environment. Also, service applications such as the Business Connectivity Service enable SharePoint to extend its reach into external systems, allowing for a true enterprise experience within the SharePoint environment.

Objectives in this chapter:

- Objective 4.1: Create and configure App Management
- Objective 4.2: Create and configure productivity services
- Objective 4.3: Configure Service Application Federation
- Objective 4.4: Create and configure a Business Connectivity Service and Secure Store application

Objective 4.1: Create and configure App Management

App Management is a new concept in SharePoint Server 2013. The concept of apps is pervasive throughout the environment. Rather than create a document library via a template, you now create a document library from a document library app. If you want to create a Contacts list, you do so from a Contacts app, and so on. Apps can come from your SharePoint farm as well as from external sources such as the Microsoft SharePoint and Office Store.

Farm administrators can also create and make App Catalogs available to users. Suppose that an internal user has created an app that he wants to make available to other users, or that an app has been purchased from a third party. Such apps can be made available to users through the App Catalog. As part of the exam, you will be expected to know the process of setting up and configuring the App Catalog as well as how to manage it.

This objective covers the following topics:

- Creating and configuring the App Store
- Creating and configuring subscriptions
- Configuring DNS entries
- Configuring wildcard certificates

Creating and configuring the App Store

The App Store allows users—either all or a subset—to acquire apps easily. This isn't something that happens automatically, which is good because otherwise users could put apps on your farm that you as a farm administrator would know nothing about. You need to configure the store based on your organization's needs, but before you can start the configuration process, you need to perform some steps.

First, you need to create at least one App Catalog site collection. Each web application can have its own App Catalog, so you can have as many as you have web applications; however, you need only one to start with. The App Catalog site has two special libraries that exist in the site—Apps for SharePoint and Apps for Office—so that the App Catalog can supply apps to both SharePoint and Office. The App Catalog can be created by a member of the Farm Administrator group by following these steps (assume that the App Management Service has been started):

1. Navigate to Central Administration with a farm administrator account.
2. Click Manage App Catalog in the Apps section.
3. Choose the web application where you want to create the App Catalog from the Web Application drop-down list.
4. Leave Create A New App Catalog Site selected, and then click OK on the Manage App Catalog page.
5. On the Create App Catalog page, enter a title in the Title text box and an optional description in the Description text box.
6. Choose the URL for the site (such as http://contoso/sites/apps) in the Web Site Address section.
7. Choose a site collection administrator in the Primary Site Collection Administrator section. Only one user login is allowed; security groups aren't supported.

8. In the End User section, specify who can see the App Catalog (such as NT AUTHORITY\authenticated users).

9. Select a quota template, if you want one, and then click OK to start the site collection process.

As soon as an App Catalog site collection exists, you can specify the store settings for the web application on which the App Catalog exists. These settings determine how users will interact with the store and give you a place to view app requests. Following these steps to configure these settings:

1. Navigate to Central Administration with a Farm Administrator account.

2. Click Apps.

3. Click Configure Store Settings in the SharePoint And Office Store section.

4. Choose whether users can get free or purchased apps from the SharePoint Store in the App Purchases section.

5. Don't touch the App Requests section. Items show up in the App Requests list if users aren't allowed to get apps directly from the SharePoint Store or if they prefer to request them (rather than pay for the app themselves).

6. In the Apps For Office From The Store section, choose whether end users are allowed to start Apps for Office from the store from a document.

7. Click OK to save changes.

IMPORTANT **If you create an App Catalog site collection, the SharePoint Store becomes available by default (although users can't add apps until more configuration is done). If this availability isn't intended, you might have users installing apps that you don't want on your SharePoint farm.**

The App Requests list in the App Catalog site collection can be accessed at the site or from Central Administration. It lists requests that users have put in because they want to install apps from the SharePoint Store. Users can request a single or multiple licenses as well as provide reasons for the app request. The relevant fields in the list and descriptions are as follows:

- **Title** The title of the app.
- **Publisher Name** The name of the app's publisher.
- **Icon URL** The picture associated with the app.
- **Content Market** Text describing the content market.
- **Billing Market** Text describing the billing market.
- **Seats** The number of licenses requested.
- **Site License** A yes/no field indicating whether a site license is requested.

- **Justification** User-entered justification for app.
- **Status** A choice field that's set to New for new requests. The reviewer can modify this to Approved, Closed as Approved, Closed as Declined, Declined, Pending, or Withdrawn.
- **Requested By** The person requesting the app.
- **Approved By** The person who approved the app.
- **Approver Comments** Any comments entered by the approver.

Administrators (members of the Owners or Designers groups) of the App Catalog site collection can also manually add apps to the catalog, making them available to all users who have permissions to the App Catalog. Follow these steps to add apps to the App Catalog:

1. Click the Apps for SharePoint link on the home page of the App Catalog site.
2. Click New on the on the Apps For SharePoint page.
3. Click Browse in the Choose A File section and select the app that you want to upload.
4. Click Open and then OK to upload the app.
5. Verify the details of the app (Name, Title, Short Description, and so forth) and make sure that the Enabled check box is selected.
6. If you want to make the app appear in the Featured section, select the Featured check box.
7. Click Save.

> ***MORE INFO*** **MANAGING THE APP CATALOG**
>
> **See** ***http://technet.microsoft.com/en-us/library/fp161234(v=office.15)*** **for more information on how to manage the App Catalog in SharePoint 2013.**

You should have an App Catalog at this point, but you still might not be able to add apps from the SharePoint Store. You can go out to the SharePoint Store and look at the apps that are available but can't add them to the catalog. Some steps and configurations still need to be verified, as described in the following sections.

Creating and configuring subscriptions

Apps rely on two services to run: the App Management service and the SharePoint Foundation Subscription Setting service. If you have an App Catalog site created, the App Management service should be running, but the SharePoint Foundation Subscription Setting service is off by default. You can turn it on by following these steps:

1. Navigate to Central Administration as a member of the Farm Administrators group and click Manage Services On Server in the System Settings section.

2. Choose the server on which you want the service to run from the Server drop-down list. This service needs to run on only one server for performance reasons; using two servers provides high availability.

3. Find the Microsoft SharePoint Foundation Subscription Settings Service service application in the Service list and click Start.

Because the Microsoft SharePoint Foundation Subscription Settings Service uses the multitenancy feature, even if you aren't providing hosting, you still need to provide a default tenant. You do so by establishing a name for the default tenant, and then any SharePoint site not specifically associated with another tenant will be part of the default tenant.

Setting up the Subscription Services service application needs to be done with PowerShell commands. This is a little more complicated than setting up a typical service application, so the details of how to go about this are as follows:

1. Open the SharePoint 2013 Management Shell with an account that has the securityadmin fixed server role on the SQL Server instance, the db_owner fixed database role on all databases to be updated, and a membership in the Administrators group on the server where the PowerShell commands are run.

2. Run the following command, where <*account*> is a member of the Farm Administrators group to get an account for the application pool:

   ```
   $account=Get-SPManagedAccount "<account>"
   ```

3. Run the following PowerShell command to create a new application pool (SettingsServiceAppPool is the name of the application pool):

   ```
   $appPool=New-SPServiceApplicationPool -Name SettingsServiceAppPool -Account
   $account
   ```

4. Create the service and proxy by using the following PowerShell commands, where <*ServiceDB*> is the name of the Subscription Service database that you want to create and <*ServiceName*> is the name you want to use for the service:

   ```
   $appService=New-SPSubscriptionSettingsServiceApplication -ApplicationPool
   $appPool -Name <ServiceName> -DatabaseName <ServiceDB>
   $proxyService=New-SPSubscriptionSettingsServiceApplicationProxy -
   ServiceApplication $appService
   ```

> ***IMPORTANT*** **The SettingsServiceAppPool application pool might already exist, in which case you can just use it by running Get-SPServiceApplicationPool SettingsServiceAppPool. Also, you might need to do an IISRESET after you create the proxy before you configure the app URLs.**

After you configure the Subscription Settings service, you can configure the app URLs. If you try to do this beforehand, you will get an error when you go to the Configure App URLs page. The two settings to configure on this page are App Domain and App Prefix. Specifying an app domain on this page defines a default tenant name. If you are hosting SharePoint instances and require multi-tenancy, you must use PowerShell to configure the app domains and the app prefixes. The app prefix is prepended to the subdomain of the app URLs. If you have a single tenant, you can use Central Administration to configure the app URLs:

1. Navigate to Central Administration with a Farm Administrator account and select Apps.
2. On the Apps page, click Configure App URLs in the App Management section.
3. On the Configure App URLs page, you need to set the app domain. The domain must already exist in your DNS servers. (The app domain is recommended to be just for apps, but that's not a strict requirement.)
4. Configure the App Prefix, which is prepended to the subdomain of the app URL so that the pattern becomes *<app prefix>-<app id>.<app domain>*.

Figure 4-1 shows the configured settings, using contoso.com as the app domain and App as the app prefix.

Configure App URLs

App URLs will be based on the following pattern: <app prefix> - <app id>.<app domain>

App domain

The app domain is the parent domain under which all apps will be hosted. You must already own this domain and have it configured in your DNS servers. It is recommended to use a unique domain for apps.

App domain:

contoso.com

App prefix

The app prefix will be prepended to the subdomain of the app URLs. Only letters and digits, no-hyphens or periods allowed.

App prefix:

App

FIGURE 4-1 Configure App URLs page

At this time, you (and users with permissions to add Apps) should be able to go out to the SharePoint Store and start adding apps to the App Catalog. When you first set this up, you should go out to the SharePoint Store yourself and see the host of available apps. It also gives you a sense of who in your organization should have access to the SharePoint Store.

EXAM TIP

Until you've configured the app URLs, apps aren't considered enabled. This concept can come up as a step in one of the exam questions, as could some of the other steps involved in setting up access to the SharePoint Store and/or enabling apps.

Configuring DNS entries

For security reasons, t is recommended that you use a different domain name for hosting apps from the domain name for the SharePoint farm or subdomain of the farm. This means that you need to configure a new name in Domain Name Services (DNS) before you start creating the App Catalog and configuring the service applications App Management and Microsoft SharePoint Foundation Subscription Settings. For the purposes of the exam, assume that you've purchased your domain name from a domain name provider.

EXAM TIP

As a SharePoint administrator, you might not have access to the domain controller where DNS entries are created, so you might have limited experience with DNS. If so, spend a little extra time on this section so that you can become familiar with the terminology and steps involved.

Configuring DNS is done differently, depending on the operating system that your DNS server uses. For this objective, you need to be concerned only with Microsoft products. Assuming that you are using Microsoft Windows Server, you should configure a forward lookup zone with the domain name (if you are using Windows Internet Name Service (WINS) forward lookup). To configure a forward lookup zone on a Windows Server instance, follow these steps:

1. Log onto a domain controller with an account that is part of the local administrators group.
2. In Administrative Tools, click DNS to start the DNS Manager.
3. Right-click Forward Lookup Zones and choose New Zone.
4. Click Next to get past the first page of the New Zone Wizard.
5. Accept the default of Primary Zone on the Zone Type page and click Next.
6. On the Active Directory Zone Replication Scope page, leave the default (To All DNS Servers In This Domain) and click Next.
7. On the Zone Name page, enter the domain name that you want for the apps (for example, contoso.com or contosoapps.com) and click Next.
8. On the Dynamic Update page, leave the default (Do Not Allow Updates) and click Next.
9. On the Completing The New Zone Wizard page, click Finish.

MORE INFO ADDING ZONES

See *http://technet.microsoft.com/en-us/library/cc754386.aspx* for more information on adding zones.

When an app is added to the App Catalog, it receives a unique new domain name. For example, if the app prefix is App and the app domain name is contoso.com, an added app might be accessed by *http://app-123ABC.contoso.com*, where 123ABC is the application ID. To support these unique domain names, a wildcard Canonical Name (CNAME) entry for the DNS entry needs to be created. Like the forward lookup zone, this is done on the domain controller. To create a CNAME record on a Windows Server instance, follow these steps:

1. Log onto a domain controller with an account that's a member of the local administrators group.
2. Open the DNS Manager in Administrative Tools.
3. Right-click the domain name you added in the Forward Lookup Zones in the DNS Manager and choose New Alias (CNAME).
4. On the New Resource Record dialog box, type * (an asterisk) in the Alias Name text box.
5. In the Fully Qualified Domain Name (FQDN) For Target Host section, enter a domain name that points to the SharePoint farm (such as home.contoso.com). You can optionally browse to the record by clicking Browse.
6. Leave the last setting cleared (Allow Any Authenticated User To Update All DNS Records With The Same Name) because it applies only to DNS records for a new name. Click OK.

After you configure the CNAME record, you can access the unique domain names that the app service creates whenever an app is added. If you've decided to use Secure Socket Layers (SSL), you still need to configure a wildcard certificate, as explained in the next section.

MORE INFO ADDING AN ALIAS (CNAME) RESOURCE RECORD TO A ZONE

See *http://technet.microsoft.com/en-us/library/cc816886* for more information on how to add an alias (CNAME) resource record to a zone.

Configuring wildcard certificates

Each app that exists in the App Catalog has a unique name, which can present some problems when using Secure Socket Layers (SSL). Each unique domain name that uses SSL requires a certificate, but you don't want to go around creating and installing certificates every time somebody puts an app in the App Catalog. To get around this, you need to obtain and install a wildcard certificate. To obtain a wildcard certificate, you can request one from your SSL certificate provider. To create a request for a wildcard certificate, follow these steps:

1. Log onto one of the WFEs in your SharePoint farm and open Microsoft Internet Information Server (IIS) 7.
2. Click the server name of the WFE and then click Server Certificates.
3. Click Create Certificate Request.
4. On the Request Certificate page, enter the information required. Make sure that the Common Name has the wildcard character at the beginning (for example, *.contoso.com) and that you don't use abbreviations for the other items, as shown in Figure 4-2.

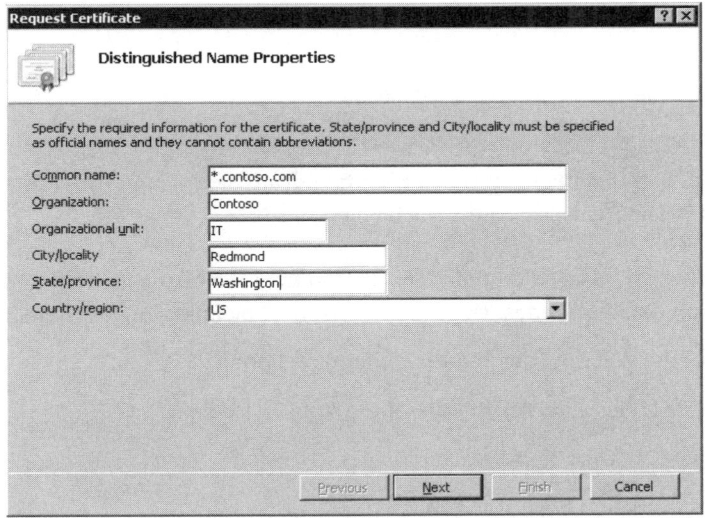

FIGURE 4-2 Request Certificate dialog box in IIS 7

5. Click Next. In the Cryptographic Service Provider Properties dialog box, choose Microsoft RSA SChannel Cryptographic Provider as the cryptographic service provider (the default) and a bit length of 2048 (which can vary depending on the needs of your SSL provider and your security requirements).
6. Click Next to move to the page where you save the certificate. Give it a name and click Finish.
7. Send the certificate to your SSL certificate provider and wait for the provider to send you the SSL certificate.

MORE INFO **REQUESTING AN INTERNET SERVER CERTIFICATE**

See *http://technet.microsoft.com/en-us/library/cc732906(WS.10).aspx* for more information on how to request an Internet server certificate in IIS 7.

When you have the SSL certificate in hand, you need to import it into IIS on each WFE. After the certificate is imported, it needs to be bound to the website where the App Catalog resides. To import an SSL certificate, follow these steps:

1. Log onto one of the WFEs in your SharePoint farm and open IIS 7.
2. Click the server name of the WFE and then click Server Certificates.
3. Click Complete Certificate Request.
4. On the Specify Certificate Authority Response page in the Complete Certificate Request dialog box, choose the filename containing the certification authority's response by clicking the button with the ellipses (...) and selecting the SSL certificate.
5. In the Friendly Name text box, enter the domain name, starting with an asterisk (for example, *.contoso.com).
6. Click OK to finish the import of the SSL certificate.

> ***IMPORTANT*** **Make sure that the friendly name starts with an asterisk; otherwise, you can't specify the host name when doing the site binding.**

After the SSL certificate is installed on the WFE, you can bind the certificate to the web application where the App Catalog resides. This is also done in IIS by following these steps:

1. Log onto one of the WFEs in your SharePoint farm and open IIS 7.
2. Open up the Sites folder and click the site of the App Catalog.
3. In the Actions section, click Bindings.
4. In the Site Bindings dialog box, click Add.
5. Select https under Type, choose the IP address to bind to, and leave Port 443 in the Port text box.
6. Choose the SSL certificate that you imported for the App Catalog (the one that begins with an asterisk).
7. Enter the base host name (for example, contoso.com).

> ***IMPORTANT*** **Some SSL certification providers don't provide wildcard certificates. Make sure that yours does before you request one and try to use it.**

Thought experiment

Ensuring high availability of the App Catalog

In the following thought experiment, apply what you've learned about this objective. You can find answers to these questions in the "Answers" section at the end of this chapter.

You've created an App Catalog and want to make sure that it's always available, even if a server goes down. That way, users can still add an app, even if a single server is down (for maintenance or hardware failure, for example).

What steps would you perform to ensure high availability of the App Catalog?

Objective summary

- You can use the App Catalog to store apps from end users as well as those obtained from the SharePoint Store.
- The app framework is designed to be used for multi-tenancy farms, so farms that are single tenancy need to define a single tenant.
- The SharePoint Store offers many beneficial apps, for free and for sale, that can be accessed as soon as Apps are enabled.
- Apps added to the App Catalog are accessed via a unique domain name.
- Unique domain names require DNS configuration to make sure that the apps can be accessed without additional configuration each time an app is added.

Objective review

Answer the following questions to test your knowledge of the information in this objective. You can find the answers to these questions and explanations of why each answer choice is correct or incorrect in the "Answers" section at the end of this chapter.

1. What types of apps can you find the App Catalog?

A. Apps from the SharePoint Store

B. Apps for Office

C. End-user customized apps

D. All of the above

2. Before apps can be considered enabled, what step must you successfully perform?
   - **A.** You need to create an App Catalog.
   - **B.** You need to create the Subscription Settings service application and proxy.
   - **C.** You need to configure the app URLs.
   - **D.** You need to create the App Management service application.
3. What reason would you have for creating a wildcard Canonical Name (CNAME) entry?
   - **A.** Because each app in the App Catalog has a unique domain name
   - **B.** To make it easier to find apps within the app catalog
   - **C.** Because all web applications need a wildcard CNAME entry
   - **D.** No reason to create a wildcard CNAME entry for an App Catalog

Objective 4.2: Create and configure productivity services

SharePoint 2013 works with productivity services via the service application framework. Productivity Services cover the Microsoft Office products as well as a new service that performs translations of content from one language to another. Each productivity service requires separate setup and configuration. The settings depend on the makeup of the SharePoint farm and the needs of the organization. For example, an organization that uses Microsoft Excel heavily will configure the Microsoft Excel Services differently from one that limits usage.

SharePoint 2013 works closely with the productivity services to provide additional functionality to help users perform their functions more efficiently and with more integration. This objective covers how to create and configure the productivity services available in SharePoint Server 2013.

This objective covers the following topics:

- Creating and configuring Microsoft Excel Services
- Creating and configuring Microsoft Access Services
- Creating and configuring Microsoft Visio Services
- Creating and configuring Microsoft Word Automation Services
- Creating and configuring Microsoft PowerPoint Conversion Services
- Creating and configuring Machine Translation Services

Creating and configuring Microsoft Excel Services

One of the most useful and powerful service applications available to SharePoint, the Microsoft Excel Services service application enables users to use Excel spreadsheets right within the browser and provides all document management benefits (versioning, security, collaboration, check in/out, and so forth) that other kinds of documents have within SharePoint. Excel Services also allows for the showing of just part of the Excel spreadsheet and the ability to display graphs and charts to users who don't have access to the spreadsheet.

Before users can start using Excel Services, you must create the service application. And before you can create the service application, you need to make sure that the following items are set up:

- A domain account needs to be set up for the application pool.
- The account used to create and configure the services needs to be a member of the Farm Administrators group.
- The domain account used for the application pool needs to have access to the content databases of the web applications that will use the service.

Access to the content databases that need Excel Services can be done at the web application level by using PowerShell, as follows:

```
$webApp=Get-SPWebApplication -identity <URL of web application>
$webApp.GrantAccessToProcessIdentity("<domain account>")
```

After the account has the proper permissions, you can begin the process of setting up Microsoft Excel Services. For the Excel Services application to be created, you need to start the Excel Calculation Services (ECS) service on at least one server (or on additional servers to provide additional resources, depending on the servers available and the resource demand expected). To start ECS, follow these steps:

1. Navigate to Central Administration with an account that's part of the Farm Administrators group.
2. Click Manage Services On Server in the System Settings section.
3. Select the server on which you want to start the service from the Server drop-down list.
4. Locate the Excel Calculation Services from the Service list and click Start.
5. Repeat steps 3 and 4 for each server on which you want the service to run.

After the ECS service starts, you can create the Excel Services application. You need only one application per SharePoint farm. Follow these steps:

1. Navigate to Central Administration with an account that's part of the Farm Administrators group.
2. Click Manage Service Application in the Application Management section.
3. Click the New button to access the drop-down list, and then select Excel Services Application.

4. Give the application a name (such as Excel Services Application) in the Name section.

5. Select the Create New Application Pool option and enter a name for the application pool (or choose one that has already been created for this application).

6. Select the Configurable option from the drop-down list (if you didn't choose a preexisting application pool) and select the account created for this application.

7. Click OK to start the creation process and wait until the process finishes.

MORE INFO CONFIGURING EXCEL SERVICES

See *http://technet.microsoft.com/en-us/library/jj219698* for more details on how to configure the Microsoft Excel Services service application in SharePoint Server 2013.

After you create the Excel Services application, you need to configure it. In fact, the Excel Services application has more options to configure than any other service application that comes with SharePoint 2013. Figure 4-3 shows the vast array of configurable options associated with this service.

Manage Excel Services Application

Global Settings
Define load balancing, memory, and throttling thresholds. Set the unattended service account and data connection timeouts.

Trusted File Locations
Define places where spreadsheets can be loaded from.

Trusted Data Providers
Add or remove data providers that can be used when refreshing data connections.

Trusted Data Connection Libraries
Define a SharePoint Document Library where data connections can be loaded from.

User Defined Function Assemblies
Register managed code assemblies that can be used by spreadsheets.

Data Model Settings
Register instances of SQL Server Analysis Services servers that Excel Services Application can use for advanced data analysis functionality.

FIGURE 4-3 The Manage Excel Services Application settings page

Configuring global settings

The first group of settings to configure are the Global Settings, which need to be configured before users start using Excel Services. The Global Settings cover settings for the following items:

- Security
- Load balancing

- Session management
- Memory usage
- Workbook cache
- External data

SECURITY SETTINGS

You can configure three options in the Security section.

The first option, File Access Method, is used only for Excel spreadsheets that aren't stored in a SharePoint database, such as those found on UNC shares or HTTP web sites. It has two settings to choose from:

- Impersonation means that when a user accesses an Excel spreadsheet, the account of the user accessing the spreadsheet is used.
- If the Process Account option is chosen, the user account isn't impersonated; instead, the account that runs the Excel Service application is used.

The second option in the Security section is Connection Encryption. Selecting Required necessitates encryption between the client computer and the front-end component running Excel Services. You can use Internet Protocol Security (IPSec) or Secure Socket Layers (SSL) for authentication. The authentication requirement also applies to the Excel spreadsheet when accessing external data sources.

The third option in the Security section is the Allow Cross Domain Access option. By default, this is turned off so that only Excel files located in the same domain can be accessed. If you want to allow cross-domain access, you need to select this check box. Keep in mind that an element of security risk exists and that cross-domain access requires more resources, especially network bandwidth.

> ***MORE INFO*** **CONFIGURING EXCEL SERVICES GLOBAL SETTINGS**
>
> **See *http://technet.microsoft.com/en-us/library/jj219683* for more information about how to plan Excel Services global settings in SharePoint Server 2013.**

LOAD BALANCING SETTINGS

The next section under Global Settings is the Load Balancing section. If only one server is running Excel Calculation Services, these setting don't apply. If more than one server are running ECS, you should choose the option that works best for your farm. The following settings are available:

- **Workbook URL** A URL in the workbook specifies which server running the ECS is used so that the specific workbook always uses the same ECS session.
- **Round Robin With Health Check** The ECS session is chosen in a round-robin fashion.
- **Local** If an ECS session is available on the server on which the workbook is opened, that session is used.

SESSION MANAGEMENT SETTINGS

In the Session Management section of Global Settings, you can choose to limit the maximum number of session per user. The default is 25, which is fairly high if you plan to have lots of people using Excel Services. It's also a high value in that it's unlikely that a single user will have more than 25 sessions open at the same time. If you want to have unlimited sessions, set the value to –1. Monitoring performance is the best way to determine whether this limit needs to be changed.

MEMORY USAGE SETTINGS

The Memory Utilization section under Global Settings deserves some special attention. Unchecked, the Excel Services can consume a significant amount of memory resources. You should spend some time evaluating these settings because the default values can result in significant memory usage for organizations that use the Excel Services significantly. The following settings are available:

- **Maximum Private Bytes** The number of megabytes allocated by the ECS process. The default is –1, which means up to 50 percent of the physical memory on the server running the ECS can be used for Excel Services.
- **Memory Cache Threshold** The percentage of the memory allocated to the ECS process that can be allocated to inactive objects. When the threshold is reached, unused objects are released from memory. The default value is 90.
- **Maximum Unused Object Age** The amount of time, in minutes, that inactive objects can remain in memory (as long as the memory cache threshold hasn't been reached). The default value is –1, which means no limit; otherwise, the limit is 34560 (24 days).

WORKBOOK CACHE SETTINGS

Another section under Global Settings that's related to memory management is the Workbook Cache section. These cache settings determine the amount of memory as well as the amount of disk space to be used on the servers running the ECS process. You need to make sure the resources specified by these settings are available on the servers running ECS. You need to review these settings to ensure that resources are allocated in the best way possible to provide optimal performance for ECS as well as typical SharePoint performance. The following settings are available:

- **Workbook Cache Location** The location of the workbook file cache. By default, this is empty, which means that the default temp location is used (usually on the C drive). Change this location to a non-system drive to help eliminate contention for hard drive resources.
- **Maximum Size Of Workbook Cache** The size (in megabytes) that can be allocated for workbooks now in use. The default value is 40960, or about 40 GB. You need to ensure that enough room is available on the drive where the workbook cache is located.

- **Caching Of Unused Files** A way to speed up spreadsheet loading for future users. This check box, selected by default, allows for the caching of unused files.

EXTERNAL DATA SETTINGS

The final section in Global Settings is for the important External Data settings. In particular, the unattended service account needs to be configured so that workbooks can use the account specified in this setting rather than have to authenticate against individual users.

The following settings are available in the External Data section:

- **Connection Lifetime** This setting specifies the amount of time, in seconds, for a connection to remain open. Connections past this value are closed. The value of –1 specifies that they never expire. The default is 1800 (30 minutes); the maximum is 2073600 (or 24 days).
- **Analysis Services EffectiveUserName** This setting applies only to external data connections based on Analysis Services with an authentication setting of Use The Authenticated User's Account. This is an alternative to Windows delegation allowing secure access to Analysis Services.
- **Unattended Service Account** All workbooks can use this account to refresh data. All workbooks that specify Use The Unattended Service Account setting requires that this value be filled in.
- **Secure Store Service Association** This value is just for reference and can't be changed. Under the value displaying which secure store application is being used, you can choose to create a new unattended service account or use an existing one.

When configuring the Global Settings, you need to either create a new unattended service account or choose a target application ID that has already been created. For either of these options to be filled in, the Secure Store Service needs to be created and configured. The unattended service account should be a low-permission account that Excel Calculation Services uses to connect to data connections that use non-Windows Single Sign-On (SSO) or no authentication method. The account used shouldn't have access to any of the SharePoint Server databases.

Defining trusted file locations

Trusted File Locations productivity services is the second settings group on the Manage Excel Services Application settings page. This group defines the locations that SharePoint can use to open an Excel workbook.

By default, Excel Services is configured to allow workbooks (or parts of workbooks) to be opened within the SharePoint environment under http://. These default settings are designed to provide the Excel Services to the broadest set of users, but they can also present some security risks. Many different Trusted File Locations can enable a high degree of control over where and how Excel Services can use Excel files. The reasons for configuring these settings are for performance and security. In the Trusted File Locations section, you can edit existing file locations or you can add a new one. For the purposes of this section, either is a valid choice for viewing the available options.

EXAM TIP

Creating a trusted file location is a prime target for questions that involve steps. It's also one of the main tasks involved with setting up a SharePoint farm. You should familiarize yourself with creating a few before the exam.

LOCATION SETTINGS

The first section, Location, is where you view or add a trusted file location:

- **Address** Enter the location, which can be a SharePoint location, a network file share, or a web folder.
- **Location Type** Choose the storage type: SharePoint, UNC, or HTTP UNC is for file shares, and HTTP is for locations accessed via the HTTP protocol.
- **Trust Children** If the check box is selected, all sublocations are also trusted. For example, if you want to trust an entire web application, you can put the top-level location in the Address field and then select Children Trusted.
- **Description** Use normal text to describe the location's purpose.

Figure 4-4 shows an example of using the http://contoso web application and all subsites and libraries.

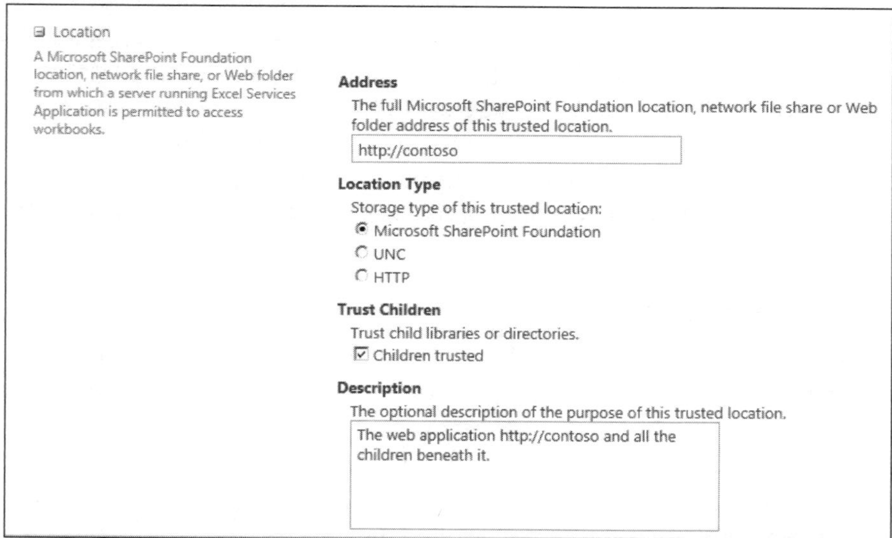

Location
A Microsoft SharePoint Foundation location, network file share, or Web folder from which a server running Excel Services Application is permitted to access workbooks.
Address
The full Microsoft SharePoint Foundation location, network file share or Web folder address of this trusted location.
http://contoso
Location Type
Storage type of this trusted location:
Microsoft SharePoint Foundation
UNC
HTTP
Trust Children
Trust child libraries or directories.
Children trusted
Description
The optional description of the purpose of this trusted location.
The web application http://contoso and all the children beneath it.

FIGURE 4-4 The Location section for the http://contoso trusted file location

SESSION MANAGEMENT SETTINGS

The next section on the Trusted File Location page is Session Management. Because each open session consumes memory resources, managing these options can help keep memory requests under control. If you are experiencing a heavy load on your servers running ECS, you probably want to determine if these properties need to be modified to provide a more responsive SharePoint experience:

- **Session Timeout** The amount of time, in seconds, that an ECS session remains open and inactive before it's shut down. The default is 450 (7.5 minutes). A value of –1 can be specified for no timeout, and the max is 2073600 seconds (24 days).
- **Short Session Timeout** The amount of time, in seconds, that an Excel session can remain open and inactive. The default values and limits are the same as for Session Timeout. The Short Session Timeout is measured from the end of the initial open request.
- **New Workbook Session Timeout** The maximum amount of time, in seconds, that an ECS session for a new workbook can remain open and inactive before it's shut down. The default value is 1800 (30 minutes). The maximum is 24 days, and a value of –1 indicates no timeout.
- **Maximum Request Duration** The maximum amount of time in seconds for a single request during an ECS session. Default is 300 (5 minutes). The maximum is 24 days, and a value of –1 indicates no timeout.
- **Maximum Chart Render Duration** The maximum amount of time in seconds to spend rendering any single chart. The default is 3 seconds. The maximum is 24 days, and a value of –1 indicates no timeout.

WORKBOOK SETTINGS

The Workbook Properties section deals with the maximum size of the workbook as well as the objects contained within. Two settings are available:

- **Maximum Workbook Size** specifies the maximum size, in megabytes, of a workbook that can be opened by ECS. The default value is 10 MB, which should be large enough for most workbooks unless they have a lot of graphics in them. The valid values are 1 through 2000.
- **Maximum Chart Or Image Size** pertains to the maximum chart size or image size that can be opened by ECS. The default is 1 MB and the maximum is any positive integer (the maximum workbook size is still the limiting factor because the workbook must be open before a chart or image contained within can be opened).

> ***IMPORTANT*** **Use caution when raising the values of the workbook properties. Opening up an extremely large workbook can cause the entire SharePoint farm to slow down, especially the server that provides the ECS session.**

SETTINGS FOR CALCULATION BEHAVIOR

Next, you consider the Calculation Behavior settings:

- **Volatile Function Cache Lifetime** specifies the amount of time, in seconds, that a volatile function is cached for automatic recalculations. The default value is 300 (five minutes). The value of –1 indicates that it's calculated once on load. The value of 0 means that it's always calculated, and the maximum value is 2073600 (24 days).
- **Workbook Calculation Mode** specifies a workbook's calculation mode. The default selection is File, which doesn't override the workbook settings (unlike all the other options). This means that whatever the workbook specifies is what is used. The next option is Manual which means that the end user needs to specify that the calculations in the workbook need to be processed. The value of Automatic means that when data is changed within the workbook then all relevant cells that use that data as part of a calculation are updated. The final selection of Automatic except data tables means that the user has to request that calculations be updated for data that is from external data sources. Choosing either one of the Automatic options puts additional strain on the ECS but also provides the most up-to-date data.

EXTERNAL DATA SETTINGS

External data sources can consume memory and CPU resources as well as be a source of security risk. The settings for this section depend heavily on how your organization treats data and the reliability of the data sources that the Excel workbooks consume:

- **Allow External Data** determines whether you should even allow external data sources. You can choose from the following values:
  - **None** prevents users from accessing external data sources.
  - **Trusted Data Connection Libraries** allows only connections available within SharePoint data connection libraries. This option allows for access to external data but provides a mechanism to control the data connections and the accounts used to access the external data.
  - **Trusted Data Connection Libraries And Embedded** is the most open and doesn't allow for oversight of data connections. This option should be allowed only in organizations where the data connections are trusted.
- **Warn Of Refresh** displays a warning before a user refreshes data from an external data source.
- **Display Granular External Data Errors** displays granular error messages (rather than a general error message) from external data failures. This option is selected by default.
- **Stop When Refresh On Open Fails** stops the open operation if the file contains a Refresh On Open operation that fails. This option is selected by default.
- **External Data Cache Lifetime** contains two fields: one for automatic refresh and one for manual refresh. The values determine the maximum amount of time that the system can use external data query results. The default is 300 for both (5 minutes). A

value of –1 means never refresh after the first query, and the maximum amount of time is 24 days.

- **Maximum Concurrent Queries Per Session** determines the maximum number of external data queries per ECS session. The default is 5.
- **Allow External Data Using REST** allows requests from REST APIs to refresh external data connections. This option is disabled by default.

SETTINGS FOR USER-DEFINED FUNCTIONS

The default setting for the User Defined Functions section is cleared. You should allow user-defined functions only if you fully trust the users creating the functions. You should probably enable this setting only in specific cases—for example, where the library that contains the Excel workbook has very limited access such as for the Finance team. Allowing user-defined functions is a very big security risk and should be allowed only in organizations that fully trust all their members.

Defining trusted data providers

The Trusted Data Providers section of the Manage Excel Services Application settings page defines the sort of data providers that can be used to provide external data to Excel workbooks. Clicking the Trusted Data Providers link takes you to the Trusted Data Providers section. SharePoint has already created many providers covering SQL Server databases all the way back to SQL Server 2000, as well as providers created for OLE DB and ODBC connections.

You can delete any of the providers listed, as well as add providers that aren't listed. To add a trusted data provider, click Add Trusted Data Provider in the Trusted Data Providers section. This opens a page where you can add providers. The following provider types are available:

- OLE DB
- ODBC
- ODBC DSN

The other fields that need to be filled in are Provider ID and Description. The Provider ID is the main one that must be filled in; don't add a provider unless it's absolutely necessary. The providers that have already been created should account for most external data sources needed.

Setting up trusted data connection libraries

Data connection libraries are special document libraries that contain connection information so that users can access external data without having direct access to the data. The Trusted Data Connection Libraries section determines which data connection libraries Excel workbooks can use to connect to external data sources. By default, no trusted data connection libraries are included. To add any that you need, click Add Trusted Data Connection Library in the Trusted Data Connection Libraries section.

The only two values for a trusted data connection library are the Address field, which contains the URL of the data connection library, and the optional Description field. Both fields are located in the Location section. As a farm administrator, you need to make sure that the connections located with the data connection libraries use secure connections with accounts that have minimal rights.

Defining user-defined function assemblies

The User Defined Function Assemblies section of the Manage Excel Services Application settings page defines what assemblies are available for Excel workbooks. Assemblies have permissions that can harm the servers they run on as well as present potential security risks because they can operate at heightened levels of security, especially if they are located in the Global Assembly Cache (GAC). Therefore, you should allow only assemblies that have been tested and validated as being secure. Also be aware of the amount of memory that the assemblies use because they can affect the performance of your SharePoint farm.

If you decide that you want to add an assembly for use by Excel workbooks, click Add User-Defined Function Assembly on the User-Defined Function Assemblies section. The following options are available:

- **Assembly** This is the full path or the strong name of the assembly that contains functions that Excel Calculation Services can call.
- **Assembly Location** An assembly can either be in the GAC or have a file path.
- **Enable Assembly** This enables you to turn off an assembly without removing the assembly from the list—for example, when the assembly needs to be tested or functionality needs to be temporarily removed.
- **Description** This is an optional description of the assembly.

Configuring data model settings

In the Data Model Settings section, you can register SQL Server Analysis Services (SSAS) that the Excel Services application can use for advanced data analysis. SQL Server 2012 Analysis Services can be used in the processing of data models created in Excel 2013. You can add one or more SQL Server instances (version 2012 SP1 or later) for use by the data models. If you do add more than one SQL Server instance, the servers are accessed in a round-robin fashion. Adding a server is straightforward—simply click Add Server in the Data Model Settings section. After that, provide the name of the server in the Server Name field and an optional description in the Description field.

MORE INFO **CONFIGURING DATA MODEL SETTINGS**

See *http://technet.microsoft.com/en-us/library/jj219780.aspx* for more information on how to plan Data Model settings for Excel Services in SharePoint Server 2013.

Creating and configuring Microsoft Access Services

Microsoft Access has been increasingly integrated into SharePoint over the last few releases, and SharePoint 2013 is no exception. Microsoft Access Services in SharePoint 2013 allows users to do the following:

- Create Access apps for use in SharePoint
- Maintain Access web databases created in SharePoint Server 2010

New in SharePoint 2013 are Access apps, which are a new type of database built into Access Services that can be shared with other users as an app within SharePoint. This provides Access functionality within the browser. SharePoint 2013 also maintains backward compatibility with Access web databases that were previously created in SharePoint 2010. These two functions each have their own service and their own service application, and they are configured separately.

Access Services 2010

Access Services 2010 is set up separately from Access Services. If you plan to use web databases that were created in SharePoint 2010 on your SharePoint 2013 farm, you need to create this service application. Although Access Services 2010 doesn't have as many options as Access Services 2013, creating this application is still a sizable task depending on your organization's needs. First, you need to consider whether you want to use reports in the Access web database(s) that you will use on the SharePoint 2013 farm. If you do need reporting capabilities, you need to have SQL Server Reporting Services added to SharePoint Server 2013. The options here depend on the version of SQL Server instance on which SharePoint 2013 is installed:

- For SharePoint farms installed on SQL Server 2008 R2, you need to install and configure SQL Server 2008 R2 Reporting Services (SSRS).
- For SharePoint farms installed on SQL Server 2012, you need to install and configure Reporting Services SharePoint Mode for SharePoint 2013.

After you configure Reporting Services (if you need to), you need to start the Access Database Service 2010 on the server or servers that will provide this service. This service isn't started by default. To start the service, follow these steps:

1. Navigate to Central Administration as a farm administrator and click Manage Services On The Server in the System Settings section.
2. Choose the server on which you want to start the service from the Server drop-down list.
3. On the Service list, find Access Database Service 2010 and click Start under the Action column.

After you start the service on the servers you choose (you can always add or remove servers as long as one server runs the service), you can create the Access Services 2010 service application. After the service application is created, you can start using the web databases. To create an Access Services 2010 service application, follow these steps:

1. Navigate to Central Administration as a farm administrator and click Manage Service Applications in the Application Management section.
2. Click the New icon on the Manage Service Applications page and choose Access Services 2010.
3. Give the application a name (such as Access Services 2010 Application) in the Access Services Application Name text box.
4. In the Application Pool section, choose whether to use an existing application pool or to create a new one.
5. Leave the Add To Default Proxy List option selected so that the application is available to all the web applications via the default proxy list.
6. Click OK to start the creation process.

Although the Access 2010 web databases are ready to use after the application is successfully created, you might want to change some of the default configuration settings, depending on your business needs. Access databases can grow quite large and use up a lot of memory and other resources on the servers in the SharePoint farm if left unchecked. To configure the settings, click the application service created in the preceding steps on the Manage Service Applications page in Central Administration (provided that you are using an account with permissions to the Access Services 2010 service application). You can configure the following settings:

The List And Queries section includes settings for queries of SharePoint lists:

- **Maximum Columns Per Query** The maximum number of columns that the query can reference, including columns automatically included. Default is 40 with a range of 1 to 255.
- **Maximum Rows Per Query** The maximum number of rows that a list can have and still be used in a query, as well as the maximum number of rows the output can have. Valid values are from 1 to 200,000 and a default of 25,000.
- **Maximum Sources Per Query** The maximum number of lists that a query can use. Range is from 1 to 20, with a default of 12.
- **Maximum Calculated Columns Per Query** The maximum number of inline calculated columns that a query or subquery can include. Values range from 0 to 32, with a default of 10.
- **Maximum Order By Clauses Per Query** The maximum number of Order By clauses allowed in a query. Range is from 0 to 8, with a default value of 4.
- **Allow Outer Joins** A check box allowing left and right outer joins. Inner joins are always allowed.

- **Allow Non-Remotable Queries** A check box indicating whether queries that can't be sent to a remote database to run. Default is that remotable queries are allowed.
- **Maximum Records Per Table** The maximum number of records that an application table can contain. The default is 500,000. A value of –1 indicates no limit to the number of records.

The Application Objects section provides limits on the types of objects an Access Services 2010 application can contain:

- **Maximum Application Log Size** The maximum number of records allowed in the log list. The range is from 1 to any valid integer. The default is 3000.

The Session Management settings determine the behavior of Access Database Service 2010 sessions:

- **Maximum Request Duration** The maximum amount of time, in seconds, allowed for a request from an application. The default is 30 seconds. The value of –1 indicates no limit, and the maximum is 2007360 (24 days).
- **Maximum Sessions Per User** The maximum number of sessions allowed per user. If the value is exceeded, the sessions are deleted until the value is reached starting with the oldest first. Default is 10. A value of –1 indicates no limit, and the range is from 1 to any positive integer.
- **Maximum Sessions Per Anonymous User** Similar to Maximum Sessions Per User but for anonymous users. The default is 25.
- **Cache Timeout** The maximum amount of time, in seconds, that a data cache is available, as measured from the end of a request. The default value is 1500 (25 minutes). A value of –1 indicates no limit, and the range is from 1 to 2007360 (24 days).
- **Maximum Session Memory** The maximum amount of memory, in megabytes, that a single session can use. The default is 64 MB. The valid values are 0, which disables session memory, to 4095 (4 GB).

The Memory Utilization section determines the allocation of memory for the Access Database Service:

- **Memory Utilization** The allocation of memory on the servers running the Access Database Service process. The default of –1 allows up to half of the physical memory to be used on the server. The maximum value is any positive integer.

The Templates section provides template management settings:

- **Maximum Template Size** The maximum size, in megabytes, allowed for Access templates. The default is 30 MB. The default value of –1 allows any size, and the limit is any positive integer.

You should exercise caution when changing these values, especially if large and/or complicated web databases exist. Depending on the configuration, you could use up at least half of the memory on the SharePoint server(s) running the Access Database Service 2010 service.

Allocating half of the physical memory to a single service isn't advisable unless you have dedicated a server to running that single service.

> ***MORE INFO*** **SETTING UP AND CONFIGURING ACCESS SERVICES 2010**
>
> **See *http://technet.microsoft.com/en-us/library/ee748653(office.15).aspx* for more information on how to set up and configure Access Services 2010 for web databases in SharePoint Server 2013.**

Access Services

Access Services is the service application in SharePoint 2013 that allows you to create Access apps that can be used and shared across the SharePoint farm. You can then create the Access apps in much the same way you would a document library or list. If you don't have any legacy Access 2010 web databases, this will be the only Access Services service application that you need to provide database functionality.

Before you start using Access Services, be aware that the requirements for Access Services exceed those of the base installation of SharePoint Server 2013. The following items are required before users can start using Access Services:

- A SQL Server 2012 instance needs to be configured for Access Services.
- The SQL Server Feature Pack needs to be installed on SharePoint.
- The Access Services service application needs to be installed and configured.
- A SharePoint site collection for Access apps needs to be created.
- Creators of Access apps need the Microsoft Access 2013 client to design Access apps.

EXAM TIP

That Access Services requires the use of SQL Server 2012 might come up on the exam because this is beyond the usual requirements for SharePoint Server 2013.

MAKING SQL SERVER 2012 AVAILABLE

The first step in getting ready to use Access Services is to make sure that SQL Server 2012 is available. If your SharePoint 2013 farm is installed on SQL Server 2008 R2 and you can't upgrade it to SQL Server 2012, you can still use an instance of SQL Server 2012 to run Access Services and attach it as a separate application database server. Assuming that you have a SQL Server 2012 instance available, you configure it for Access Services.

The account that runs Access Services must have certain built-in server roles on the SQL Server instance:

- dbcreator
- securityadmin

SQL Server 2012 must also have certain components installed before it can be used by Access Services. You might already have these services installed on SQL Server, but you still want to double-check to make sure. The required components—in addition to the database engine and SQL Server Management Studio—are as follows:

- Full-Text and Semantic Extractions for Search
- Client Tools Connectivity

The next step in configuring SQL Server 2012 is to ensure that the following properties and settings are configured:

- **Mixed Mode Authentication** In SQL Server Management Studio (SMSS), you can configure this setting through the server's properties in the Security section.
- **Enable Contained Database** In SMSS, you can configure this setting through the server's properties in the Advanced section. Under the Containment heading, set Enable Contained Databases to True.
- **Allow Triggers To Fire Others** In SMSS, you can configure this setting through the server's properties in the Advanced section. Under the Miscellaneous heading, set Allow Triggers To Fire Others to True.
- **Named Pipes** This needs to be enabled through the SQL Server Configuration Manager. Under SQL Server Network Configuration, select Protocols For MSSQLSERVER and set Named Pipes to Enabled. This change requires a restart of MSSQLSERVER.
- **Firewall settings** You need to open TCP 1433, TCP 1434, and UDP in the Windows Firewall (or other firewall product) if they haven't already been opened.

When the components are available and the settings are configured correctly, SQL Server 2012 should be ready for Access Services. Each Access app creates its own database, so you should keep an eye on the number of databases and the memory that they are using.

SharePoint 2013 servers running Access Services also need SQL Server components installed on them. The necessary components can be found in the Microsoft SQL Server 2012 Feature Pack:

- Microsoft SQL Server 2012 Local DB
- Microsoft SQL Server 2012 Data-Tier Application Framework
- Microsoft SQL Server 2012 Native Client
- Microsoft SQL Server 2012 Transact-SQL ScriptDom
- Microsoft System CLR Types for Microsoft SQL Server 2012

MORE INFO **DOWNLOADING THE MICROSOFT SQL SERVER 2012 FEATURE PACK**

You can download the Microsoft SQL Server 2012 Feature Pack at *http://www.microsoft.com/en-us/download/details.aspx?id=29065*.

STARTING THE ACCESS SERVICES SERVICE

The next step (although this step could have been done earlier as well) is to start the Access Services service. Follow these steps:

1. Navigate to Central Administration with a farm administrator account and click Manage Services On Server in the System Settings section.
2. Choose the server on which you want the Access Services service running by choosing it from the drop-down list next to the word Server.
3. Click Start under the Action column on the line that has Access Services under the Service Column.
4. Wait for the service to start, and then repeat steps 2 and 3 for any other servers that you want running the Access Services service.

CREATING THE ACCESS SERVICES SERVICE

As soon as the Access Services service is running, you can create the Access Services service application. This is set up similarly to other service applications:

1. Navigate to Central Administration with a farm administrator account and click Manage Service Applications in the App Management section.
2. Click New and choose Access Services from the list of service applications.
3. In the Name section, enter an appropriate name (for example, Access Service Application).
4. In the New Application Database Server section, enter the name of the SQL Server 2012 instance where Access app databases will be created.
5. Leave Windows Authentication selected under the Application Database Authentication heading (unless your organization has specified a strong reason not to).
6. Leave Validate The Application Database Server selected if you want to check the SQL Server instance to ensure that it has been configured correctly.
7. In the Application Pool section, choose to use an existing application pool or create a new one.
8. Leave the default proxy list settings as is, unless you don't want the proxy to show up in the default list. Click OK.

If the SQL Server instance hasn't been configured correctly, you should receive an error message describing what you need to fix. If the instance has been configured correctly, the service application is created.

CONFIGURING THE APPLICATION POOL

After creating the Access Services service application, you still need to configure the application pool that's used with the service application. You can perform this step earlier if you plan to use an existing application pool. The application pool needs to be configured in Internet Information Services (IIS), and the Load User Profile setting needs to be set to True. Follow these steps to configure the application pool:

1. In the Start text box, type **IIS** or select it from Administrative Tools.
2. Open the server where the application pool exists and click Application Pools.
3. Right-click the application pool that starts with a GUID and has multiple applications (the Access Services pool application also starts with a GUID but has only a single application) and select Advanced Settings.
4. In the Process Model section, select True for the Load User Profile setting.
5. Click OK and perform an IISRESET.

CREATING A SITE COLLECTION

Now you need to create a site collection where users can create Access apps. The site collection is just a typical site collection based on any template you want (such as Team Site). This is the location that you specify when you create an Access app.

CONFIRMING THE SETTINGS

At this point, you should look at the configuration of the Access Services service application and make sure that the settings are in line with your business needs. Also, if you set up a SQL Server 2012 instance because SharePoint Server 2013 is installed on SQL Server 2008 R2, you need to specify the SQL Server 2012 instance in the settings of the service application. You need to make fewer decisions than with the Access Services 2010 application, but they can still have a major effect on the resources of your SharePoint farm. The following configuration items are available:

- **Maximum Request Duration** The maximum amount of time, in seconds, allowed for a request. The default is 30 seconds. A value of –1 indicates no limit, and the maximum value is 2073600 (24 days).
- **Maximum Sessions Per User** The maximum number of sessions allowed per user, with the oldest ones being deleted as new requests come in. The default is 10. A value of –1 indicates no limit, and the maximum is any positive integer.
- **Maximum Sessions Per Anonymous User** The same as Maximum Sessions Per User, except it's for anonymous users. The default is 25.
- **Cache Timeout** The maximum amount of time, in seconds, that data can remain cached as measured from the end of the last request. Default is 300 seconds (5 minutes). A value of –1 indicates no limit, and the maximum value is 2073600 (24 days).

- **Query Timeout** The maximum amount of time, in seconds, for a query to complete before it's canceled. A value of 0 indicates no limit, and the maximum value is 2073600 (24 days).
- **Maximum Private Bytes** The maximum amount of server memory that can be allocated by the Access Services process. A value of –1 indicates that up to 50 percent of the memory can be allocated. The maximum value is any positive integer.
- **New Application Database Server** Where you can add a new database server (an additional server or the first one if you aren't using the SQL Server instance on which SharePoint is installed). You enter the database information in the same way as when creating the service application (see Figure 4-5).

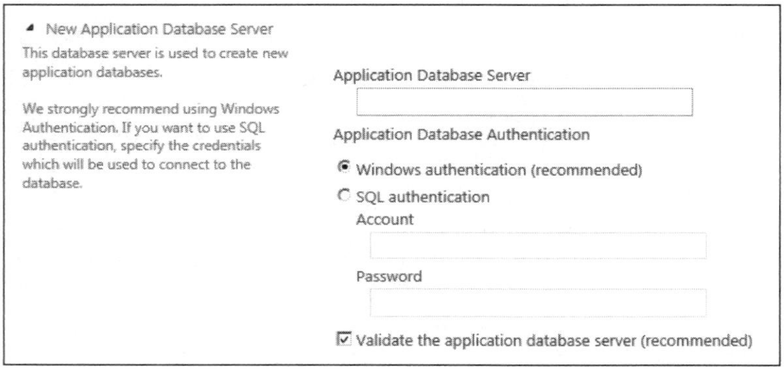

FIGURE 4-5 Adding an additional (or new) application server for Access Services

As with Access Services 2010, you should be thoughtful in how you modify the settings. Unchecked, Access Services can easily consume half of the resources available to the SharePoint farm just from a single user (depending on your farm's configuration). If you expect heavy usage of Access Services, you should dedicate at least one SharePoint server to the Access Services service.

After you set up Access Services, users can start creating Access apps, as follows:

1. Open the Microsoft Access 2013 desktop application. (The Access Service service application doesn't have an open API, so you can't use code to create Access apps.)
2. Choose Custom Web App from the choice of templates.
3. In the Custom Web App dialog box, enter the App Name. For the Web Application, use the site collection you created earlier for the purpose of managing Access apps.

If an error occurs during app creation, you should go back and double-check all the steps to make sure that you didn't miss anything. The Validate The Application Database Server option discussed earlier in the section "Creating the Access Services service" doesn't catch all the required items.

MORE INFO WHAT'S NEW IN ACCESS 2013?

See *http://msdn.microsoft.com/en-us/library/fp179914(v=office.15).aspx* to learn about the new features in Access 2013.

Creating and configuring Microsoft Visio Services

The Visio Services service application allows users to interact with Visio drawings. Users can load, display, interact programmatically with, and connect Visio drawings to the Business Connectivity Services. With SharePoint 2013, users can now save Visio files directly to SharePoint without having to export them to a Visio web drawing (.vdw). Users still need Microsoft Visio 2013 to save drawings this way, however.

Two different file types can be saved directly to SharePoint. The first file type has a .vsdx extension and is based on the Open Packing Conventions (OPC) standard. The second file type uses the XML-based file format with a .vsdm extension and is similar to the Visio 2010 file format. Both .vsdx and .vsdm files are displayed in raster format, whereas the .vdw files are displayed via Silverlight.

IMPORTANT **Silverlight is going away. It's not even supported in the Microsoft Windows 8 Modern UI. Although Silverlight probably isn't on the test, you should plan on users possibly not being able to display Visio web drawings.**

Be aware of several new features in Visio Services when configuring the service application. Diagrams can now be connected to external lists via the Business Connectivity Services. An additional related benefit is that the Visio diagrams can be refreshed as the data in the external lists is updated. Visio 2013 drawings can have comments attached to individual shapes and pages. This comment framework can be accessed through a JavaScript API allowing users to retrieve comments so they can be displayed on the web page.

MORE INFO USING VISIO SERVICES IN SHAREPOINT 2013

See *http://msdn.microsoft.com/en-us/library/jj164027.aspx* for more information on using Visio Services in SharePoint 2013.

Creating an unattended service account

The first step in creating and configuring Visio Services is to create an unattended service account for it to use. Although doing so isn't required before the actual creation of the service application, it will save you time because it's one of the configuration items.

Creating an unattended service account requires that the Secure Store service application already be created, configured, and started. Then you can create the account by following these steps:

1. Create or use an Active Directory account that has been given the SQL Server built-in server role of db_datareader.
2. Navigate to Central Administration with a farm administrator account and click Manage Service Application in the Application Management section.
3. Click the Secure Store Service service application.
4. Click New on the ribbon.
5. Enter a name (such as VisioAccount) in the Target Application ID text box.
6. In the Display Name text box, enter a user-friendly name.
7. In the Contact E-mail box, enter an email address of a monitored account.
8. In the Target Application Type drop-down list, select Group.
9. Click Next twice, leaving the default credential fields as they are.
10. Enter the administrator(s) of the account in the Target Application Administrators text box in the Specify The Membership Settings section.
11. In the Members text box, type **Everyone** (unless you want to limit Visio Services to a subgroup, but remember that each Visio Services service application can have only one unattended service account).
12. Click OK to save changes and return to the Secure Store Service Application page.
13. Set the credentials by hovering over the target application ID that was created in step 5 and click the down arrow that appears. Select Set Credentials.
14. Enter the Active Directory account that you created for the unattended service account in the Windows User Name text box.
15. Enter the password for the account and click OK.

Creating the Visio Graphics Service service application

Creating the Visio Graphics Service service application is straightforward:

1. Start it on the Services On Server page in Central Administration on all servers that will run the service.
2. On the Manage Service Applications page, create a new Visio Graphic Services service application. Give it a name and designate or create a new application pool for it to use. The account used to run the Visio Graphic Services service shouldn't be the same account as the one used for the unattended service account.

Configuring Visio Graphics Service settings

After you create the service application, you should configure its settings to meet your organization's needs. To configure the settings, open the Manage Services Applications page and clicking the service application you created. This takes you to the Manage The Visio Graphics Service page. The two sections on the page are Global Settings and Trusted Data Providers, as shown in Figure 4-6.

Manage the Visio Graphics Service

Global Settings
Manage settings for performance, security, and refreshing data connections.

Trusted Data Providers
Add or remove data providers that can be used when refreshing data connections.

FIGURE 4-6 Setting categories for the Visio Graphics Service

GLOBAL SETTINGS

You should review the default global settings to ensure that they meet the needs of your organization. Like with most service applications, these settings can affect the performance of not just the Visio Graphics Service but also that of the entire SharePoint farm. The following global settings are available:

- **Maximum Web Drawing Size** The size, in megabytes (between 1 and 50), of the largest web drawing that can be rendered. The default is 25 MB.
- **Minimum Cache Age** The minimum number of minutes, between 0 and 34560 (24 days), that a web drawing remains in cached memory. The default value is 5.
- **Maximum Cache Age** The maximum number of minutes, between 0 and 34560 (24 days), that a web drawing remains in cached memory. After this value, the cache is purged of the web drawing. The default value is 60.
- **Maximum Recalc Duration** The amount of time, in seconds (between 10 and 120), before a data operation times out. The default is 60.
- **Maximum Cache Size** The maximum size, in megabytes (between 100 and 1024000), that can be used for the cache. The default is 5120 (5 GB).

> ***NOTE*** **BOOST THE CACHE SIZE**
>
> **While not as memory intensive as Excel or Access, Visio can still consume considerable resource in organizations where it's used extensively. The default cache size of 5 GB can be a considerable burden on servers that have limited amounts of memory.**

- **External Data** Where the unattended service account is entered. Enter the application ID in the text box provided. It's used whenever Visio connects to external data sources.

> ***MORE INFO*** **CONFIGURING GLOBAL SETTINGS FOR THE VISIO GRAPHICS SERVICE**
>
> **See *http://technet.microsoft.com/en-us/library/ee524061.aspx* for more information on how to configure the global settings for the Visio Graphics Service in SharePoint Server 2013.**

TRUSTED DATA PROVIDERS

The second group of settings for the Visio Graphics Service service application is Trusted Data Providers. This list is similar to that in the Excel Services service application, but notice that several additional data providers aren't part of the Microsoft suite of products. That this list of trusted providers is longer is probably because of Visio being more trusting of external data, due to the nature of what it can do (draw diagrams). One source is even for Excel Web Services, in case the values for some of the drawings exist in Excel workbooks. In fact, Visio Graphics Service allows for six different types of data providers for Excel, instead of just three.

If the data provider that you need isn't available, you can add it by clicking Add A New Trusted Data Provider on the Visio Graphics Service Trusted Data Providers page and configure the following settings:

- **Trusted Data Provider ID** The name used by Visio to connect to external data
- **Trusted Data Provider Type** An integer between 1 and 6—1 for OLE DB, 2 for SQL, 3 for ODBC, 4 for ODBC with DSN, 5 for SharePoint Lists, and 6 for Visio Custom Data Providers—that specifies the type of data provider
- **Trusted Data Provider Description** A description that appears in the Trusted Data Provider list

Creating and configuring Microsoft Word Automation Services

Word Automation Services enables users to automate the conversion of Word documents into other sorts of documents. You can think of it as a way to automate the Save As command. For example, if you want to convert thousands of word documents into single file web pages (with the .mht or .mhtml extension), you can use Word Automation Services. Enabling Word Automation Services begins by starting the Word Automation Services service application:

1. Navigate to Central Administration with a farm administrator account.
2. Click Manage Services On Server in the System Settings section of the home page.
3. Choose the server on which you want to start the services from the Server drop-down.

4. Find Word Automation Services under the Service column and click Start in the action column.
5. Repeat steps 3 and 4 for each server on which you want Word Automation Services to run.

Creating the service application

As soon as Word Automation Services is running on all SharePoint servers that you want it to (you can always add or remove more at a later date), you can create the Word Automation Services service application. As with other service applications, this one can be created through the Central Administration interface as well as through PowerShell commands. The steps involved with using Central Administration are as follows:

1. Navigate to Central Administration with a farm administrator account.
2. Click Manage Service Applications in the Application Management section.
3. Click the New icon on the Manage Service Applications page to drop down the list of service applications and select Word Automation Services.
4. In the Create New Word Automation Services Application dialog box, enter a name (such as Word Automation Services Application) in the Name text box.
5. Choose an existing application pool or create a new one in the Application Pool section.
6. Choose the Partitioned Mode Only option if you are creating a multi-tenant SharePoint farm.
7. Select the Add To Default Proxy List option if you want to add the proxy to the default proxy list.
8. Click Next.
9. On the Database Page, enter the name of the database server as well as the name of the database to be created for the service application in the Database Name text box.
10. Click Finish to create the Word Automation Services Application service application.

Modifying properties

After you create the service application, you can modify its properties. Word Automation Services can open not only Microsoft Word documents but also the same kinds of documents that Microsoft Word can open, such as Rich Text Format files and single file web pages. The kinds of files that can be opened as well as settings that can affect the performance of the server(s) running the Word Automation Services service can be modified by clicking the Word Automation Services service application on the Manage Service Applications page in Central Administration. The following settings are available:

- **Supported File Formats** In this section, you specify which supported file formats will be allowed for use by Word Automation Services. Figure 4-7 shows the supported file types.

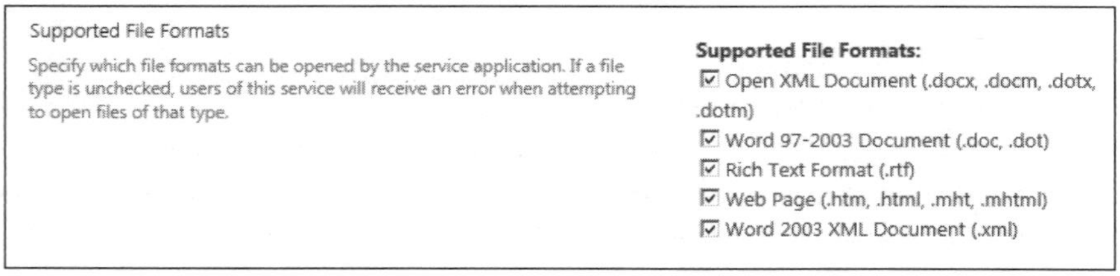

Supported File Formats

Specify which file formats can be opened by the service application. If a file type is unchecked, users of this service will receive an error when attempting to open files of that type.

Supported File Formats:

- [x] Open XML Document (.docx, .docm, .dotx, .dotm)
- [x] Word 97-2003 Document (.doc, .dot)
- [x] Rich Text Format (.rtf)
- [x] Web Page (.htm, .html, .mht, .mhtml)
- [x] Word 2003 XML Document (.xml)

FIGURE 4-7 Supported file formats

- **Embedded Font Support** This option enables you to choose whether to embed fonts (to help preserve consistency across different machines). It's enabled by default.
- **Maximum Memory Usage** This is the percentage of system memory made available to the Word Automation Service service application. The default is the maximum, 100 percent.
- **Word 97-2003 Document Scanning** This option provides added security when loading Word 97-2003 documents. This process requires extra resources but should be disabled only if you fully trust all Word 97-2003 documents being loaded.
- **Conversion Processes** This is the number of concurrent documents that can be converted at the same time per server running Word Automation Services. The default is 1, and the maximum is 1000.
- **Conversion Throughput** This is the frequency at which groups of conversions are started and the number of conversions allowed per group. The default frequency is every 15 minutes (range is 1 to 59). The default number of conversions per group is 300 (range is 1 to 1000).
- **Job Monitoring** This is the length of time, in minutes, before the conversion status is monitored and, if necessary, restarted. Default is 5 minutes (range is 1 to 60).
- **Maximum Conversion Attempts** This is the maximum number of times Word Automation Services tries to convert a document before its status is set to failed. The default number of times is 2 (range is 1 to 10).
- **Maximum Synchronous Conversion Requests** This is the maximum number of conversion requests that can be processed at a time per server. Default is 25 (range is 1 to 1000).

As you can tell by the setting values (particularly the 100 percent for the Maximum Memory Usage setting), you need to plan resource allocation if you expect to convert a large number of documents. You can easily bring the SharePoint farm to a grinding halt if these settings aren't properly set.

Configuring file conversions

SharePoint Server 2013 provides two options for how a conversion is started. In SharePoint 2010, conversions are placed into a queue that's processed by a timer job that runs up to once a minute (or up to 59 minutes). In SharePoint 2013, conversions can be processed "on demand," in which they are started right away and pushed ahead of the conversions in the queue. This allows for a much more responsive user experience. For example, you might have a web part that converts Word documents to web pages for end users. Users would much prefer to have the document converted right away rather than have to wait until the timer job starts.

> ***IMPORTANT*** **On-demand file conversions can be done synchronously, on only one file at a time.**

The server that Word Automation Services uses doesn't have to be the one that the SharePoint farm is installed on. You can use a different server to help take the load off the SharePoint farm database. You can also move the database, after you create it, to another SQL Server instance if you decide that the load is too much on the server where it is located. You need to edit the Word Automation Services service application properties if you do move the database. This can be done in Central Administration or via PowerShell.

> ***MORE INFO*** **MOVING THE WORD AUTOMATION SERVICES DATABASES**
>
> **See *http://technet.microsoft.com/en-us/library/jj729799.aspx* for more information on how to Move the Word Automation Services service application databases in SharePoint Server 2013.**

Another new feature in SharePoint Server 2013 for Word Automation Services is the ability to perform file conversions on streams. This means that you can now convert files that aren't stored in SharePoint. This feature has many uses, especially if you are converting the file before it goes into SharePoint. This would save you from having to put the file into SharePoint and then deleting it after it is converted (resource-expensive operations that also take a lot of transaction log space). The drawback to this new feature is that it can be used only with on-demand file conversion jobs, which means that only one stream can be converted at a time.

> ***MORE INFO*** **WHAT'S NEW IN WORD AUTOMATION SERVICES FOR DEVELOPERS?**
>
> **See *http://msdn.microsoft.com/en-us/library/office/jj163073.aspx* for more details on the new developer features in Word Automation Services.**

Creating and configuring Microsoft PowerPoint Conversion Services

Microsoft PowerPoint Conversion Services is a new feature in SharePoint 2013. In concept, it's similar to Word Automation Services in that it provides the capability for automated conversions of PowerPoint documents to other types of documents. For example, if you wanted to convert a series of PowerPoint documents to a series of JPG files, you could use PowerPoint Conversion Services to automate this. The following files are supported for conversion by PowerPoint Conversion Services:

- Open XML File Format (.pptx)
- PowerPoint 97-2003 (.ppt)

PowerPoint Conversion Services can take these supported files and convert them into various formats, as follows:

- Open XML File Format (.pptx)
- Portable Document Format (.pdf)
- Open XML Paper Specification (.xps)
- Portable Network Graphics (.png)
- Joint Photographic Experts Group (.jpg)

MORE INFO **USING POWERPOINT AUTOMATION SERVICES**

See *http://msdn.microsoft.com/en-us/library/fp179894.aspx* for more information on using PowerPoint Automation Services and PowerPoint Conversion Services in SharePoint 2013.

The PowerPoint Conversion Services service application relies on the PowerPoint Conversion Service. If you expect to convert many files, you should probably have this service running on more than one server. If you expect heavy and regular conversion usage, you should dedicate one or more servers to running this service. You can start the service on the required servers by following these steps:

1. Navigate to Central Administration as a farm administrator and click Manage Services On Server in the System Settings section.
2. Select the server on which you want the service running from the Server drop-down list.
3. Find the PowerPoint Conversion Service under the Service column and click Start under the Action column.
4. Repeat steps 2 and 3 for every server that you want running the PowerPoint Conversion Service.

After you start the services on the servers, you need to create the PowerPoint Conversion Service service application. This can be done by running the Farm Configuration Wizard and choosing the PowerPoint Conversion Service Application in the list of service applications.

(If this is the only service application that you want configured, make sure that all the other options that can be changed are cleared.) The Farm Configuration Wizard uses the default settings; if you don't want to use the default settings or just prefer to use PowerShell, you can use the following commands to create the service application and its proxy:

```
$account=Get-SPManagedAccount "<account>"
$appPool=New-SPServiceApplicationPool -Name PowerPowerAppPool -Account $account
$appService=New-SPPowerPointConversionServiceApplication -ApplicationPool $appPool -Name
<ServiceName>
$proxyService=New-SPPowerPointConversionServiceApplicationProxy -ServiceApplication
$appService
```

After you create the PowerPoint Conversion Service service application and proxy, it's ready to be used by programmers. You don't need to configure any user settings.

EXAM TIP

PowerPoint Conversion Services was also known as PowerPoint Automation Services but in the final release of SharePoint Server 2013, it's referred to as PowerPoint Conversion Services. It could be referred to either way on the exam.

Creating and configuring Machine Translation Services

The Machine Translation Services service application is a powerful new tool in SharePoint 2013 that allows documents to be sent to Microsoft for translation from one language to another. This can be done for files and pages as well as for whole sites. This remarkable new service allows owners of SharePoint to deliver much of its content in wide variety of languages. Architecturally, the Machine Translation Service is similar to the Word Automation Service in that it has timer jobs and queues.

NOTE **LANGUAGE PACKS AREN'T APPLICABLE HERE**

The Machine Translation Services service application isn't connected to the language packs that enable the user interface elements to be displayed in the language of the browser.

IMPORTANT **Information sent to Microsoft for translation can be used to help improve the translation process (and only for that reason). You should let users know that this is possible so that they can decide whether they want to use the service.**

Creating and configuring the Machine Translation service is a little more complicated than most of the service applications, mainly because it has to connect to the Internet. The following prerequisites must exist before you can use the Machine Translation service:

- The App Management service needs to be running.
- Server-to-server authentication needs to be configured.

- The default proxy group must have a User Profile service application proxy.
- Any server running the Machine Translation service needs to be connected to the Internet.

The App Management Service is probably already running on your server, but if it isn't, you need to create the App Management Service service application and start the App Management service as you did when creating and configuring the App Catalog in Objective 4-1, "Create and configure App Management."

> ***MORE INFO*** **CONFIGURING AUTHENTICATION**
>
> **Configuring server-to-server authentication and app authentication isn't covered in detail here for the Machine Translation service. For the exam, however, you should still know that they are required. See *http://technet.microsoft.com/en-us/library/jj219532.aspx* for information on how to configure server-to-server authentication in SharePoint 2013. For information on how to configure app authentication in SharePoint Server 2013, see *http://technet.microsoft.com/en-us/library/jj655398.aspx*.**

Creating a Machine Translation Services service application

Any server that runs the Machine Translation service needs Internet access. This generally means opening up an Internet Explorer browser window on the server and going to Tools | Internet Options. On the Connections tab, click LAN Settings and then define a proxy server and port that will allow access out to the Internet. Your organization might already have this set up, or you might want to use a configuration script to make this happen. In any case, the server needs to send and receive files from the internet.

After you make sure that the perquisites are met and that the Machine Translation service is running on the appropriate servers, you can begin the process of creating a Machine Translation Services service application in Central Administration. Follow these steps:

1. Navigate to Central Administration as a member of the Farm Administrators group and click Manage Service Applications in the Application Management section.
2. Click the New icon on the Manage Service Applications page and then choose Machine Translation Service.
3. Enter a name (such as Machine Translation Service Application) in the Name text box.
4. In the Application Pool section, either select an existing application pool or create a new one.

NOTE Application pool and User Profile service application

If you used a different account for the application pool that's used to run the Machine Translation service, you need to add that account to the list of users who can use the User Profile service application in the permissions settings.

5. In the Partitioned Mode section, select Run In Partitioned Mode only if you will be hosting.
6. Choose whether to add the service application to the default proxy list in the Add To Default Proxy List section.
7. In the Database section, choose the database server and the database name (use the SharePoint SQL Server instance unless you have a good reason to do so otherwise, such as heavy SQL Server loads and the need for load balancing). Leave Windows Authentication selected unless specified by your SQL Server administrator or for some other overriding business reason.
8. Click OK to finish.

Configuring the settings

After the Machine Translation Services service application is created, you should review the settings. Because the actual work of translation isn't done on the SharePoint farm, the Machine Translation service doesn't have the same resource requirements as Access Services or Word Automation Services. You should still make sure that the settings don't overly burden the servers running the service, however, especially if you need to translate a large number of files into a multitude of languages. To access the settings, click the name of the Machine Translation service on the Manage Service Applications page. The following settings are available:

- **Enabled File Extensions** A list of file extensions that are allowed to be sent to the Machine Translation service, grouped into four sets: Microsoft Word Documents, HTML, Plain-Text, and XLIFF.
- **Maximum File Size For Binary Files In KB** In the Item Size Limits section, but specifies the maximum size for those files in the Microsoft Word Documents section. The default value is 51200 (range is 100 to 524288).
- **Maximum File Size For Text Files In KB** Limit in the Item Size Limits section for plain-text, HTM, and XLIFF files. The default is 5120 (range is 100 to 15360).
- **Maximum Character Count For Microsoft Word Documents** Limit in the Item Size Limits section for the maximum number of characters. The default is 500000 (range is 10,000 to 10,000,000).

- **Web Proxy Server** In the Online Translation Connection section, in case you want to specify a specific proxy server for the service to use.
- **Translation Processes** The number of translation processes per server, meaning the number of translations that can occur at the same time per server. The default is 1 (range is 1 to 5).
- **Frequency With Which To Start Translations** In the Translation Throughput section; determines the frequency at which groups of translations are started. The default is 15 (range is 1 to 59).
- **Number Of Translations To Start** In the Translation Throughput section; determines the number of translations that can be sent per group (per translation process). Default is 200 (range is 1 to 1000).
- **Maximum Translation Attempts** In the Maximum Translation Attempts section; specifies the attempts to translate before a translation status is set to Failed. Default is 2 (range is 1 to 10).
- **Maximum Number Of Synchronous Translation Requests** In the Maximum Synchronous Translations Requests section; specifies the maximum number of synchronous translations that can be processed per server. Default is 10 (range is 0 to 300).
- **Maximum Number Of Items Which Can Be Queued Within A 24-Hour Period** In the Translation Quota section; specifies the maximum number of items in a 24-hour period. Default is No Limit (range is 100 to 1,000,000).
- **Maximum Number Of Items Which Can Be Queued Within A 24-Hour Period Per Site Subscription** In the Translation Quota section; determines the limit per site description. Default is No Limit (range is 100 to 1,000,000).
- **Recycle Threshold** In the Recycle Threshold section; specifies the number of documents translated by a translation process before it's restarted. Default is 100 (range is 1 to 1000).
- **Disable Office 97-2003 Document Scanning?** In the Office 97-2003 section; determines whether extra checks are done on Office 97-2003 documents before the documents are opened. Disable this setting only if you fully trust all documents loaded by the Machine Translation service.

> ***MORE INFO*** **CREATING AND CONFIGURING MACHINE TRANSLATION SERVICES**
>
> See *http://technet.microsoft.com/en-us/library/jj553772(v=office.15).aspx* for more information on how to create and configure Machine Translation Services in SharePoint Server 2013.

Running Machine Translation Services

The Machine Translation service can operate asynchronously, in which case the timer job values listed in the settings determine when the translations are processed. It can also operate synchronously. If you want to start translation processing immediately, you can do so by using the following PowerShell commands:

```
$timerjob = Get-SPTimerJob "Machine Translation Service - Machine Translation Service
Timer Job"
$timerjob.Runnow();
```

Several methods are available to make use of Machine Translation Services. The service application can be accessed through server-side code such as C#, through client-side code such as Jscript, or even through Representational State Transfer (REST) services. Within the SharePoint farm, Machine Translation Services has been integrated into variations. Translations can be requested by site owners manually, or they can be automated.

EXAM TIP

Because Machine Translation Services is new to SharePoint Server 2013, you can expect some sort of question about it on the exam. Pay attention to the pieces required to make it work, such as an Internet connection requirement and that it can run synchronously or asynchronously.

Thought experiment

Converting Word Automation Service servers

In the following thought experiment, apply what you've learned about this objective. You can find answers to these questions in the "Answers" section at the end of this chapter.

You are getting complaints from users that SharePoint has been slower than usual lately. You realize that a large Word conversion task is occurring and will continue for several months. You suspect that this has something to do with the slowness that users are experiencing. You also know that the Word conversion task is critical because a deadline is scheduled.

Your farm consists of two application servers and three WFEs. After some investigation, you've noticed that the memory on the application servers is being maxed out but that the WFEs aren't even using 50 percent of their resources.

What would you do improve the end-user experience without negatively affecting the Word conversion project and without adding any new servers?

Objective summary

- Excel Services is a powerful way to display Excel data wholly or partially in a controlled manner.
- Access Services allows complex queries of SharePoint data as well as external data sources.
- The Visio Graphics Service can provided raster-formatted data from Visio 2013 as well as display older Visio drawings using Silverlight.
- Word Automation Services allows for unattended processing of document conversions via timer jobs as well as on-demand conversions.
- PowerPoint Conversion Services can allow for the conversion of PowerPoint presentations into a wide variety of other types of documents, but configuration is limited.

Objective review

Answer the following questions to test your knowledge of the information in this objective. You can find the answers to these questions and explanations of why each answer choice is correct or incorrect in the "Answers" section at the end of this chapter.

1. The Excel Services application can use Excel files from which of the following locations?
   A. SharePoint sites
   B. Network file shares
   C. Non-SharePoint websites
   D. All of the above
2. Access Services requires SQL Server to store its data. Which version of SQL Server is required to use Access Services on SharePoint Server 2013?
   A. SQL Server 2008 Express
   B. SQL Server 2008 R2
   C. SQL Server 2012
   D. All of the above
3. What's the maximum amount of physical memory that Access Services can use on an individual SharePoint server?
   A. 25 percent
   B. 50 percent
   C. 75 percent
   D. All available up to 100 percent

4. Visio Services can display several types of drawing formats in the web browser. What types of drawings can't be displayed in raster format?
   - **A.** Visio web drawings (.vdw)
   - **B.** Visio 2013 drawings saved with the .vsdx extension (files saved in Open Packing Convention)
   - **C.** Visio 2013 drawings saved in the XML format with the .vsdm extension
   - **D.** All of the above
5. Both Visio Graphics Services and Excel Services can access external data through trusted data providers. What type of provider type can neither of these service applications use?
   - **A.** ODBC
   - **B.** Access
   - **C.** OLE DB
   - **D.** DBC with DSN
6. Which of the following file types can't be opened and converted by using the Word Automation Services?
   - **A.** Word 2003 documents
   - **B.** HTML pages
   - **C.** Excel workbooks
   - **D.** Rich Text Format files

Objective 4.3: Configure Service Application Federation

SharePoint Server 2013 farms can provide some of its services to other farms, otherwise known as a federation of services. If you are in an organization with more than one SharePoint farm, you can use federation of services to keep data consistent or use dedicated farms to provide services so that other SharePoint farms can use their resources for other tasks.

The first step in federating services is to determine which services should be federated. When this is determined, you need to set up a trust between the consuming farm and the publishing farm. After the trust is set up, one farm can publish the service and the other farm can consume it.

This objective covers the following topics:

- Planning services to federate
- Performing a certificate exchange
- Managing trusts
- Managing service application permissions
- Publishing service applications
- Consuming service applications

Planning services to federate

The first step in planning to federate services is to determine what services need to be federated. In SharePoint, a service on a farm can be published, and then one or more farms can consume this service. You might have various reasons to federate services. For example, if you want every farm to be able to search the same sets of data (thus providing consistent search results), you would want to set up a farm just for Search so that each farm won't crawl the same set of data and store duplicate indexes, thereby saving storage space, memory, and CPU. The business needs of your organization should determine which services to federate; however, only certain services can be federated:

- Business Data Connectivity
- Machine Translation
- Managed Metadata
- Search
- Secure Store
- User Profile

SharePoint 2010 farms can also consume services from a SharePoint 2013 farm, but not the other way around. This allows for SharePoint 2010 farms to be migrated in stages but still maintain consistency and services. For example, the Managed Metadata service application could be migrated to the SharePoint 2013 farm, and SharePoint 2010 farms could still consume the migrated managed metadata. SharePoint 2010 farms can consume only the services available in SharePoint 2010. For example, because Machine Translation doesn't exist in SharePoint 2010, the farm couldn't consume that service.

IMPORTANT **The User Profile service application and the content that it supports must reside in the same data center. This means that the My Site Host, the personal sites (SkyDrive Pro storage), team sites, and community sites must all be in the same data center.**

To use federated services, the farms involved need to be set up to trust one another and then the services themselves need to be published and consumed. The order in which the process of federating service applications should occur is as follows:

1. Exchange trust certificates between the farms (consuming and publishing) involved in the federation process.
2. Publish the service application on the publishing farm.
3. Set appropriate permissions on the consuming farm for the federated service application.
4. Connect to the publishing farm service application from the consuming farm.
5. Add the shared service application to a Web Application proxy group (that is, default proxy group) on the consuming farm.

EXAM TIP

The preceding steps are exactly the kind of ordering you might be asked to do on the exam. You can expect to see at least one question or case study (and perhaps more) about federating services.

Determining which services should be federated, which farms should be consumers, and which should be publishers is up to you and whoever else is architecting the farm. Switching to a federated service or switching back can take a considerable amount of time—hours or even days, depending on what data and/or settings need to be transferred to restore functionality. This would, of course, cause significant disruption in a production environment. To avoid these disruptions, try to test the scenarios that you might use before you implement them in production.

MORE INFO **SHARING SERVICE APPLICATIONS ACROSS FARMS**

See *http://technet.microsoft.com/en-us/library/ff621100.aspx* for more information on how to share service applications across farms in SharePoint 2013.

Performing a certificate exchange

Before two SharePoint farms can federate service applications, they must trust each other. For the SharePoint farms to trust each other, trust certificates must be exchanged between them. The consuming farm needs to provide two trust certificates to the publishing farm:

- Root certificate
- Security Token Service (STS) certificate

Whereas the consuming farm needs to provide two trust certificates to the publishing farm, the publishing farm needs to provide to the consuming farm just one certificate: the root certificate. These certificates must be created, copied over to the corresponding server, and then imported. The act of exporting the certificates varies somewhat, depending on the type of certificate being exported. To export the root certificate on the consuming farm, follow these steps:

1. Log onto a SharePoint server on the consuming farm with an account that is a member of the Administrators group. The account must also have the securityadmin and the db_owner fixed database roles on the consuming SharePoint farm's SQL Server instance.
2. Open the SharePoint 2013 Management Shell.
3. Run the following PowerShell commands, where *<Root Cert Path>* is the path and filename where you want to create the root certificate (for example, c:\Consuming-RootCert.cer):

   ```
   $rootCert = (Get-SPCertificateAuthority).RootCertificate
   $rootCert.Export("Cert")|Set-Content <Root Cert Path> -Encoding byte
   ```

While you are in the SharePoint 2013 Management Shell, you can export the security token (the STS certificate). Use the following PowerShell commands, in which *<STS Cert Path>* is the path and filename where you want to create the security token (STS) certificate:

```
$stsCert = (Get-SPSecurityTokenServiceConfig).LocalLoginProvider.SigningCertificate
$stsCert.Export("Cert")|Set-Content <STS Cert Path> -Encoding byte
```

After you export the certificates, you need to copy the consuming farm certificates to the publishing farm and the publishing farm certificate to the consuming farm.

> ***MORE INFO*** **EXCHANGING TRUST CERTIFICATES BETWEEN FARMS**
>
> **See *http://technet.microsoft.com/en-us/library/ee704552.aspx* for more information on how to exchange trust certificates between farms in SharePoint 2013.**

Managing trusts

After the certificates are created and exchanged, you can manage the trust between the consuming SharePoint farm and the publishing farm. Managing trusts requires that trust be established between the two farms. Establishing trust is done by importing certificates on the respective servers. On the publishing farm, you must import both the root and the STS certificates from the consuming farm. On the consuming farm, you need to import just the root certificate from the publishing farm. These tasks can be accomplished using Central Administration or through PowerShell commands. To import the certificates on the publishing farm, follow these steps:

1. Navigate to Central Administration with an account that's part of the Farm Administrators group.

2. Click the Security link on the home page.
3. Click Manage Trust in the General Security section.
4. Click New on the Trust Relationship page.
5. On the Establish Trust Relationship page, enter a name for the trust relationship (such as Farm A trust) in the General Setting section.
6. Click Browse in the Root Certificate For The Trust Relationship section and select the exported consuming farm's root certificate.
7. Select the Provide Trust Relationship check box in the Security Token Service (STS) Certificate For Providing Trust section.
8. Click the Browse button next to the Token Issuer Certificate box and select the exported consuming farm's STS certificate.
9. Click OK to save changes.

On the consuming farm, you would follow steps 1 through 6, except that you would choose the exported publishing farm's root certificate and then click OK. You don't need to import an STS certificate on the consuming farm, so you would leave the Provide Trust Relationship box cleared. When the two farms have their certificates imported, trust is considered to be established.

You can also use PowerShell commands to establish trust. To import the consuming farm's root certificate onto the publishing farm, follow these steps:

1. Open the SharePoint 2013 Management Shell on the publishing farm with an account that has the same level of permissions required for creating a certificate.
2. Run the following PowerShell commands, where *<name of the consuming server>* is the name of the consuming server (or another unique way to identify the consuming farm) and *<root cert path>* is the location of the consuming farm's root certificate:

   ```
   $rootCert=Get-PfxCertificate <root cert path>
   New-SPTrustedRootAuthority <name of the consuming server> -Certificate $rootCert
   ```

That takes care of importing the root certificate. Now you need to import the exported STS certificate from the consuming farm. You can do this by staying in the SharePoint 2013 Management Shell and using the following PowerShell commands, where *<sts cert path>* is the location of the consuming farm's STS certificate:

```
$stsCert=Get-PfxCertificate <sts cert path>
New-SPTrustedServiceTokenIssuer <name of consuming server> -Certificate $stsCert
```

The certificates on the publishing farm should be complete at this point. You can verify that they are set up correctly by looking at the Manage Trusts page in Central Administration. As with the Central Administration method, the consuming farm needs to import only the publishing farm's root certificate, and you can use the same set of PowerShell commands as you did on the publishing farm (except that you would use the path to the publishing farm's exported root certificate and use a unique name that represents the publishing farm).

Managing service application permissions

Before a consuming farm can actually consume any service applications from a publishing farm, the publishing farm has to give the consuming farm permissions to the Application Discovery and Load Balancing service application. After this is complete, the publishing farm can give permissions to the consuming farm for other service applications. Setting permissions on the publishing server can be done either in PowerShell or in Central Administration, but in either case you need the consuming farm ID, which you must obtain by using PowerShell commands. Follow these steps:

1. Log onto the consuming farm with an account that's a member of the Administrators group and also has the securityadmin role on the SQL Server instance that the consuming farm is running on.
2. Start the SharePoint 2013 Management Shell.
3. Run the following PowerShell command and store the ID (for example, in a text file) that's returned.

   ```
   Get-SPFarm | Select Id
   ```

Now that you have the ID of the consuming farm, you can provide permissions to the Application Discovery and Load Balancing service application. This can be done on the publishing farm using PowerShell commands as follows:

1. Log onto the publishing farm with an account that's a member of the Administrators group and also has the securityadmin and db_owner roles (on any database being updated) on the SQL Server instance that the publishing farm is running on.
2. Run the following PowerShell commands, where *<consuming farm ID>* is the ID of the consuming farm that you obtained earlier:

   ```
   $security=Get-SPTopologyServiceApplication|Get-SPServiceApplicationSecurity
   $claimprovider=(Get-SPClaimProvider System).ClaimProvider
   $principal=New-SPClaimsPrincipal -ClaimType
   http://schemas.microsoft.com/sharepoint/2009/08/claims/farmid -ClaimProvider
   $claimprovider -ClaimValue <consuming farm ID>
   Grant-SPObjectSecurity -Identity $security -Principal $principal -Rights "Full
   Control"
   Get-SPTopologyServiceApplication|Set-ServiceApplicationSecurity -ObjectSecurity
   $security
   ```

EXAM TIP

You might have noticed the Get-SPTopologyServiceApplication command in the preceding PowerShell code. This is because the Application Discovery and Load Balancing service application is also known as the Topology service. You might see the terms used interchangeably on the exam and in documentation.

If you want to use Central Administration (and save yourself a lot of typing) to set permissions on the Application Discovery and Load Balancing service application, you still need the consuming farm ID that you got from PowerShell earlier in this section. Assuming that you have the ID available, you can set permissions by following these steps:

1. Log onto a publishing server that's running Central Administration with an account that's a member of the Farm Administrators group.
2. Click Manage Service Applications in the Application Management section on the Central Administration home page.
3. Click the row that contains Application Discovery and Load Balancing Service Application.
4. On the ribbon, click the Permissions icon.
5. In the Connection Permissions dialog box, paste the consuming farm ID in the claims box, as shown in Figure 4-8.

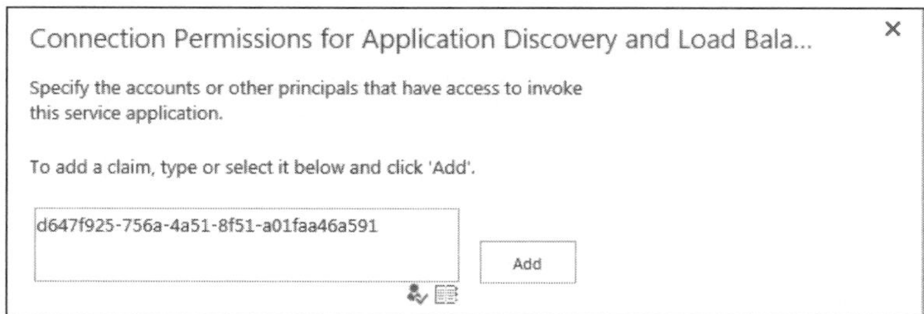

FIGURE 4-8 Connection Permissions dialog box with a farm ID pasted in it

6. Click the check names icon to resolve the farm ID, and then click the Add button.
7. Select the consuming farm ID in the box below where it was added and then select Full Control (the only option that can be selected).
8. Click OK.

After permissions are added to the Application Discovery and Load Balancing service application, you need to add permissions in the same way in Central Administration to any of the service applications that you want to publish to the consuming farm. If you want to use PowerShell commands to add these permissions, you would use similar commands as the earlier ones but instead use the service application's GUID with Get-SPServiceApplication, not Get-SPTopologyServiceApplication.

> ***MORE INFO*** **SETTING PERMISSIONS TO PUBLISHED SERVICE APPLICATIONS**
>
> **See *http://technet.microsoft.com/en-us/library/ff700211.aspx* for more information on how to set permissions to published service applications in SharePoint 2013.**

Publishing service applications

By now, you've exchanged certificates between the consuming and publishing farms, imported the certificates, and set permissions on the service applications. Now you need to actually publish the service applications so that they can be consumed by one or more farms.

The act of publishing a service application provides a Universal Resource Name (URN) that can be passed to consuming farm(s). This URN provides schema and authority information needed by the consuming farm.

You can use either Central Administration or PowerShell commands to publish service applications. The following steps use the Central Administration method:

1. Log onto Central Administration with a Farm Administrator account.
2. Click Manage Service Applications in the Application Management section.
3. Select the service application that you want to publish (do *not* to click the link but just *select* the line so that it's highlighted) on the Manage Service Applications page.
4. Click the Publish button on the ribbon to open the Publish Service Application dialog box.
5. Select the type of connection (http or https) that you want to use from the Connection Type drop-down list.
6. Select the check box for Publish This Service Application To Other Farms.
7. Copy the published URN so that it can be used later. A published URN look something like this:

   ```
   schemas-microsoft-com:sharepoint:service:196807c3bb0f4eea9b10afb70793a16
   7#authority=urn:uuid:daf0ec20a27a44c7abe5104b5d516637&authority=https://
   publishingserver:32844/Topology/topology.svc
   ```

8. Optionally, enter a Description and a link to an information page if you want to provide consuming farms with that information.
9. Click OK to start publishing.

The service application should be published at this point and you should have the published URN for use on the consuming farm. If you didn't set up your trust with the consuming farm(s) earlier, you could have done it from the Publish Service Application dialog box by clicking the Click Here To Add A Trust Relationship With Another Farm link. You can also publish a service application by using PowerShell commands, as follows:

1. Log onto a server in the SharePoint publishing farm with an account that's a member of the Administrators group and has the securityadmin fixed server role on the publishing farm's SQL Server instance.
2. Open the SharePoint 2013 Management Shell.
3. Run the PowerShell command Get-SPServiceApplication to get a list of service applications and their associated GUIDs. Find the GUID associated with the service application that you want to publish and copy it for later.
4. Run the following PowerShell command, where *<Service App GUID>* is the GUID you copied from step 3.

   ```
   Publish-SPServiceApplication -Identity <Service App GUID>
   ```

5. The service is published at this point if the command was successful. Use the PowerShell command Get-SPTopologyServiceApplication to get the load-balancing URN of the topology service that's needed for consuming the service.

> ***MORE INFO*** **PUBLISHING SERVICE APPLICATIONS**
>
> **See *http://technet.microsoft.com/en-us/library/ee704545.aspx* for more information on how to publish service applications in SharePoint 2013.**

Consuming service applications

Now you should be ready to start consuming service applications and using that functionality on the consuming SharePoint farm. To consume a service application, you need the published URN from the service application on the publishing farm. You can use Central Administration or PowerShell commands to consume the service application. If you want to consume the service application with Central Administration, follow these steps:

1. Open Central Administration with an account that's a member of the Farm Administrators group.
2. Click Manage Service Applications in the Application Management section.
3. On the ribbon, click the Connect icon and then choose the type of service application to which you want to connect (such as Machine Translation Service Proxy).
4. On the Connect To A Remote Service Application page, enter the Farm or Service Application address (for example, the value from the Published URN field that starts with *urn*).

5. Click OK. If you can connect to the published service application, you should get a confirmation screen; otherwise, you should get an error.
6. On the next screen you should see the service application. Select whether you want to add the service to the consuming farm's default proxy list.
7. Make sure that the service is highlighted and click OK to connect.
8. A confirmation screen appears. Click OK again.

The remote service application should be available for use now if everything is configured correctly.

If you want to use PowerShell commands to connect to the remote service application, follow these steps:

1. Log onto a server in the SharePoint publishing farm with an account that's a member of the Administrators group and has the securityadmin fixed server role on the publishing farm's SQL Server instance.
2. Open the SharePoint 2013 Management Shell.
3. Run the following PowerShell command, where *<Published URL>* is the publishing farm topology URL that you can get from Central Administration or from the PowerShell command Get-SPTopologyServiceApplication:

   ```
   Receive-SPServiceApplicationConnectionInfo -FarmURL <Published URL>
   ```

4. You need to use a different command depending on the type of service application you are connecting to. Regardless of the command, you still need to supply a name and the Published URL (same one as in step 3). The different commands available are as follows:

   ```
   New-SPBusinessDataCatalogServiceApplicationProxy
   New-SPEnterpriseSearchServiceApplicationProxy
   New-SPMetadataServiceApplicationProxy
   New-SPProfileServiceApplicationProxy
   New-SPSecureStoreServiceApplicationProxy
   ```

At this point, you should be able to consume the service application. If an error occurred in the configuration, you need to pinpoint it starting with the trust certificates, then going to permissions, and also verifying that you're using the correct published URL. All these items have to be done without error for federation to work. Troubleshooting can be difficult, so it might be easiest to start over from the beginning if it's not working.

MORE INFO CONNECTING TO SERVICE APPLICATIONS ON REMOTE FARMS

See *http://technet.microsoft.com/en-us/library/ee704558.aspx* for more information on how to connect to service applications on remote farms in SharePoint 2013.

Thought experiment

Upgrading service applications

In the following thought experiment, apply what you've learned about this objective. You can find answers to these questions in the "Answers" section at the end of this chapter.

You are migrating your SharePoint 2010 farms over to SharePoint 2013. Because of scheduling and budget issues, you can migrate only one farm over at this time. You want the remaining SharePoint farms to use the Search service on the SharePoint 2013 farm, to free up server resources on the SharePoint 2010 farm as well as provide a single source for querying and indexing.

What steps are required to make this happen?

Objective summary

- You can use federation to keep data consistent, reduce duplication of data, offload resource-intensive tasks to other farms, and increase security.
- Two certificates from the consuming farm and one from the publishing farm are required to establish trust between two SharePoint farms.
- Trust relationships can be viewed in Central Administration on the Manage Trust page, which can be found through the General Security section on the Security page.
- The Application Discovery and Load Balancing service application—also know as the Topology service—must be published on the publishing farm.
- The consuming farm must be given permissions to the publishing farm's Application Discovery and Load Balancing service application as well as the service application that it's consuming.
- The published URL for a service application on the publishing farm is needed by the consuming farm to connect to the published service application.

Objective review

Answer the following questions to test your knowledge of the information in this objective. You can find the answers to these questions and explanations of why each answer choice is correct or incorrect in the "Answers" section at the end of this chapter.

1. Which of the following services can't be consumed by a SharePoint 2010 farm from a SharePoint 2013 farm?
   - **A.** Search
   - **B.** Secure Store
   - **C.** Machine Translation
   - **D.** Managed Metadata
2. For a trust to be established between two SharePoint farms, certificates must be exchanged between the consuming farm and the publishing farm. Which certificate(s) must be created by the consuming farm and copied over to the publishing farm?
   - **A.** A root certificate and a security token certificate
   - **B.** Just a root certificate
   - **C.** Just a token certificate
   - **D.** A subordinate certificate
3. Which PowerShell commands should you use when importing a root certificate from another farm?
   - **A.** Get-SPCertificateAuthority
   - **B.** Get-PfxCertificate
   - **C.** Get-RootCertificate
   - **D.** Get-SPServiceApplicationSecurity
4. Which of the following steps must you perform before a consuming farm can consume a service application from a publishing farm?
   - **A.** The consuming farm must be given permissions to the Application Discovery and Load Balancing service application.
   - **B.** The consuming farm must be given permissions to the service application that's to be consumed.
   - **C.** Both the root and the STS certificates from the consuming farm must be imported on the publishing farm.
   - **D.** All of the above.

Objective 4.4: Create and configure a Business Connectivity Service and Secure Store application

The Business Connectivity Service (BCS) is used to connect to external data so that it can be exposed as a SharePoint list or be used in SharePoint application. It works with the Secure Store service application to provide users secure access to the data. The Secure Store also works with other service applications, such as the Visio Graphics Services and Excel Services service applications, but it's included in this objective because it is integral to the BCS service application.

Many kinds of data are better stored directly in databases such as SQL Server, but this data might also need to be exposed to users. The BCS can expose this data securely by exposing only the data that's truly needed, as well as using the Secure Store to access the data with an account that has only limited rights so that end users never have direct access to the underlying data. With proper permissions, end users can even update the underlying data through SharePoint.

This objective assumes that the BCS and Secure Store service applications have already been created on the SharePoint farm. The BCS requires considerable configuration before you can start displaying and interacting with external data. Proper configuration will ensure secure exposure of data and provide optimal performance. This objective covers how to create and configure both the BCS and the Secure Store service applications.

This objective covers the following topics:

- Importing and configuring BCS models
- Configuring BCS model security
- Generating a Secure Store Master Key
- Managing the Secure Store Master Key
- Creating Secure Store target applications
- Managing Secure Store target application permissions

Importing and configuring BCS models

BCS models—also known as Business Data Catalog (BDC) models—are XML files that describe an external data source. The XML file outlines the data available, the data type, and the data location for one or more external content types. The BCS model can be used with a wide variety of different types of data sources:

- Open Data (OData)
- Windows Communication Foundation (WCF) endpoints
- SQL Server

- Web services
- Cloud-based services
- .NET assemblies
- Custom connectors

The ability to use OData data sources is new to SharePoint. SharePoint lists have been available as OData to other programs that can consume OData sources, but this is the first version of SharePoint that has built-in support for consuming OData. Data is accessed with OData by using a specially formed URL.

MORE INFO **USING ODATA SOURCES WITH BCS**

See *http://msdn.microsoft.com/en-us/library/sharepoint/jj163802(v=office.15)* for more information on using OData sources with Business Connectivity Services in SharePoint 2013.

EXAM TIP

Because using OData data sources is new to SharePoint 2013, you can expect to see it in some fashion on the exam. OData also requires that Visual Studio (2010 or later) be used to create BCD models that use it, whereas usually you can choose between Visual Studio and SharePoint Designer.

After a model is created and imported, the BCS can expose the data as a SharePoint list, use it in a SharePoint application, or even use it in Microsoft Office 2013. The BCS models can be created with SharePoint Designer or with Visual Studio. Depending on permissions and how the BCS model is designed, users can create, read, update, and delete data (known as *CRUD operations*). Users can also create queries that use the data. Regardless of how a model is created, it can be imported into the Business Data Connectivity Services (BDCS) service application using Central Administration or with PowerShell commands. To import a BCS model using Central Administration, follow these steps:

1. Open Central Administration with an account that has permissions to use the BDCS service application (a farm administrator or an administrator of the BDCS service) and has Edit permissions on the metadata store.
2. Click Manage Service Applications in the Application Management section.
3. Find the BDCS service application (Business Data Connectivity Service Application) and click it.
4. Click the Import icon, as shown in Figure 4-9.

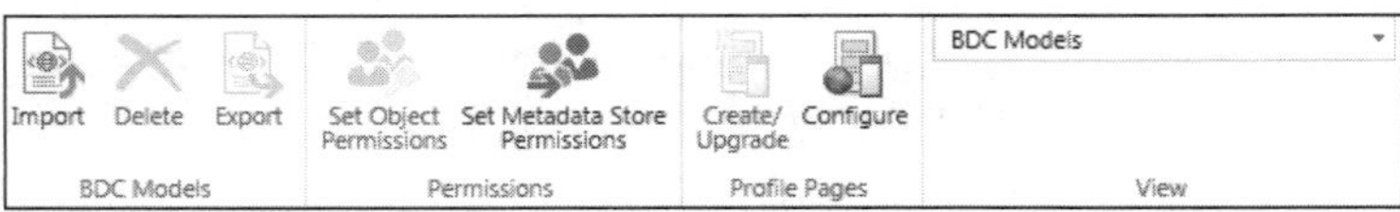

FIGURE 4-9 Ribbon for Business Data Connectivity Services service application

5. On the Import BDC Model page, click Browse in the BDC Model section and choose the exported model file that you want to import.
6. Under File Type, choose whether it's a Model (a definition file that contains the base metadata) or a Resource (a definition file that contains any combination of localized names, properties, and permissions).
7. In the Advanced Settings section, choose which resources to import (if you are importing a resource file) and configure any custom environment settings that you want to use.
8. Click Import to begin importing the file. The file is validated and, if it was successfully imported, you can click OK to finish.

> ***IMPORTANT*** **Use caution when importing permissions. The permissions imported are added to the security objects for the existing model. If an entry for a particular access control list (ACL) entry already exists, it will be overwritten.**

After you import the model, it appears on the Business Data Connectivity page. Notice that three views can exist on the page: BDC Models, External Systems, and External Content Types. If you don't see the data you are expecting, check to make sure that the view is correct.

You can also import models by using PowerShell commands in the SharePoint 2013 Management Shell, assuming that the account used has the proper permissions. You need to get a reference to the metadata store using the command Get-SPBusinessDataCatalogMetadataObject and then use the command Import-SPBusinessDataCatalogModel to import the model into the BDCS service application. In the following example, *<context>* is a web app that uses the metadata store you want to associate your model to (such as http://contoso) and *<BDCM Path>* is the file path to the exported model (for example, c:\model.bdcm):

```
$meta=Get-SPBusinessDataCatalogMetadataObject -BdcObjectType "Catalog" -ServiceContext
<context>
Import-SPBusinessDataCatalogModel -Path <BDCM Path> -Identity $meta
```

> ***MORE INFO*** **USING IMPORT-SPBUSINESSDATACATALOGMODEL**
>
> **See *http://technet.microsoft.com/en-us/library/ff607757.aspx* for more information on how to use the PowerShell command Import-SPBusinessDataCatalogModel.**

As soon as a model is in the Business Data Catalog service application, it can be exported out. You might want to do this when you are moving from development to production or from one farm to another. If you created the model with SharePoint Designer 2013, you should use that to export the model. If you created the model with Visual Studio, you can import through Central Administration or through the SharePoint 2013 Management Shell by using the PowerShell command Export-SPBusinessDataCatalogModel.

MORE INFO USING EXPORT-SPBUSINESSDATACATALOGMODEL

See *http://technet.microsoft.com/en-us/library/ff607696(v=office.15).aspx* for more information on the PowerShell command Export-SPBusinessDataCatalogModel.

To use Central Administration to export a BDC model or resource file, follow these steps:

1. Open Central Administration with an account that has permissions to use the BDCS service application (a farm administrator or an administrator of the BDCS service) and has Edit permissions on the metadata store.
2. Click Manage Service Applications in the Application Management section.
3. Click the BDCS service application (Business Data Connectivity Service Application).
4. Make sure that the view is set to BDC Models.
5. From the list of models and resources, select the one you want to export.
6. Click the Export button that should now be enabled.
7. Select Model or Resource in the File Type section and then choose which resources you want to export (see Figure 4-10). You can also specify the name of any custom environment settings.

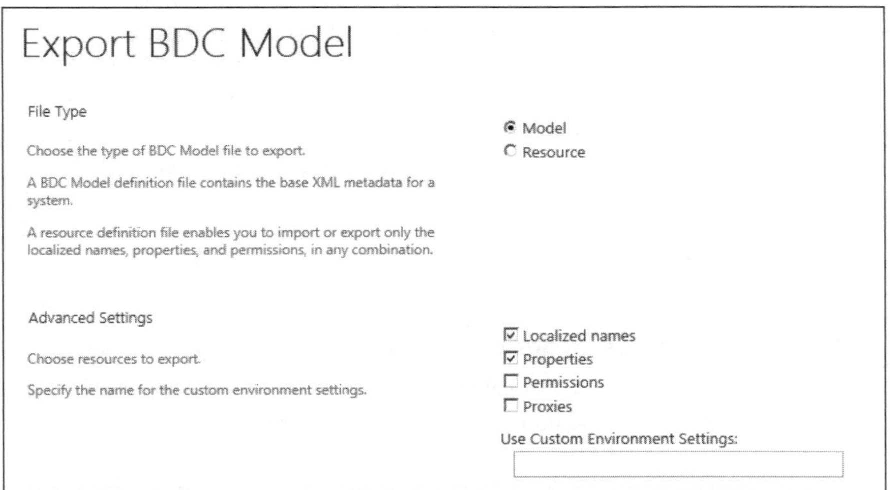

Export BDC Model
File Type
Choose the type of BDC Model file to export.
A BDC Model definition file contains the base XML metadata for a system.
A resource definition file enables you to import or export only the localized names, properties, and permissions, in any combination.
Model
Resource
Advanced Settings
Choose resources to export.
Specify the name for the custom environment settings.
Localized names
Properties
Permissions
Proxies
Use Custom Environment Settings:

FIGURE 4-10 Export BDC Model page, showing export options

8. Click Export to begin the process of saving the model or resource to a file. You are prompted where to save the file.

EXAM TIP

This exam won't cover creating the models in any detail; the other exams go into deeper detail in that area. You just need to know how to make the models available securely to developers and end users.

The BCS uses profile pages to enable end users to see data related to a particular record. For example, a user could see all the details related to a catalog item such as price, quantity, weight, and so on. All the data related to the particular record appears on the profile page just by clicking the View Profile Action link that shows up on any SharePoint list where the business data is displayed. You can set the location of where the profile pages will reside, which can be any SharePoint site in the farm, but for maintenance and security reasons you are recommended to use one site for all the profile pages used by the BCS. You don't have to enable profile page creation, but if you do, you need to specify a location. To configure profile pages for a BCD model, follow these steps:

1. Open Central Administration with an account that has permissions to use the BDCS service application (a farm administrator or an administrator of the BDCS service) and has Edit permissions on the metadata store.
2. Click Manage Service Applications in the Application Management section.
3. Click the Business Data Connectivity Services Application link.
4. Click the Configure icon in the Profile Pages section of the ribbon.
5. Leave the Enable Profile Page Creation check box selected and provide the location of the site to create the pages, as shown in Figure 4-11.

FIGURE 4-11 Configure External Content Type Profile Page Host page

6. Click OK to save changes.

After you supply a Host SharePoint site URL and enabled profile page creation, you can create the profile pages by following these steps, assuming that you are already on the Business Data Connectivity Service Application properties page:

1. Change the view to External Content Types.

2. Select the External Content Types for which you want to create profile pages.
3. Click the Create/Upgrade icon in the Profile Pages section.
4. A page appears that has several warnings on it. If you still want to create the page, click OK.
5. Either a success page or an error page that indicates something is wrong with your model (such as a warning that SpecificFinder isn't defined) appears. Click OK to continue.

> ***IMPORTANT*** **Creating a profile page overwrites any previous profile page (such as one that you might have customized). If the External Content Type has a Custom Action as its Default Action, creating a profile page changes that Default Action to View Profile.**

In a situation where profile pages already exist, they are either upgraded or replaced. If they are replaced, you will lose any customizations. If they are being upgraded from SharePoint 2010 profile pages, they are simply upgraded; if they are being upgraded from SharePoint 2007 profile pages, a new action, called View Profile (SharePoint 2007), is added to point to the old profile page. View Profile points to the newly created profile page.

Profile pages are regular SharePoint pages that can be modified after they are created. You can provide additional information about the record, modify the look and feel of the page, and put links to more information on the page. You can add/remove web parts and customize the page to fit your organization's needs. You can also modify the templates on which the profile pages are based, but remember that all future profile pages will use these modified templates.

Configuring BCS model security

Security in general should be kept to a least-privileged model. This means that only those users who need access to a BCS model (also known as a BDC model) and the components associated with it (External Systems and External Content Types) should have access to it.

Depending on the size and complexity of your organization, you probably don't want the SharePoint farm administrators to manage the security on the BCS models. In fact, you might not want the farm administrators to have anything to do with the management of the BCS models. As a BCS administrator, you can apply permissions to each of the following items directly:

- Metadata store
- BDC models
- External systems
- External content types

The BDC models, external systems, and external content types are all stored in the metadata store. It not only provides a place for storage but also a mechanism for permissions inheritance. If a BDC model, external system, or external content type isn't given explicit permissions, they inherit their permissions from the metadata store. An external content types can also inherit its permissions from the external system to which it's connected.

Permissions inheritance can happen in one of two ways. Whenever an item is added, it automatically inherits the permissions of the metadata store. You can also forcibly overwrite any set of custom permissions by using the Propagate Permissions To All option when modifying the metadata store permissions. To modify the metadata store permissions, follow these steps:

1. Open Central Administration with an account that has permissions to use the BDCS service application (a farm administrator or an administrator of the BDCS service) and has Edit permissions on the metadata store.
2. Click Manage service Applications in the Application Management section.
3. Click the Business Data Connectivity Services Application link.
4. Click the Set Metadata Store Permissions icon in the Profile Pages section on the EDIT tab of the ribbon.
5. Add an account or accounts to the Permissions box and click Add.
6. Choose Edit and/or Set Permissions in the Permissions section, as shown in Figure 4-12. (Execute and Selectable In Clients have no meaning here.)

FIGURE 4-12 Permission section of the Set Metadata Store Permissions dialog box

7. Select the Propagate Permissions To All BDC Models, External Systems And External Content Types In The BDC Metadata Store check box if you want to overwrite all existing permissions.
8. Click OK to save changes.

You can make changes to each of the three components (BDC Models, External Systems, and External Content Types) individually depending on your organization's security needs. You would set the permissions similarly, but you would first select the view corresponding to the item that you want to change (such as BDC models) and then select the items to which you want to assign permissions. After selecting the items, click Set Object Permissions in the Permissions section of the EDIT tab on the ribbon. Then add users and permissions in the same way as you would with the metadata store. Any set of permissions that you set on the object will override the permissions set at the metadata store level unless the permissions are forcefully propagated down. The types of permissions and what they mean are as follows:

- **Edit** Users who have this permission can edit the object.
- **Execute** This is required for users of the external content type to perform CRUDQ (create, read, update, delete, and query) operations.
- **Selectable in Clients** This allows users or groups to expose external content types in external lists and apps within SharePoint by making them available in the external item picker.
- **Set Permissions** This allows users to set permissions on the object. At least one user or group must have this permission for each object.

Having a very limited set of users (or even just one user) at the metadata store level is generally advisable, and as is using the Propagate permissions to all early on and then not use it again. For the individual objects, give permissions explicitly to the users that are responsible for how the objects will be used. Periodically, you should review the permissions on all objects in BCS as you would with any secured area of your organization.

> ***MORE INFO*** **OVERVIEW OF BUSINESS CONNECTIVITY SERVICES SECURITY TASKS**
>
> **See** ***http://technet.microsoft.com/en-us/library/jj683116.aspx*** **for an overview of Business Connectivity Services security tasks in SharePoint 2013.**

Generating a Secure Store master key

The Secure Store is a service application that provides an authorization service to other service applications. Credentials are stored securely in a database on the SQL Server instance that the SharePoint farm uses. The BCS uses the Secure Store to provide secure access to external systems that don't use Active Directory or use Active Directory but want to impersonate as a different user. The security placed on BCS objects has no relation to the permissions that are set in Secure Store.

Before the BCS can start using the Secure Store, a master key needs to be generated. This master key is used to encrypt the credentials so that even if someone had access to the Secure Store database, they couldn't retrieve the credentials. After the Secure Store service application is created, you need to create the master key:

1. Navigate to Central Administration with a farm administrator account.
2. Click Manage Service Applications in the Application Management section.
3. Click the Secure Store service application.
4. On the Secure Store Service Application page is a message indicating that you must first generate a new key. If you don't see this message, a master key has already been created or something is wrong with the Secure Store service.

5. Click Generate New Key in the Key Management section of the EDIT tab, as shown in Figure 4-13.

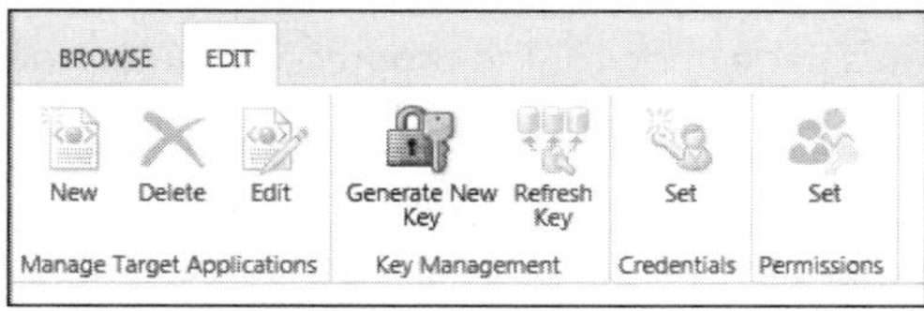

FIGURE 4-13 EDIT tab of the Secure Store service application

6. In the Generate New Key dialog box, enter a passphrase in the Pass Phrase text box. A passphrase is a case-sensitive password that's required to add new store service servers and needed for restoring a Secure Store database. It's not stored, so record it somewhere safe. The passphrase must meet the following requirements:
   - It's at least eight characters long.
   - It contains at least three of the following character groups: English uppercase characters (A through Z), English lowercase characters (a through z), numerals (0 through 9), and non-alphabetic characters (such as !, $, #, and %).
7. Reenter the passphrase in the Confirm Pass Phrase text box and click OK.

After you generate a new key, you should back up both the Secure Store database as well as the Secure service itself (which contains the key). These backups should be stored in separate locations for security reasons; the key is necessary to decrypt the database. If a new key is generated, you should repeat the backup process so that the backups of the key and the database are kept in sync.

> ***IMPORTANT*** **The Secure Store service application isn't backed up as part of the usual database backup procedure. If the Secure Store service application is lost, you can't decrypt the Secure Store database and all the data in there will be unusable.**

You use Central Administration or PowerShell commands to back up the Secure Store service. To back up the service with Central Administration, follow these steps:

1. Navigate to Central Administration as a farm administrator.
2. Click Perform A Backup in the Backup and Restore section.
3. On the Select Component To Back Up page, expand the Shared Services section if it's not already expanded.
4. Expand the Shared Services Applications section and select Secure Store Service Application.
5. Click Next to open the Select Backup Options page.

6. In the Backup Type section, select Full (the default).
7. Enter a backup location in the Backup File Location and click Start Backup.
8. On the Backup And Restore Job Status page, monitor the progress until the procedure is complete.
9. Move the backup file to a secure location—not on the SharePoint farm and not with the backups of the Secure Store database.

You can back up the Secure Store service application with PowerShell also. As with the Central Administration backup method, the backup should be done locally for performance reasons but then it should be moved to a separate secure location. You can use the following PowerShell command in the SharePoint 2013 Management Shell to back up the Secure Store service application, where *<path>* is the network folder location and *<service name>* is the name of the Secure Store service application:

```
Backup-SPFarm -Directory <path> -BackupMethod Full -Item <service name>
```

If for some reason the key is compromised, a new one should be created. If this is done, any backups of the old Secure Store database and any backups of the old Secure Store service application (which contains the key) should be deleted as well, assuming that new backups have been done.

> ***MORE INFO*** **BACKING UP THE SECURE STORE SERVICE**
>
> **See *http://technet.microsoft.com/en-us/library/ee748648.aspx* for more information on how to back up the Secure Store service in SharePoint 2013.**

Managing the Secure Store master key

Managing the Secure Store master key means keeping the backed-up key (the backup of the Secure Store service application) and the passphrase in a secure location and, if necessary, restoring the master key. Keeping the master key and passphrase in a secure location depends on your organization and the options that you have available. Storing it on physical media such a thumb drive and putting it in a locked storage area is recommended.

You might need to restore the Secure Store service application (and therefore the master key) if the key is compromised or the service application becomes corrupted because of hardware or software failures. You can use Central Administration or PowerShell commands to restore the Secure Store service application, but in either case you need the passphrase. To perform the restore operation using Central Administration, follow these steps:

1. Navigate to Central Administration as a farm administrator.
2. Click Restore From A Backup in the Backup And Restore section.

3. On the Select Backup To Restore page, enter the path to the backup of the Secure Store service application and click Refresh.
4. Select the backup from the list of backups and click Next.
5. On the Select Component To Restore page, expand the Shared Services section if it's not already expanded.
6. Expand the Shared Services Applications section and select Secure Store Service Application.
7. Click Next to open the Select Restore Options page. Check that the name of the Secure Store service application appears in the Restore Component section (preceded by Farm\Shared Services\Shared Services Applications\).
8. In the Restore Options section, select Same Configuration under Type Of Restore. Click OK to confirm.
9. Click Start Restore and wait for the job to complete.
10. Go to the Service Applications page and click the Secure Store service application.
11. On the Secure Store Service page, click Refresh Key.
12. Enter the passphrase in the Pass Phrase text box when asked, and then click OK.

After you restore a Secure Store service application, you should probably generate a new key and do another backup.

If you want to use PowerShell commands to restore the Secure Store service application, you can do so by using the following commands in the SharePoint 2013 Management Shell, where *<service name>* is the Secure Store service application name, *<path>* is the folder where the backup is stored, and *<passphrase>* is the passphrase:

```
Restore-SPFarm -Directory <path> -Item <service name> -RecoveryMethod Overwrite
Update-SPSecureStoreApplicationServerKey -Passphrase <passphrase>
```

This method restores the most recent backup (if more than one exist). To retrieve a specific backup, use the PowerShell command Get-SPBackupHistory.

> ***MORE INFO*** **RESTORING THE SECURE STORE SERVICE**
>
> **See *http://technet.microsoft.com/en-us/library/ee748602.aspx* for more information about how to restore the Secure Store service in SharePoint Server 2013.**

Creating Secure Store target applications

A *target application* is defined as a collection of information used to map a user or group of users to a set of credentials that's used to access data. The user name and password stored in the credentials is what's used to access the external data, instead of the user's credentials used to access SharePoint. The following information is stored as part of the target application:

- Credentials (user name and password) used to connect to the external application
- Any additional fields that might need to be sent to the external system
- Whether it's an individual or group mapping
- User(s) that can administer the target application
- Users or groups that can use the target application

One of the most import decisions when creating a target application is whether to use individual mappings or group mappings. Individual mapping is when each user has a unique set of credentials, whereas group mapping is where everyone has the same set of credentials. You can use individual mapping when you want to keep logging information about the user, but doing so requires more resources. Group mapping uses fewer resources and requires less work, but everyone is treated as the same person.

The second main decision to make is who will access the target application and therefore be able to use it and its account. After you open the target application to users, they can use it on multiple SharePoint solutions, potentially overloading the external system that it's accessing.

Target applications can be created within the context of the Secure Store service application. Follow these steps:

1. Navigate to Central Administration as a farm administrator or with an account that has full control of the Secure Store service application.
2. Click Manage Service Applications in the Application Management section.
3. Click the Secure Store service application in the Name column of the Service Application list.
4. Click the New Icon in the Manage Target Application section of the EDIT tab.
5. On the Create New Secure Store Target Application page, enter a unique name for the target application in the Target Application ID text box. This is the name to be used in the application and can't be changed.
6. Enter a user-friendly name in the Display Name text box.
7. Enter the email address of the primary contact for the target application in the Contact E-mail text box.
8. In the Target Application Type section, select one of the application types: Individual, Individual Ticket, Individual Restricted, Group, Group Ticket, or Group Restricted.

9. For the Target Application Page URL, choose the target application page where credentials can be set.
10. Click Next to open the field page.
11. Configure the Field Name and Field Type, as shown in Figure 4-14. The default field names and field types are Windows User Name and Windows Password.

FIGURE 4-14 Field page of the Secure Store Target Application process

12. Use the Add Field link to add more fields (and then enter a field name and choose the field type).
13. Because field names and types can't be changed in the future, make sure they are correct. Then click Next to open the Target Application Administrators page.
14. Enter the users who can administer this target application in the Target Application Administrators text box. Users who have full control of the Secure Store service application or have All Target Applications permissions can also administer this target application.
15. If the target type is one of the group target types, enter the member(s) or group(s) in the Members text box.
16. Click OK to save.

The target application is ready to have its credentials set at this point (and any of the other fields added). Unless you are working with customized solutions, you should stick with either Individual or Group for the Target Application type. The Ticketing options are used with systems that can use tickets and requires the IssueTicket and GetCredentialsUsingTicket methods to be used in the code accessing the external system. The Restricted options are used when the code calling the external system requires a restricted context.

MORE INFO CONNECTING TO AN EXTERNAL SYSTEM VIA THE SECURE STORE SERVICE

See *http://msdn.microsoft.com/en-us/library/ee554863.aspx* for more information on how to use the Secure Store service to connect to an external system.

Managing Secure Store target application permissions

Target applications have two different types of applicable permissions: permissions that determine who can administer the target application and credentials that are set for access to the external data. The permissions on who can administer a target application are entered when it is created. You can change these permissions at any time, though, by using Central Administration. Follow these steps:

1. Navigate to the Secure Store service application in the same manner as you did when you created a target application.
2. Either click in the space next to the Target Application ID to open the drop-down list and then choose Set Permissions, or select the check box next to the Target Application ID and click the Set icon in the Permissions section on the EDIT tab.
3. On the Edit Secure Store Target Application page, enter the user(s) or group(s) that you want to be able to administer the target application.
4. If the target type is one of the group types, modify the user(s) and/or groups(s) in the Members text box.
5. Click OK to save changes.

The next permissions-related item is setting the credentials. The default type of credentials is Windows (Active Directory), but several different types of credential types can be used, such as the following:

- Generic
- PIN
- Certificate
- Windows

Whatever type of credentials you choose, you need to set the values along with the values of any fields that have been added. These additional fields could be items such as default language or which database to use. You can set the values for these fields in the Secure Store service application. Follow these steps:

1. Navigate to the Secure Store service application in the same manner as you did when you created a target application.

2. Either click in the space next to the Target Application ID to open the drop-down list and then choose Set Credentials, or select the check box next to the Target Application ID and click the Set icon in the Credentials section on the EDIT tab.
3. On the Set Credentials For Secure Store Target Application page, fill in the values for the fields and confirm any masked fields, as shown in Figure 4-15.

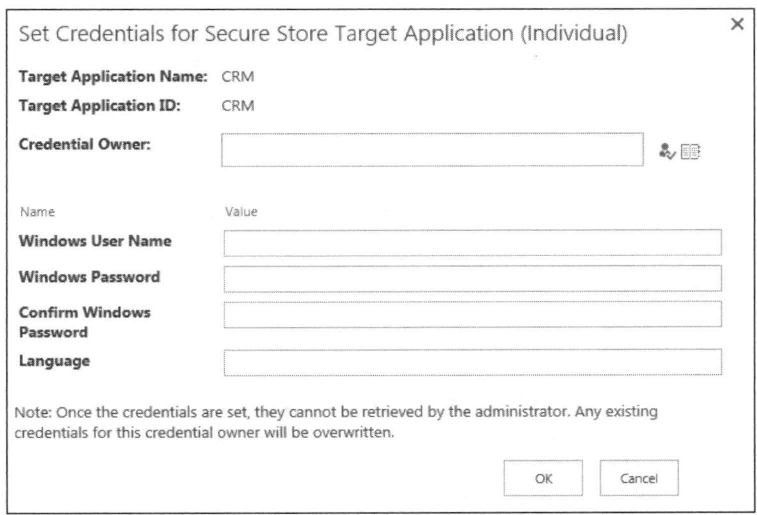

FIGURE 4-15 Setting the credentials of a target application using the Individual target type

4. Click OK to save changes.

This example showed a target application type of Individual. This set of credentials would map to an individual, and each individual who wanted to use the target application would need her own set of credentials. If it had been a target application type of Group, the credential members would be shown but you couldn't edit them here; you would have to edit the target application to change the members.

> ***MORE INFO*** **PLANNING THE SECURE STORE SERVICE**
>
> **See *http://technet.microsoft.com/en-us/library/ee806889(v=office.15)* for more information on how to plan the Secure Store service in SharePoint Server 2013.**

Thought experiment

Accessing Windows Live data

In the following thought experiment, apply what you've learned about this objective. You can find answers to these questions in the "Answers" section at the end of this chapter.

As part of a new social endeavor, you have decided to provide data from your users' Windows Live contacts from their Windows Live accounts. You want to expose these contacts as a SharePoint list so that users can have access to them without leaving SharePoint.

How would you expose the Windows Live data so that SharePoint designers can show this data for the end user?

Objective summary

- The BCS uses models to define the metadata associated with a data source.
- BDC models, external system information, and external content types are stored in the metadata store.
- Permissions are inherited from the metadata store unless they are explicitly changed at the object level (BDC models, external systems, and external content types).
- The Secure Store provides secure storage for credentials used to access external data in objects called target applications.
- Individual target application types provide individual logging and the ability to provide differing security levels, but they also require more resources than the Group target applications.
- Credential fields can contain additional information that might be needed by the external system.

Objective review

Answer the following questions to test your knowledge of the information in this objective. You can find the answers to these questions and explanations of why each answer choice is correct or incorrect in the "Answers" section at the end of this chapter.

1. You can use Business Data Catalog models for which kind of data type?
   - **A.** OData
   - **B.** WCF
   - **C.** .NET assemblies
   - **D.** All of the above
2. Which of the following BCS objects can't have permissions directly given through Central Administration?
   - **A.** BDC model
   - **B.** Methods
   - **C.** External content types
   - **D.** External system
3. For somebody (not on the SharePoint farm) to decrypt the credentials stored in the Secure Store database, that person would need which of the following items, assuming that he didn't have a huge supercomputer and tons of time in which to break the encryption?
   - **A.** The Secure Store database and the password of the account used to install SharePoint
   - **B.** The Secure Store database and the master key
   - **C.** The Secure Store database, the master key, and the passphrase
   - **D.** The Secure Store database and the passphrase
4. Which of the following is an invalid target application type?
   - **A.** Individual Group
   - **B.** Individual
   - **C.** Individual Ticket
   - **D.** Individual Restricted

Chapter summary

- SharePoint apps are now the preferred model for developing custom solutions.
- End users go to the App Catalog or the SharePoint Store to obtain SharePoint apps to be installed on their sites.
- Service applications extend the base functionality of SharePoint but need to be installed and configured correctly to keep them from affecting overall performance.
- The Secure Store provides a mechanism to store credentials that can be used by service applications such as Excel Services and Visio Services so that users don't have to have direct access to external data sources.
- A SharePoint farm can provide services to other farms, assuming that a trust has been set up between the farms and the publishing farm has published the service.
- The Business Connectivity Services service application allows SharePoint to connect to and interact with data from external sources in a wide variety of formats such as OData, WCF, and cloud-based services.
- The Secure Store service application should be backed up individually and stored in a different location than the master key and the password, all of which are needed for restoration.

Answers

This section contains the solutions to the thought experiments and answers to the lesson review questions in this chapter.

Objective 4.1: Thought experiment

In this thought experiment, you were asked what it would take for an App Catalog to remain available even though a SharePoint server was down for maintenance or because of hardware failure. The purpose behind this thought experiment was to reiterate the concept of high availability regarding apps.

First, you would probably want to take is to make sure that the App Management Services service application and the Microsoft SharePoint Foundation Subscription Settings Service service application are both running on more than one server. This ensures that the services needed by the App Catalog are available.

Second, you would want to make sure that more than one front end are available for and DNS entries that you created for use by the App Catalog. This should enable the App Catalog to be highly available so that users can get to the apps they need, even when a server is down.

Objective 4.1: Review

1. **Correct answer:** D
   - **A. Incorrect:** Apps from the SharePoint Store can be added to the App Catalog, but it's just one of the right answers.
   - **B. Incorrect:** Apps for Office can be made available in the App Catalog, but it too is just one of the right answers.
   - **C. Incorrect:** End users can create their apps and ask that they be added to the App Catalog for other users to add to their SharePoint sites. However, this is only one of the right answers.
   - **D. Correct:** Answers A, B, and C are all valid answers.
2. **Correct answer:** C
   - **A. Incorrect:** An App Catalog needs to be created, but you can have an App Catalog and apps still be disabled.
   - **B. Incorrect:** The Subscription Settings service application needs to be created with PowerShell commands before you can configure the app URLs, so apps are still considered to be disabled.
   - **C. Correct:** After the app URLs are configured, apps should be enabled.

D. **Incorrect:** The App Management service application doesn't enable apps by itself. It's just one of the steps involved.

3. **Correct answer:** A

A. **Correct:** Each app in the App Catalog has a unique domain name that starts with an app prefix appended with the application ID. To keep from having to create an entry in DNS for each app, you can use a wildcard Canonical Name (CNAME) entry.

B. **Incorrect:** A CNAME entry has nothing to do with finding an app.

C. **Incorrect:** Most web applications don't need wildcard CNAME entries, except only those that have multiple prefixes such as the App Catalog.

D. **Incorrect:** The reason is stated in answer A.

Objective 4.2: Thought experiment

In this thought experiment, you were told to figure out how to solve the slowness experienced by end users without compromising the Word conversion project. By default, the Word Automation Services service consumes 100 percent of the available memory on the servers that run the service. You could lower this percentage to give other applications more memory and ease up the load on the application servers, but this will probably slow down the Word conversion project. Another solution might be to delay the Word conversions until after hours or on the weekends. This might be a solution if you work with the developers to delay the requests and add only enough conversions so that they finish before the users come into work.

Perhaps the best solution is to use one of the WFEs as a dedicated Word Automation Services server and remove the service from the application servers. Because the WFEs aren't even being used at 50 percent, removing one of them would still provide redundancy and the WFEs still wouldn't be maxed out. Because the Word Automation Services server wouldn't have to compete with other applications on the WFE server, it would most likely provide even better performance than if it was running on the both of the application servers. You wouldn't have redundancy, but if the server should happen to fail, you could always start it up on one of the other SharePoint servers until it could be replaced or repaired.

Objective 4.2: Review

1. **Correct answer:** D

A. **Incorrect:** Although SharePoint sites are a valid option, this isn't the best answer because other answers are also correct.

B. **Incorrect:** Although network file shares can be used, this isn't the only right answer.

C. **Incorrect:** Non-SharePoint websites can be used as long as the account running the Excel Calculation Service can access them, but this isn't the only right answer.

D. **Correct:** A, B, and C are all valid answers.

2. **Correct answer:** C
   - **A. Incorrect:** The Express version of SQL Server 2008 doesn't support Access Services.
   - **B. Incorrect:** Although you can install SharePoint 2013 on SQL Server 2008 R2, you need SQL Server 2012 Standard or Enterprise editions to run Access Services.
   - **C. Correct:** Access Services requires SQL Server 2012, even if SharePoint 2013 is installed on SQL Server 2008 R2.
   - **D. Incorrect:** Because A and B are both incorrect, D is also incorrect.
3. **Correct answer:** B
   - **A. Incorrect:** The only way that 25 percent would be the limit is if that amount of physical memory was entered in the Maximum Physical Bytes setting, but it wouldn't be the maximum allowed.
   - **B. Correct:** No matter what value is entered in the Maximum Physical Bytes setting, the limit is 50 percent of the physical memory available. A value of –1 sets it at 50 percent, no matter what the size of the memory on the server.
   - **C. Incorrect:** The limit is 50 percent, no matter what value is entered into the Maximum Physical Bytes setting.
   - **D. Incorrect:** The limit is 50 percent. A value of 100 percent wouldn't allow the other programs necessary for the server to function correctly.
4. **Correct answer:** A
   - **A. Correct:** Visio web drawings are displayed using Silverlight.
   - **B. Incorrect:** Visio 2013 drawings saved with the .vsdx extension are displayed using the raster format.
   - **C. Incorrect:** Visio 2013 drawings saved with the .vsdm extension are displayed in the raster format.
   - **D. Incorrect:** Because B and C use the raster format, D can't be correct.
5. **Correct answer:** B
   - **A. Incorrect:** Visio Graphics Service and Excel Services can both use ODBC data providers.
   - **B. Correct:** Neither application service can use Access data providers.
   - **C. Incorrect:** Both application services can use OLE DB data providers.
   - **D. Incorrect:** Both application services can use ODBC with DSN (although in Excel Services it's referred to as ODBC DSN).
6. **Correct answer:** C
   - **A. Incorrect:** Word Automation Services can open Microsoft Word documents all the way back to Word 97.

B. **Incorrect:** HTML documents can be opened and converted to other types of documents.

C. **Correct:** Microsoft Excel documents can't be converted to other documents using Word Automation Services.

D. **Incorrect:** Rich Text Format files can be converted to other types of documents.

Objective 4.3: Thought experiment

In this thought experiment, you were asked what steps would be required to be able to use the Search service of a SharePoint 2013 farm by an unspecified number of SharePoint 2010 farms. The steps required for connecting one consuming farm to one publishing farm were covered in the objective. The process for connecting more than one consuming farm is basically the same procedure repeated for each farm. You have to create the publishing farm root certificate only once. The same certificate can be used on all the consuming farms.

To use the Search service, follow these steps:

1. Create root and STS certificates on the consuming farms (one set per farm) and copy them to the publishing farm.
2. Import the certificates on the publishing farm.
3. Create the root certificate on the publishing farm and copy it to the consuming farms.
4. Import the publishing farm's root certificate on each consuming farm.
5. Obtain the farm ID of each consuming farm.
6. Use the farm IDs to provide permissions to the Application Discovery and Load Balancing service application on the publishing farm.
7. Publish the Application Discovery and Load Balancing service application on the publishing farm.
8. Use the consuming farm IDs again to provide permissions to the Search service application on the publishing farm.
9. Publish the Search service application on the publishing farm and obtain the published URL.
10. Connect to the publishing farm's Search service application by using the published URL on each consuming farm.

At this point, the consuming farms should be able to use the SharePoint 2013 farm's Search service just as they would their own Search service. Management of any search settings needs to be done on the SharePoint 2013 farm, and any Search service crawling account needs permissions on the SharePoint 2010 farms to crawl them.

Objective 4.3: Review

1. **Correct answer:** C
   - **A. Incorrect:** The Search service application can be published by a SharePoint 2013 farm and consumed by a SharePoint 2010 farm.
   - **B. Incorrect:** The Secure Store service application can also be consumed by a SharePoint 2010 farm.
   - **C. Correct:** Because the Machine Translation service application doesn't exist on a SharePoint 2010 farm, it can't be consumed.
   - **D. Incorrect:** The Managed Metadata service application can also be consumed by a SharePoint 2010 farm.
2. **Correct answer:** A
   - **A. Correct:** Both certificates must be created on the consuming farm, but only the root certificate needs to be created on the publishing farm.
   - **B. Incorrect:** The security token (STS) certificate also needs to be created.
   - **C. Incorrect:** The root certificate also needs to be created.
   - **D. Incorrect:** A subordinate certificate doesn't need to be created on either the consuming farm or the publishing farm.
3. **Correct answer:** B
   - **A. Incorrect:** The PowerShell command Get-SPCertificateAuthority is used for getting a certificate.
   - **B. Correct:** The PowerShell command Get-PfxCertificate is used when importing a root certificate and when importing the STS certificate.
   - **C. Incorrect:** The PowerShell command Get-RootCertificate doesn't exist.
   - **D. Incorrect:** The PowerShell command Get-SPServiceApplicationSecurity is used when giving permissions to a service application.
4. **Correct answer:** D
   - **A. Incorrect:** The consuming farm needs permissions to the Application Discovery and Load Balancing service application, but this is just one of the right answers.
   - **B. Incorrect:** The consuming farm also needs permissions to the service application that it will consume, but this is just of the correct answers listed.
   - **C. Incorrect:** The publishing farm needs both the STS certificate and the root certificate from the consuming farm, but this is just one of the correct answers.
   - **D. Correct:** Because the items in A, B, and C are all needed before a consuming farm can consume a published service, this is the right answer.

Objective 4.4: Thought experiment

In this thought experiment, you were asked to provide a way to expose a user's contacts from Windows Live in a SharePoint list. Because Windows Live is an OData provider, you can use OData as your data type when you create the BCD model. This most likely is the most straightforward way to reach this goal.

You need Visual Studio 2012 to create the OData model because SharePoint Designer can't create OData models. You would create the model defining the Windows Live data source and then import it into the Business Data Connectivity service application. You would then provide permissions to the model and use Secure Store to provide pass through authentication. SharePoint Designers could then use an external content type to expose the contact information in a SharePoint list.

Using REST to expose the Windows Live data would also be possible because Windows Live exposes its endpoints via REST. Another option would be that a programmer could write a .NET assembly that pulls data from Windows Live and exposes it as SharePoint list data. However, OData is being embraced by SharePoint and, going forward, will likely be the most compatible with future releases. It's also an open system that's used by other organizations, so it is likely to become even more prevalent.

Objective 4.4: Review

1. **Correct answer:** D

   A. **Incorrect:** Although OData is a supported data type as of SharePoint 2013, it's just one of the right answers.

   B. **Incorrect:** WCF is a supported data type just as it was in SharePoint 2010, but it too is just one of the correct answers.

   C. **Incorrect:** .NET assemblies can be used as a data type, assuming that they have been created for that purpose. However, it's just one of the right answers.

   D. **Correct:** Because all three of the previous answers are correct, that makes "All of the above" the best answer.

2. **Correct answer:** B

   A. **Incorrect:** The BDC model can be assigned permissions directly on the Business Data Catalog Service Application page by going to the BDC Models view, selecting a BDC model, and clicking the Set Object Permissions icon.

   B. **Correct:** Methods inherit their permissions from the external content type and therefore can't be given permissions directly in Central Administration.

   C. **Incorrect:** External content types can be assigned permissions directly similarly to the BDC Model but under the External Content Types view.

   D. **Incorrect:** External system objects can be assigned permissions just like BDC models by going to the External Systems view, selecting the external system(s), and clicking the Set Object Permissions icon.

3. **Correct answer:** C

   A. **Incorrect:** The Secure Store database is where credentials are stored in an encrypted format and therefore is required if you want to retrieve those credentials. However, the account used to install the SharePoint farm has nothing to do with decrypting the data.

   B. **Incorrect:** The master key is required, but you still need the passphrase to be able to use it with the Secure Store database.

   C. **Correct:** If you have the Secure Store database, the master key, and the passphrase, you can decrypt the credentials. That's why it's important to keep the backups of these items in separate locations if you want to keep the credentials stored in them secure.

   D. **Incorrect:** The master key would still be needed to decrypt the credentials. The master key is backed up as part of the Secure Store service application, which isn't part of the usual database backups.

4. **Correct answer:** A

   A. **Correct:** Target application types fall into two different categories, group or individual, but they can't be both. Therefore, Individual Group is an invalid target application type.

   B. **Incorrect:** The Individual target application type is valid.

   C. **Incorrect:** The Individual Ticket target application type is valid and used for target applications that can assign tickets.

   D. **Incorrect:** The Individual Restricted target application type is valid and used for target applications that require a restricted security context.

CHAPTER 5

Manage SharePoint solutions, BI, and systems integration

This chapter covers a diverse set of objectives that didn't fit into the any of the previous chapters but represent important topics relevant to advanced solutions in SharePoint. This chapter covers how to manage customizations that programmers and developers have created as well as how to upgrade these solutions from SharePoint 2010. Another important topic covered is the business intelligence (BI) framework that SharePoint provides to give users and developers a powerful set of tools to analyze and present data. The final part of the chapter covers how to configure SharePoint to work with other systems, such as Exchange Server and Project Server. These systems greatly extend SharePoint but require planning and configuration to be able to use them productively and securely.

Objectives in this chapter:

- Objective 5.1: Manage SharePoint solutions and applications
- Objective 5.2: Manage and configure a BI infrastructure
- Objective 5.3: Create and configure work management

Objective 5.1: Manage SharePoint solutions and applications

This objective covers issues with configuring, deploying, and upgrading customizations, including sandboxed solutions, farm solutions, and SharePoint apps. Sandboxed solutions and farm solutions were available in SharePoint 2010 and are still available in SharePoint 2013. Whereas farm solutions don't seem to be going anywhere, sandboxed solutions are being deprecated—at least, as of this writing. Best practices dictate that any future development be done within the apps framework or in the context of a Farm Solution.

The main difference between farm solutions and SharePoint apps is that server-side code isn't allowed to run inside SharePoint-hosted apps. SharePoint apps can run on a non-SharePoint server and even in the cloud, but in some cases you will still need to run code within a SharePoint worker process. In these cases, you need to develop a farm solution, but otherwise you should be developing apps because this is the direction SharePoint is headed. This exam doesn't cover creating any of these customizations but rather what to do after the solution or app is handed over from the developers.

This objective covers the following topics:

- Managing sandbox solution quotas
- Configuring sandbox solution management
- Deploying farm solutions
- Upgrading farm solutions
- Deploying apps
- Upgrading apps

Managing sandboxed solution quotas

Sandboxed solutions run as a very restricted set of code. The whole purpose of the sandboxed solutions was to allow deployment of solutions that wouldn't affect the rest of SharePoint. For example, an errant web part couldn't take all the resources of the SharePoint farm. SharePoint accomplishes this by making all the sandboxed solutions run within the User Code Service and by setting quotas on how much of the system resources the sandboxed solutions could consume.

Quotas are set at the site collections level both for the amount of space they can use and how many points can be allocated to sandboxed solutions. When a sandboxed solution or set of solutions uses up the resource points within a single day, all sandboxed solutions in the site collection are stopped until the Solution Daily Resource Update timer job runs (typically late at night or early morning) or the quota is removed or increased.

MORE INFO **SANDBOXED SOLUTIONS OVERVIEW**

See *http://technet.microsoft.com/en-us/library/ee721992(v=office.14).aspx* for an overview of sandboxed solutions.

Determining the resource quota for sandboxed solutions is accomplished by modifying an individual quota for a site collection or by modifying or creating a quota template and then applying it to a site collection. When modifying a quota, you set the maximum number of points that can be used by all sandboxed solutions that run in the site collection before sandboxed solutions are disabled. You can also set a warning level that sends out an email as soon as it has been reached. You can set the quotas for an individual site collection in Central Administration by following these steps:

1. Navigate to Central Administration as a farm administrator.
2. Click Application Management to open the Application Management page.

3. Click Configure Quotas And Locks.
4. Choose the site collection that you want to set quotas on in the Site Collection section.
5. In the Site Quota Information section, select the quota template that you want from the Current Quota Template drop-down list, or select Individual Quota if you want to configure the values yourself. If you don't choose Individual Quota, you can review the values and click OK to finish.
6. In the Sandboxed Solutions Resource Quota section, enter the maximum allowed points that sandboxed solutions can use in the Limit Maximum Usage Per Day To box, as shown in Figure 5-1 (the default is 300 points).

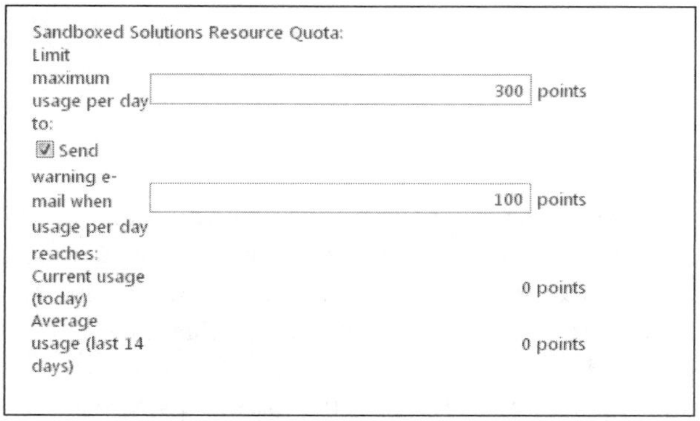

Sandboxed Solutions Resource Quota:
Limit maximum usage per day to: 300 points
Send warning e-mail when usage per day reaches: 100 points
Current usage (today) 0 points
Average usage (last 14 days) 0 points

FIGURE 5-1 Sandboxed Solutions Resource Quota section

7. Choose whether to send an email warning and at what value to send the warning in the Send Warning E-mail When Usage Per Day Reaches text box.
8. View the current usage and the average of the last 14 days before clicking OK to save.

In these steps, you could have chosen a template rather than sett directly for an Individual Quota. You can also set a quota template by running the following PowerShell command in the SharePoint 2013 Management Shell, where <*site collection*> is the URL or GUID of the site collection and <*template name*> is the name or the GUID of the template:

```
Set-SPSite -Identity "<site collection>" -QuotaTemplate "<template name>"
```

In the quotas, you were setting the number of points that could be accumulated in a day before the sandboxed solutions were disabled. A point is determined by a collection of up to 15 resource counters. For example, after the sandboxed solutions in a site collection use up a certain number of CPU cycles, that counts as a point and is added to the total for the day. As a farm administrator, you can change what these values are by using PowerShell commands. You can see the current resource point allocations by using the following PowerShell commands as a farm administrator in the SharePoint 2013 Management Shell:

```
$rpa=[Microsoft.SharePoint.Administration.SPUserCodeService]::Local
$rpa.ResourceMeasures | Select-Object Name,ResourcesPerPoint,AbsoluteLimit
```

Running the commands lists the names of the resource measures, the amount of resources per point, and the absolute limit of points per resource:

```
Name                                     ResourcesPerPoint              AbsoluteLimit
-------------------------------------------------------------------------------------
AbnormalProcessTerminationCount                          1                          1
CPUExecutionTime                                       200                         60
CriticalExceptionCount                                  10                          3
IdlePercentProcessorTime                               100                         10
InvocationCount                                        100                        100
PercentProcessorTime                                    85                        100
ProcessCPUCycles                              100000000000               100000000000
ProcessHandleCount                                   10000                       5000
ProcessIOBytes                                    10000000                  100000000
ProcessThreadCount                                   10000                        200
ProcessVirtualBytes                             1000000000                 4000000000
SharePointDatabaseQueryCount                           400                        100
SharePointDatabaseQueryTime                             20                         60
UnhandledExceptionCount                                 50                          3
UnresponsiveprocessCount                                 2                          1
```

You can use the names in the preceding list to modify the values if you want to change the respective weights of the resources. For example, you might want to make CPU execution time more important than Process IO Bytes. You would do this by lowering the CPUExcecutionTime property from 200 down to something less, like 100, so that the points would accumulate twice as fast as they did before you changed it. You can change the values of the resource measures in the same Management Shell by using the following PowerShell commands, where *<resource name>* is the name of the resource measure to be changed, *<limit value>* is the absolute limit value, and *<point value>* is the resource per point value:

```
$rpa=[Microsoft.SharePoint.Administration.SPUserCodeService]::Local
$rpa.ResourceMeasures["<resource name>"].AbsoluteLimit = <limit value>
$rpa.ResourceMeasures["<resource name>"].ResourcesPerPoint = <point value>
$rpa.ResourceMeasures["<resource name>"].Update()
$rpa.Update()
```

EXAM TIP

That you will need to know this level of detail about resource point allocations for the exam is doubtful, especially because sandboxed solutions are being deprecated. However, this information might help you with planning and controlling the resources consumed by sandbox solutions on your SharePoint 2013 farm.

Whatever values you use, you might want to keep track of the points by referring back to the Configure Quotas And Locks page to see how many points are being consumed. Any sandboxed solutions that you are using and deem as valuable in the long term for your business should be marked for migration to an app solution or a farm solution if an app solution isn't feasible.

Configuring Sandboxed Solution Management

Sandboxed solutions (or *user solutions*, as they are sometimes called) can be managed at the farm level. Since SharePoint 2010 introduced sandboxed solutions, they have been the preferred development solution. Thousands and thousands of sandboxed solutions are available.

Even though SharePoint 2013 recommends that you now use SharePoint apps instead of sandboxed solutions, most organizations won't have enough time and/or money to convert these applications before upgrading to SharePoint 2013. This means that you need to test and manage these solutions as they are migrated to the new farm(s).

The preceding section covered setting quotas, which can limit how many resources are used by sandboxed solutions per site collection. Sandbox Solution Management allows for blocking of certain sandboxed solutions as well as determining how servers are used to provide resources. This way, you can remove certain solutions that might be consuming more resources than they should be without affecting the other solutions. It also allows you to determine which servers are used to provide solution services. To delete sandboxed solutions, follow these steps:

1. Navigate to Central Administration as a farm administrator and click System Settings.
2. Click Manage User Solutions in the Farm Management section. (Remember that sandboxed solutions are also referred to as user solutions.)
3. Click the Browse button in the Solution Restrictions section (see Figure 5-2). You need to browse to and select the solution package that was used to install the sandboxed solution. Solutions are blocked based on the contents of the solution and not the name of the solution file.

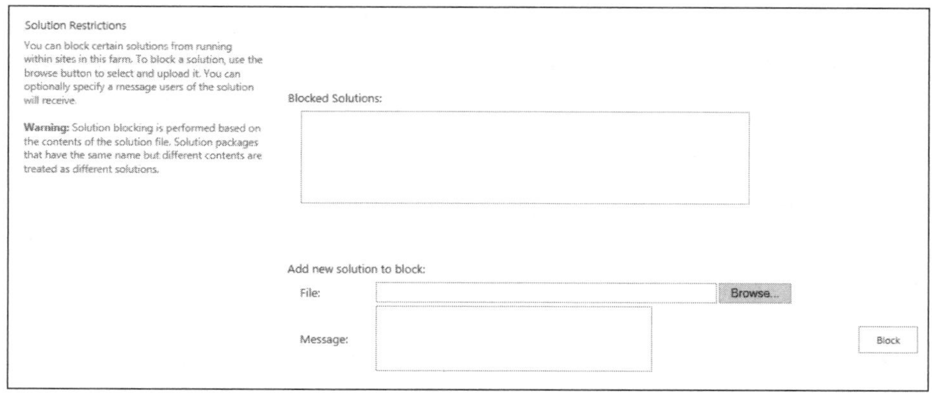

FIGURE 5-2 Solution Restrictions section of Sandboxed Solution Management

4. Enter a message that will appear when a user tries to use the solution.
5. Click Block to add the solution to the list of blocked solutions.
6. Click OK to save changes.

In the Load Balancing section, the option to run the sandboxed code on the same server as requests can help improve performance and requires that all WFEs run the Sandboxed Code Service. If you want to specify servers to run the Sandboxed Code Service, you need to use the Requests To Run Sandboxed Code Are Routed By Solution Affinity option. This can also help you isolate the sandboxed solutions so that they don't potentially use many resources on the WFEs, but doing so also can cause something of a performance hit because the WFEs have to communicate across servers.

Deploying farm solutions

Farm solutions are also known as *full trust solutions* because they have full trust on the servers on which they are installed. When you deploy a farm solution, it can place the dynamic link libraries (DLLs) that it uses in the global assembly cache (GAC). This gives farm solutions a high degree of access to the server.

Only fully tested and trusted farm solutions should be deployed into a production environment. Despite the push for SharePoint apps, server-side code is still needed for many solutions, which means that you will continue to need to deploy farm solutions.

Deploying farm solutions is much more different in SharePoint 2013 from what it is in SharePoint 2010, because of the ability of SharePoint 2013 to run SharePoint 2010 mode alongside SharePoint 2013 mode. SharePoint 2013 accomplishes this by having different areas in the root folder. It has a folder that starts with 14 for SharePoint 2010 files and a folder that starts with 15 for SharePoint 2013 files.

If you deploy a farm solution in the same way that you did in SharePoint 2010—by using the PowerShell commands Add-SPSolution and Install-SPSolution—the farm solution files that are part of the TEMPLATES directory are installed only under the 14 folder and therefore aren't accessible to SharePoint 2013 mode. The files that aren't part of the TEMPLATES directory are still installed in the same places they were in SharePoint 2010—that is, in binaries, DLLS, ISAPI files, and so on. If you want the farm solution files available to both the SharePoint 2010 mode and the SharePoint 2013 mode, you need to install the files into both folders.

SharePoint 2013 uses the CompatibilityLevel property that you can include as part of the Install-SPSolution command or define in the solution file (although values in the solution file will be overridden by those of the Install-SPSolution command). Following are the valid values for the CompatibilityFile property:

- **14** installs the solution into the 14 folder for SharePoint 2010 mode compatibility.
- **15** installs the solution into the 15 folder for SharePoint 2013 mode compatibility.
- **"14,15"** or **"All"** installs the solution into both the 14 and 15 folders.
- **"Old"** or **"OldVersions"** installs the solution to the old (14) folder.
- **"New"** or **"NewVersions"** installs the solution to the new (15) folder.

MORE INFO USING INSTALL-SPSOLUTION

See *http://technet.microsoft.com/en-us/library/ff607534(office.15).aspx#detail* for more information on how to use the PowerShell command Install-SPSolution.

If a solution file doesn't contain a Compatibility Level property, it defaults to 14. You can install a farm solution into both the 14 and 15 folders with a single command; if you try to install a solution by using two different commands, you will get an error. If you try to use the -Force option, you can cause the solution to malfunction. You should uninstall it by using the Uninstall-SPSolution and then reinstall by using the "14,15" or the "All" Compatibility Level, as shown in the following example where <*solution name*> is the name of the solution:

```
Install-SPSolution -Identity <solution name> -CompatibilityLevel "14,15"
```

IMPORTANT The CompatibilityLevel property is available for features as well. The values for the CompatibilityLevel property and concepts of which folders they deploy into are the same as for solutions.

To have functionally different solutions for the SharePoint 2010 and SharePoint 2013 modes, you should create two different solutions and make sure that their compatibility levels are different. If you want two different solutions but also want them to share a set of global files, you can create three solution files: one set for files that go in the 14 folder, one for files that go in the 15 folder, and one for files that are shared globally.

IMPORTANT When uninstalling a solution (using the Uninstall-SPSolution command), be sure to use the appropriate Compatibility Level. If you use the wrong one, the files in the TEMPLATE folder will be left behind, but the global files will be removed.

If you want to use Central Administration to deploy a farm solution and want to control what folder the solution is deployed into, you need to set the version in the solution itself. This is done by setting the SharePointProductVersion attribute of the Solution property in the solutions manifest file (manifest.xml). Now, the only valid values for SharePointProductVersion are 14.0 and 15.0. By default, if no version is set, SharePoint 2013 assumes that the solution will be installed into the 14 folder. You can add the SharePointProductVersion attribute to the manifest files if you want ensure that people installing it with Central Administration install it into the right folder. If you want to install (deploy) it into both the 14 and the 15 folders, you need to use the PowerShell command Install-SPSolution or create two solutions. If you still want to deploy your farm solution with Central Administration, add it first by using the PowerShell Add-SPSolution command and then follow these steps:

1. Navigate to Central Administration as a farm administrator.
2. Click System Settings to open the System Settings page.

3. Click Manage Farm Solutions in the Farm Management section.
4. Click the name of the .wsp (such as contososolution.wsp) file that was added under the Name column on the Solutions Management page.
5. On the Solutions Properties page, click Deploy Solution.
6. On the Deploy Solution page, choose whether you want to deploy the solution immediately or in the future. Either situation will create a timer job that will actually deploy the solution.
7. On the same page, choose which web application (or all Web applications) that the solution will be deployed to.
8. Click OK to create the timer job. You are returned to the Solution Management page, where you can see the deployment's progress. When the status for the solution says Deployed, the solution is ready to use.

EXAM TIP

The concept of side-by-side folders (the 14 folder and the 15 folder) to implement two different SharePoint modes is new to SharePoint 2013, and you can expect to see it on the exam. It was covered in Chapter 3, "Upgrade and migrate a SharePoint environment," but knowing how it affects solutions is also important.

Upgrading farm solutions

This exam doesn't cover programming, but you need to be aware of some aspects of upgrading farm solutions. The good thing about bringing farm solutions over to SharePoint 2013 is that most of them will run because of the separate 14 and 15 folders. The farm solution defaults into the 14 folder when it's installed. That the solution might even be available in SharePoint 2013 mode is highly likely. You should still upgrade your farm solutions when you can, though. SharePoint 2013 uses .NET 4.0 and if you want your farm solutions to be natively compatible with SharePoint 2013, they need to be compiled with .NET 4.0. If you want the farm solution to be deployed to the 15 folder, follow these steps to modify your old solution:

1. Open the solution in Visual Studio 2012 (or higher).
2. Right-click Package.Package under Package in the Solution Explorer.
3. Change the SharePoint Product Version to 15.0.
4. Rebuild your solution.

After rebuilding a solution, you need to deploy it, upgrading the solution to the most current version. When upgrading a farm solution, you have two options: replace or update.

In the replacement method, the solution is retracted and optionally removed. The new solution is then added and deployed. If you uninstalled but didn't remove the solution, you need to use a new (and unique) filename for the .wsp file and a new GUID. If you plan to install the solution into the same folder, you should use the replacement method if any of the following is true:

- Addition or removal of a feature
- Changed ID of a feature
- Changed scope
- Changed version of a feature receiver
- Any changes to elements.xml
- Addition/removal of an elements.xml file
- Addition/removal of Property element in feature.xml
- Changed Property value in Feature.xml

When updating a farm solution, SharePoint automatically detects that the GUID already exists and retracts the existing solution before deploying the new solution. It keeps a backup of the old solution in case the new one fails to deploy (only one copy of a backup is kept at a time). You use the Update-SPSolution PowerShell command to perform this type of upgrade. You can update a 14 solution in the 14 folder or a 15 solution in the 15 folder, but you can't cross the folders because it must contain the same set of files and features as the existing solution.

MORE INFO USING UPDATE-SPSOLUTION

See *http://technet.microsoft.com/en-us/library/ff607724* for more information on the PowerShell command Update-SPSolution.

Deploying apps

Chapter 4, "Create and configure service applications," covered the topic of creating an App Catalog. The App Catalog stores apps that SharePoint users can then install on their SharePoint sites. An App Catalog is scoped to the web application level, so any apps that you want to be available to a site must be in the App Catalog that's for the web application that contains the site. Adding a SharePoint app to the App Catalog can be done by navigating to the App Catalog site and following these steps:

1. Verify that the user adding the SharePoint app is a member of the site Owners or Designers group.
2. Click the Apps For SharePoint link.
3. On the Apps For SharePoint page, click New Item.
4. Click the Browse button in the Choose A File dialog box and select the SharePoint app to be added.

5. Click Open.
6. Click OK to upload the SharePoint app.
7. Validate the values in the Item Details section.
8. Make sure that Enabled is selected so that users can see the SharePoint app on their sites.
9. Optionally, select Featured so that the SharePoint app will appear in the featured section when a user adds an app.
10. Click Save.

> ***MORE INFO*** **MANAGING THE APP CATALOG**
>
> **See *http://technet.microsoft.com/en-us/library/fp161234.aspx* for more information on how to manage the App Catalog in SharePoint 2013.**

An App Catalog is scoped to the web application level, but that doesn't mean that only one web application can use it. An App Catalog can be used by all or several of your web applications. This means that you can use a single App Catalog for all the web applications on the SharePoint farm. This has a drawback in that you might be showing users SharePoint apps that aren't applicable to the web application, but it has the benefit of allowing for app management in a single location. If you have an App Catalog per web application and want a particular SharePoint app to be available to all web applications, you have to add it to each App Catalog. If you want to attach an App Catalog to a different web application, you can do so in Central Administration by following these steps:

1. Navigate to Central Administration as a member of the Farm Administrators group.
2. Click Manage App Catalog in the Apps section.
3. On the Manage App Catalog page, choose the web application to which you want to assign the App Catalog by clicking the down arrow next to the Web Application drop-down list and then selecting the web application's name. The dialog box should close.
4. Back on the Manage App Catalog page, select Enter A URL For An Existing App Catalog Site and then enter the location of the App Catalog (for example, http://contoso.com/appcatalog).
5. Click OK to save changes.
6. Repeat for all the web applications to which you want to assign the App Catalog.

Upgrading apps

A SharePoint app package can contain various items, depending on where it's located (that is, where the code runs). If an App runs in the cloud, the app package might consist of only an app manifest, which contains a product ID and a version number. For you to update an app the product ID must be the same as the existing app that you want to upgrade, and the version number must be higher. Migrating from an old app to a new one is also possible. In the migration scenario, the app would have a different product ID but could still have the same friendly name. In either case, you upgrade an app the same way that you deploy it for the first time.

After a SharePoint app is updated, end users will see an indication that an update is available on the Site Contents page of every web site on which the app is installed. Clicking the link to update the app starts the update process, and if it fails, it's completely rolled back. The following series of events will occur in no particular order and, in some cases, will even occur in parallel:

- If permissions are changed, the user is asked to approve the changes.
- The SharePoint app becomes temporarily unavailable while it's being updated.
- If a schema change is made to a SQL Azure database, the database is backed up before the change is made so that it can be rolled back, if needed.
- If an app is auto-hosted and a Windows Azure Web Site component is changed, a transaction occurs that allows a full rollback.
- If the app contains a solution package (a .wsp file) and the contents are changed, SharePoint makes a backup of the app web, tests the update, and then either updates the app package or rolls it back, depending on the success of the test.
- Assuming that the app is provider hosted, any update logic on non-SharePoint components can occur in the PostUpdate web service or in the first-run logic of the app itself.
- The PostUpdate web service is executed.

Any updates that SharePoint 2013 can't make need to go in the PostUpdate web service or in the first-run logic (code that runs the first time the app is run but not after that). This process of updating app code gives more power to end users (or to the site owner, at least) and away from farm administrators. This means that additional communication is needed for site owners to be aware of any app updates.

Migrating an app to a new one requires that the app use a new product ID in its manifest. Although the new app can have the same friendly name as the old app, they both will show up in the App Catalog as two distinct apps until the old app is removed. If data needs to be migrated, it needs to be handled by the app code via the PostInstall event, which runs after the app is installed. The new app can use any components (such as external data sources) that aren't installed by the old app because when the old app is removed, it also removes any components that were installed with it.

MORE INFO UNDERSTANDING THE APP FOR SHAREPOINT UPDATE PROCESS

See *http://msdn.microsoft.com/en-us/library/fp179904.aspx* for more information on the App for SharePoint update process.

Thought experiment

Migrating a farm solution

In the following thought experiment, apply what you've learned about this objective. You can find answers to these questions in the "Answers" section at the end of this chapter.

You have a farm solution that runs on your SharePoint 2010 farm that you want to migrate over to your SharePoint 2013 farm. The solution uses server-side code and is a critical application that you can't get rid of. You want the solution to be available to the web applications running in either SharePoint 2010 mode or SharePoint 2013 mode. For the web applications running in SharePoint 2013 mode, you want to be able to take advantage of new functionality provided by SharePoint 2013. Users still using the solution in SharePoint 2010 won't get any additional updates after the initial install. You have developer resources that can be used to implement the new features specific to SharePoint 2013 and/or to rewrite the solution as a SharePoint app.

What is a possible solution to this request?

Objective summary

- SharePoint 2013 supports sandboxed solutions, but development on them shouldn't be continued because they are being deprecated.
- The Compatibility Level determines which SharePoint modes can use a farm solution when it's installed.
- To target a farm solution to the 15 folder, you need to rebuild the solution in Visual Studio and set the SharePoint version to 15.0.
- An updated farm solution must contain the same set of files and features as the deployed solution.
- Apps added to the App Catalog are available to all web applications that use that particular App Catalog.
- After an app is updated in the App Catalog, the sites that use that App Catalog can manually upgrade the app by updating it on the Site Contents page.
- If an app doesn't update successfully, it automatically rolls back.

Objective review

Answer the following questions to test your knowledge of the information in this objective. You can find the answers to these questions and explanations of why each answer choice is correct or incorrect in the "Answers" section at the end of this chapter.

1. SharePoint Server 2013 supports which of the following?
    - **A.** Sandboxed solutions
    - **B.** Farm solutions
    - **C.** SharePoint apps
    - **D.** All of the above
2. You are installing a farm solution on SharePoint 2013 and want it available only for SharePoint 2010 mode. Which of the following Compatibility Level options for the Install-SPSolution command can you use for this purpose?
    - **A.** 14
    - **B.** "14,15"
    - **C.** "Old"
    - **D.** "All"
3. Which of the following can you change in a farm solution and still do an update rather than a replacement upgrade?
    - **A.** Add a feature
    - **B.** Modify a DLL
    - **C.** Update the elements.xml file
    - **D.** Change the scope of the solution
4. Which of the following is true about upgrading a SharePoint app by using the update method?
    - **A.** The product ID stays the same.
    - **B.** The app remains fully functional throughout the process.
    - **C.** The app is automatically updated on the sites that use it.
    - **D.** If the app fails to update, the previous version must be reinstalled.

Objective 5.2: Planning and configuring a BI infrastructure

SharePoint 2013 provides a wide range of powerful business intelligence (BI) tools to use. Chapter 4 has already discussed some of these tools, such as Excel Services, but several others haven't been discussed, such as Performance Point, PowerPivot, and Power View. These tools can be used to do BI analysis of the data in SharePoint lists as well as data from external sources. As powerful as these tools are, they can also consume many resources; as a result, you must carefully plan implementation of these BI tools to ensure not only that users can access them, but also that the tools don't overburden the SharePoint server so that other users can't use it. This objective covers how to plan for and implement the SharePoint infrastructure that will enable users to perform BI analysis securely on a wide range of data sources.

This objective covers the following topics:

- Planning and configuring PerformancePoint
- Planning and configuring Reporting Services
- Planning and configuring PowerPivot
- Planning and configuring Excel Services Data Modeling
- Planning and configuring Power View

Planning and configuring PerformancePoint

In SharePoint Server 2013, the PerformancePoint service application can be used to create BI dashboards. These dashboards can contain custom reports, key performance indicators (KPIs), filters, tabular data sources, and scorecards made up of SharePoint data as well as data from external sources.

You need to start the PerformancePoint service, create the PerformancePoint service application, and configure it before you can start using PerformancePoint services. Follow these steps:

1. Navigate to Central Administration as a farm administrator.
2. Click Manage Services On Server in the System Settings section.

3. Select the server on which you want to run the PerformancePoint service by clicking the down arrow and selecting Change Server (or leave the default server selected).
4. Scroll down until you find PerformancePoint Services and click Start in the Action column.
5. Repeat steps 3 and 4 for each server on which you want to run the PerformancePoint service.
6. Back on the Central Administration home page, click Manage Service Applications in the Application Management section.
7. Click the New icon and choose the PerformancePoint Service Application.
8. Enter a name for the PerformancePoint service application (such as PerformancePoint Service Application) in the Name text box.
9. Select the default proxy list check box if you want the service application to be in the default proxy list (leave it cleared if you want to specify manually which web applications can use this service application).
10. Enter the name of the database server in the Database Server text box; use the default database server for performance reasons.
11. Enter the name of the database in the Database Name text box. A non-GUID based name makes entering the name into scripts and identifying it in backups easier.
12. Leave the Database Authentication method set to Windows Authentication unless you have to use SQL Authentication (due to business requirements or governance).
13. If a failover server is available, enter its name in the Failover Database Server text box.
14. Choose to create a new application pool or use an existing application pool in the Application Pool section.
15. Click Create.

SharePoint lets you know when the creation process is completed by displaying the screen shown in Figure 5-3, indicating that the PerformancePoint service application has been created, the steps necessary to complete the configuration, and a warning about connecting to Microsoft SQL Server Analysis Services.

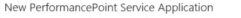

New PerformancePoint Service Application

The PerformancePoint Service application was successfully created.

- The PerformancePoint Service Application, PerformancePoint Service Application, and the associated service proxy were successfully created. The settings for this service can be modified through manage service applications in SharePoint Central Administration.
- The service will use application pool, SharePoint Web Services Default, to run instances of the service application, PerformancePoint Service Application.
- SharePoint Web Services Default is running

Additional configuration steps:

- To access data sources using shared credentials instead of per-user identity, configure the PerformancePoint Unattended Service Account and/or create Target Applications in the Secure Store using SharePoint Central Administration.
- The PerformancePoint web application and site collection features must be enabled in order to use the PerformancePoint capabilities.
- Trusted locations should be configured through manage service applications to prevent use of any site collection or sites, with PPS features enabled, that could allow for unauthorized access to data sources.

Connecting to Microsoft SQL Server Analysis Services:

- In order for PerformancePoint to connect to Analysis Services data sources (including PowerPivot workbooks), you may need to install the PowerPivot for SharePoint installation package (2013 or later). This package must be installed on every farm server that runs the PerformancePoint service.

FIGURE 5-3 PerformancePoint Service Application confirmation page

EXAM TIP

Pay special attention to the additional configuration steps to be done after the PerformancePoint service application is created. This information could show up on the exam in the form of an "items required" or "steps to take" type of question.

You also can create the PerformancePoint service application by using PowerShell commands in the SharePoint 2013 Management Shell.

Configuring the unattended service account

As indicated in Figure 5-3, after the PerformancePoint service application is created, you need to perform additional configuration steps before users can start using the PerformancePoint services. First, configure the unattended service account, which is stored in the Secure Store service application. Before you can do so, you must create the Secure Store service application and generate a master key, as explained in Chapter 4. After the Secure Store is ready to be used, you can configure the unattended service account in Central Administration by following these steps:

1. Navigate to Central Administration as a farm administrator.
2. Click Manage Service Applications in the Application Management section.
3. Select PerformancePoint from the list of service applications.
4. Click the PerformancePoint Service Application Settings link on the Manage PerformancePoint Services page, as shown in Figure 5-4.

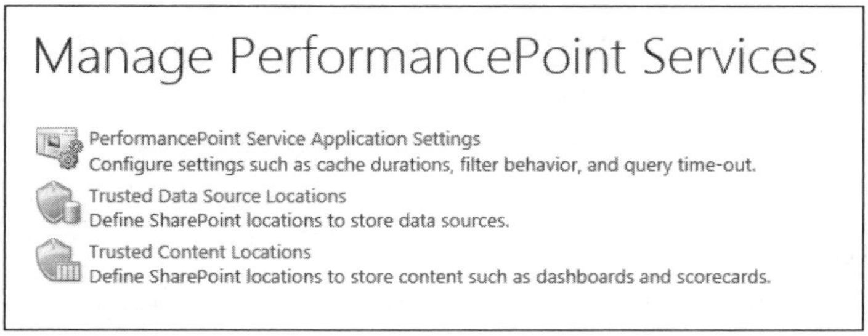

Manage PerformancePoint Services

PerformancePoint Service Application Settings
Configure settings such as cache durations, filter behavior, and query time-out.

Trusted Data Source Locations
Define SharePoint locations to store data sources.

Trusted Content Locations
Define SharePoint locations to store content such as dashboards and scorecards.

FIGURE 5-4 Manage PerformancePoint Services page

5. Enter the user name and password of the account that you want to be the unattended service account in the Secure Store And Unattended Service Account section and click OK.
6. Verify that the account used for the unattended service account has db_datareader permissions on any databases that it needs to access, read access to any SharePoint data that will be used (including Excel workbooks used by Excel Services), and read access to any cubes that might be used if you plan to use SQL Server Analysis Services.

MORE INFO **CONFIGURING THE UNATTENDED SERVICE ACCOUNT**

See *http://technet.microsoft.com/en-us/library/ee836145* for more information on how to configure the unattended service account for PerformancePoint Services.

PerformancePoint dashboards can also use Secure Store target applications to access external data sources. You use the Dashboard Designer to connect to the external data sources, using the name of the target application after it's created in the Secure Store. Creating a target application for PerformancePoint is similar to creating one for other service applications such as Excel Services or the Business Connectivity Services. The main difference is in the permissions required. PerformancePoint Services only reads data, so the Target Application account needs only the db_datareader role on the SQL Server databases it will access. If you are connecting to other data sources, the account still needs only read access to the data being reported on, but the actual permissions given depend on the data source. In general, the account has only these minimal permissions (and therefore is more secure). For security concerns, you should audit the account to make sure that it doesn't receive more permissions than required to provide the necessary BI information required.

The Dashboard Designer tool gets installed on users' local machines and helps them design dashboards that can contain a wide variety of BI-related information, such as analytic charts, strategy maps, key performance indicators (KPIs), and so forth. Although you don't need to know how to use Dashboard Designer for the exam, it can bring a better understanding of how users are using the tool and help you determine the best way to configure it.

> ***MORE INFO* USING PERFORMANCEPOINT SERVICES TO CREATE DASHBOARDS**
>
> **See *http://technet.microsoft.com/en-us/library/jj571736.aspx* for more information on how to create dashboards by using PerformancePoint Services.**

Configuring trusted data sources

After you configure the unattended service account, you should consider configuring the trusted data source locations. By default, PerformancePoint trusts all SharePoint locations. If this is the configuration you want, you don't have to do anything. If you don't want to trust all SharePoint locations—for example, you don't want users to be able to report on certain data in SharePoint—you need to specify each location that PerformancePoint Services trusts for SharePoint data. The locations can be site collections, sites, and/or document libraries. To change the trusted data source locations in Central Administration, follow these steps:

1. Navigate to the Manage PerformancePoint Services page as a farm administrator or with an account that has full control of the PerformancePoint service application.
2. Click the Trusted Data Source Locations link.
3. Select Only Specific Locations and click Apply.
4. Click the Add Trusted Data Source Location link that should have appeared below the Apply button.
5. On the Edit Trusted Data Source Location page, enter the full URL of the SharePoint location to be trusted in the Address text box and then validate the URL by clicking the validate icon to the right of the text box, as shown in Figure 5-5.

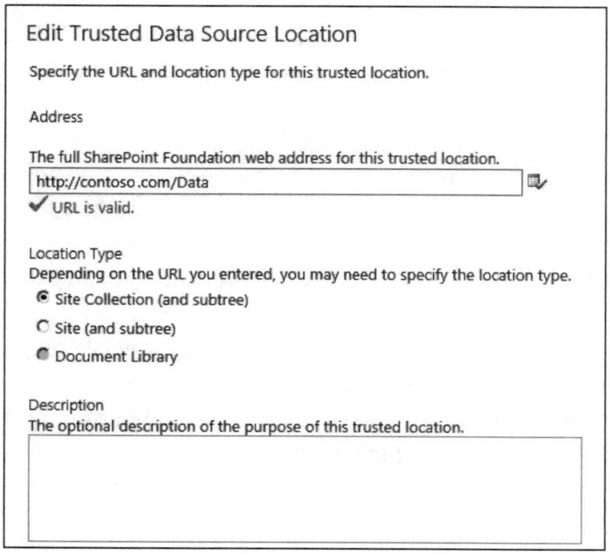

Edit Trusted Data Source Location

Specify the URL and location type for this trusted location.

Address

The full SharePoint Foundation web address for this trusted location.

http://contoso.com/Data

URL is valid.

Location Type

Depending on the URL you entered, you may need to specify the location type.

Site Collection (and subtree)

Site (and subtree)

Document Library

Description

The optional description of the purpose of this trusted location.

FIGURE 5-5 Edit Trusted Data Source Location page

6. Choose which type of location the SharePoint URL is (Site Collection, Site, or Document Library) in the Location Type section.
7. Enter an optional description in the Description field.
8. Click OK to save.
9. Repeat steps 4 through 8 for each additional SharePoint location that you want to trust.

You can also configure where PerformancePoint components (such as dashboards and scorecards) are allowed to be created. By default, PerformancePoint allows components to be stored in any SharePoint location (although the creator of the content would still need contribute rights to the location). If you want to limit where users can create Performance-Point content, you need to add each location that's allowed, similar to way the trusted data source locations were added. Although PerformancePoint Services are extremely useful for a wide range of BI-related tasks, you might want to limit the locations for performance and security reasons. You can limit the locations allowed in Central Administration by following these steps:

1. Navigate to the Manage PerformancePoint Services page as a farm administrator or with an account that has full control of the PerformancePoint service application.
2. Click Trusted Content Locations.
3. On the Trusted Content Locations page, select Only Specific Locations and click Apply.
4. Click the Add Trusted Content Location link.
5. On the Edit Trusted Content Location page, enter the full URL of the SharePoint location in the Address text box and click the verify icon.
6. **In the Location Type section, choose the location type:** site collection, site, or document library.
7. Enter an optional description in the Description text box and click OK to save.
8. Repeat steps 4 through 7 until all desired locations are added.

> ***MORE INFO*** **ENABLING TRUSTED LOCATIONS FOR PERFORMANCEPOINT SERVICES**
>
> **See *http://technet.microsoft.com/en-us/library/ee836148.aspx* for more information on how to enable trusted locations for PerformancePoint Services in SharePoint Server 2013.**

Configuring site collections to use PerformancePoint

After configuring PerformancePoint services, you can turn on the PerformancePoint feature on existing site collections to allow PerformancePoint content to be created. SharePoint 2013 provides a site template designed to help guide users in the development of dashboards and scorecards, as well as the items contained within. If you users aren't familiar with

PerformancePoint, the site collection's home page has some helpful directions as well as a link to install the Dashboard Designer.

As mentioned in the confirmation dialog box when you created the PerformancePoint service application, information from SQL Server Analysis Services can be displayed in PerformancePoint dashboards and scorecards. This powerful capability requires some additional setup and works with PowerPivot. Because PowerPivot is covered in this objective, the configuration of the connection between SharePoint and SQL Server Analysis Services is covered in the section covering PowerPivot. Note that the PowerPivot installation package needs to be installed on every server that runs the PerformancePoint service.

Planning and configuring Reporting Services

SQL Server Reporting Services can be used in SharePoint 2013, assuming that both SQL Server and SharePoint have been configured correctly. After Report Services is configured, SharePoint can display and interact with SQL Server reports. This provides end users access to these reports without giving them access to the underlying data used to generate the reports. It also allows the full power of SQL Server to be used to generate reports (such as those based on millions of lines of data and/or complex relationships) that might not otherwise be feasible if they were pulled from SharePoint lists. Some reports have to be generated periodically rather than on demand. Regardless of the type of report created, it can be exposed within SharePoint.

Before you start configuring Reporting Services in SharePoint, you need to install it on the SQL Server instance that will provide Reporting Services to SharePoint (SQL Server can provide reports without SharePoint using Reporting Services).

> ***IMPORTANT*** **An instance of a compatible SQL Server version (such as SQL Server 2012) with Reporting Services needs to exist on each SharePoint WFE as well as all SharePoint servers running the Reporting Services service application. This can be the Express edition, but neither Reporting Services nor SharePoint can store their databases in the Express versions.**

Installing Reporting Services on SQL Server

Configuring Reporting Services for SharePoint on SQL Server 2012 requires that you go through the setup process and add features (if they aren't already installed). This means that SQL Server won't be available during part of the installation. Also, the account that installs the software needs to be a member of the local administrators group during the installation. The account should be removed from the group after installation if it's also an account that has access to SQL Server or the SharePoint farm. Follow these steps to add the Reporting Services feature to SQL Server 2012:

1. Log onto the server where SQL Server 2012 is installed with an account that's a member of the Local Administrators group.
2. Start the SQL Server Installation Wizard by navigating to All Programs | Microsoft SQL Server 2012 | Configuration Tools and clicking SQL Server Installation Center.
3. In the SQL Server Installation Center dialog box, click Installation and then click New SQL Server Stand-Alone Installation or Add Features To An Existing Installation.
4. If necessary, browse to the SQL Server 2012 Installation Media and click OK.
5. Wait for the Setup Support Rules check to finish and click OK.
6. The Product Updates page automatically checks for updates if that's enabled. Wait for the check to finish and then click Next.
7. The process for installing setup files should take just a moment. Wait until it finishes and the SQL Server 2012 Setup dialog box appears.
8. Wait for the Setup Rules check to run and click Next.
9. On the Installation Type page, select Add Features To An Existing Instance Of SQL Server 2012 and choose the SQL Server instance on which to install Reporting Services. Click Next.
10. In the Features Selection, choose the Reporting Services - SharePoint feature under the Shared Features. If the server is also running SharePoint, choose Reporting Services Add-in For SharePoint Products (as shown in Figure 5-6) and click Next.

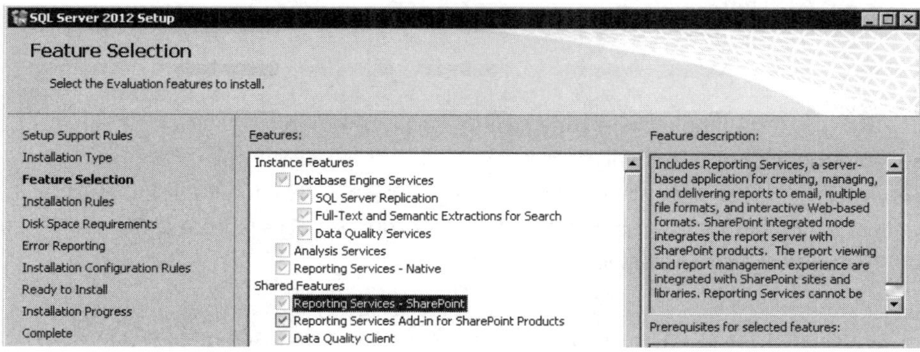

FIGURE 5-6 Feature Selection page in SQL Server 2012 Setup

11. On the Disk Space Requirements page, make sure that enough space is available to install the feature, and then click Next.
12. On the Error Reporting page, select whether you want to send error reports to Microsoft (the default is cleared) and click Next.

13. On the Installation Configuration rules page, wait for the rules check to finish (a second or two) and then click Next.
14. On the Ready To Install page, verify the features and configuration and then click Install to begin the installation of the features.
15. On the Complete page, click Close to finish the installation and close the wizard.

Configuring SharePoint for Reporting Services

After Reporting Services is installed on SQL Server, you need to configure the SharePoint servers for Reporting Services by registering and starting the Reporting Services SharePoint Service. Unlike many of the other service applications, you need to use PowerShell commands rather than the Central Administration UI:

1. Open the SharePoint 2013 Management Shell as a farm administrator.
2. Run the PowerShell command Install-SPRSService to install the service and wait for the command prompt to return.
3. Run the PowerShell command Install-SPRSServiceProxy to install the service proxy.
4. Run the following PowerShell command to start the service:

```
Get-spserviceinstance -all | where ($_.TypeName -like "SQL Server
Reporting*")|Start-SPServiceInstance
```

> ***IMPORTANT*** **If the Install-SPRSService command isn't found, it's most likely caused by the version of SQL Server. You need at least Service Pack 1 installed for the command to be found.**

After you install the service, you can also start it by going to the Manage Services On Server page in Central Administration. It should be listed as SQL Server Reporting Services Service. If the server that you want to start it on doesn't show it in the list, it must be installed on that server before it can be started (and Reporting Services feature of SQL Server 2012 SP1 or greater must also be installed on the server).

> ***MORE INFO*** **INSTALLING AND STARTING THE REPORTING SERVICES SHAREPOINT SERVICE**
>
> **See *http://msdn.microsoft.com/en-us/library/gg492276.aspx#bkmk_install_SSRS_shared-service* for more information on how to install and start the Reporting Services SharePoint service.**

Now that the SQL Server Reporting Services service is running, you can create the Reporting Services service application. Follow these steps:

1. Navigate to Central Administration as a farm administrator.

2. Click Manage Service Applications in the Application Management section.
3. On the Manage Service Applications page, click the New icon and select SQL Server Reporting Services Service Application.
4. Enter a name (such as SQL Server Reporting Services Service Application) in the Name text box.
5. Choose to use an existing application pool or create a new application pool in the Application Pool section.
6. In the SQL Server Reporting Services (SSRS) Service Database section, enter the name of the SQL Server to be used for Reporting Services (it can't be an Express version) in the Database Server text box.
7. In the same section, give the Reporting Services database a name in the Database Name text box.
8. Choose whether to use Windows Authentication or Stored Credentials (if you are using SQL authentication). If you choose Stored Credentials, specify whether the credentials are Windows credentials.
9. Choose one or more web applications with which to associate the SQL Server Reporting Services service application. Disabled and cleared web applications have already been associated to a different SQL Server Reporting Services service application.
10. Click OK to finish. If you were successful, you should see a screen indicating that you might need to provision Reporting Services to allow access to the SQL Server agent (see Figure 5-7).

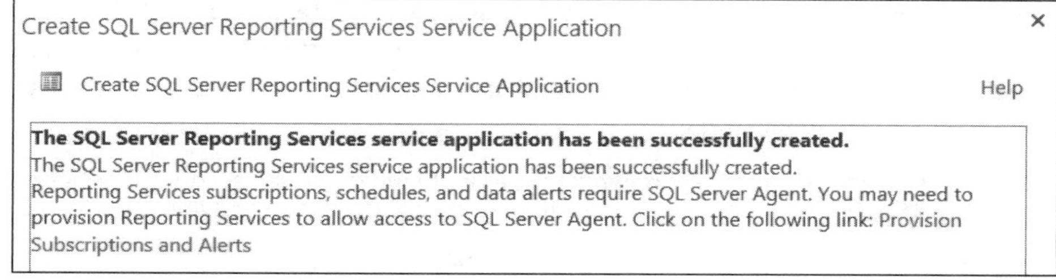

FIGURE 5-7 Confirmation page for SQL Server Reporting Services service application creation

Provisioning subscriptions and alerts

After creating the SQL Server Reporting Services service application, you should go ahead and provision subscriptions and alerts. Doing so requires that the SQL Server Agent run on the SQL Server instance that will host the Reporting Services databases. You also need to download a script and enter credentials for the account used to access the SQL Server Agent.

The account needs sufficient permissions to grant the RSExecRole execute permissions to the following databases:

- Reporting Services service application databases
- MSDB
- Master

The Provision Subscriptions and Alerts page should look similar to Figure 5-8. It shows you whether the SQL Server Agent is running, gives you a link to download the necessary script, and provides a place to enter the necessary credentials.

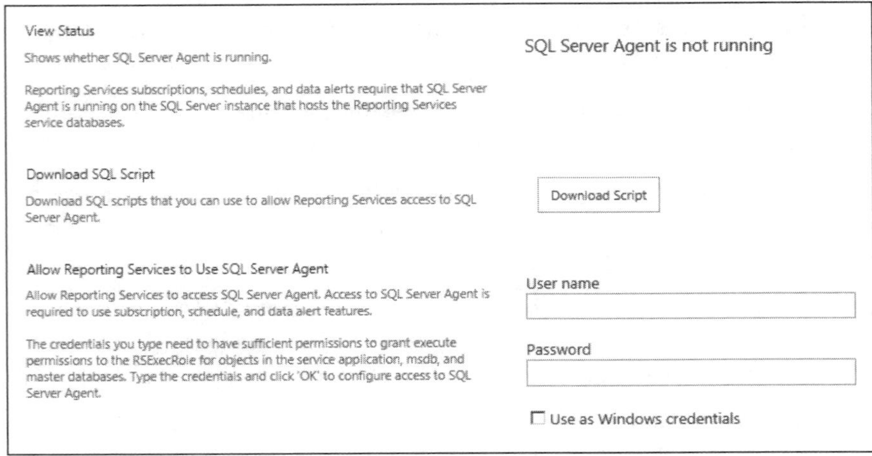

View Status
Shows whether SQL Server Agent is running.
Reporting Services subscriptions, schedules, and data alerts require that SQL Server Agent is running on the SQL Server instance that hosts the Reporting Services service databases.
SQL Server Agent is not running
Download SQL Script
Download SQL scripts that you can use to allow Reporting Services access to SQL Server Agent.
Download Script
Allow Reporting Services to Use SQL Server Agent
Allow Reporting Services to access SQL Server Agent. Access to SQL Server Agent is required to use subscription, schedule, and data alert features.
The credentials you type need to have sufficient permissions to grant execute permissions to the RSExecRole for objects in the service application, msdb, and master databases. Type the credentials and click 'OK' to configure access to SQL Server Agent.
User name
Password
Use as Windows credentials

FIGURE 5-8 Subscriptions and alerts page for provisioning

After the SQL Server Agent is started on the SQL Server instance that hosts the Reporting Services database(s) and an account is provided to allow Reporting Services to use the SQL Server Agent, you should execute the script that was downloaded. You can do this through SQL Server Management Studio:

1. Open an instance of SQL Server Management Studio with an account that has appropriate permissions (same or higher than those of the credentials that were entered on the Provision subscriptions and alerts page).
2. In the Connect To Server dialog box, enter the name of the server hosting the Reporting Services database(s) in the Server Name text box, select Database Engine from the Server Type list, and select an authentication mode (and enter credentials if necessary).
3. Click Connect.
4. From the toolbar of SQL Server Management Studio, choose File | Open | File.
5. Navigate to the downloaded script (for example, SQL Server Reporting Services Application-GrantRights.sql), select the file, and click Open.
6. Click the Execute icon and wait for the command to complete successfully.

At this point, the subscriptions and alerts for SQL Server Reporting Services (SSRS) service application provisioning should be done. You also can generate the script with PowerShell and to run the script with the command line.

> ***MORE INFO*** **PROVISIONING SUBSCRIPTIONS AND ALERTS FOR SSRS SERVICE APPLICATIONS**
>
> **See *http://msdn.microsoft.com/en-us/library/hh231725.aspx* for more information on how to provision subscriptions and alerts for SSRS service applications.**

Configuring Reporting Services

Reporting Services is up and running at this point (or should be) but still needs to be configured. Several options can be configured, as shown on the Manage Reporting Services Application page in Figure 5-9. You can get to the page via Central Administration by navigating to Manage Service Application in the Application Management section and clicking the name of the Reporting Services service application (for example, SQL Server Reporting Services Service Application).

Manage Reporting Services Application

System Settings
Define system settings for the Reporting Services application

Manage Jobs
Manage jobs that are currently running

Key Management
Backup, restore, change, or delete keys

Execution Account
Manage execution account

E-mail Settings
Configure the e-mail settings

Provision Subscriptions and Alerts
Use this page to determine if the Reporting Services service application can use SQL Server Agent for subscriptions, schedules, and data alerts. Download scripts that allow access to SQL Server Agent or use the page to configure access to SQL Server Agent.

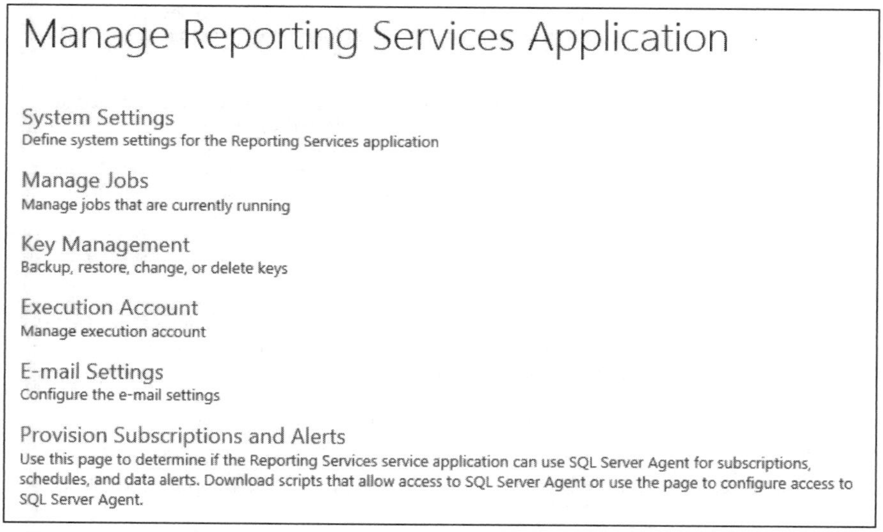

FIGURE 5-9 Manage Reporting Services Application page

CONFIGURING SYSTEM SETTINGS

The first link you should visit is on the System Settings page, which offers the settings shown in Table 5-1.

TABLE 5-1 System Settings for configuring Reporting Services

Setting	Page section	Description
External Images Timeout	Reporting	Determines the length of time, in seconds, before a timeout occurs when retrieving external images. The default value is 600 (10 minutes). The range is any positive value.
Snapshot Compression	Reporting	Defines how snapshots are compressed: SQL, None, or All.
System Report Timeout	Reporting	Determines the time, in seconds, before a report times out. It can be overridden at the report level. The default is 1800 (30 minutes). A value of –1 is for no limit, and the max is any positive integer.
System Snapshot Limit	Reporting	Sets the maximum number of snapshots stored for a report. The default is –1 (no limit), and the range is any positive integer.
Stored Parameters Lifetime	Reporting	Determines the number of days that stored parameters can be stored. The default is 180 days, and the range is any positive integer.
Stored Parameters Threshold	Reporting	Determines the threshold, in days, for a parameter. The default is 1500 days. The range is any positive integer.
Session Timeout	Session	Determines the length of time, in seconds, that a session remains active. The default is 600 (10 minutes), and the range is any positive integer.
Use Session Cookies	Session	Indicates whether cookies can be used when communicating with client browsers. This option is selected by default.
RDLX Report Timeout	Session	Determines the amount of time, in seconds, before an RDLX report times out. The default is 1800 (30 minutes), and the range is any positive integer.
Enable Execution Logging	Logging	Lets you choose whether to enable report execution logging.
Execution Log Days Kept	Logging	Determines how many days to keep report execution information. The default value is 60 days, and valid values are –1 to any positive integer. A value of 0 indicates that entries won't be deleted.
Enable Integrated Security	Security	Determines whether integrated security is enabled.
Enable Load Report	Security Definition	Determines whether users can perform impromptu queries from a Report Builder report.
Enable Remote Errors	Security	Determines whether remote information is included with the error messages returned from remote computers. This setting is disabled by default.
Enable Test Connection Detailed Errors	Security	Determines whether detailed error messages are sent to the client computer when the data source connection is tested.
Enable Report Builder Download	Client	Indicates whether users can download Report Builder from sites in the SharePoint farm.

Setting	Page section	Description
Report Builder Launch URL	Client	Requires a URL if the Report Service doesn't use the default Report Builder URL.
Enable Client Printing	Client	Specifies whether the RSClientPrint ActiveX control is available for download from the report server. Note that some browsers and/or browser settings can prohibit ActiveX controls.
Edit Session Timeout	Client	Specifies the number of seconds before a report edit session times out. The default is 7200 (2 hours), and the range is any positive integer.
ExecutionLogLevel	User-Defined	Defines the execution log level with a default of Normal. The other valid option is Verbose.

MANAGING JOBS

Clicking the Manage Jobs link of the Manage Reporting Services Application page takes you to the Manage Jobs page, where you can view any running Reporting Services jobs. You can also select jobs to delete on this page (for example, if a particular job or set of jobs is taking too long). This page has nothing to configure, but if you set your timeout to be particularly high, you might need this page to end errant jobs.

MANAGING KEYS

The next link on the Manage Reporting Services Application page is Key Management. SharePoint encrypts the data in the Reporting Services databases with an encryption key that you can back up, restore, and change.

If you have to restore a Reporting Services service application, you also need to restore the encryption key. When you back up the encryption key, you provide a password that must meet the complexity requirements set by the domain policy. This password is also needed to restore the encryption key, so keep it in a safe location separate from the backup of the encryption key. For security purposes, you should also store the encryption key in a physically separate location from the SharePoint farm as well as from the backups of the Reporting Services service application. You should change the encryption key occasionally, but the process can take several hours depending on the amount of content. Therefore, you should schedule this so that users are minimally affected, and you should back up the key immediately after changing it (as well as back up the service application itself, because the two backups work in tandem).

The final option on the Key Management page is to delete encrypted content. Deleted content (which can include stored connection strings, subscription information, and information necessary to connect to external data sources) can't be recovered after it's deleted. This action is non-reversible, so make sure that users aren't caught unaware by it. All four actions—backup, restore, change, and delete—are available on the Key Management page, as shown in Figure 5-10.

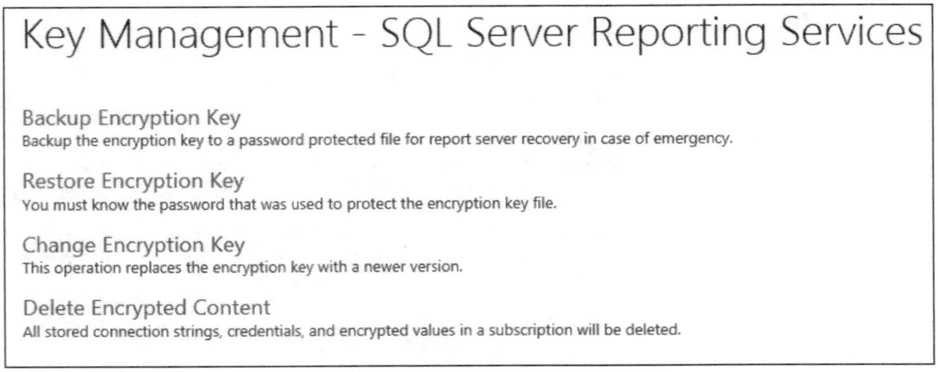

Key Management - SQL Server Reporting Services

Backup Encryption Key
Backup the encryption key to a password protected file for report server recovery in case of emergency.

Restore Encryption Key
You must know the password that was used to protect the encryption key file.

Change Encryption Key
This operation replaces the encryption key with a newer version.

Delete Encrypted Content
All stored connection strings, credentials, and encrypted values in a subscription will be deleted.

FIGURE 5-10 Key Management page of the SQL Server Reporting Services service application

CONFIGURING THE EXECUTION ACCOUNT

The fourth item on the Manage Reporting Services Application page is the Execution Account. This account is used when connecting to data sources that don't use credentials or when connecting to another server to retrieve external image files or resources. The account is also used when a data source specifies None as the credential type. It shouldn't be the same account used to run the Reporting Services service because of security concerns. Also, it should have minimal access, such as read-only, if any access at all is required (to external servers, for example).

You are recommended to use a domain user account that has network logon permissions, so that it can access other servers. You can set the account by clicking Execution Account to get to the Execution Account page. You need to select Specify An Execution Account, provide a user name and password, and then confirm the password before clicking OK (it doesn't verify that the password is correct, so make sure that it's valid and not just matching). If you are building out more than one Reporting Services application, you will need to make sure that all the Execution Accounts are the same on all the service applications.

CONFIGURING EMAIL SETTINGS

The fifth link on the Manage Reporting Services Application page is E-mail Settings. This might seem confusing at first because you also set up email settings for the SharePoint farm. Email settings for Reporting Services are separate from the SharePoint farm. The Reporting Services email system can deliver reports and/or notifications through email subscriptions. Email in Reporting Services requires that you use a Simple Mail Transport Protocol (SMTP) server, so you must have access to one or set one up. You can configure the settings by following these steps:

1. Click E-mail Settings on the Manage Reporting Services Application page in Central Administration.
2. Select the Use SMTP Server check box—otherwise, you can't enter the other values.

3. Enter the name of the SMTP server (such as smtp.contoso.com) in the Outbound SMTP Server text box (no inbound traffic is allowed).
4. In the From Address text box, enter an email address. This doesn't have to be valid or monitored, but you might want to use a valid email address for replies.
5. Click OK to save settings.

PROVISIONING SUBSCRIPTIONS AND ALERTS

The Provision Subscriptions And Alerts link is the same one shown when the Reporting Services service application was created. If you want to make changes or didn't go through the provisioning right after creating the service application, you can us this link to perform that task.

MONITORING RESOURCES

Reporting Services should be ready to use at this point. When users start creating and deploying reports, you should monitor the resources consumed so that you can modify the settings and/or topology to meet your organization's demands.

> ***MORE INFO*** **MANAGING A REPORTING SERVICES SERVICE APPLICATION**
>
> **See *http://technet.microsoft.com/en-us/library/gg492284.aspx* for more information on how to manage a Reporting Services service application.**

Planning and configuring PowerPivot

You can use the powerful PowerPivot tool for data mash-ups and data exploration. PowerPivot can be used to explore millions or even billions of rows of data. SharePoint has taken this powerful tool and made it accessible through its service application infrastructure.

In general, the users of PowerPivot won't be your typical end users but, depending on the types of operations they are performing, they can end up use many resources. As a result, you must plan out what servers will provide these resources, who will use them, and what the settings will be on the service application.

PowerPivot doesn't come with SharePoint Server 2013—at least, not in the initial release. You must download and install it, or find the latest version of the software to install.

> ***MORE INFO*** **DOWNLOADING POWERPIVOT**
>
> **See *http://www.microsoft.com/en-us/download/details.aspx?id=35577* to download Microsoft SQL Server 2012 SP1 PowerPivot for Microsoft SharePoint.**

After you download the PowerPivot installation file, you can install it on a SharePoint server on your farm. You need to be a local administrator as well as a member of the Share-

Point Farm Administrators group to completely install PowerPivot. The following items are installed on the server when you install the installation package:

- PowerPivot for SharePoint 2013
- Analysis Services OLE DB Provider for SQL Server 2012
- ADOMD.NET
- SQL Server 2012 Analysis Management Objects

As soon as the PowerPivot service application is installed and configured, users can start using it. SharePoint shows that a new site template can be used for sites dedicated to PowerPivot functionality. Also, a feature is available on the site collection level that enables PowerPivot functionality on any site collection. Because PowerPivot is a specialized tool that's typically used only by a small group of users, dedicating a site collection to those users is best so that PowerPivot is easier to manage.

Running the Configuration tool

After the PowerPivot for SharePoint package is installed, you can run the PowerPivot for SharePoint 2013 Configuration tool. You can use this tool to configure, repair, or remove PowerPivot on a SharePoint server. When you run the tool for the first time, the only option is to configure, which you can do by following these steps, using an account that is both local administrator and a SharePoint farm administrator:

1. On the server on which you installed Microsoft SQL Server 2012 SP1 PowerPivot for Microsoft SharePoint, navigate to All Programs | Microsoft SQL Server 2012 | Configuration Tools and select PowerPivot for SharePoint 2013 Configuration.
2. The tool examines your system, which can take a minute or so. Afterward, the first screen allows you to choose only to Configure Or Repair PowerPivot For SharePoint. Click OK to continue.
3. A PowerPivot Configuration Tool window should appear, as shown in Figure 5-11. You need to consider many values, and the screen might vary depending on your SharePoint installation. Make sure that everything is configured correctly before you click Run.

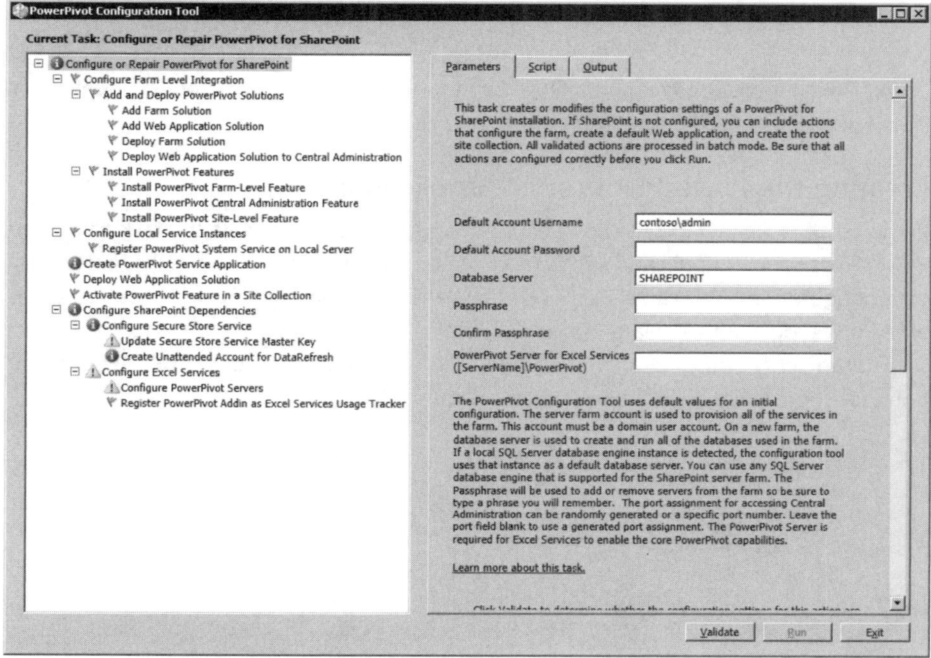

FIGURE 5-11 PowerPivot Configuration Tool window

4. After you enter the necessary values, click Validate to test the values that you've entered. Make sure that the items that you don't want to run at this time are excluded; for example, if you want to create the PowerPivot service application manually through Central Administration or PowerShell, you can clear the Create PowerPivot Service Application option.

5. If the validation comes back as a success, click Run to begin the batch job that will run all the tasks. An Activity Progress bar appears, showing the progress of the tasks being completed. On completion, click OK and then click Exit to close the configuration tool.

You don't need to configure everything here; you can come back later or configure the PowerPivot Service Application in Central Administration and/or with PowerShell. However, although the PowerPivot Configuration Tool provides many options, you should be sure to have the correct values for at least the following:

- **Default Account** This account is used to provision the PowerPivot service application pool and create the service application (if that step is done here). It can't be a built-in account.
- **Passphrase** If the SharePoint farm hasn't been created, create a new passphrase that will become the SharePoint farm passphrase. If the SharePoint farm already exists, use the SharePoint farm passphrase, the one used when you add a new server to the farm.

- **Database Server** This is the name of a SQL Server 2012 SP1 PowerPivot Server running in SharePoint mode.
- **Port** If you are creating a SharePoint farm, you can specify the port number or let SharePoint create one randomly.

Creating the PowerPivot service application

In the list of tasks that exist in PowerPivot Configuration Tool, notice the task called Create PowerPivot Service Application. This task creates the PowerPivot Service Application as part of the configuration. (You can also choose to create the PowerPivot Service Application at a later time.) If you do want to create the service application with the tool, you should click the task so you can verify and/or change the values. Clicking the Create PowerPivot Service Application task should display a screen similar to Figure 5-12.

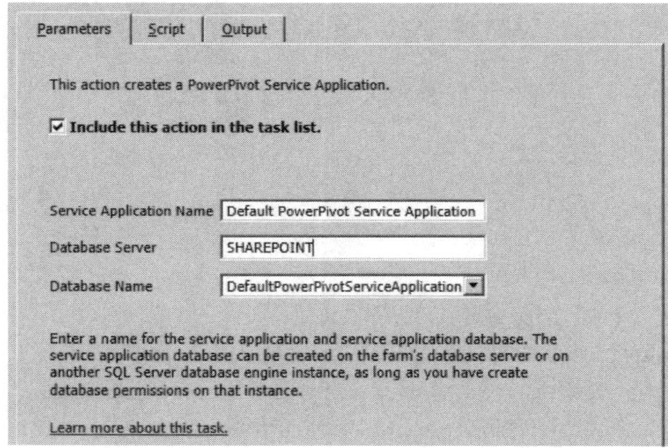

FIGURE 5-12 Create PowerPivot Service Application task pane

You should change the values in the Create PowerPivot Service Application task pane depending on your needs. The name in the Database Name field actually has a GUID in it, but that part is hidden because the name is so long. If you're using scripting or multiple PowerPivot service applications, you should modify the name to make it easier to type and distinguish. The database server doesn't have to be on the SharePoint farm; it can be any PowerPivot-capable database that the default account has access to.

EXAM TIP

Because PowerPivot isn't a widely used SharePoint feature, it's an easy one to overlook when studying for the exam. This is especially true because it has to be downloaded, installed, and configured. You should at least be aware of what's required to install it as well as what the configuration tool can do.

You later might want to do (or have already done) several other tasks rather than have the configuration tool do them for you, such as configuring the Secure Store and Excel Services. If you're connecting to an existing farm, more than likely these already exist and you don't need to have them created.

> ***MORE INFO*** **CONFIGURING OR REPAIRING POWERPIVOT**
>
> **See *http://technet.microsoft.com/en-us/library/jj820150.aspx#bkmk_steps* for more information on how to configure or repair PowerPivot for SharePoint 2013 using the PowerPivot Configuration Tool.**

You also can create the SQL Server PowerPivot service application within Central Administration. The SQL Server PowerPivot System service should also be running on the server on which the configuration tool was run. If you want the service to run on other servers, you should run the configuration tool on those servers and choose only the task that installs the service (Configure Local Service Instance). Creating the service application can be done in Central Administration by following these steps:

1. Navigate to Central Administration as a farm administrator and click Manage Service Applications in the Application Management section.
2. Click the New icon and select SQL Server PowerPivot Service Application.
3. Enter a name for the PowerPivot service application (such as PowerPivot Service Application) in the Name text box.
4. Create a new application pool or select an existing one in the Application Pool section.
5. In the PowerPivot Service Application Database section, enter the name of the database server to be used in the Database Server text box and a database name in the Database Name text box. The database doesn't have to be the same one used for the SharePoint farm.
6. In the same section, select the authentication method used to connect to the database server and credentials, if necessary.
7. If you want this service application to be added to the default proxy group, leave the check box selected in the Default section and click OK (if this is the first PowerPivot service application on the SharePoint farm, you need to add the PowerPivot service application to the default proxy for the PowerPivot Management Dashboard to work properly).

Working with additional PowerPivot settings

After the PowerPivot service application is created, it has a default set of configuration settings. You are recommended to leave these settings alone unless you're experiencing performance problems or you to change them for a specific web application (such as a separate PowerPivot service application for a web application dedicated to PowerPivot functionality).

You change the settings in the PowerPivot Management Dashboard, but note that an IISRESET might be needed after the service application is created before the dashboard can work.

You can get to PowerPivot Management by clicking the PowerPivot service application on the Manage Service Applications page in Central Administration. This opens the dashboard, where you can get to the settings page by clicking Configure Service Application Settings in the Actions Settings section. Table 5-2 lists the available settings and their descriptions.

TABLE 5-2 PowerPivot service application settings

Setting	Section	Description
Data Load Timeout	Data Load Timeout	Determines the number of seconds before a data load attempt times out. The default is 1800 (30 minutes), and the range is from 1 to 3600.
Connection Pool Timeout	Connection Pools	Determines the number of seconds before an idle connection is removed from the connection pool. The default is 1800, and the range is from 1 to 3600.
Maximum User Connection Pool Size	Connection Pools	Determines the maximum number of connections in the user connection pool. The default is 1000, and the range is from –1 to 10000, with a value of –1 meaning unlimited and 0 meaning that user connection pooling is disabled (every connection is created new).
Maximum Administrative Connection Pool Size	Connection Pools	Determines the maximum number of connections in the administrative connection pool. The default is 200, and the range is –1 to 10000, with –1 meaning unlimited and 0 meaning that administrative connection pooling is disabled.
Business Hours	Data Refresh	Specifies the usual business hours so that data refreshes can be scheduled to occur after business hours and can include the data from the current day.
PowerPivot Unattended Data Refresh Account	Data Refresh	Enables you to put a Secure Store target application in here for unattended data refreshes. The value should be the name of the target application, not the ID.
Allow Users To Enter Windows Credentials	Data Refresh	Allows users to enter arbitrary Windows credentials for a data refresh. SharePoint will automatically create a target application for the set of credentials.
Refresh Jobs To Run In Parallel	Data Refresh	Specifies the maximum number of data refresh jobs that can run in parallel. The default is 1 and the range is from 1 to 5.
Maximum Processing	Data Refresh History Length	Specifies the maximum number of days to keep the processing history. The default is 365 and the range is 1 to 5000.
Disable Data Refresh Due To Consecutive Failures	Data Refresh	Specifies the number of times a data refresh can consecutively fail before it's disabled.
Disable Data Refresh For Inactive workbooks	Data Refresh	Determines how many times a data refresh can occur for workbooks that aren't used interactively before they are disabled. The default is 10, and the range is 0 to any positive value. A value of 0 means they are never disabled.

Setting	Section	Description
Keep Inactive Database In Memory (In Hours)	Disk Cache	Specifies the number of hours to keep an inactive PowerPivot database in memory. The default is 48 hours and the range is any positive integer.
Keep Inactive Database In Cache (In Hours)	Disk Cache	Determines the number of hours to keep an inactive database in cache. Must be greater than the Keep Inactive Database In Memory setting. The default is 120, and the range is any positive integer.
Load To Connection Ratio	Health Rule Settings	Determines the value for the health rule for the number of workbooks being loaded relative to the number of user connections. High values indicate a high memory load. The default is 20, and the range is 1 to 99.
Data Collection Interval (In Hours)	Health Rule Settings	Specifies the interval in hours to count load and connection events to determine the Load To Connection Ratio. The default is 4, and the range is 1 to 24.
Check For Updates To PowerPivot Management Data.xlsx File	Health Rules Settings	Specifies the threshold in days before a warning is created to indicate that the data file used by reports in the PowerPivot Management Dashboard is not being updated. The default is 5, and the range is 1 to 30.
Query Reporting Interval	Usage Data Collection	Indicates the number of seconds to gather response statistics before reporting it as a usage event. The default is 300 (5 minutes), and the range is any positive integer.
Usage Data History	Usage Data Collection	Determines the number of days to retain usage data and server health statistics. The default is 365 (a year), and the value is from 0 to any positive integer, with 0 meaning indefinitely.
Trivial Response Upper Limit	Usage Data Collection	Determines the maximum number of milliseconds allowed to complete a trivial request (trivial requests are excluded from report data). The range is from any positive integer to a number less than the Quick Response Upper Limit. The default is 500 (half a second).
Quick Response Upper Limit	Usage Data Collection	Determines the upper limit in milliseconds for a completing a quick request. A quick request could be considered querying a small dataset. The default is 1000 (one second), and it must be greater than the Trivial Response Upper Limit and lower than the Expected Response Upper Limit.
Expected Response Upper Limit	Usage Data Collection	Specifies another threshold in milliseconds for completing a query in an expected amount of time. Most PowerPivot data queries will fall into this category. The default is 3000 (3 seconds), and the value must be greater than the Quick Response Upper Limit and less than the Long Response Upper Limit.
Long Response Upper Limit	Usage Data Collection	Sets the threshold, in milliseconds, for long-running requests. Very few requests should fall into this category; otherwise, performance will be affected. The default number is 10000 (10 seconds), and it must be greater than the Expected Response Upper Limit.

As you can see from Table 5-2, many settings can be configured. However, you should use caution when modifying these settings because you can greatly curtail the performance of both SharePoint and PowerPivot if you misconfigure them.

> ***MORE INFO*** **CREATING AND CONFIGURING A POWERPIVOT SERVICE APPLICATION**
>
> **See *http://technet.microsoft.com/en-us/library/ee210685.aspx* for more information on how to create and configure a PowerPivot service application in Central Administration.**

Planning and configuring Excel Services data modeling

Chapter 4 covers how to set up and configure Excel Services, but this section focuses on the data models created in Excel 2013. With Excel Services, you can specify one or more instances of Microsoft SQL Server 2012 SP1 to use for processing these data models. Excel Services can use Analysis Services to work with the data models; in fact, if you use Excel workbooks that store imported data in multiple tables, you need to have Analysis Services to be able to interact with the data in SharePoint. An Analysis Service instance doesn't have to be on the same SQL Server instance as the SharePoint farm, but it does have to be on the same network and in the same domain. If the load on your Analysis Services instance becomes too great to meet the demands of your users, you can add more servers as needed.

You configure the data model settings inside the context of the Excel Services service application. The settings allow you to register one or more servers to be used for Analysis Services. Follow these steps to register a SQL Server instance to the data model settings:

1. Navigate to Central Administration as a farm administrator or as an administrator of the Excel Services service application.
2. Click Manage Service Applications in the Application Management section.
3. Click the Excel Services service application under the Name column to open the Manage Excel Services Application page.
4. Click Data Model Settings.
5. Click Add Server on the Excel Services Application Data Model Settings page.
6. In the Server Name text box, enter the name of the SQL Server instance (the server must be running SQL Server Analysis Services 2012 SP1 or higher in SharePoint deployment mode).
7. Enter an optional description in the Description text box and click OK.

After you add the Analysis Services server, you have only two options for further configuration of the item you just added. You can edit the server name and/or description, or you can unregister the Analysis Services server. These tasks can also be done from the Excel Services Application Data Model page.

> ***MORE INFO*** **MANAGING THE EXCEL SERVICES DATA MODEL SETTINGS**
>
> **See *http://technet.microsoft.com/en-us/library/jj219780.aspx* for more information on how to manage the Excel Services data model settings.**

Planning and configuring Power View

The Power View tool can be used for interactive exploration of data. It provides a visual way to explore large sets of data, using various different charts and graphs. You even can connect Bing maps to data, giving users a way to map out their data by region (such as sales data per state).

Power View is installed as part of the Reporting Services add-on for SharePoint found in Microsoft SQL Server 2012 SP1 (or greater). So when you installed Reporting Services for SharePoint, you also installed the capability to use Power View. Power View reports can be created from PowerPivot workbooks or tabular data in SQL Server 2012 Analysis Services.

Power View requires that Analysis Services be installed in Tabular mode when you are installing an instance of SQL Server. If you've already installed Analysis Services in Multidimensional and Data Mining mode, you need to install another instance of SQL Server or change the mode to be unsupported. (You also could remove SQL Server and reinstall it, but that might not be feasible.) To install Analysis Services in Tabular mode, follow these steps when you are installing an instance of SQL Server:

1. When you get to the Feature Selection page during the installation of the SQL Server instance, be sure to choose Analysis Services, as shown in Figure 5-13. Also choose the other features that you want to install.

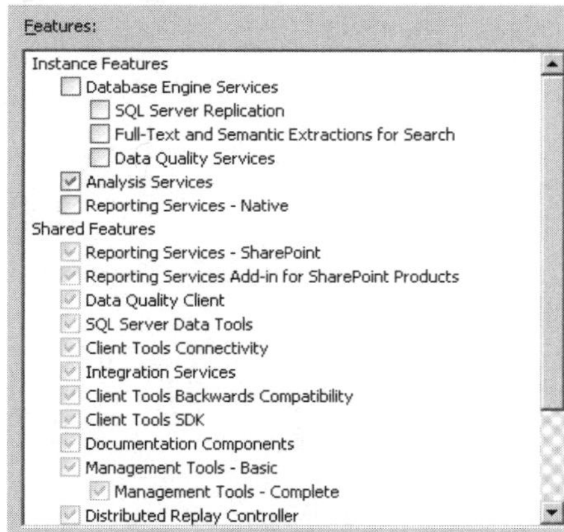

FIGURE 5-13 Feature selection page that's part of a SQL Server installation.

2. Continue with the installation until you get to the Analysis Services Configuration page, where you need to select Tabular Mode in the Server Mode section.
3. Finish the installation of the SQL Server instance.

MORE INFO INSTALLING ANALYSIS SERVICES IN TABULAR MODE

See *http://msdn.microsoft.com/en-us/library/hh231722.aspx* for more information on how to install Analysis Services in Tabular mode.

After you ensure that SharePoint has access to Analysis Services in Tabular mode, ensure that Power View is working with Analysis Services. To do this, Analysis Services needs to have a data model in it to report on. You can do this by following these steps:

1. Navigate to a PowerPivot site (or a site with the PowerPivot site collection feature enabled).
2. Go to the Library Settings of the Documents Library and click Advanced Settings.
3. Click Yes to Allow Management Of Content Types? in the Content Types section and click OK to save the settings.
4. Back on the Library Settings page, click Add From Existing Site in the Content Types section.
5. On the Add Content Types page, select BI Semantic Model Connection from the list of Available Site Content Types and click Add, as shown in Figure 5-14.

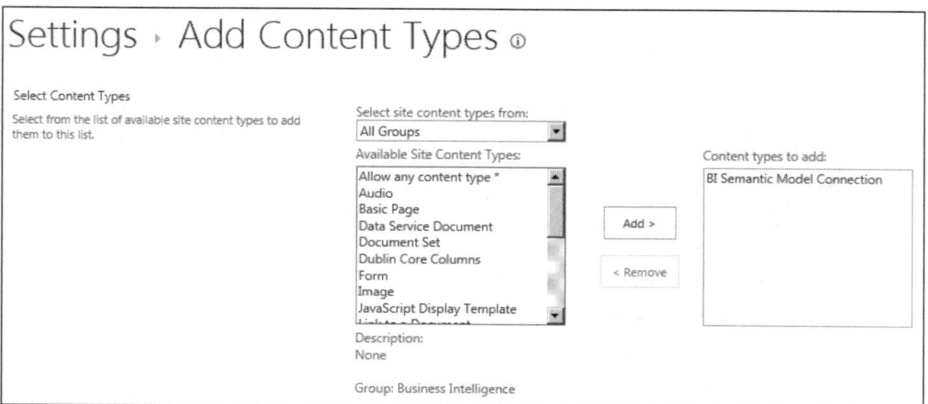

FIGURE 5-14 Add Content Types page

6. Click OK on the Add Content Types page to add a BI Semantic Model Connection document to the Document library.
7. Add a new BI Semantic Model Connection by returning to the Documents library, clicking the Files tab, and then selecting BI Semantic Model Connection from the New Icon drop-down list.
8. Enter a filename (the file to be created) in the File Name text box for the BI Semantic Model Connection and a description in the Description text box.

9. Enter the name of a workbook URL or server name (the Analysis Services in Tabular Mode server) in the Workbook URL Or Server Name text box.
10. If you entered a server name in step 9 (and you should have if using Analysis Services), enter the name of the database to connect to in the Database text box and click OK.
11. After the file is created, click the three dots next to the newly created document and then choose Create Power View Report.
12. Install Silverlight if necessary (if you have to install it, you need to return to this page to continue after restarting the browser). Return to the document, click the three dots again, and then click Create Power View Report.

You and your users should be able to use Power View at this point. You might see the following error when you try to create the BI Semantic Model Connection:

```
Could not load type 'Microsoft.AnalysisServices.Sharepoint.Integration.ASLinkFilePage'
```

This error probably means that the PowerPivot farm solution hasn't been deployed on the web application on which the PowerPivot site (or site collection that has the PowerPivot feature installed) resides. You can solve this issue by following these steps:

1. Navigate to Central Administration as a farm administrator and click System Settings.
2. Click Manage Farm Solutions.
3. Click the powerpivotwebapplicationsolution.wsp link under the Name column.
4. Click Deploy Solution on the Solution Properties page.
5. In the Deploy To? Section, choose the web application to deploy to and then click OK to deploy the solution.

If you still have issues, you need to do some troubleshooting. Getting to this point involves many steps and configurations. In some cases, redoing steps might be easier than trying to fix them. Installing Power View seems to involve many steps, but it will be worth it in the end and your power users will have a great set of tools to do some outstanding data analysis.

Thought experiment

Providing PowerPivot to end users

In the following thought experiment, apply what you've learned about this objective. You can find answers to these questions in the "Answers" section at the end of this chapter.

You have a SharePoint 2013 farm installed that uses a SQL Server 2008 R2 database. The data analysis team knows that you have SharePoint installed and that PowerPivot is an option, but it's not currently installed or configured. The data analysis team members are now using SQL Server 2012 SP1 Analysis Services for their dedicated projects.

How would you best go about providing to the team PowerPivot for SharePoint without buying any additional hardware or software?

Objective summary

- PerformancePoint is a powerful reporting tool for both SharePoint data and external data that needs to be configured to prevent the accidental reporting of secure data.
- Reporting Services requires SQL Server 2012 SP1 Reporting Services installed on each SharePoint server required to run Reporting Services.
- Reporting Services content is encrypted with a key along with a password to restore the service application in case of a disaster.
- PowerPivot requires a separate download that comes with a configuration tool that works with SQL Server 2012 SP1 to install PowerPivot on SharePoint.
- PowerPivot provides many configuration options, but you should rely on the defaults unless performance becomes an issue.
- Power View works with SQL Server Analysis Services and PowerPivot workbooks to provide end users powerful interactive charts and graphs.

Objective review

Answer the following questions to test your knowledge of the information in this objective. You can find the answers to these questions and explanations of why each answer choice is correct or incorrect in the "Answers" section at the end of this chapter.

1. Which of the following isn't a requirement to be able to use PerformancePoint services with shared credentials?
   - **A.** Provide credentials to the PerformancePoint service application for the Unattended Service Account
   - **B.** Create a target application for PerformancePoint
   - **C.** Ensure that the PerformancePoint service is running on at least one server
   - **D.** Create the PerformancePoint service application
2. Which of the following isn't needed to restore a Reporting Services service application?
   - **A.** A backup of the Reporting Services service application
   - **B.** A copy of the encryption Key for Reporting Services
   - **C.** A farm password
   - **D.** An encryption key password
3. The PowerPivot for SharePoint 2013 Configuration tool can do which of the following tasks?
   - **A.** Create the SQL Server PowerPivot Service Application
   - **B.** Create a web application
   - **C.** Configure the Secure Store service application
   - **D.** All of the above
4. Power View can report on Analysis Services data models. What minimum version and mode of Analysis Services is required for Power View in SharePoint 2013?
   - **A.** Microsoft SQL Server 2012 Analysis Services in Tabular mode
   - **B.** Microsoft SQL Server 2012 Analysis Services in Multidimensional and Data Mining mode
   - **C.** Microsoft SQL Server 2012 SP1 Analysis Services in Tabular mode
   - **D.** Microsoft SQL Server 2012 SP1 Analysis Services in Multidimensional and Data Mining mode

Objective 5.3: Creating and configuring work management

This section covers interacting with other servers, such as Microsoft Project Server and Microsoft Exchange Server. Interactions between these systems require the applications to trust each other so they can have access to the information they need to perform certain functions. For example, if you're performing eDiscovery with SharePoint and part of the eDiscovery process involves having access to a user's mailbox, the SharePoint farm needs to trust the Exchange farm and the Exchange farm must trust the SharePoint farm. This level of security ensures that applications can't have access, even if the user might actually have access. This is not only for security reasons but also for performance reasons because unfettered access to an application could slow it down or even bring it to a halt.

This objective covers the following topics:

- Planning and configuring Microsoft Project Server 2013
- Configuring a connection to Exchange for eDiscovery and Resource Sharing

Configuring a connection to Microsoft Project Server

Microsoft Project Server 2013 is installed as part of SharePoint. Several versions ago, Project Server didn't even know that SharePoint existed, but gradually it became more integrated with SharePoint until Project Server 2010, when it became a service application that ran on the SharePoint infrastructure. Although it's not completely integrated—Project Server has its own security structure in addition to the one provided by SharePoint—Project Server can leverage the power of SharePoint for document management and project storage and allow for users to interact with projects through a browser interface.

You can use a client-side program called Project Professional to open and work with projects from a local computer or from a SharePoint server. Project files can be saved onto a SharePoint farm with or without Project Server being installed. Conceptually, this can be thought of in the same way as how other products with client-side programs (such as Word, Excel, and PowerPoint) work with SharePoint. You can use Project Server to deliver and receive project-related information without end users having to purchase a copy of Project Professional for their client machine, potentially saving your organization a considerable amount of money. Project Server doesn't come with the SharePoint Server software, but it can be downloaded for evaluation (and eventual purchase, if desired) so that you can prepare for the exam.

MORE INFO **DOWNLOADING MICROSOFT PROJECT SERVER 2013**

See *http://technet.microsoft.com/en-us/evalcenter/hh973403.aspx* to download Microsoft Project Server 2013.

Installing Project Server

Assuming that you've obtained the installation software for Project Server, you can begin to install it. Installing Microsoft Project Server 2013 on SharePoint is a multistep process that needs to be done correctly; otherwise, it could leave your SharePoint farm in an unstable state. Also, installation can take several hours, depending on how many servers are in your farm. The principal steps required are as follows:

1. Install Project Server 2013 on every SharePoint server in the farm.
2. Run the SharePoint Products Configuration Wizard for each sever in the farm.
3. Start the Project Server Application service.
4. Create a Project Server service application.

As with any software, you should install Project Server on a test farm before you install it in production. You also should back up the entire SharePoint farm (databases and farm configuration) before installing Project Server. After you have taken care of all the prerequisite tasks, you can begin to install Project Server by following these steps:

1. Log onto a SharePoint server with an account that can be used to install software. You should run the Project Server installation software with the same account that you used to install SharePoint (but you can do Run As to accomplish this).
2. Start the Project Server installation software to get to the splash screen, as shown in Figure 5-15.

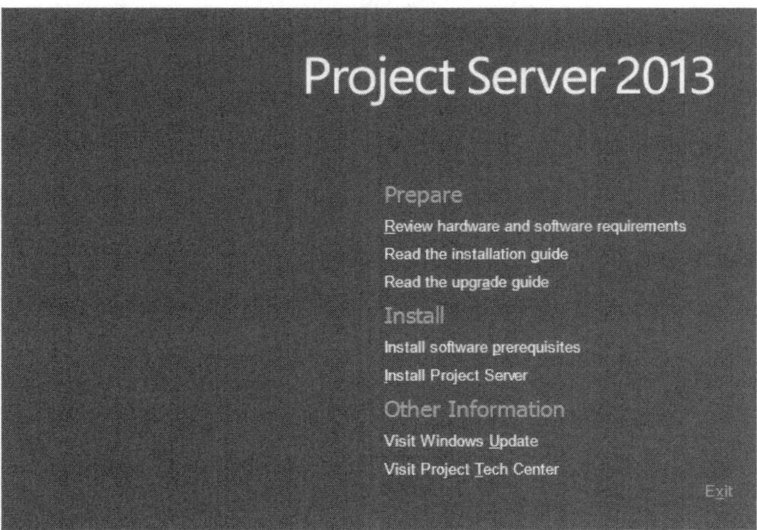

FIGURE 5-15 Project Server 2013 installation splash screen

3. Because you're installing onto a server that already has SharePoint 2013 installed, you can skip Install software Prerequisites (they are covered by the SharePoint 2013 installation) and click Install Project Server.
4. After the setup process initializes, enter a valid product key (note that you can't install an evaluation version of Project Server 2013 on a production version of SharePoint 2013) and click Continue.
5. On the End User License Agreement page, review the agreement, select I Accept The Terms Of This Agreement (if you agree to them), and then click Continue.
6. On the Choose A File Location page, click Install Now to begin the installation process (the actual browse buttons should be disabled).
7. When the installation process is complete, clear the Run The SharePoint Products And Technologies Configuration Wizard Now check box (unless you have only one server in your SharePoint farm).
8. Click Close.
9. Repeat steps 1 through 8 until you've installed Project Server on each SharePoint server in the SharePoint farm.
10. On one of the SharePoint servers in the SharePoint farm, start the SharePoint 2013 Products Configuration Wizard.
11. On the Welcome page, click Next.
12. A list of services appears, warning that the services might have to restart. Click Yes to continue.
13. Select Do Not Disconnect From This Server Farm on the Modify Server Farm Settings page and click Next.
14. If you are on a server that hosts the Central Administration website, select No, This Machine Will Continue To Host The Web Site on the Modify SharePoint Central Administration Web Application page. Click Next to continue.
15. Click Next on the Completing The SharePoint Products Configuration Wizard page.
16. Wait until the process completely finishes before moving on.
17. Click Finish on the Configuration Successful page.
18. Repeat steps 10 through 17 for each SharePoint server in the SharePoint farm.

IMPORTANT **RUNNING THE SHAREPOINT 2013 PRODUCTS CONFIGURATION WIZARD**

Make sure that you wait until the SharePoint 2013 Products Configuration Wizard is completely finished on one SharePoint Server before moving to the next SharePoint server. Failing to do so could leave the SharePoint farm in an unstable state.

Starting the Project Server Application Service

After you install Project Server on all the SharePoint servers and run the SharePoint 2013 Products Configuration Wizard on each SharePoint server in turn, you are ready to start the Project Server Application service and then create the Project Server service application, either via Central Administration or with PowerShell commands. The first task is to start the Project Server Application Service, as follows:

1. Navigate to Central Administration with a farm administrator account.
2. Click Manage Services On Server in the System Settings section.
3. Select the server on which you want to start the service from the Server drop-down list and click the Start link on the line that says Project Server Application Service in the Service column.
4. Repeat steps 2 and 3 for every server that you want running the Project Server Application Service.

If possible, you should have the Project Service Application Service running on at least two servers for redundancy; except for very heavy Project Server loads, two should be sufficient.

Creating the Project Server service application

Now that the service is running, you are now ready to create the Project Server service application. You can do this in Central Administration by following these steps:

1. Navigate to Central Administration as a farm administrator and click Manage Service Applications in the Application Management section.
2. Click the New icon to open the drop-down menu and select Project Server Service Application.
3. Enter a name (such as Project Server Service Application) in the Project Server Application Name text box.
4. Choose whether to create a new application pool or use an existing one in the Application Pool Settings section.
5. In the Service Application Proxy section, leave the Create A Proxy For This Service Application? check box selected if you want the service application in the default proxy group.
6. Click OK to create the service application.

> ***MORE INFO*** **INSTALLING AND CONFIGURING PROJECT SERVER 2013**
>
> **See *http://technet.microsoft.com/en-us/library/ee662109.aspx* for more information on how to Install and configure Project Server 2013.**

Creating a Project Server web app

You are almost ready to start using Project Server, but you still need to create a Project Server web app in a new site collection or within an existing site collection. Creating the web app within its own site collection (and its own content database) is probably a good idea for the purposes of management and disaster recovery. Project Server is a complex program with data that changes frequently. The odds of having to recover data are much higher with this type of data than your typical document management data. Isolating the Project Server to its own site collection and content database greatly speeds up the recovery process.

Users of the Project Server web app need read permissions to the site collection that contains the web app. To create a site collection to be used by the Project Server web app, follow these steps:

1. Create a site collection for the Project Server web app. Project Server doesn't require a certain template because the team site template will work fine.
2. Navigate to the site collection that you created and click Share.
3. On the Share page, click Show Options and choose the Visitors group (<site> Visitors [Read]) from the Select A Group Or Permission Level drop-down list.
4. Type **Everyone** in the Enter Names Or Email Addresses text box (or the user group that you want to have access to the underlying Project Server data).
5. Click Share.

You are finally ready to create a Project Server web app. That you create a new content database for the Project Server web app site and the associated workspaces is highly recommended. For this to happen, you need to create the site collection during a time when other users aren't trying to create sites within the web application. Then, you need to perform the following steps (if the web application houses only the Project Server web app and the top-level site collection, you can have both site collections in the same content database):

1. Lock down the existing content databases (set content database to Offline).
2. Create a new content database for the web application hosting the Project Server web app.
3. Create the Project Server web app.
4. Lock down the content database created for the Project Server web app.
5. Unlock the other content databases for the web application.

Creating the actual Project Server web app can be done in Central Administration by following these steps:

1. Navigate to Central Administration as a farm administrator.
2. Click Manage Service Applications in the Application Management section.

3. Select the Project Server Service Application from the list of service applications to open the Manage Project Web Apps page, as shown in Figure 5-16.

Manage Project Web Apps

Project server provisioning timer job status: Online. Last Run Time: 2/19/2013 6:12:02 AM

Create Project Web App Instance | Refresh Status | Manage Queue Settings for Project Web App

There are no items to show in this view.

FIGURE 5-16 Manage Project Web Apps page

4. Click Create Project Web App Instance.
5. In the Web Application section, select the web application (the one where you created the site collection for this web app) where you want the web app instance to reside from the Web Application drop-down list.
6. Enter the path from the root site. (You can leave it as PWA if installing at the root.)
7. Select a language from the Select A Language drop-down list (pulled from the installed language packs) for the user interface.
8. Enter an administrator account in the Administrator Account text box. This user is who initially handles setting up permissions for the site.
9. Enter a database server and project web app database name in the Database Settings section. The database doesn't have to be on the same SQL Server instance where the SharePoint farm is installed, but you can experience reduced performance if it's not.
10. In the Site Quota section, enter the values (in megabytes) for the Quota For SharePoint Content and the Quota Warning.
11. Click OK. You are returned to the Manage Project Web Apps page, where the status displays Waiting For Resources. Wait until the status shown says Provisioned. It might take a while (a few minutes usually), depending on the resources available. If you don't have enough resources (like low on memory), the process will fail, but it can be started again after you correct the resource issue.

MORE INFO **DEPLOYING A PROJECT WEB APP WITH A NEW SITE COLLECTION**

See *http://technet.microsoft.com/en-us/library/ee662105.aspx* for more information on how to deploy a Project web app with a new site collection.

You can also create a Project Server web app in an existing site collection for relatively small projects. In this case, the Project Server web app site would be part of the existing site collections content database, which should factor into any performance and disaster recovery considerations. The steps involved with this process are straightforward:

1. Enable the site collection feature Project Web App.
2. Create a site using the Project Web App site template.

After creation, the site is ready to use either through the browser or with the Project Professional 2013 client application, as long as users have access to it.

> ***MORE INFO*** **DEPLOYING A PROJECT WEB APP IN AN EXISTING SITE COLLECTION**
>
> **See *http://technet.microsoft.com/en-us/library/jj200304.aspx* for more information about how to deploy a Project web app in an existing site collection.**

After you create your project web app site, you can navigate to it and verify that it was created correctly. It should appear as it does in Figure 5-17. You should also verify that users who need to use the site can get to it; they have to have at least read permissions to the site.

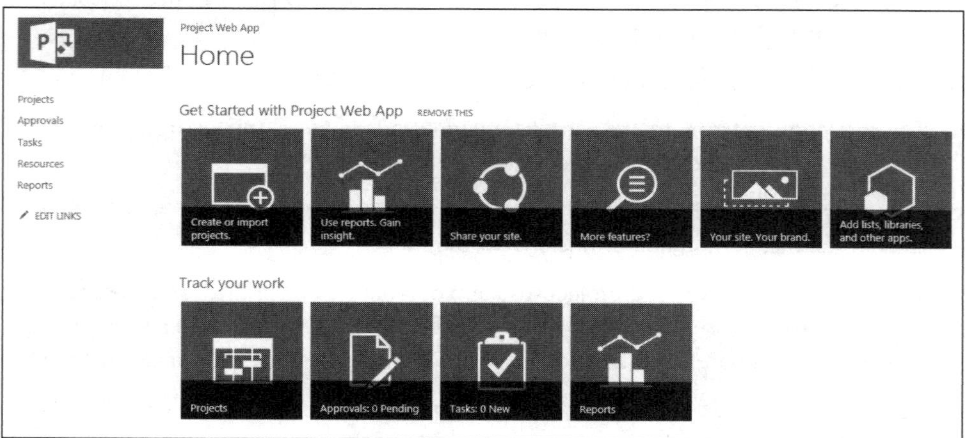

FIGURE 5-17 Project Server web app site home page

From the Project web app, users can create or import projects and do all the work on the project right from the browser. This eliminates the need for having the Project Professional client application work on projects, but some licensing issues exist. Project Server 2013 is licensed separately from SharePoint Server 2013, and you need to determine how many licenses you need for your organization before allowing users access to the Project web apps. Typically, Project Server 2013 has one license for itself and then additional client-access licenses (CALs) for each user who accesses the Project Server data, either directly or indirectly.

EXAM TIP

That you need to install Project Server on all SharePoint servers before you run the SharePoint 2013 Products Configuration Wizard is a prime example of a question that will lend itself to one of the "put-the-steps-in-order" questions. Note that some documentation mentions that Project Server is needed only on the app servers, but it actually needs to be installed on the WFEs also.

Configuring a connection to Exchange for eDiscovery and Resource Sharing

SharePoint 2013 can be used for eDiscovery both for SharePoint content as well as content in Microsoft Exchange. It can query emails, put holds on them, and export their content as part of the overall eDiscovery process. The process of enabling SharePoint to be able to perform these functions takes configuration on both the SharePoint farm and the Exchange farm. Chapter 2, "Plan a SharePoint environment," covered how to configure an eDiscovery center in some detail, but only briefly covered the steps involved on the Exchange server. This objective covers the Exchange portion in more detail.

Communication between SharePoint and Exchange requires that the two systems trust each other. This trust needs to be established on each system separately. SharePoint trusts the Exchange server by making it a security token issuer and granting the Exchange service principal full control to SharePoint site subscription. You can make an Exchange farm a security token issuer by logging onto a SharePoint server and running the following PowerShell command in the SharePoint 2013 Management Shell as a farm administrator, where *<exchange server>* is the Exchange 2013 server name (or FQDN):

```
New-SPTrustedSecurityTokenIssuer -Name Exchange -MetadataEndPoint https://<exchange
server>/autodiscover/metadata/json/1
```

While you are still in the Management Shell, you can grant the Exchange service principal full control to SharePoint site subscription by running the following PowerShell commands, where *<sharepoint server>* is the server on which you are running the commands:

```
$exch=Get-SPTrustedSecurityTokenIssuer "Exchange"
$app=Get-SPAppPrincipal -Site http://<sharepoint server> -NameIdentifier $exch.NameId
$site=Get-SPSite http://<sharepoint server>
Set-SPAppPrincipalPermission -AppPrincipal $app -Site $site.RootWeb -Scope
sitesubscription -Right fullcontrol -EnableApplyOnlyPolicy
```

IMPORTANT **SharePoint and Exchange must be in the same forest if SharePoint is going to perform eDiscovery on the Exchange mailboxes.**

Configuration with regards to server trust is complete on the SharePoint server at this point; configuring the Exchange server is next. Typically, the administrator accounts on the SharePoint farm aren't administrators on the Exchange farm—nor should they be. You need to make sure that the account configuring the trust on the Exchange server has the Organization Management permission to perform the necessary steps. You can use the following PowerShell command on the Exchange 2013 server to provide the necessary trust, where *<sharepoint server>* is a server on the SharePoint farm or the FQDN of the server:

```
cd c:\'Program Files'\Microsoft\'Exchange Server'\V15\Scripts
.\Configure-EnterprisePartnerApplication.ps1 -AuthMetadataUrl "http://<sharepoint
server>/15/_layouts/metadata/json/1" -ApplicationType SharePoint
```

This script works as long as Exchange is installed on the C drive; otherwise, point to the where it is installed. The preceding command is a script that relies on the PowerShell command New-AuthServer to specify a new trusted server.

> ***MORE INFO*** **USING NEW-AUTHSERVER**
>
> **See *http://technet.microsoft.com/en-us/library/jj215704.aspx* for more information on the PowerShell command New-AuthServer.**

Any user who will perform eDiscovery on Exchange mailboxes needs the appropriate permissions on the Exchange server. The needed permissions are provided by adding the SharePoint users performing In-place eDiscovery to the Discovery Management role group on the Exchange 2013 server.

> ***IMPORTANT*** **Users who are part of the Discovery Management role group will have access to all the mailboxes on the Exchange server. This could potentially give users access to sensitive and confidential information.**

By default, nobody is part of the Discovery Management role group. You can add users to the Discovery Management role group via the Exchange Administration Center by following these steps:

1. Open the Exchange Administration Center with an account that is a member of the Role Management group.
2. Navigate to Permissions and click Admin Roles.
3. Select Discovery Management from the list view and then click Edit.
4. Under Members, click Add+ in the Role Group.
5. Select one or more users in the Select Members list box.
6. Click Add and then click OK.
7. Click Save.

MORE INFO ADDING A USER TO THE DISCOVERY MANAGEMENT ROLE GROUP

See more *http://technet.microsoft.com/en-us/library/dd298059* for more information on how to add a user to the Discovery Management role group.

At this point, you have configured users for eDiscovery. As soon as the eDiscovery process is complete, you should remove all users from the Discovery Management role group. The elevated permissions represent a security risk that should be minimized as soon as possible.

Thought experiment

Installing Project Server

In the following thought experiment, apply what you've learned about this objective. You can find answers to these questions in the "Answers" section at the end of this chapter.

Your assignment is to add a Project Server web app to the SharePoint Server 2013 farm. Currently, your farm doesn't have Project Server 2013 installed. Your farm has two web front ends (WFEs), an application server, and a backend database. The path to the Project Server web app should be *http://www.contoso.com/pwa*. The site collection at *http://www.contoso.com* already exists.

What steps do you have to perform to get a Project Server web app installed at the desired location?

Objective summary

- Project Server 2013 is installed as a service application that runs on SharePoint Server 2013.
- Project Server web apps are best installed on their own content database to improve backup and restore performance as well as to help troubleshoot any issues.
- Users who are performing eDiscovery on Exchange mailboxes have access to all mailboxes on the Exchange server.
- To use eDiscovery on Exchange via SharePoint, the SharePoint and Exchange farms must trust each other.

Objective review

Answer the following questions to test your knowledge of the information in this objective. You can find the answers to these questions and explanations of why each answer choice is correct or incorrect in the "Answers" section at the end of this chapter.

1. By default, which of the following users are members of the Discovery Management role group on the Exchange Server?

   A. Exchange administrators

   B. Members of the local Administrators group on the Exchange server

   C. Nobody

   D. Members of the Role Management group

2. You want to install and configure Project Server 2013 on your SharePoint 2013 farm. On which SharePoint servers do you need to install Project Server?

   A. All the servers running SharePoint

   B. Just the application servers

   C. Just the web front ends

   D. Just the servers running the Project Server service

3. For SharePoint 2013 to perform eDiscovery on Exchange mailboxes, which of the following must be true?

   A. The SharePoint farm needs to trust the Exchange farm, but the Exchange farm doesn't need to trust the SharePoint farm.

   B. The Exchange farm needs to trust the SharePoint farm, but the SharePoint farm doesn't need to trust the Exchange farm.

   C. As long as the Exchange farm and SharePoint farm are in the same domain, establishing trust isn't necessary.

   D. The Exchange farm and the SharePoint farm must trust each other through the exchange of certificates.

4. A Project web app has a parent site or site collection. What rights do users need to the parent site collection to use the Project web app (which has its own set of permissions)?

   A. Read

   B. Read and Write

   C. Full Control

   D. Users only need permissions to the Project web app and not the parent.

Chapter summary

- SharePoint 2013 allows for website collections to run in either SharePoint 2010 mode or SharePoint 2013 mode by having directories for each mode.
- Sandboxed solutions and farm solutions can be deployed to both 2010 and 2013 mode, but SharePoint apps can be used only in 2013 mode.
- Many of the business intelligence (BI) features of SharePoint Server 2013 require SQL Server 2012 SP1 or higher components to be installed on the SharePoint servers.
- SharePoint provides many powerful BI tools, but care must be used in planning and usage because some of the BI features can put a heavy load on the backend databases.
- Project Server 2013 allows users of SharePoint Server 2013 to get the functionality of Microsoft Project without needing the client application.
- Exchange and SharePoint Server must trust each other before SharePoint can perform eDiscovery on Exchange mailboxes.

Answers

This section contains the solutions to the thought experiments and answers to the lesson review questions in this chapter.

Objective 5.1: Thought experiment

In this thought experiment, you are assigned to help facilitate the migration of a farm solution. Because you need to make it available to both the SharePoint 2010 mode and the SharePoint 2013 mode, you need to plan out how you will install and potentially upgrade it.

Because the SharePoint 2010 mode has no idea about the SharePoint 2013 features, you can just go ahead and install the farm solution as usual on the SharePoint 2013 farm. It defaults to the 14 folder and is available for use without any modification.

Because you want the SharePoint 2013 mode users to have access to SharePoint 2013 features, you need to modify the code for the farm solution or potentially convert it into a SharePoint app. The main issue with trying to convert the farm solution into a SharePoint app is that it's using server-side code, and apps can't use that. Unless the functionality of the solution can be done with server-side code, you are stuck with a farm solution and because they are still fully supported in SharePoint 2013, you will be fine for the next version of SharePoint.

Assuming that you are sticking with a farm solution, you should rebuild the solution and change the target SharePoint version to 15.0 so that when you deploy the solution, it will go into the 15 folder and not overwrite the SharePoint 2010 mode. You could force it into the 15 folder by using the CompatibiltyFolder property, but you should go ahead and change the target with Visual Studio. You then can add features specific to SharePoint 2013 to the farm solution without worry of overwriting the old SharePoint 2010 mode version. Even if the SharePoint 2013 features aren't added right away, you should at least rebuild the solution with the updated target. Because you aren't planning to keep the SharePoint 2010 mode version updated, this will mark the separation of the two farm solutions going forward.

Objective 5.1: Review

1. **Correct answer:** D
    - **A. Incorrect:** Sandboxed solutions are supported, even though SharePoint apps are the preferred code solution. However, this is just one of the right answers.
    - **B. Incorrect:** Farm solutions are supported and will probably continue to be supported because SharePoint apps can't have server-side code. This is just one of the right answers, though.
    - **C. Incorrect:** SharePoint apps are the preferred method for developing code solutions for SharePoint 2013, but this too is just one of the right answers.
    - **D. Correct:** All the preceding answers are supported fully in SharePoint Server 2013.

2. **Correct answers:** A and C

   A. **Correct:** The Compatibility Level value of 14 installs the solution into the 14 folder for the SharePoint 2010 mode.

   B. **Incorrect:** The Compatibility Level of "14,15" installs the solution into both the 14 and 15 folders, which allows for the solution to be used for the SharePoint 2010 mode and the SharePoint 2013 mode.

   C. **Correct:** The Compatibility Level of "Old" is equivalent to 14 in SharePoint 2013, although this might change in future versions of SharePoint.

   D. **Incorrect:** "All" is the equivalent of "14,15" in SharePoint 2013. In future versions of SharePoint, "All" might include more modes.

3. **Correct answer:** B

   A. **Incorrect:** Any changes to features require that you use the replacement method to update a farm solution.

   B. **Correct:** Changes to DLLs are allowed with the Update method of upgrading a farm solution.

   C. **Incorrect:** Any changes to the elements.xml file requires the replacement method of upgrading. Adding or removing an elements.xml file also requires the replacement method.

   D. **Incorrect:** Changes in scope require that the replacement method be used to upgrade a farm solution.

4. **Correct answer:** A

   A. **Correct:** To use the update method of upgrading a SharePoint app, the product ID must remain the same.

   B. **Incorrect:** During the upgrade process, the SharePoint app becomes non-functional so that the app can be swapped out.

   C. **Incorrect:** SharePoint apps are usually updated when the update link is clicked next to the app on the Site Contents page. In any event, the process isn't automatic.

   D. **Incorrect:** When a SharePoint app fails to update, it automatically rolls back and the old version is restored.

Objective 5.2: Thought experiment

In this thought objective, you have to provide PowerPivot for SharePoint to the data analyst team without spending any money on hardware or software. PowerPivot for SharePoint is a free download but requires SQL Server 2012 SP1; however, the SharePoint Server is running on SQL Server 2008 R2. Depending on the licensing, which was not specified, it can cost money to upgrade the database and in any case would cause a major disruption to services if SharePoint is heavily used.

Fortunately you could install the components necessary using the SQL Server 2012 SP1 Express edition on one of the servers in the SharePoint farm. This server would run the PowerPivot service as well as be the server where the PowerPivot configuration tool is run. You would still need a full version of SQL Server 2012 SP1 to host the PowerPivot databases, though. The PowerPivot service application can use a separate database than the one SharePoint is installed on, so this would solve your problem. Although performance won't be quite as good from a connection standpoint, you will gain some benefit from balancing the overall SharePoint load across two database servers. After configuration, you should monitor the server running the PowerPivot service to make sure that it's not being overtaxed. If it is, you might consider removing services from that server and/or configuring the PowerPivot settings.

Objective 5.2: Review

1. **Correct answer:** B
   - **A. Incorrect:** You need to configure the unattended service account before you can use shared credentials.
   - **B. Correct:** You don't need to create a target application to use shared credentials. Target applications are used to impersonate specific accounts to connect to external data.
   - **C. Incorrect:** You need to make sure the PerformancePoint service is running on at least one of the SharePoint servers on the farm.
   - **D. Incorrect:** You need to have a PerformancePoint service application created before users can use PerformancePoint Services.
2. **Correct answer:** C
   - **A. Incorrect:** You need to restore the service application from a backup of the service application and not just the associated Reporting Services database.
   - **B. Incorrect:** You need to restore the Encryption Key as well as the Reporting Services service application.
   - **C. Correct:** The farm password, used to add servers to the SharePoint farm, isn't needed.
   - **D. Incorrect:** A password is associated with the encryption key that will be needed when you restore it.
3. **Correct answer:** D
   - **A. Incorrect:** The PowerPivot for SharePoint 2013 Configuration tool can create the SQL Server PowerPivot service application for you, rather than you take care of it

through Central Administration or PowerShell. However, this is just one of the correct answers.

   B. Incorrect: The configuration tool can actually create a couple of different web applications. It can create a Central Administration web application and one specifically for PowerPivot. However, this is just one of the right answers.

   C. Incorrect: The configuration tool can also be used to configure the Secure Store service application, but this is just one of the right answers.

   D. Correct: Because A, B, and C are all true, "All of the above" is the best answer.

4. **Correct answer:** C

   A. Incorrect: Tabular mode is the correct mode, but Microsoft SQL Server 2012 SP1 or greater is required.

   B. Incorrect: Multidimensional and Data Mining mode is the wrong mode and the SQL Server version is wrong.

   C. Correct: SQL Server 2012 SP1 is the right version of SQL Server and Tabular mode is the correct mode.

   D. Incorrect: The SQL Server version is correct, but the Multidimensional and Data Mining mode is the wrong mode.

Objective 5.3: Thought experiment

In this thought experiment, you were asked to add Project Server 2013 functionality to the SharePoint 2013 farm and create a Project Server web app at *http://www.contoso.com/pwa*. Because you don't have Project Server 2013 installed, that's the first thing you need to take care of. You need to install Project Server on the two WFEs and the application server (but don't run the SharePoint 2013 Products Configuration Wizard at the end of the setup). You don't need to install Project Server on the database server because it's not running SharePoint.

After you install Project Server on each SharePoint server, you need to go back and run the SharePoint 2013 Products Configuration Wizard on each of the SharePoint Servers one at a time, waiting until one server is completely done before starting on another. You should now start the Project Server Application Service and create a Project Server service application. You are restricted by the path you were instructed to use, so you could activate the Project Server site collection feature and then create a site using the Project Server site template at *http://www.contoso.com/pwa*. You could also go to the Project Server service application and create a Project Server web app from the Manage Project Web Apps page. This would create a site collection at *http://www.contoso.com/pwa* and allow for designating a database for the Project Server content as well as allowing you to set quotas specifically for the Project Server web app site. This has the additional benefit of being easier to back up and restore, greatly increasing the speed of recovery in case of a disaster. It also helps isolate issues for troubleshooting, should the need arise.

Objective 5.3: Review

1. **Correct answer:** C

   A. **Incorrect:** Exchange administrators aren't members of the Discovery Management role group because it has no members by default.

   B. **Incorrect:** Local administrators aren't members of the Discovery Management role group.

   C. **Correct:** The Discovery Management role group is empty by default because it allows access to all mailboxes and therefore access to potentially confidential and sensitive information.

   D. **Incorrect:** Members of the Role Management Group aren't members of the Discovery Management role group, but they can add users, including themselves, to the group.

2. **Correct answer:** A

   A. **Correct:** Project Server needs to be installed on all the servers in the SharePoint farm that are running SharePoint.

   B. **Incorrect:** The application servers need Project Server installed on them, but so do all the other servers running SharePoint.

   C. **Incorrect:** The WFEs also need Project Server installed on them, but so do all the other servers running SharePoint.

   D. **Incorrect:** The Project Server service determines which servers process requests from the Project Server service application, but you still need to install Project Server on the other SharePoint servers.

3. **Correct answer:** D

   A. **Incorrect:** The trust needs to be established in both directions through the exchange of certificates.

   B. **Incorrect:** Like with answer A, the trust needs to be established in both directions.

   C. **Incorrect:** Being in the same domain doesn't do away with the trust requirement. The Exchange farm and the SharePoint farm don't need to be in the same domain, but they do need to be in the same forest.

   D. **Correct:** The Exchange and SharePoint farms must exchange certificates to establish trust before the SharePoint farm can perform eDiscovery on mailboxes located on the Exchange farm.

4. **Correct answer:** A

   A. **Correct:** The users of the Project web app need at least Read access to the parent site or site collection. This is separate from the permissions on the Project web app site.

- **B. Incorrect:** Write permissions can be given in addition to Read permissions, but they aren't needed to use the Project web app.
- **C. Incorrect:** Users don't need Full Control, although that would give them the necessary Read permissions. Also, for security reasons, regular users shouldn't have full control of the site or site collection that hosts the Project web app.
- **D. Incorrect:** Giving users permissions to only the Project web app site and not the parent site or site collection will prohibit them from getting to the Project web app site.

Index

A

B

D

E

F

G

H

I

J

K

L

M

N

O

P

Q

R

S

T

U

V

W

About the Author

MICHAEL DOYLE, MCTS, MCSD, MCSE, and a senior architect at a major company, has been working with SharePoint almost exclusively for a decade. He is a frequent speaker and blogger. Michael is the author of *Microsoft SharePoint 2010: Customizing My Site* and co-author of *Microsoft SharePoint Foundation 2010 Inside Out.*